Concordia Popular Commentary

1 Corinthians

Gregory J. Lockwood

Concordia Publishing House • Saint Louis

3558 S. Jefferson Ave., St. Louis, MO 63118-3968
1-800-325-3040 • www.cph.org

Concordia Publishing House thanks the Reverend Dr. Paul E. Deterding for editing this volume.

Manufactured in the United States of America

Library of Congress Cataloging-in-Publication Data

Lockwood, Gregory J.
1 Corinthians / Gregory J. Lockwood.
p. cm. — (Concordia popular commentary)
ISBN 978-0-7586-2545-8
1. Bible. N.T. Corinthians, 1st--Commentaries. I. Title. II. Title: First Corinthians. III. Series.

BS2675.53.L63 2010
227'.2077—dc22 2010029469

---

1 2 3 4 5 6 7 8 9 10 19 18 17 16 15 14 13 12 11 10

CONTENTS

EDITORS' PREFACE

What may a reader expect from the Concordia Popular Commentary?

This commentary series brings faithful Christian Bible scholarship to the people. Based on the Concordia Commentary series, its goals are similar: to help Christians understand and talk about God's Word with greater clarity, understanding, and faithfulness to the divine intent of the text.

The commentaries in this popular commentary series are designed for Christians that have an intermediate-level familiarity with Scripture and with the teachings of historic Christianity, especially those of the Lutheran Church. These volumes offer the insights of the scholarly Concordia Commentary series without the need to know foreign languages like Greek, Hebrew, and Aramaic. The central points from the scholarly series remain the same. Some differences include the removal of foreign-language textual notes. Footnote references and extensive interaction with certain technical, academic sources also have been removed. If the reader wishes to consult a list of sources, he or she is encouraged to look at the bibliography in the corresponding Concordia Commentary volume.

Jesus Christ is the content of the scriptural testimony. The Lord himself has said, "The Scriptures . . . testify to me" (Jn 5:39). The message of the Scriptures is the Good News of God's work to reconcile the world to himself through the life, death, resurrection, ascension, and everlasting session of Jesus Christ at the right hand of God the Father. Under the guidance of the same Spirit who inspired the writing of the Scriptures, these commentaries seek to find in every passage of every canonical book "that which promotes Christ" (as Martin Luther's hermeneutic is often described). They are Christ-centered, "Christological" commentaries.

Even as the God of the Gospel came into this world in Jesus Christ (the Word in human flesh), the scriptural Gospel has been given to and through the people of God, for the benefit of all humanity. God did not intend his Scriptures to have a life separated from the church. He gave them through servants of his choosing: prophets, sages, evangelists, and apostles. He gave them to the church and through the church for admonition and comfort, for preaching and teaching. The living context of Scripture is always the church, where the Lord's ministry of preaching, baptizing, forgiving sins, teaching, and celebrating the Lord's Supper continues. This series remains aware of the close union of Scripture and church, of Word and Sacraments, a result of God taking up human flesh in Christ.

This Gospel Word of God creates a unity among all those in whom it works the obedience of faith and who confess the truth of God revealed in it. This is the unity of the one holy Christian and apostolic church, which extends through world history. The church is to be found wherever the marks of the church are present: the Gospel in the Word and the Sacraments. These have been proclaimed, confessed, and celebrated in many different cultures and are in no way limited or especially attached to any single culture or people. These commentaries seek to promote concord, in the best sense of the terms, to be confessional, ecumenical, and "catholic" (universally Christian).

All of those convictions and characteristics describe the theological heritage of Martin Luther and of the confessors who subscribe to the *Book of Concord* (1580)—those who have come to be known as Lutherans. The editors and authors forthrightly confess their subscription to the doctrinal exposition of Scripture in the *Book of Concord*. As the publishing arm of The Lutheran Church—Missouri Synod, Concordia Publishing House is bound to doctrinal agreement with the Scriptures and the Lutheran Confessions and seeks to herald the true Christian doctrine to the ends of the earth.

As they unfold the scriptural testimony to Jesus Christ, these commentaries talk about Law and Gospel. These are the overarching doctrines of the Bible. Understanding them in their proper distinction and relationship to one another is a key for understanding the self-revelation of God and his plan of salvation in Jesus Christ. God's Law condemns our sin, and his Gospel forgives our sin. However, Law and Gospel do not always appear simply labeled as such in Scripture. The language in Scripture is multicolored, with many and rich hues. A Bible passage may express Law and Gospel by the themes of the fallen creation and the new creation in Christ; darkness and light; death and life; wandering and the promised land; exile and return; ignorance and wisdom; demon possession and the kingdom of God; sickness and healing; being lost and then being found; guilt and righteousness; flesh and Spirit; fear and joy; hunger and feast; or Babylon and the new Jerusalem. But the common element is God's gracious work of restoring fallen humanity through the Gospel of his Son. This stress on the Gospel proclamation makes these commentaries, in the proper sense, evangelical.

Scripture is God's vehicle for communicating the Gospel. The editors and authors accept without reservation that the canonical books of the Old and New Testaments are, in their entirety, the inspired, infallible, and inerrant Word of God. The triune God is the ultimate author of the Bible, and the Holy Spirit breathed forth every word in the original Hebrew, Aramaic, and Greek through the holy authors in a supernatural process of divine inspiration. This is much more profound than the common use of "inspired" to describe a person who is moved by a poignant event in life, a great idea, a brilliant speaker, and so on. God is the one who inspired the authors of Scripture. He worked through those men and achieved his goal in every respect, so that the Scriptures are God's Word, without blemish, error, or falsehood.

Yet in the mysterious process by which the Scriptures were divinely inspired (e.g., 2 Tim 3:16; 2 Pet 1:21), God made use of the human faculties, knowledge, interests, and styles of the biblical writers, whose individual books surely are marked by distinctive features. At the same time, the canon of Scripture has its own inner unity, and each passage must be understood in harmony with the larger context of the whole. This commentary series pays heed to the smallest of textual details because of its acceptance of plenary and verbal inspiration.

Authors in this series interpret each text in accord with the analogy of faith, following the principle that Scripture interprets Scripture. Passages that are clearer, such as when Jesus explains a parable, guide the interpretation of passages that are not as transparent, such as the parable itself. One always looks first at the clear passages for the meaning and intent of the Lord. One then looks to related passages that have similar themes and language. Obscure passages should never be interpreted in a way that conflicts with well-understood passages. Doctrine is established by the plain sense of clear passages. Literal passages include Mt 28:19–20 and the Lord's Words instituting the Lord's Supper in Mt 26, Mk 14, Lk 22, and 1 Cor 11. Even though "this is my body" may not be captured by human reason, nevertheless, the passage has Jesus, the elements, and the congregation of disciples. That is as real as the pastor, the elements, and today's congregation.

Scripture passages do not exist in isolation. One can find the literal sense of a difficult passage in a clearer parallel text, a passage where prophecy is fulfilled, or the accumulated evidence concerning a topic in Scripture. The Bible is replete with passages covering all aspects of human life from before birth to after death, from the house of worship to the outhouse. No one can find a situation so unique or so bad into which a loving, forgiving God will not enter. God really means "all nations." God wants to save you, and his Word speaks to where you are in life.

Sometimes one can find both a literal meaning and an additional, spiritual meaning called the "mystical sense." This spiritual meaning always rests on and connects with the literal sense, as orthodox Lutheran theologians like Johann Gerhard describe. There may indeed be ways of applying Scripture to oneself, to cultural changes, and to political events. For example, a Christian identifies the sin of the prodigal son with his own and therefore hears the forgiveness of the gracious, loving father as God's forgiveness to him. The parable is more than a mere story. It plays a vital role in the application of Law and Gospel. Figures of speech, allegory, morality, and heavenly revelation all connect with this spiritual sense. Yet this sense can be abused, a caution that Lutheran biblical interpretation has always sounded.

Such application may be very helpful, for example, in cross-cultural communication. After the fall of Rome and the huge upheaval of migrant nations with different languages, the Church relied heavily on allegory to help Germanic and Slavic peoples to identify with the literal meaning of Scripture using ideas familiar to them. Allegory unfortunately became the dominant method of interpretation and got separated from the literal sense. People began to read all kinds of meaning into Scripture, which is contrary to God's intent.

In many passages one can see a moral sense where the literal meaning of a passage also establishes a universal moral principle revealed by God to curb the unrighteous, mirror brightly our sin, and guide our steps. Additionally, one may encounter a heavenly sense in some passages that speaks not only to how God literally deals with us here and now, but also to heavenly realities that pass beyond human understanding and to our eternal home with God. All these other senses, as Gerhard describes in Topic II, On the Interpretation of Scripture, in his 1610 *Loci Theologici* and in Topic IV, On Christ, in the 1625 *Exegesis*, rest on the fundamental, literal sense.

The authors and editors stand in the exegetical tradition of Martin Luther and the other Lutheran reformers, who in turn stand in continuity with faithful theologians of the early and medieval church. All remain rooted in the hermeneutics of the Scriptures themselves (evident, for example, by how the New Testament interprets the Old). This method, practiced also by many non-Lutherans, includes (1) interpreting Scripture with Scripture in harmony with the whole of Christian doctrine revealed in the Word; (2) giving utmost attention to the grammar of the original language of the text; (3) seeking to discern the intended meaning of the text, the "plain" or "literal" sense as it connects to different literary genres and figures of speech; (4) drawing on linguistics, archaeology, literature, philosophy, history, and other fields as they help one understand the text; (5) considering the history of the church's interpretation; (6) applying the text as authoritative also for today's interpreter, and (7) above all, seeing the present application and fulfillment of the text in terms of Jesus Christ and his corporate church; upholding the Word, Baptism, and the Supper as the means through which Christ imparts salvation today; and affirming the inauguration, already now, of the eternal benefits of that salvation that is yet to come.

Author's Preface

"Be steadfast, immovable, always abounding in the work of the Lord, knowing that in the Lord your labor is not in vain" (1 Cor 15:58). These words of personal encouragement concluded a letter I received in the mid 1970s from the Lutheran education secretary in Papua New Guinea, Ray Blacklock. Ray knew that his rookie missionary had been going through a stressful period of adjustment to the culture and the church situation in the western highlands of Papua New Guinea. What he could not know was how that great Pauline text, based on our resurrection hope in Christ, would stay with me through life's ups and downs as a firm "anchor of the soul" (Heb 6:19).

My formal studies in 1 Corinthians had begun in 1968 at Luther Seminary, Adelaide, in South Australia. Our lecturer, Dr. Victor Pfitzner, left me with an abiding interest in the epistle and a desire to understand the text as a coherent whole. Recent reading of works by commentators such as Richard Hays has further stimulated my desire to appreciate Paul as an apostle with a coherent message. For a Lutheran commentator, such an approach is especially congenial because of the traditional Lutheran insistence on the clarity, consistency, and persuasive power of the Scriptures. At a time when the apostle and his message have been subjected to criticism and even shameless repudiation, an empathetic approach to Pauline studies—a hermeneutic of appreciation—is, I believe, sorely needed. Peter Brunner was surely right in his judgment that a church which rejects Paul's message and instructions in 1 Corinthians will lose its "apostolic character" and degenerate into "a syncretistic sect."

During the final stages of the commentary process, I became increasingly impressed by the relevance of 1 Corinthians to the contemporary church, in particular the remarkable similarity between the cultural and religious situation of first-century Corinth and the world at the dawn of the twenty-first century. To take only the clearest example, on every side we hear the voices of modern individualism, in tones reminiscent of ancient Stoicism, proclaiming the need for autonomy, independence, self-fulfillment, putting oneself first, being "in charge" and "in control" of one's life. To this culture Paul throws out the challenge, as he challenged the Corinthians, that true fulfillment is found only through loving, self-sacrificing *fellowship* with others—with the one who was crucified on Calvary (1 Cor 1:9), and with our fellow members of his body. "Don't you know that . . . you are not your own? For you were bought for a price" (1 Cor 6:19–20).

Among the sons (and daughters) of encouragement (cf. Acts 4:36)—the Ray Blacklocks—who helped along the way, I would especially like to thank the following: Dr. Jonathan Grothe, my New Testament adviser during my graduate studies at Concordia Seminary, St. Louis, and now president of Concordia Lutheran Theological Seminary in St. Catharines, Ontario, gave constant encouragement and asked stimulating questions during the early stages. Another unfailing source of encouragement was Dr. Christopher Mitchell of Concordia Publishing House, who edited the manuscript with great care and offered many helpful suggestions in the most congenial manner. Mrs. Julene Dumit, the commentary series copy editor, left no stone unturned in checking sources and references. Dr. Jeffrey Gibbs, associate professor of New Testament at Concordia Seminary, St. Louis, and the New Testament editor of the commentary series, also read the manuscript and gave constructive advice. Rev. Jerald Joersz of the Commission on Theology and Church Relations of The Lutheran Church—Missouri Synod took a great interest in the commentary and pointed me to some helpful literature. Finally, I would thank the administration of Concordia Theological Seminary, Fort Wayne, for the necessary study leave, my colleagues on the faculty for their encouragement, the staffs of Walther Library, Fort Wayne, and Loehe Memorial Library, Adelaide, and the students it has been my privilege and joy to teach on the Fort Wayne and Adelaide campuses.

My constant prayer is that by God's grace this commentary may serve for the edification of the church (1 Cor 14:26) and the glory of Christ crucified (2:2).

PRINCIPAL ABBREVIATIONS

BOOKS OF THE BIBLE

Gen	2 Ki	Is	Nah	Rom	Titus
Ex	1 Chr	Jer	Hab	1 Cor	Philemon
Lev	2 Chr	Lam	Zeph	2 Cor	Heb
Num	Ezra	Ezek	Hag	Gal	James
Deut	Neh	Dan	Zech	Eph	1 Pet
Josh	Esth	Hos	Mal	Phil	2 Pet
Judg	Job	Joel	Mt	Col	1 Jn
Ruth	Ps (pl. Pss)	Amos	Mk	1 Thess	2 Jn
1 Sam	Prov	Obad	Lk	2 Thess	3 Jn
2 Sam	Eccl	Jonah	Jn	1 Tim	Jude
1 Ki	Song	Micah	Acts	2 Tim	Rev

BOOKS OF THE APOCRYPHA

1 Esdras	Judith	Sirach	Add Dan	Manasseh
2 Esdras	Add Esth	Bar	Sus	1 Macc
Tobit	Wisdom	Ep Jer	Bel	2 Macc

OTHER ABBREVIATIONS

ET English translation (Shows differences in verse numbers between the Greek text and common English translations.)

INTRODUCTION

THEOLOGICAL THEMES

Martin Luther gives a concise summary of the theological purpose of 1 Corinthians: "In this epistle St. Paul exhorts the Corinthians to be one in faith and love, and to see to it that they learn well the chief thing, namely, that Christ is our salvation, the thing over which all reason and wisdom stumbles. . . . For it was as in our day, when the gospel has come to light. There are many mad saints (we call them factious spirits, fanatics, and heretics) who have become wise and learned all too quickly and, because of their great knowledge and wisdom, cannot live in harmony with anybody" (AE 35:380–81).

Paul states the epistle's theme in 1:18: "For the word of the cross is foolishness to those who are being destroyed, but to us who are being saved it is the power of God." Immediately he supports his theme from the OT: "For it has been written: 'I will destroy the wisdom of the wise, and the understanding of the understanding I will reject.' " Thus, what Luther calls "the theology of the cross" forms the epistle's foundation. Salvation is found through faith in the "weak" and "foolish" word of "Jesus Christ and him crucified" (1:18, 25; 2:2). Faith in the Christ who died for their sins and rose again for their justification will also restore the congregation's unity by inspiring loving concern (cf. 1 Corinthians 13) for the brother "for whom Christ died" (8:11).

In proclaiming the theology of the cross, Paul opposes a theology of glory which had become endemic in Corinth. Some members of the church had fallen prey to a secular spirit (2:12) which displayed itself in constant "boasting," becoming "puffed up" with self-importance, strife, jealousy, disorder (3:3; 14:33), and a putting down of fellow Christians who were considered to have fewer gifts or advantages. This secular spirit had no sense for spiritual things (2:10–16); its only concern was what received human applause.

In contrast to this secular spirit, "the Spirit which is from God" (2:12) leads its recipients to find "grace" and "peace" (1:3) in Christ crucified. Appreciative of all the spiritual gifts that are theirs in the Gospel, in their Baptism in one Spirit, and in the sustaining spiritual food and drink of Holy Communion (2:12; 10:3–4; 12:13), they are built up in the one communion (1:9; 10:16) of Jesus Christ and his body and blood. They understand themselves as fellow members of Christ's body, a body marked by big-hearted, longsuffering love (12:27; 13:4), peace, and good order (12:27; 13:4; 14:33, 40; 16:14, 24).

This is a love that can wait. Paul faced the challenge of teaching the Corinthians the tension of Christian existence between the Lord's two advents.

Already saints, already spiritually endowed people, they still must wait for the Lord's final coming and the resurrection of their bodies (1:7–8; 11:26; 15:1–58). And living patiently in this tension—not trying to get out from under it—meant joining the apostles in living under the cross (4:9–13), and disciplining their bodies, marked for resurrection, in holy and humble service of the brother.

Paul's approach to the manifold aberrations of the Corinthians is a model of pastoral wisdom. His tone throughout is that of a father who dearly loves his erring children. His chief concern is not to apply the Law (although he certainly does at times speak the Law in all its sharpness), but to administer the healing medicine of the Gospel.

In our time, when factious spirits again threaten to tear the church apart, when a so-called postmodern age encourages each person to set up what "I think" or "I feel" as the final criterion of truth, so that each is inclined to do what is "right in his own eyes" (Judg 21:25), there is an urgent need to hear afresh the apostolic encouragement to Christian harmony in faith and love.

THE CITY OF CORINTH

Geography and History

Corinth is situated on the narrow isthmus (four and a half miles wide) that links the Greek mainland in the north to the Peloponnese peninsula in the south (where ancient Sparta was located). The city possessed strategic advantages, with its citadel, the Acrocorinth, rising to 1,886 feet (575 meters) above sea level, and economic advantages through its position as a gateway between northern and southern Greece, and between the Corinthian Gulf to the west and the Saronic Gulf to the east. It possessed two harbors, Lechaeum (facing Italy) and Cenchreae (facing Asia). Rather than transporting goods by the dangerous route around the southern tip of Achaia, merchants could have smaller ships placed on wheeled platforms and dragged across the isthmus along a kind of tramway. The customs duties levied on this trade contributed greatly to the city's wealth. Its fertile hinterland also contributed to Corinth's prosperity; indeed, our word "currant" derives from the name "Corinth."

In 146 BC, the Roman consul Lucius Mummius razed the city to the ground, as a reprisal for Corinth leading the other Achaean cities in revolt. For more than a century the city lay dormant, until Julius Caesar rebuilt it in 44 BC. Corinth swiftly regained and exceeded its former prominence, becoming the largest city in Roman Greece and attaining a population of approximately 100,000. During the reign of Augustus (27 BC–AD 14), it was adorned with numerous public buildings. The city also resumed its role as host of the biennial Isthmian games conducted at the nearby sanctuary of Poseidon. It became an important center of Roman culture; prominent citizens from neighboring towns coveted magistracies in the city and became its benefactors. Latin became the official language. By 27 BC, Corinth had clearly been reinstated as capital of the senatorial province of

Achaia. Thus, it is the provincial proconsul, Gallio, who hears the case brought against Paul before the Corinthian "judgment seat" (Acts 18:12–16). Along with Gallio and other civil and military officers, the new city was settled by ex-soldiers and freedmen from Rome, an influx of people from neighboring areas, and numerous slaves.

Morality

The city was also quick to regain its former unsavory reputation. Old Corinth had been known for sexual vice, to the extent that the comic poet Aristophanes (450–385 BC) coined the verb "to behave like a Corinthian," i.e., "to be a fornicator." The geographer Strabo claimed that 1,000 temple prostitutes were employed at the temple of Aphrodite. This is probably an exaggeration; besides Strabo was not speaking of the new Roman city. However, the Corinth of Paul's day, like many harbor cities, was undoubtedly a center for prostitution (cf. 6:12–20). And the city maintained her ties with Aphrodite: three temples of the goddess adorned the new foundation.

Religious Pluralism

Not only did the city have a reputation for sexual promiscuity and other forms of immorality (cf. the list in 1 Cor 6:9–10 and the catalog of Greco-Roman vices in Rom 1:18–32, penned while Paul was in Corinth), but it was also known for religious promiscuity. Like its sister-city Athens, Corinth was "very religious" (or "very superstitious," Acts 17:22). Thus, there is evidence of sanctuaries and statues honoring Apollo, "Black Aphrodite," Athena, Zeus, Poseidon (Neptune), Tyche (Fortune), the healing god Asklepios, Demeter and Kore (or Persephone; the sanctuary of Demeter and Kore has been excavated), Dionysus, the Egyptian gods Isis and Serapis, the "mother of the gods," and last but not least, the imperial cult. Accustomed as they were to this pluralistic and tolerant milieu, the Corinthian Christians found it difficult to adjust to the exclusive claims of their new faith and were tempted to lapse into syncretism (cf. Paul's warnings against idolatry in 1 Cor 5:10; 6:9; and especially 8:1–10:22).

Stoicism and Epicureanism

In Athens, Paul found himself contending not only with religious pluralism but also with "some of the Epicurean and Stoic philosophers" (Acts 17:18). Almost certainly these philosophical movements were well represented in nearby Corinth. Epicureanism encouraged the pursuit of pleasure and tranquility, and the avoidance of pain, passions, and superstitious fears, especially the fear of death. It was not Epicurus' intention to foster immorality—disturbing passions were, after all, to be subdued—but his emphasis on pleasure as the chief goal of human life could easily become an excuse for self-indulgence. Another aspect of Epicureanism which may have influenced some Corinthian Christians (cf. 1 Cor 15:12) was the attempt to overcome the fear of death by insisting that it simply meant nothingness—the dissolution of body and soul into their constituent atoms. Epicureans were truly "without hope and without God in the world" (Eph 2:12).

The Stoics believed humans could achieve freedom and autonomy by living in a rational manner consistent with the nature of the universe. They greatly prized individual self-sufficiency. At its best, Stoicism encouraged the individual to realize one's self by working for universal ends. At its worst, it fostered a spiritual pride and (like Epicureanism) a self-centered individualism totally antithetical to the Christian emphasis on the body of Christ, whose members build each other up in love.

At a number of points in 1 Corinthians, Paul seems to be echoing—and countering—Stoic philosophy:

1. The phrase "all things are yours" in 3:21–22 echoes Stoics like Seneca, who repeatedly used the slogan "all things belong to the wise man." Paul initially expresses his agreement: all things do belong to those in Christ (3:22). But then Paul adds this corrective: "But you are Christ's" (3:23). The phrase, with Paul's balancing corrective, is similar to a pair of theses expressed by Luther: "A Christian is a perfectly free lord of all, subject to none," but a Christian is also "a perfectly dutiful servant of all, subject to all" (AE 31:344).

2. In showing so little concern for self-assessment (4:3–5), Paul may be deliberately rejecting the Stoic practice of detailed self-scrutiny at the end of each day. Some of the Corinthians may have been encouraged to practice such self-criticism in order to cultivate their character. For Paul, however, only the Lord's judgment matters.

3. Both Cynic and Stoic philosophers sometimes claimed to be rich men and kings by virtue of their philosophy. Thus, when Paul ironically chides the Corinthians for being "full," "rich," and "kings" (4:8), it is likely that he is grappling with the impact of Stoic ideas on his people.

4. Another Corinthian slogan that may stem from Stoic or Cynic tendencies is "all things are possible for me" (6:12; 10:23). According to the philosophers, the wise person enjoys autonomy and may do as he pleases. Some of the Corinthians may have thought Paul would support their slogan. For the apostle, however, the overriding concern is what benefits and edifies the church.

"I will not be dominated (come under the authority of) anything" (6:12b) may be another Stoic expression of the individual's freedom. Paul first concedes the validity of the slogan but proceeds to point out that if it is true, then they should not be surrendering their bodies to the control of prostitutes (6:13–20).

5. Finally, the asceticism Paul seeks to counter in 7:3–5 may have been fuelled, at least to some extent, by Stoic and Cynic philosophy. These schools debated whether marriage or the unmarried state was more conducive to wisdom.

Many of those characteristics of ancient Greek philosophical schools are also found in modern cultural movements. Paul's responses to them in 1 Corinthians therefore are relevant for our own cultural context.

THE SOPHISTIC MOVEMENT IN CORINTH

While many in Corinth were captivated by philosophy, even more, it seems, came under the spell of the polished rhetorical performances ("wisdom of word," 1 Cor 1:17) of the sophists. The sophists ("wise, skillful men") had first come to prominence in the fifth century BC, when men like Protagoras (known for his dictum "man is the measure of all things") set themselves up as professional teachers of clear thinking and oratory. They prepared young men for public life, charging fees for their services. In the first century AD the sophistic movement came to a new flowering. Cities and provinces found it worthwhile to hire sophists as ambassadors; parents made use of them in training their sons in the arts of persuasion necessary for success in administrative, legal, and teaching positions. In 1 Corinthians, Paul seems to be concerned over the influence on the fledgling congregation of sophistic values that were antithetical to "the word of the cross" (1 Cor 1:18).

The sophists came from society's upper echelons; they were "wise, powerful, and well-born" (cf. 1 Cor 1:26), and their movement helped perpetuate their class. They were also known for boastfulness and fierce competitiveness (cf. "zeal and strife," 1 Cor 3:3) against one another for influence and students.

Upon his arrival in a city, a sophist would give a sample oration upon which depended his chances for endorsement and employment in the city. In this, he would (1) attempt to project an image of himself as likeable and trustworthy, (2) play on his hearers' emotions, and (3) convince them of his reasoning ability (cf. 1 Cor 2:4). By contrast, when Paul arrived in Corinth, he deliberately eschewed the deceitfulness which characterized the sophists' rhetoric, concentrating instead on a straightforward presentation of the weak and foolish message of the cross (2:1–5).

1 Corinthians points to the intrusion of secular, sophistic mores into the congregation. It was natural, for example, that Christians of a sophistic mind-set would place the eloquent Apollos on a pedestal and express the hope that Paul would never come back (4:18–19). Paul's practice of working with his hands to support himself, refusing to accept financial support from the Corinthians, may well have been his way of distancing himself from the avaricious sophists.

BROADER SECULAR INFLUENCES

Some members of the Corinthian church may have belonged to the elite classes of Corinthian society and hence imported secular ways and leadership models into the church. These secular approaches would have included the importance of patronage and loyalty between pupil and teacher as well as an emphasis on status. Thus, the rivalry among Corinthian Christians ("I belong to Paul," 1:12, and so on) may have stemmed in part from secular patterns whereby a young man would attach himself to a greater man as a way of eventually making his own mark in society.

Such patterns could have provoked Paul's response in chapters 1–4. Similar dynamics may also lie behind the congregation's failure to censure the incestuous man (5:1–13): he may have been of high social standing, and thus considered to be exempt from criticism. It was most likely Christians of higher status who brought litigation against fellow Christians (6:1–8) in order to advance their own interests—a common practice in Greco-Roman society.

Thus, both the sophist movement and secular leadership practices tempted Christians in Corinth to make an ideal of status rather than service. In countering this secular mind-set, Paul used non-status imagery (agricultural and artisan language and household imagery, 1 Cor 3:5–15; 4:1–2) and held before them the patterns of pastoral servanthood exhibited by himself, Apollos, Timothy, and Stephanas (1 Cor 2:1–16; 3:5–9; 4:16–17; 16:15–16).

THE CORINTHIANS' QUEST FOR SPIRITUAL POWER

In many of these ways, Corinthian society—like ours—was characterized by the feverish quest for power. In this climate, the gift of the Spirit offered by the Christian faith was easily misconstrued, in the sense of pagan enthusiasm, as the offer of personal spiritual power. This was the pattern followed by Greek pagan religion and Stoicism, which spoke of the "spirit" as a divine or cosmic force inspiring and infilling certain persons like poets or the priestesses of Apollo in Delphi. The infilling with the spirit was perceived as liberating the person, making him or her one who is caught up out of the ordinary circumstances of life.

By contrast, the NT never suggests that the gift of the Spirit is given to satisfy anyone's personal quest to become so powerfully possessed by God as to be beyond life's normal misfortunes. The Spirit is not to be cut loose from the Jesus who died on the cross. The Christ who was "crucified in weakness" (2 Cor 13:4) is preached by his apostle "in weakness and in fear and in much trembling" (1 Cor 2:3; 2 Cor 13:4). Spiritual people live and struggle in weakness under the shadow of the cross. Gifted with "the Spirit of faith" (2 Cor 4:13), they live in the present aeon by faith, not by sight: they put up with the cruciform ministry of apostles and pastors who may not shine (or choose not to shine) as orators; they endure the tensions of their "already but not yet" existence as saints who long to be delivered from weakness and put on their spiritual bodies; they wait for the hope of righteousness which will only be experienced at the revelation of the Lord Jesus; and they constantly bear with others in longsuffering love. Thus, the Spirit does not endorse a self-centered focus on works, feelings, or empowerment. The Spirit orients the Christian in faith toward Christ crucified and toward other people in love.

THE FOUNDING OF THE CHURCH IN CORINTH

Toward the end of his second missionary journey, which took him through Macedonia and Achaia, Paul became the founding father of the church in Corinth (see the account in Acts 18:1–22). Some weeks after his arrival, he was joined by Silas and Timothy. Their hosts in the city were Aquila and Priscilla, who with their fellow Jews had recently been expelled from Rome by an edict of Claudius. Aquila, Priscilla, and Paul practiced the same trade, the making and repairing of tents. It has been suggested they may have been occupied with making awnings for the Isthmian games, held in April–May AD 51. Another suggestion is that they made awnings for the theater and other venues in Corinth itself.

After their expulsion from the synagogue in Corinth, Paul and his companions continued to preach in the home of Titius Justus. Their ministry bore fruit, as Crispus, a leader of the synagogue, and many other Corinthians believed and were baptized. Encouraged by a nighttime vision, Paul remained among them for eighteen months, teaching the Word of God (Acts 18:6–11).

Not satisfied with ejecting him from the synagogue, the Jews rose up against Paul and brought him before the tribunal of the Roman procurator, Gallio, a brother of the philosopher Seneca. Perceiving that Paul was not guilty of any crime, and that the charges against him concerned (from Gallio's perspective) merely fine points of the Jewish religion, the procurator dismissed the case (Acts 18:12–17). For some years, at least in Achaia, this ruling helped ensure protection for Christianity as simply a sect of Judaism enjoying the status of a legal religion under Roman law.

The reference to Gallio (Acts 18:12–17) enables us to date Paul's ministry in Corinth with some precision. An inscription discovered at Delphi records the emperor Claudius' commendation of "my friend [Lucius] Junius Gallio, proconsul of Achaia." The inscription must stem from the first seven months of AD 52, for Claudius describes himself as emperor for the twenty-sixth time; his twenty-seventh acclamation came on August 1. Scholars judge it unlikely that Gallio would have taken office in June 52; more likely he came to Corinth in 51. Thus, Paul's eighteen-month stay in Corinth probably may be dated to 50–52.

Most likely, then, it was early in 52 that Paul left Corinth for Syria (Acts 18:18). After brief visits to Ephesus, Caesarea, Jerusalem, and Antioch (Acts 18:19–22), he set out on his third missionary journey, of which the focal point was a three-year ministry in Ephesus (Acts 18:23–20:38). Toward the end of this period (the period ca. 52–55), he received word of the troubles in Corinth and wrote his first epistle in an attempt to calm the waters. From 1 Cor 16:8, we gather that he wrote some weeks before Pentecost. Thus, the letter's most likely date is early 55.

THE CHURCH'S RELIGIOUS AND SOCIAL STRUCTURE

Religious Composition

The Lord's "many people" in Corinth (Acts 18:10) seem to have been mainly former pagans, and, in particular, "God-fearers" who had attached themselves to the synagogue because of their respect for Jewish monotheism and its high moral standards. The aberrations Paul addresses (e.g., sexual immorality, litigiousness, frequenting heathen temples, denial of a bodily resurrection) were typical of Gentile paganism.

On the other hand, the congregation must have contained a significant Jewish-Christian minority. Crispus, the synagogue leader and his whole household joined the church (Acts 18:8), and if the synagogue leader Sosthenes, mentioned in Acts 18:17, is the same Sosthenes who helped Paul write his epistle (1 Cor 1:1), then at least two prominent Jewish families were founding members. The presence of a Jewish synagogue in the city is attested not only by Acts 18:4–17, but also by the discovery of a lintel bearing the inscription "Synagogue of the Hebrews."

Socioeconomic Status

Turning to the socioeconomic circumstances of the Corinthian Christians, the best starting point is Paul's statement in 1 Cor 1:26: "Not many [of you] were wise by human standards, not many were powerful, not many were of noble birth." It is likely that some, although "not many" (1:26), of the city's elite belonged to the church. Gaius, who could host the whole church in his home, and Erastus, a city official, are probably to be reckoned among this small group (Rom 16:23). Other Christians in that upwardly mobile society would have been at least moderately well to do, among them the tent-making couple Aquila and Priscilla, the synagogue leaders Crispus and Sosthenes, and Stephanas (1 Cor 1:16; 16:15–17). While others may have been craftsmen or small businessmen, a significant number must have been slaves (7:21–22).

Communal Gatherings

According to the descriptions of Roman Corinth supplied by Dio Chrysostom, Galen, and Plutarch, the city was known for its wealth and opulence. The spacious suburb of Craneion in particular was celebrated as a desirable residential area. While the archaeological evidence is sparse—only four private residences have been excavated—it confirms the literary evidence that a number of the homes must have been sizeable, with spacious atriums and dining rooms.

Next door to the Jewish synagogue stood one of the more spacious homes, belonging to one of the church's founding members, Gaius (Acts 18:7). In the home of this man, whom Paul describes as "my host and the host of the whole church" (Rom 16:23), it was possible for the whole church—the whole Corinthian "parish"—to come together (1 Cor 11:20; 14:23). In addition, there may have been smaller churchly gatherings in homes like those of Aquila and Priscilla (cf. Acts 18:1–3; 1 Cor 16:19) and of Phoebe, the church's protector and patroness, in nearby Cenchrea (Rom 16:1–2).

On the basis of Acts 18 and 1 Corinthians, we may identify Stephanas, Fortunatus and Archaicus, Gaius Titius Justus, Aquila and Priscilla, Crispus, Sosthenes, and Chloe's people as members of the congregation; on the basis of Rom 16:21–23, we may add Lucius, Jason, Sosipater, Tertius, Erastus, and Quartus. In addition to these, there were surely other families and individuals worshiping in Corinth who are not mentioned in the biblical record. Estimates of the total number of worshipers range as high as 100 individuals. To accommodate such a number would, indeed, have required a very spacious home.

THE OCCASION OF THE EPISTLE

Two developments in particular seem to have prompted Paul to write this epistle. First, he had received reports from "Chloe's people" about the rise of at least four factions, grouping themselves around the names of Paul, Apollos, Cephas, and Christ (1 Cor 1:10–12). This growing disunity is the chief topic addressed in chapters 1–4. Similarly, the problems addressed in the following chapters (5–6) probably came to Paul's attention through Chloe's people. Her people may have also reported that some were denying the bodily resurrection (15:12). Whether 11:2–34 (women's head-coverings; conduct at communal meals and the Lord's Supper) was also prompted by information from the same source is difficult to say.

Second, Paul needed to respond to several questions put to him in a letter from the Corinthians ("now about the things you wrote," 7:1). This accounts for his discussion of marital issues in chapter 7, and probably also of meat offered to idols (8:1–11:1) and spiritual gifts (12:1–14:40). Those topics are introduced by "now about" (7:1, 25; 8:1; 12:1). Whether the same formula in 16:1 ("now about the collection") and 16:12 ("now about Apollos") also introduces Paul's responses to a letter from Corinth must be considered more doubtful.

THE EPISTLE'S EXTERNAL ATTESTATION AND INTEGRITY

External attestation to the epistle's Pauline authorship appears as early as 1 Clement (ca. AD 95 or 96): "Take up the epistle of the blessed Paul the apostle . . . Truly he wrote to you in the Spirit about himself and Cephas and Apollos, because even then you had split into factions" (47:1–3). In the "maranatha" of Didache 10:6, we hear a clear echo of 1 Cor 16:22. Ignatius (ca. AD 110) cites the epistle frequently (Ephesians 10:3; 16:1; 18:1; Trallians 2:3; 12:3; Romans 5:1; 9:2), as does Polycarp, also ca. AD 110 (Philippians 2:2; 4:3; 5:3; 10:1; 11:2). There may be allusions to 1 Cor 3:1, 16, 18 in the Epistle of Barnabas (e.g., 4:11; 6:15).

See also Justin Martyr, *Dialogue with Trypho*, chapter 35. There are numerous 1 Corinthians citations and allusions in Irenaeus, Clement of Alexandria, and Tertullian.

The canonicity of 1 Corinthians seems never to have been in doubt. Marcion accorded it canonical status, as did the Muratorian Canon. Finally, it is listed with 2 Corinthians among the canonical books of the NT in Athanasius' Thirty-ninth Festal Letter (AD 367).

The epistle's integrity has been questioned by some scholars. Observing that at times it seems disjointed, they have proposed that an editor has pasted together various Pauline fragments. But the sometimes abrupt transitions from topic to topic may be explained by the way in which Paul periodically received information and reacted to it. See the section above entitled "The Occasion of the Epistle." These partition theories have rarely called into question the Pauline origin of the various "pieces." Recently, however, the authenticity of 14:34–35 has come under fire. The text-critical and other issues involved are discussed in the commentary on those verses and the excursus "The Ordination of Women."

THE COMMENTARY PROCESS

Translating the Greek Text into English

This commentary offers a literal translation of the Greek based primarily on the writer's own reading of the text, and secondarily on a comparison with the translation options offered by selected English versions. A particular translation sometimes signals a particular interpretation that needs to be evaluated in light of the evidence. If the translation/interpretation is misleading, it may have an unfortunate impact on the church's understanding of that text for generations. For example, who knows how many Christians may have been kept away from the Lord's Supper by the dire warning given in the King James Version translation of 1 Cor 11:29: "he that eateth and drinketh unworthily, eateth and drinketh *damnation* to himself" (emphasis added)? Unworthy eating and drinking, according to the original text, does not result in "damnation" but in "judgment," or chastening designed to bring undiscerning recipients to their senses and thus help them escape final damnation. Most modern versions have picked up Paul's distinction in 11:29–32 between "judgment" (11:29) and "damn/condemn" (11:32) and here translated 11:29 correctly: "eats and drinks *judgment*" (emphasis added).

Commentaries

Some commentators eschew, as far as possible, any reflection on current issues in the church, believing it is the exegete's duty simply to re-present what the text says. After all, the text itself has a force of its own and should be allowed to speak to modern readers directly, without telling them which applications they need to make. Other commentators make frequent and even lengthy applications to the contemporary church. The present work tries to steer a middle course, giving top priority to listening to the text, but not hesitating to point periodically to its implications for the church's theology and practice.

In a commentary of this scope, it is not possible to deal with, or even note, every view that diverges from one's own. The writer has attempted to give the thread of his own reading of Paul in as clear and uncluttered a fashion as possible, paying attention only to the most significant divergent viewpoints. Hopefully, the simplicity of this commentary's style and approach will make it accessible to a wide readership.

A major part of the difficulty in interpreting 1 Corinthians is our sketchy knowledge of the situation into which Paul was speaking. If only we knew how the worship services ran (Paul hasn't supplied us with a liturgy and agenda)! If only we had a guide outlining how the communal meals related to celebration of the Sacrament! If only we had some audio recordings of their tongues-speaking or prophecies! Whereas Paul's original hearers would have known exactly what he meant, on so many issues all the modern interpreter can do is make a judgment on the basis of the indications we have. This is part of the delight and challenge, but also the frustration, of exegesis! This commentary, then, goes out with the hope and prayer that it has been faithful to the words of the apostle and that the readers will be given greater confidence in the Christ proclaimed by "the word of the cross" (1:18).

Commentary

1 CORINTHIANS 1:1–17

EPISTOLARY OPENING

1 CORINTHIANS 1:1–3

Greetings

TRANSLATION

1 [1]Paul, a called apostle of Christ Jesus by the will of
God, and Sosthenes the brother, [2]to the church of
God that is in Corinth, having been sanctified in
Christ Jesus, called saints, together with all who call
on the name of our Lord Jesus Christ in every place—
both their [Lord] and ours: [3]grace to you and peace
from God our Father and the Lord Jesus Christ.

COMMENTARY

CALLED APOSTLE (1:1)

With great care Paul has designed every detail of his introduction (1 Cor 1:1–9) to combat the rising factionalism and to restore the Corinthians again to the one fellowship of Jesus Christ. To this end, he begins by asserting his authority as Jesus' designated envoy, who in carrying out his commission had become the spiritual father of every Christian in Corinth (4:15). Although Paul saw himself as the least of the apostles (15:8–9), his apostleship was, nevertheless, beyond dispute. He had seen the risen Lord (9:1)! This Lord had called him as his chosen vessel to be the apostle to the Gentiles (Acts 9:15; Rom 11:13), including those in the largely Gentile city of Corinth.

But Paul knew that he was nothing in himself (2 Cor 12:11). He had no intention of building a personal following and deplored the formation of a "Paul" faction as much as he deplored any other faction (1 Cor 1:12). He saw himself simply as servant and witness of the crucified and risen Lord, Christ Jesus, Israel's promised Messiah and the Savior of the world (Mt 1:21; Jn 4:42). Now, the former persecutor of the church (1 Cor 15:9) had found his great vocation in betrothing others to Christ (2 Cor 11:2); his most important labor was in ensuring that Christ was formed in others (Gal 4:19). His concern to advance the name and cause of Christ emerges clearly in the opening verses of this epistle, where "Christ" occurs ten times in the first ten verses. As he wrote to the Philippians, "For me to live is Christ" (Phil 1:21).

It was "not from men nor through a man" that Paul had been commissioned to serve Christ (Gal 1:1), but "through the will of God" (2 Cor 1:1; Eph 1:1; Col 1:1; cf. 1 Tim 1:1). Unlike the false apostles who commended themselves and sought to impose their own will on the church (2 Cor 10:18; 11:13), Paul's ministry bore the divine stamp of approval.

Despite his standing as a divinely called apostle, Paul never operated as a "one-man band." His ministry was always a team effort, whether he was associated with Barnabas, with Silas and Timothy (1 Thess 1:1; 2 Thess 1:1), with various "brothers" (Gal 1:2), or, as here, with Sosthenes. This is probably the same Sosthenes who had been serving as synagogue ruler during Paul's first visit to Corinth (Acts 18:17). Like another synagogue ruler before him (Crispus, Acts 18:8), Sosthenes found Paul's preaching compelling. But his Christian leanings incurred the hostility of his fellow Jews, who inflicted a beating on him before the proconsul Gallio's tribunal (Acts 18:17). Thereupon, Sosthenes seems to have left the city, making his home in Ephesus. As a former synagogue official, and moreover one who had been beaten for the sake of Christ, Sosthenes would have been honored by the Corinthian church.

Sosthenes probably wrote down most of the letter (i.e., through 1 Cor 16:20) at Paul's direction. But this may have involved more than accepting mechanical dictation. The two men probably talked over the letter's contents and came to a consensus on what should be transmitted. Nevertheless, it is clear that Paul is the primary human author. The ultimate author is God, whose Spirit inspired the writing of the Scriptures (2 Tim 3:16; 2 Pet 1:21), and so Paul's canonical writings are part of the sacred Scriptures (2 Pet 3:16). The exact method and circumstances of the human authors in no way compromises the divine authorship of the Scriptures (cf. the commentary on 1 Cor 1:16).

CALLED SAINTS (1:2)

Paul and Sosthenes address "the church of God that is in Corinth" (1:2). The church does not belong to Paul or Apollos or anyone else; it is God's. Paul, Apollos, Sosthenes, and the other church workers all belong to God. They are "God's co-workers," and the Corinthian saints are "God's field, God's building" (3:9; cf. 3:22–23). Thus, Paul tries to lift the Corinthians' sights above any limited conceptions of the church as a merely human institution, or an arena for human power plays, to a proper understanding of its character as a divine institution. The apostle of Christ Jesus, called by the will of God, is writing to the church of God, consisting of saints who are also called by God. This is the great vision of the church Paul wants the Corinthians to catch, the vision of God's "one holy catholic and apostolic church" (Nicene Creed), of which the church in Corinth is a manifestation.

On the one hand, the church in Corinth is fully church, with no gifts or graces missing. On the other hand, it is only one manifestation of God's church among many others, one outcropping, the one that happens to be in Corinth. So the Corinthians should not see themselves as superior to other Christians because of their intellectual attainments or spiritual gifts or unique cultural situation. They are to obey the same apostolic Word that sustains all the churches (cf. 4:17;

7:17; 10:32; 11:16; 14:33). Thus, Paul constantly reminds the Corinthians of their place in the larger Christian family (cf. 16:19). After all, the Word of God did not originate with them (14:36)!

How paradoxical that the one church of God was present in corrupt Corinth! Paul now elaborates on the church's nature: it consists of those in a state of "having been sanctified in Christ Jesus" (1:2). The sanctification of God's people does not result from their efforts at self-improvement, their moral accomplishments; it is God's gift in Christ. The church received her holiness in Baptism: "But you were washed, but you were sanctified, but you were justified in the name of the Lord Jesus Christ and in the Spirit of our God" (6:11; see also 12:13). On the basis, then, of the sanctification conferred on the church, Paul constantly appeals to the Corinthians: "Become what you are!"

Another epithet follows, "called saints" (1:2), which balances "a called apostle" in 1:1. God's people in Corinth had become saints, "a holy nation," by virtue of the divine summons "out of darkness into His marvelous light" (1 Pet 2:9; cf. Ex 19:5–6). In Paul's letters, the word "saints" always embraces all believers.

The Corinthians are saints "together with all who call on the name of our Lord Jesus Christ in every place" (1 Cor 1:2). Again, Paul is reminding the Corinthians that they belong to a great spiritual fellowship of Christians throughout the world. To "call on the name of the Lord" (1:2) means to believe in Jesus as Lord, appeal to him in prayer, and praise him in worship. The attentive listener in Corinth would have been able to complete the text Paul is citing from Joel 3:5: "Everyone who calls on the name of the Lord will be saved." In no other name was salvation to be found (Acts 4:12; cf. Acts 3:16). No doubt the text had become more precious to Paul since his Baptism, when Ananias admonished him, "Rise, be baptized, and wash away your sins, *calling on his name*" (Acts 22:16). The Roman statesman Pliny the Younger testified (*Letters*, 10.96.7) that Christians were characterized by the practice of singing hymns to Christ "as to God."

The phrase, "in every place" (1 Cor 1:2), evokes the grandeur of the universal church and its mission in echoes of Malachi: " 'From the rising of the sun even to its setting, my name shall be great among the nations; and in every place incense shall be offered to my name, and a pure offering, for my name shall be great among the nations,' says the Lord of hosts" (Mal 1:11).

The final phrase in 1 Cor 1:2, "both their [Lord] and ours," reminds the Corinthians again of what they have in common with fellow Christians everywhere. They are not unique; they share the same Lord Jesus Christ as do their brothers and sisters around the world (cf. Rom 10:12).

CONFERRAL OF GIFTS (1:3)

Paul now confers his apostolic blessing of "grace" and "peace" (1 Cor 1:3). These scriptural blessings are not merely wishes. They convey what the words say. The first blessing, "grace," is the highest gift of God, his free favor and forgiveness to undeserving people. Grace, then, is the source of peace, the state of being reconciled to God (Rom 5:1–11). Since the death of God's Son brought us forgiveness and reconciliation to God (Rom 5:10), Christians are inspired to live in a forgiving and peaceful manner with one another and, so far as it lies with them (Rom 12:18), with all people. How sorely the strife-torn Corinthian congregation needed this blessing of peace and the conciliatory spirit that flowed from it! Often God's peace also bears fruit in a sense of inner peace, though this "feeling" is not essential. The objective condition of a peaceful relationship with God through Jesus Christ is paramount in Paul's concept of "peace" (Rom 5:1–2; Eph 2:14–18).

The gifts of grace and peace are conferred both by "God our Father and the Lord Jesus Christ" (1 Cor 1:3). "The Lord Jesus Christ" is accorded equal status with the Father as the bestower of divine gifts. When he is called "Lord," he is given an ascription belonging to God (e.g., 1:31).

1 CORINTHIANS 1:4–9
THANKSGIVING

TRANSLATION

**1 [4]I thank my God for you always, because of the grace
of God given you in Christ Jesus. [5][I am thankful]
that in everything you were enriched in him, in all
speech and all knowledge, [6]as the testimony to Christ
was confirmed among you. [7]Thus you are not lacking
in any gift of grace as you eagerly await the revelation
of our Lord Jesus Christ, [8]who will also confirm you
until the end, blameless on the day of our Lord Jesus
Christ. [9]God is faithful, by whom you were called into
the communion of his Son, Jesus Christ our Lord.**

COMMENTARY

Faced by the host of problems in the Corinthian congregation, Paul might naturally be expected to begin on a note of complaint. But he takes care not to let the abundant aberrations loom so large in his mind that they sour his relationship with the church and make him lose sight of the far more abundant grace of God (cf. Rom 5:20). As their faithful apostle, pastor, and intercessor, he first assures the Corinthians that he always thanks God for them.

While it was standard practice in ancient letters and speeches to begin by expressing one's gratitude to the audience, a practice which could degenerate to hollow flattery (cf. Acts 24:1–3), there is nothing hollow about Paul's words of thanksgiving to God for the grace he has poured out on the Corinthians. From the fullness of the unspeakable gift of Christ himself (2 Cor 9:15), the congregation had received "grace upon grace" (Jn 1:16). Ever since their Baptism (1 Cor 6:11; 12:13), they had enjoyed a rich and full spiritual life. For all this the apostle is deeply grateful.

In Christ they had been enriched "in all speech and all knowledge" (1:5). Their rich endowment in "speech" included the gift of tongues and its interpretation, prophecy and the weighing of prophecy, teaching, and the composing of hymns (12:10, 28–30; 14:26). Following the pattern of their teacher, Apollos, an "eloquent" man (Acts 18:24), the Corinthians had been enriched in all "eloquence, speech" (1 Cor 1:5).

This gift of speech flowed from the "knowledge" that was in their hearts. Like "speech," "knowledge" is a comprehensive word. It includes the Corinthians' Spirit-given understanding of the wisdom of the cross, their appreciation of all

God's gifts, their ability to exercise spiritual judgment, and the specific gift of prophetic knowledge (2:6–16; 13:2; 14:6). These two gifts—the utterance of the mouth and the knowledge of the heart—find an echo in the two parts of Rom 10:9: "If you confess with your mouth the Lord Jesus and believe in your heart that God raised him from the dead, you will be saved."

For the congregation's outstanding endowment with these gifts, Paul thanks God. Some commentators have detected a trace of irony in his thanksgiving, for it was precisely these gifts of speech (especially the gift of tongues) and of knowledge which had led many Corinthians to become puffed up. But there can be little doubt that Paul's thanksgiving is thoroughly genuine. The gifts of grace (12:4, 9, 28, 30, 31) in themselves were signs of God's rich gift of grace (1:7). The problems had arisen because some were letting their gifts "go to their heads," as though they had acquired them through their own efforts or brilliance. Later, Paul would remind them, "What do you have that you have not received?" (4:7).

Thus, in praising God for the Corinthians' giftedness "in all speech and all knowledge" (1:5), Paul is not only giving God his due but also signaling to the Corinthians that it is to these two gifts that he will be paying most attention. *Throughout the epistle, everything he says will be aimed at correcting distortions and developing the right understanding of Christian speech and knowledge.*

Their rich spiritual gifts served as evidence that the apostolic testimony to Christ had created Christian faith in the hearers. Through the Holy Spirit's testimony, it had been brought home to their deepest convictions that the Gospel message was true, leading to these rich results.

1 Cor 1:7 is a result clause, balancing the positive statement of 1:5 ("in everything you were enriched in him") with its double-negative corollary ("thus you are not lacking in any gift of grace"). Paul is probably not comparing the Corinthians with other Christians ("you are not lacking in comparison with others"), but simply saying that the gifts of grace they had received were sufficient.

This is the first time Paul has used the word "gifts of grace" (1:7). While the Corinthians themselves seem to have preferred the word "spiritual gifts" (12:1), Paul prefers "gifts of grace" as a reminder that all they have is by grace.

At the same time, Paul gently reminds them not to let their giftedness lull them into complacency. They must not become so focused on present blessings that they lose sight of their Christian hope. They should still be filled with longing for "the revelation of our Lord Jesus Christ" (1:7). Their gifts are to serve a church which is still on the way, but the Corinthians are in danger of falling into a self-centered intoxication with their gifts, so that later Paul must reproach them: "Already you are satiated! Already you have begun to be rich! Without us you have begun your reign!" (4:8). As a result, not only are they no longer eagerly anticipating the Lord's final coming, but their hope for the final resurrection of their bodies has also faded (1 Corinthians 15). They need to join Paul in praying the prayer with which he closes the epistle, "Our Lord, come!" (1 Cor 16:22).

Just as the testimony to Christ had been confirmed among them in the past (1:6), so Paul gives thanks that in the future God would continue to strengthen the Corinthians in faith. He could be counted on to keep doing this "until the end" (1:8; cf. Phil 1:6; Jude 24–25).

Thus, on the day when all must appear before Christ's judgment seat (2 Cor 5:10), the Corinthians could be assured that they would be "holy, pure, and blameless" before him (Col 1:22). That day and the assessment of his life which would take place on that day were, for Paul, far weightier matters than any human assessment of his ministry (1 Cor 4:3). For the Corinthians also, preoccupied as they were with the present age and its gifts, it was essential to keep the Last Day continually before their eyes. Our death may transpire before Jesus' final coming, but the resurrection of the body and eternal life in the new creation will commence only then, at his return. We need a proper "apocalyptic" perspective—a sense that our brief lives are always lived in the shadow of eternity. Then we will not become too myopically engrossed in the joys, gifts, and cares of this world, "for the form of this world is passing away" (7:31).

When Paul says that God will keep them "blameless" (1 Cor 1:8), he does not mean, of course, that the last advent will find them morally perfect. His assurance is that no one will be able to bring a charge against them (Rom 8:33), for Christ Jesus has become their righteousness (1 Cor 1:30). Moreover, Paul is confident that God will keep them from falling in times of temptation (10:13; 2 Cor 1:10).

He can assure them that God will sustain them to the end because he knows "God is faithful" (1 Cor 1:9). God's faithfulness is one of his outstanding attributes, according to the Scriptures (Deut 7:9; 2 Cor 1:18–20; Titus 1:2). Thus, he is worthy of the Christian's total confidence.

As a sign that the one who had called them would see his good work through to the end (cf. Phil 1:6), Paul points to the blessed fellowship the Corinthians already enjoyed in Christ. This "communion" involved far more than some kind of vague relationship with Christ. It meant, rather, an actual participation in him, a union with him through faith and Baptism into his body, so that their bodies were now in a mysterious way members of his body (6:15; 12:13). This deep communion was constantly nourished by the Gospel and Christ's true body and blood in the Sacrament of Holy Communion (9:23; 10:16).

Communion with Christ is, in turn, the basis for communion among Christians (Acts 2:42; 1 Jn 1:3). In drawing people into communion with his Son as members of his body, God draws them into a close and deep relationship with one another. From the outset, Paul is reminding the Corinthians that their "communion" (1 Cor 1:9) in Christ rules out all factionalism and individualism (1:10–11). Paul would have no time for the modern attitude that "my Christianity is something between me and my God."

1 CORINTHIANS 1:10–17

PAUL APPEALS FOR UNITY IN CHRIST

TRANSLATION

1 [10]I urge you, brothers, by the name of our Lord Jesus
Christ, that you all say the same thing and there
be no factions among you, but that you be restored
to the same mind and the same conviction. [11]For it
was made clear to me concerning you, my brothers,
by Chloe's people that there are quarrels among
you. [12]What I mean is that each of you is saying:
"I belong to Paul," or "I belong to Apollos," or "I
belong to Cephas," or "I belong to Christ." [13]Is Christ
divided? Paul was not crucified for you, was he? Or
were you baptized into the name of Paul? [14]I thank
God I did not baptize any of you except Crispus
and Gaius, [15]lest anyone say you were baptized into
my name. [16]Oh yes, I also baptized the family of
Stephanas. Beyond that, I do not know if I baptized
anyone else. [17]For Christ did not send me to baptize
but to preach the Gospel, not by wisdom of word,
lest the cross of Christ be emptied [of its power].

COMMENTARY

BE OF ONE MIND (1:10–12)

Paul turns now to address the first big issue of the epistle: the need to restore the church's unity. This topic will be his chief concern throughout the first four chapters (1:10–4:21). While he can sometimes be stern (4:21!), the chief basis of his appeal is the Gospel of the crucified and risen Lord Jesus Christ, whose name the Corinthians call upon (1:2). Their faith and fellowship in Christ, he points out, have clear implications for their unity.

The Corinthians had been called into communion with Christ (1:9). Paul now urges them to maintain that unity. Calling them "brothers," a term he will use thirty-nine times in the epistle, his appeal comes to them "by the name of our Lord Jesus Christ" (1:10), the one name that should completely overshadow any party names and loyalties. After all, this was the name into which they had been baptized. Paul is here, no doubt, anticipating the baptismal argument in 1:13. The Corinthians belong to Christ and only to Christ, for they have been baptized in his name, not the name of Paul or anyone else.

On the basis of their common bond in Christ, Paul encourages the church "to say the same thing" (1:10). It had become apparent that the Corinthians, proud of their intellectual ability, delighted in debating with one another, taking a variety of positions on issues like sexuality and marriage, food laws, spiritual gifts, and the role of women in worship. Paul's plea for unity does not mean he envisaged a colorless uniformity, with no room for individual insights and accents. On the other hand, neither would he have condoned the principle of "reconciled diversity," the pluralism in doctrine and practice endorsed by the modern ecumenical movement. That would not be compatible with saying the same thing. Paul is pleading for a "great consensus" (AC I 1) in the church, so that the congregation will glorify God "with one voice" (Rom 15:6) and be eager to "maintain the unity of the Spirit in the bond of peace" (Eph 4:3; cf. Ps 133:1; Jn 17:17–21).

Thus, there should be "no factions" in the congregation. The word "faction" may mean a "tear" in a garment (Mk 2:21). Although the congregation is not yet so divided that Paul cannot address the Corinthians as a unified whole, it seems they are on the verge of being torn apart. Like his Lord in the high priestly prayer, Paul is concerned that they should "continue to be one" (Jn 17:21, 23). They should not let their loyalty to their favorite leaders rend the community any further.

Continuing his appeal, Paul urges the Corinthians to be "restored to the same mind and the same conviction" (1 Cor 1:10). The verb "restore" is used for the mending of fishing nets (Mk 1:19). The Corinthians are to "patch things up" among themselves (cf. 2 Cor 13:11).

In 1:11, Paul models a wise pastoral approach in naming the source of his information. This is no mere rumor. His informants may have been Chloe's relatives or her servants. Chloe herself was almost certainly a Christian or at least sympathetic to the church. Whether she lived in Corinth or Ephesus is not indicated.

Chloe's people had informed Paul that there were "quarrels" (1:11) among the Corinthians. The word "quarrels" is almost synonymous with "factions" in 1:10. The presence of quarreling and jealousy was a sign that the Corinthians were still "fleshly" people (3:3), controlled by their unregenerate human nature. Paul's list of "the works of the flesh" in Gal 5:19–20 includes "quarreling" and closely related sins like "enmities . . . jealousy, anger, and selfish ambition." Anyone who habitually indulged in these sins was in danger of forfeiting his share in God's kingdom (Gal 5:21).

The regrettable tendency to quarreling had become widespread in Corinth. Most unfortunate was the egotism which Paul brings out by the four-times repeated "I": "*I* belong to Paul," "*I* belong to Apollos," "*I* belong to Cephas," "*I* belong to Christ" (1:12).

It is clear that none of these "leaders" encouraged the development of a faction around himself. What is not so clear is the motivation that led to the formation of each group.

A significant group seems to have stood by Paul as the church's founding father who had labored among them for a year and a half (Acts 18:11). They believed he should be held in honor as the first missionary to have reached them. They may also have preferred his more direct and unpretentious style of teaching. But Paul disapproves of this group as much as the others. As he perceives, the Paul-people are not motivated by concern for the truth of the Gospel. Rather, in a self-interested and boastful fashion, they are busy forming a personality cult around the apostle, just as the other groups for their own selfish purposes are putting Apollos or Cephas or Christ on a pedestal.

After Paul had planted the church in Corinth, Apollos, the gifted and eloquent Alexandrian, was encouraged by the church in Ephesus to travel to Achaia (Greece). "On his arrival he greatly helped those who by grace had believed" (Acts 18:27). Apollos was thus honored as the one who "watered" what Paul had planted in Corinth (1 Cor 3:6). By comparison with Apollos' rhetorical skills, Paul's preaching seemed—to some at least—unimpressive and simplistic (2:1–3; 2 Cor 10:10; 11:6). But there is no suggestion that Apollos ever encouraged the formation of a faction bearing his name. All the evidence indicates that he and Paul worked in harmony (cf. 16:12, where Paul informs them he has been urging his "brother" Apollos to pay them another visit).

The "Paul" and "Apollos" factions may have been the largest. Certainly the dispute between them seems to have weighed most heavily on Paul's mind. In chapters 3 and 4, he returns to the question of a proper evaluation of the role of Apollos and himself (3:4–9; 4:6). But the "Cephas" and "Christ" groups are not mentioned again.

The group that had formed around Cephas is more difficult to account for than the Paul and Apollos groups. It is possible that Cephas had made a personal visit to Corinth accompanied by his wife, for the Corinthians were familiar with his habit of taking his wife along on his travels (9:5). If the church had been host to both Peter and his wife, this would more readily explain some members' attachment to him. But it is difficult to say whether the Corinthians knew about his travel habits from personal observation or simply from reports. It is also possible that some, especially those Corinthians who were Jewish-Christian in background, had been baptized by Peter, and on that basis had formed a personal attachment to him. Some of these Jewish Christians may have arrived in Corinth proudly carrying letters of recommendation from the chief apostle (cf. 2 Cor 3:1).

But more than this we cannot say. There is not one piece of evidence in the epistle that the "Cephas" group was a Judaizing faction upholding a stricter attitude to Jewish law, particularly food laws.

Finally, the "Christ" group is the most difficult to account for. Numerous theories have been advanced as to their identity, including those who had known Jesus, Judaizers like those who troubled the churches of Galatia, those who rejected any apostolic authority, spiritualists who followed "Christ" but disavowed following the human Jesus, and those who claimed a special knowledge and freedom from any authority.

What does seem certain is that the "Christ" faction was reacting against the other three. Rather than advocating any distinctive doctrine or practice, they may have been individuals proclaiming themselves to be weary of the bickering, and saying in a superior fashion, "a pox on all your houses; I belong to Christ." On the other hand, their critical attitude toward their faithful pastors suggests that the "Christ" group may have seen themselves as a particularly "spiritual" group, claiming to have direct access to Christ apart from any human proclaimers of his word. Proud of their giftedness and their "knowledge" (1:5), they may have been especially prone to a theology of glory in which there was little room for the crucified Christ and cruciform pastors. But one cannot belong to Christ while rejecting the apostolic ministry instituted by God himself. Thus, Paul also opposes this group.

THREE RHETORICAL QUESTIONS (1:13)

Paul's response to the news from Chloe's people begins with three rhetorical questions: "Is Christ divided? Paul was not crucified for you, was he? Or were you baptized into the name of Paul?" (1:13). Paul asks incredulously whether Christ could possibly have been divided into competing factions. To ask the question is to answer it; the idea is preposterous! Obviously the Lord Jesus is one indivisible person. And just as his person cannot be fragmented, so it is inconceivable that his body, the church, should be factionalized.

Taking only his own party to task, and allowing the other groups to fill in the blanks, Paul shows the absurdity of their position: "Paul was not crucified for you, was he? Or were you baptized into the name of Paul?" Now, for the first time in this letter, he points to the pivotal role of Christ's crucifixion and of Baptism into Christ and Christ's name as the appropriation of Christ's death. From the beginning, the heart of the Gospel preached to the Corinthians had been "Christ died for our sins" (15:3). In the light of their faith in Christ crucified, how could they make so much of Paul or any other minister of the Gospel? After all, they had not been purchased by the blood of Paul. The great foundation of their faith remained Jesus Christ and him crucified (2:2; 3:11).

Baptism in the name of Jesus was the other foundational event in the life of the church. Through Baptism, the believers had appropriated the salvation Christ won on the cross. Thus, it was absurd for the "Paul" faction to idolize Paul as if their salvation and identity were to be found in him.

PAUL AS BAPTIZER (1:14–16)

Naturally, Paul did not approach his work in Corinth with the intention of baptizing as few people as possible. However, in retrospect, he is grateful to God for his providence in not letting him baptize more families than he did.

God had seen to it that Paul baptized only Crispus and Gaius. Crispus was the synagogue official who had been one of Paul's early converts in Corinth, believing in the Lord "with his whole household" (Acts 18:8). Presumably Paul baptized the whole family, but here he only mentions Crispus as the family's head.

Gaius is probably the man Paul describes in his epistle to the Romans (written from Corinth) as "my host and the host of the whole church" (Rom 16:23). His full name may have been Gaius Titius Justus. Titius Justus is mentioned in Acts as the God-fearing Gentile who welcomed Paul into his home after he had been driven from the synagogue in Corinth (Acts 18:7). Like Crispus, then, he belonged to the first group of converts, and for that reason had been baptized by the apostle himself. He was probably a man of means, which made it possible for him to host the whole church. In this respect, he and Crispus were different from most members of the Corinthian congregation (1 Cor 1:26–29). Gaius may have been one of the Roman freedmen who came to Corinth and made their wealth in commerce.

For a moment, Paul entertains the possibility that someone could say he had been baptized into Paul's name (1:15). Whether such claims had actually been made or not, it is conceivable that some of his converts from paganism, impressed by the miracles that attended his preaching, had come to regard him as a godlike figure (cf. the Lycaonians in Acts 14:8–18). But Paul rules any such grandiose ideas about himself out of court. In the first place, since Baptism *by* someone is not Baptism *into* someone, *no one* baptized by Paul could claim to be baptized into Paul. Baptism was always "into the name of Jesus" (a brief way of referring to Christian Baptism in the name of the Holy Trinity, Mt 28:19). Moreover, since Paul had baptized only Crispus and Gaius (and the household of Stephanas, 1 Cor 1:16), only they could even come close to claiming—if that were at all proper—that they had been baptized into Paul's name.

Finally, Paul recalls "the family of Stephanas" (1:16). This family had been "the firstfruits of Achaia" (16:15). They were noted for their significant service to the saints (16:15). Why then did Paul momentarily forget him, when Stephanas was with him at the time in Ephesus, together with the other members of the Corinthian delegation, Fortunatus and Achaicus (16:17)? One suggestion is that it may have been precisely because Stephanas was with Paul that Paul forgot him. Preoccupied with recalling names back in Corinth, Paul momentarily failed to consider the Corinthians who were in Ephesus. We might even imagine there may have been some amusement as Stephanas himself or one of the other delegates jogged Paul's memory. After this lapse, Paul was not confident he had included everyone, so he adds, "Beyond that, I do not know if I baptized anyone else" (1:16). Keeping a tally of those he had baptized apparently was not high on his agenda.

That the Scriptures allow us to see an apostle struggling with his memory reminds us not to conceive of biblical inspiration in terms of some mechanical process of dictation, as though the writer's mind were not involved. At the same time, this apparent glimpse of an apostle's human weakness does not detract from the nature of the apostolic Scriptures as the Word of God written for our edification and comfort.

PAUL AS PREACHER OF THE GOSPEL/WORD OF THE CROSS (1:17)

Baptism had not been the apostle's top priority, "for Christ did not send [him] to baptize but to preach the Gospel" (1:17). The verb "sent" is related to the word "apostle." Christ's commission to Paul had not placed Baptism as the major component. Jesus himself did not baptize; he entrusted baptizing to his disciples (Jn 4:1–2). The apostles Peter and John did not baptize the Samaritan converts; that had already been done by the deacon Philip (Acts 8:12–17). To say this is not to depreciate the Sacrament of Baptism and the gifts received there. The point is that the task of administering Baptism could be carried out by any of the apostles' assistants. On the other hand, it is significant that the apostle Paul did baptize some people; the NT pattern is that the preaching of the Gospel is accompanied by Christian Baptism (e.g., Acts 2:38–41; 8:12–13, 36–38; 10:47–48).

Paul had been entrusted with "the priestly service of the Gospel" of Christ (Rom 15:15–16). To this task he had been set aside from his mother's womb. He was to preach the Gospel of God's Son among the Gentiles, reaching out into regions where Christ had not yet been named (Rom 15:20–21; 2 Cor 10:14–16; Gal 1:15–16). Paul and his fellow apostles had a unique pioneering role in spreading the Gospel as widely as possible. It was a task that required special gifts.

On the other hand, the "elders" (pastors) whom Paul began to appoint from the time of his first missionary journey (Acts 14:23) had much more limited local responsibilities. Their duties have always included not only preaching but the administration of Baptism and the Lord's Supper.

Having praised preaching so highly, Paul hastens to add that the preacher should not rely on his "wisdom/cleverness of word" (1 Cor 1:17). His "way with words" may be a fine servant of the Gospel, if he employs it humbly to that end. But if he uses it to focus attention on his eloquence rather than the cross, then the good servant has become the bad master. The expression "wisdom of word" includes the ability to communicate with charm and eloquence, a skill in which Paul did not excel, at least in comparison with Apollos. He had come to the Corinthians "in weakness and fear and much trembling" (2:3). While they granted that his letters were "weighty and strong," they thought he had no presence in public and no ability as a speaker (2 Cor 10:10; 11:6). Their superficial judgments focused on the manner of his presentation rather than its substance.

While "wisdom of word" does include oratorical ability, the context implies that much more is involved. The expression embraces both form and content, both human rhetorical skills *and human philosophy.* Note the antagonism of a group of Greek philosophers toward Paul and the Gospel in Acts 17:18, and also Paul's critique of "philosophy and empty deceit" in Col 2:8. Paul contrasts the Gospel with worldly wisdom more pointedly in 1 Cor 1:18–25. In 1:21, for example, where Paul says, "the world did not know God through wisdom," "wisdom" primarily means philosophy. Paul is thus rejecting the traditional approach of the Greek philosophers and sophists with their "wise" ideas to peddle and their "wisdom" or "cleverness" in presenting them.

Any reliance on human wisdom, whether in formulating arguments or in presenting them, would empty the cross of Christ of its power (1:17), for its power is in its weakness (cf. 2 Cor 12:9; 13:4). The failure to present the word of the cross in a straightforward manner robs that word of any opportunity to do its powerful work. All that the speaker has accomplished is to focus people's attention on himself and his own ability with words. To this issue Paul will turn next.

PREACHING AS "THE HIGHEST OFFICE IN CHRISTENDOM"

Paul's call and highest ambition in his role as apostle to the Gentiles was to preach the Gospel in places where Christ had never been named (Rom 15:20). Thus, his ministry took him from province to province as he evangelized, taught, and exhorted the new converts until Christ was formed in them (Gal 4:19). With his broad responsibilities and extensive travels, it was impossible for him to attend to the ongoing pastoral care and administration of the Sacraments required in each place. As already noted, these local responsibilities he entrusted, from the beginning of his missionary journeys, to "elders" (pastors) appointed in each church (Acts 14:23).

In telling the Corinthians that Christ did not send him to baptize, it is clearly not Paul's intention to encourage any disregard for the Sacraments or the regular pastoral ministry. His point, simply, is that baptizing was not the chief part of the specific charge of his apostolic office.

Luther (AE 39:313–14) cited 1 Cor 1:17 in support of his view that good preaching was the highest of a pastor's responsibilities:

> The spiritual tyrants despised and underestimated the office of preaching and made a great separation between it and the spiritual government, even though it is the highest office, on which all others depend and from which they follow. On the other hand, where there is no office of preaching, none of the others can follow. For John says, John 4[:2],

that Jesus did not baptize, he only preached. And Paul boasts, I Corinthians 1[:17], that he was not sent to baptize but to preach.

Therefore, whoever has the office of preaching imposed on him has the highest office in Christendom imposed on him. Afterward he may also baptize, celebrate mass, and exercise all pastoral care; or, if he does not wish to do so, he may confine himself to preaching and leave baptizing and other lower offices to others—as Christ and all the apostles did, Acts [6:1–4].

EXCURSUS
MODERN DENOMINATIONS

How does the tendency Paul deplores in 1 Cor 1:10–17 manifest itself in the contemporary church? In response to this question, many scholars naturally think of our denominational divisions. It is indeed true—and it cannot be stated too strongly—that wherever Christians take a chauvinistic pride in their own denomination, there Paul's warnings and judgment must be heeded. However, we cannot simply draw a straight line from Paul's text to the modern denominational scene without some qualifications.

First, an analysis must take into account the way tags have sometimes been foisted on Christians and churches, even against their will, by those who disagreed with them. Such may have been the origin of "Christian" and "Nazarene" in the NT era. In 1521, Luther (AE 45:70) echoed Paul in 1 Cor 1:10–17 and 3:4–6, 22 when he requested,

> In the first place, I ask that men make no reference to my name; let them call themselves Christians, not Lutherans. What is Luther? After all, the teaching is not mine. . . . Neither was I crucified for anyone. . . . St. Paul, in I Corinthians 3, would not allow the Christians to call themselves Pauline or Petrine, but Christian. How then should I—poor stinking maggot-fodder that I am—come to have men call the children of Christ by my wretched name? Not so, my dear friends; let us abolish all party names and call ourselves Christians.

However, members of a denomination named after an individual do not necessarily pledge allegiance to every opinion of that individual over against the Word of God. Nor does such a denominational name imply disagreement with other Christians throughout history who have confessed the Gospel. Rather, an individual's name may be appropriated precisely because he confessed the truth of the Gospel with exceptional clarity, and perhaps also in contradistinction to others who were obscuring or even denying the Gospel. In such cases, the label may help signify one's agreement with the true Gospel confessed also by all believers of all times. For example, the Lutheran church, in calling itself "Lutheran," identifies itself as a confessor of the one catholic faith expressed in the three ecumenical creeds and the Lutheran Confessions.

Moreover, it should be recognized that the differences between churches frequently do involve important differences in doctrine and practice, whereas there is no evidence that the factions Paul describes in 1 Corinthians 1 represented any differences in doctrine or practice. The way Paul describes the problem, it seems the factions simply were the result of personal preferences for one of the unwilling factional "leaders": Paul, Apollos, Cephas, or Christ (1 Cor 1:12). Paul condemns the divisions because there was no valid, substantive basis for them.

All the excitement was being generated by their followers in their overcharged enthusiasm for one leader over another. But later in 1 Corinthians, when Paul refers to "divisions" (11:18, the same word as in 1:10 and 12:25) that involve differences regarding the Lord's Supper, Paul actually commends the existence of such divisions, saying, "For there must be divisions among you, in order that those who are genuine may be manifested among you" (11:19). In other words, the divisions revealed which members were remaining faithful and which were not. In another context, Paul himself also did not hesitate to take a firm stand against Peter and rebuke him publicly when a disagreement arose about church fellowship (Gal 2:11–21).

Taking all of the above into account, one must say that the tragedy behind the existence of divisions and denominations today is that many in Christendom have departed from the apostolic Gospel in various matters of doctrine and practice. The scandal is caused by departure from the truth, and the restoration of the church's unity requires all parties to return to the one catholic and apostolic faith. The union of visible church bodies does not necessarily accomplish that return to unity in the true faith. The word of the cross, the Gospel of Jesus Christ, defines what the church is and what the church must be if it is to remain Christ's. On the basis of the Gospel, Paul will order the excommunication of the incestuous man and forbid fellowship with immoral persons (1 Corinthians 5). The apostle will spell out the implications of the Gospel for marriage and sexuality, the Lord's Supper, worship, spiritual gifts, and the role of women (1 Corinthians 6–14). He will repeat the apostolic tradition about the resurrection, without which faith is in vain (1 Corinthians 15). The dominical and apostolic Gospel is now recorded in the Scriptures. For modern denominations and congregations, as for the Corinthian church, the practice of fellowship must be based on fidelity to that authoritative teaching. No article of the Christian faith can be abandoned or compromised as unimportant or irrelevant for the church's unity.

The modern phenomenon in Christendom that most resembles the situation in Corinth probably is the tendency to idolize the "brilliant" (or even the not-so-brilliant) theologian or the outstanding churchman or evangelist. Such movements can assume cultic features, and the dynamics can be operative apart from any organization or name.

Paul himself wrote that neither he nor Apollos was anything; all glory belonged to God, who alone caused his Word to bear fruit (3:7; cf. 2 Cor 12:11). It is the one Spirit who leads us into all truth (Jn 16:13). And that truth is found only in Jesus (Eph 4:21; cf. Col 2:3).

1 CORINTHIANS 1:18–4:21

THE WORD OF THE CROSS IS THE BASIS FOR THE CHURCH'S UNITY

1 CORINTHIANS 1:18–25

The Theme: The Word of the Cross Is God's Power for Salvation

TRANSLATION

1 18 For the word of the cross is foolishness to those
who are being destroyed, but to us who are being
saved it is the power of God. 19 For it has been
written: "I will destroy the wisdom of the wise,
and the understanding of the understanding I will
reject." 20 Where is a wise man? Where is a scribe?
Where is a debater of this age? Has not God made
foolish the wisdom of the world? 21 For since in God's
wisdom the world did not know God through its
[own] wisdom, it was his good pleasure to save those
who believe through the foolishness of preaching.
22 Since Jews ask for signs and Greeks look for
wisdom, 23 we preach Christ crucified, to Jews a
stumbling block and to Gentiles foolishness, 24 but
to the called themselves, both Jews and Greeks,
Christ [whom we preach is] God's power and God's
wisdom. 25 For God's folly is wiser than people
and God's weakness is stronger than people.

COMMENTARY

THE WORD OF THE CROSS (1:18–19)

Paul has been arguing that reliance on one's skill as a speaker can rob the cross of Christ of its power. He now sets out to cure the Corinthians of their fascination with rhetoric. After all, they should know that no matter how well they dress up the word of the cross, the world will always find it unpalatable, for the world marches to a different drummer. Its enthusiasm always is for whatever seems attractive and successful. Its basic orientation is toward what has aptly been called "the theology of glory." But now, in opposition to the world's lust for glamour, success, and "image," Paul sets forth "the word [the theology] of the cross"

(1:18–25). Only that sobering word will provide the Corinthians with a basis for overcoming their divisions and restoring their fellowship in Christ.

"The Theology of Glory" and "The Theology of the Cross"

These expressions derive from Luther's Heidelberg Disputation of 1518 (AE 31:39–70). In thesis 20 (AE 31:52–53), for example, Luther cites 1 Cor 1:21, 25, and continues: "It is not sufficient for anyone, and it does him no good to recognize God in his glory and majesty, unless he recognizes him in the humility and shame of the cross. Thus God destroys the wisdom of the wise. . . . For this reason true theology and recognition of God are in the crucified Christ." He adds, then, in thesis 21 (AE 31:53): "God can be found only in suffering and the cross. . . . It is impossible for a person not to be puffed up by his good works unless he has first been deflated and destroyed by suffering and evil until he knows that he is worthless and that his works are not his but God's." The *power* of God is visible in creation (Rom 1:18–32), but the *grace* of God can only be found in God's Word and Sacraments, on the cross and in the Supper, which to the world appear weak and foolish.

The Corinthians need to be realistic that "the word of the cross" will always be "foolishness to those who are being destroyed" (1 Cor 1:18). In itself, of course, the Gospel is not foolishness; only to those who are being destroyed is it foolishness. There was a period when even Jesus' mother and brothers thought he was "beside himself" (Mk 3:21). Many of his Jewish opponents claimed that he was insane (Jn 10:20). Later, the Roman governor Festus charged Paul with insanity (Acts 26:24). Through the centuries, the message of the cross has drawn similar abuse from Christianity's cultured and less cultured despisers. In their view, Christians "are of all people most to be pitied" (1 Cor 15:19).

So long has the cross been a centerpiece in churches that Christians can easily forget the shame and offensiveness it represented in the ancient world. Only criminals and recalcitrant slaves were crucified. Indeed, Matthew's gospel portrays Jesus' death as that of a slave worth thirty pieces of silver (Mt 26:15; cf. Ex 21:32), and Paul draws a connection between Jesus' taking the form of a slave and dying the death of the cross (Phil 2:7–8).

But Paul underlines that rejection of the word of the cross brings tragic consequences. Those who despise it are actually in the process of condemning themselves to eternal death; they are "being destroyed" (1 Cor 1:18). The rejected Gospel, as "a fragrance from death to death," is having its effect on them (2 Cor 2:15–16).

On the other hand, "to us who are being saved it [the word of the cross] is the power of God" (1 Cor 1:18). Note that despite the divisions he has just deplored, Paul does not classify the Corinthians among those being lost. The words "to us" assure them that they and he are united as the blessed recipients of salvation. For them, as for him, the word of the cross is a "fragrance from life to life" (2 Cor 2:16).

According to Pauline theology, believers are surrounded by salvation—past, present, and future. Having been saved by grace in the past (Eph 2:5, 8; cf. Rom 8:24; Titus 3:5), they are now, day by day, in the process of being saved (1 Cor 1:18; 15:2; 2 Cor 2:15), a process which continues until they are finally saved on the last day (Rom 5:9; 11:26). Above all, it is this sure hope of rescue from God's wrath on the Last Day which lends the words "save" and "salvation" their color.

Our salvation is accomplished by "the power of God" effective in "the word of the cross" (1 Cor 1:18). The voice of the Gospel is not foolishness, but "the power of God for salvation" (Rom 1:16). Thus, Paul's ministry was "a demonstration of the Spirit and power" (1 Cor 2:4). Through his preaching, God established his kingdom "in power" (4:20). Hence, Paul was not interested in how well his spiritually "inflated" opponents could talk, but in their power (4:19). While outwardly he and his co-workers appeared to be weak, he rejoiced in weakness and blessed God when there was no more room for self-reliance (2 Cor 1:8–9), for then he knew the power of Christ would rest on him (2 Cor 12:9–10; 13:4).

Indeed, according to Paul's Gospel, human cleverness and self-reliance were an abomination to God (1 Cor 1:19). Paul supports his thesis from Is 29:14:

> I will destroy the wisdom of the wise
> and the understanding of the
> understanding I will reject.

The quotation is word for word from the Greek version of Is 29:14, except for the change from "I will hide" to "I will reject." "The wise" in Isaiah 29 are the complacent priests and prophets who had no idea that God would perform amazing deeds of judgment and salvation in their day. Those people drew near to God with their mouths and honored him with their lips, while their hearts were far from him (Is 29:13). It is very likely that Paul, in citing Is 29:14, was recalling the whole context and suggesting to the Corinthians that all their "prized speech gifts," including the gift of tongues, would only incur God's judgment if their hearts were far from him.

THE WORLD'S FOLLY (1:20–21)

Although Paul may no longer be formally quoting the OT, we still hear the voice of Isaiah in the series of rhetorical questions which mock the wisdom of this age (1:20). The first two questions Paul draws directly from Isaiah, whom he has just cited and will cite another five times in the epistle (2:9, 16; 14:21; 15:32, 54), for that prophet also had a keen sense for the difference between reliance on human strength and wisdom, and a quiet reliance on God (e.g., Is 7:4; 25:9; 26:3–4; 30:15).

The first three questions all begin with the interrogative "where." In its original context in Isaiah, the first question ("where is a wise man?") mocks the wise counselors of Pharaoh for their failure to foresee the divine judgments coming upon Egypt (Is 19:12). The second question from the prophet ("where is a scribe?") targets foreign scribes, men of strange speech, who would tally tribute levied on Israel (Is 33:18). The third question ("where is a debater of this age?") is Paul's own free formulation, targeting anyone who raises arguments against the knowledge of God revealed in Jesus Christ (cf. 2 Cor 10:4–5).

Adapting Isaiah to his own day, Paul's first target is probably the typical sage of Greek culture, the philosopher or rhetorician, while the second object of his mockery, the "scribe," is the Jewish rabbi, and the "debater of this age" is any clever person opposed to the true knowledge of God. Although some think this analysis is too subtle, it suits the context, which goes on to speak of Jews and Greeks (1 Cor 1:22). What seems especially clear is that the second question refers to Jewish teachers of the Law. The Greeks never referred to a scholar as a "scribe;" they used that word for a civil officer like the "town clerk" of Acts 19:35.

The wise man, the scribe, and the debater all belong to "this age" (1 Cor 1:20). Human wisdom, like this age, is transitory and prone to evil, in contrast to the eternal wisdom of God in Christ (Ephesians 1; Colossians 2). God has "made foolish the wisdom of the world" (1 Cor 1:20; cf. Is 44:25; Job 12:17) with all its pretensions.

Paul now sets out to demonstrate what he has just asserted by means of his rhetorical questions. His argument and terminology anticipate his epistle to the Romans, 1:18–22 (cf. "knowing God," "claiming to be wise," "being made foolish," Rom 1:21–22). Even more, they echo Jesus' words of thanksgiving to the Father in Mt 11:25–26: "I thank you, Father, Lord of heaven and earth, because you have hidden these things [insight into the person and work of Christ] from *the wise and understanding* [cf. 1 Cor 1:19] and revealed them to babies. Yes, Father, for this was your *gracious will* [corresponding to "good pleasure" in 1 Cor 1:21]." Thus, Paul underscores what both Isaiah and his Lord had said about the way God surprises the world by rejecting its values and elevating what it despises. For centuries, Greek philosophers and Jewish rabbis had been engaged in the quest to know God. "Through . . . wisdom" (1 Cor 1:21), the pre-Socratic Greek philosophers had sought to understand the structure of the universe, and Socrates and his successors had tried to understand human beings in relation to their world. But with all their intellectual ingenuity, they had missed the mark. Meanwhile, the rabbis had busied themselves with the minute study of Torah, but over their hearts lay a veil which is only removed when a person turns to the Lord (2 Cor 3:15).

THE FOOLISH PREACHING OF CHRIST CRUCIFIED (1:22–25)

Because of the folly of human thinking about how to attain the knowledge of God, it was God's gracious and sovereign decision to lead people to the right knowledge of himself by that most unimpressive means, "the foolishness of preaching" (1 Cor 1:21). By "preaching," Paul does not mean merely the act of preaching; he constantly bears in mind its content, the cross of Christ (1:18). As he goes on to say (1:23), "we preach Christ crucified."

Nonbelievers, on the other hand, set up themselves as the arbiters of truth. Thus, they demand to be convinced by evidence that falls within the parameters of their own experience. This nonbelieving world is classified by Paul into two groups, Jews and Greeks. What they had in common was a quest for impressive signs of outward success, whether that be a display of power (like the plagues against Egypt, the parting of the Red Sea, the raining down of bread from heaven, or the ejecting of the Romans from Palestine; compare modern demands for health and wealth) or a brilliant show of intellectual prowess. The Jews, for example, constantly demanded that Jesus give them a powerful sign from heaven to prove his messianic claims (Mt 12:38; 16:1; Lk 23:8; Jn 2:23; 4:48; 6:30). In response, Jesus told them: "An evil and adulterous generation seeks a sign, and no sign will be given it but the sign of the prophet Jonah. For just as Jonah was in the belly of the fish for three days and three nights, so the Son of Man will be in the heart of the earth for three days and three nights" (Mt 12:39–40). In other words, when the Jews demanded a sign, Jesus pointed to his death and resurrection. Of course, to those with eyes to see, the miracles performed by Jesus and the apostles were powerful confirmations of the word of the cross. But those miracles were always gracious gifts; they were never performed on demand.

The Greeks on their part looked for wisdom. The Greek historian Herodotus (*History*, 4.77) had said of them: "All Greeks were zealous for every kind of learning." Paul could speak from firsthand experience, having encountered the Epicurean and Stoic philosophers in Athens (Acts 17:18). But we should not think only of the Greeks of Corinth and Athens. From the parallel "Gentiles" in 1 Cor 1:23, we see that Paul uses the word "Greeks" to include all non-Jewish peoples of the Roman Empire, where the influence of the Greek language and culture was widespread (cf. Rom 1:16).

In direct opposition to Jews and Greeks, who continue their unfulfilled quest for divine power and wisdom, Paul and his associates proclaim with joyful certainty the gift that has already been given to them: "We preach Christ crucified" (1:23). The expression "Christ crucified" (or "a crucified Messiah") is paradoxical, for while the title "Messiah" denotes a person of royal dignity, to describe him as "crucified" denotes the very opposite, an executed criminal bereft of any claim to human dignity and status. As Paul will write in his second epistle, "he was crucified in weakness" (2 Cor 13:4).

The tense of "having been crucified" should not be overlooked. Christ continues to live as the crucified one; in his risen and glorified state, he still bears the marks of his crucifixion (Jn 20:24–29). The triumphant "Lion of the tribe of Judah" (Rev 5:5) is at the same time "the Lamb who was slain" (Rev 5:6, 12; 13:8).

"To Jews," a crucified Messiah was "a stumbling block" (1 Cor 1:23). While there was a great diversity of messianic expectations among first-century Jews, those expectations consistently were for a *powerful* figure. Moreover, anyone who had been crucified was repugnant, having been cursed by God (Deut 21:22–23; cf. Gal 3:13).

To Gentiles, enmeshed in a culture enamored of power and success, it also made no sense that a crucified criminal was held up as Savior of the world (cf. 1 Cor 1:18). There is probably significance in the shift from "Greeks" (1:22) to "Gentiles" (1:23). Greeks were known for their wisdom. But not only Greeks, but especially Romans with their thirst for power would find the notion of a crucified Messiah ridiculous; Cicero, (*Pro Rabirio*, chapter 5), Tacitus (*Annals*, 15.44), and Pliny the Younger (*Letters*, 10.96.8) were among those who expressed this view.

The sad description of the Gospel's rejection by most Jews and Gentiles (1:23b) gives way to a note of joy as Paul describes its impact on the addressees of his epistle (1:24). A third grouping of people had been formed, called from among both Jews and Gentiles. To this group, "the called themselves" (1:24), belonged the Corinthians, together with all other Christians (1:2), and, of course, Paul himself (1:1). For them, Christ was neither an offense nor foolishness, but "God's power and God's wisdom" (1:24). Paul is saying: "If you are a Jew looking for signs and wonders as a display of God's power (1:22), you will find that power displayed in Christ crucified. And if you are a Greek on a quest for wisdom, you will find God's wisdom perfectly revealed in the word of the cross" (cf. 1:30; Col 2:3).

Paul has been arguing that the crucified Christ displays God's power and wisdom. He now concludes his argument with a general principle: "For God's folly is wiser than people, and God's weakness is stronger than people" (1 Cor 1:25).

By the cross, God outsmarted and overpowered all human wisdom and power. He did not consult human beings. For, as he proclaims through Isaiah in a context concerned with the forgiveness of sins (Is 55:6–7) and the efficacy of his Word (Is 55:10–11),

> "My thoughts are not your thoughts,
>   nor are your ways my ways," says the Lord.
> "For as the heavens are higher than the earth,
>   so are my ways higher than your ways
>   and my thoughts than your thoughts." (Is 55:8–9)

1:26–2:5

The Theme Illustrated

1 CORINTHIANS 1:26–31

God's Election of Unsophisticated People

TRANSLATION

1 [26]For consider your call, brothers, that not many were
wise by human standards, not many were powerful,
not many were of noble birth. [27]But God chose the
foolish things of the world so that he might humiliate
the wise people, and God chose the weak things of the
world so that he might humiliate the strong things,
[28]and God chose the lowly things of the world and
the despised things—the things that are not—so that
he might reduce to nothing the things that exist, [29]so
that no one may boast in the presence of God. [30]By his
doing you are in Christ Jesus, who became wisdom
for us from God—righteousness and sanctification
and redemption—[31]to bring about what has been
written: "Let the one who boasts boast in the Lord."

COMMENTARY

Paul now provides two illustrations of his argument that God's mysterious way of bringing salvation through the "foolish" and "weak" word of the cross is infinitely higher than—and stands in contradiction to—the human tendency to make much of human wisdom and power (cf. Is 55:8–9). First, Paul points to the status (or lack of status) of most members of the church at the time of their call (1 Cor 1:26–31). Second, he points to his own weaknesses and approach as a speaker (2:1–5).

Paul first urges the Corinthians to consider their situation when they were called: "Not many were wise by human standards, not many were powerful, not many were of noble birth" (1:26). There were, indeed, exceptions to the rule, prominent men like Stephanas (1:16; 16:17), Sosthenes, Crispus (1:1, 14), the hospitable Gaius, and the city treasurer, Erastus (Rom 16:23). Other well-to-do members may have been the ones who despised "the have-nots" and went ahead with their own meals during the dinners that accompanied the Lord's Supper (1 Cor 11:21–22). Church membership certainly was not confined to the lower classes. There are always some camels who, by the grace of God, pass through the eye of the needle (Mt 19:24).

But the majority of converts in places like Rome and Corinth had humble origins. Many were either slaves or freed slaves (cf. 1 Cor 7:21–23). Thus, the church attracted people from the entire sociological spectrum. The history of Christian missions down to the present time, with notable gains among less developed peoples, such as the untouchables of India, amply confirms Paul's observation.

At the same time, although God's gracious call does tend to attract people who, for the most part, do not belong to the well-educated, powerful, and noble social classes, whether a person becomes a Christian or not does not depend upon his sociological status, but upon coming to realize that everything of which he may like to boast—education, prestige, noble birth, moral standing—is worthless rubbish in comparison with knowing Jesus Christ (Phil 3:4–10). Whatever Crispus or Gaius or Stephanas may have been or had, they needed to realize that, in God's sight, they were "wretched, pitiable, poor, blind, and naked" (Rev 3:17). Only then would they learn to boast in the Lord. This theme becomes more explicit in 1 Cor 1:27–28.

Human merit and worth did not enter God's calculations (1 Cor 1:27–28). The pattern of Paul's ministry in Corinth had followed the pattern set by Jesus. Not many of Jesus' followers came from the privileged classes; they came rather from the poor, the tax collectors, and sinners (Lk 15:1–2; 19:10). Indeed, Jesus praised the Father for hiding the mysteries of his kingdom from the wise and understanding, and revealing them to babies (Mt 11:25). God's kingdom belongs to the poor in spirit, not those proud of their intellect, wealth, or prestige (Mt 5:3). This divine pattern was repeated in Corinth. By the preaching of the cross, people like Gaius and Crispus, together with those of a lower social status, had come to regard themselves as foolish, weak, lowly, and insignificant—indeed, as babies.

To describe "those of low degree" in 1 Cor 1:27–28, Paul uses a series of neuter plural adjectives: "the foolish things . . . the weak things . . . the lowly things . . . the despised things—the things that are not." This choice of the neuter ("things" rather than "people") may be due to his concern not to suggest that the Corinthians are in reality foolish, weak, lowly, and of no account. To be sure, the world may place them in that category, dismissing them as nonpersons. But God's call has turned the tables on the world and its values. His called saints are not "nobodies," but people endowed with divine wisdom, power, and true nobility as royal heirs of God's kingdom (Acts 17:11; 1 Cor 2:6–16; 2 Cor 12:9–10).

Paul finally summarizes the Corinthians' lowly status in the eyes of the world by calling them nonentities ("the things that are not," 1 Cor 1:27). God has chosen insignificant people like the Corinthians to "reduce to nothing the things that exist" (1:28). He gives life to the dead and delights to create out of nothing (Gen 1:1–2:25; 1 Sam 2:5–6; cf. Rom 4:17—"calling into being the things that are not"—where similar creation terminology is applied to God creating Isaac in Sarah's barren womb).

God's overarching goal in choosing the lowly (1 Cor 1:27–28) is that "no one may boast" in his presence (1:29). As Paul explains to the Romans and Ephesians, all boasting is excluded by the doctrine of justification through faith in Christ crucified (Rom 3:27; Eph 2:9). Not even Abraham, the human father of the Jewish people, is entitled to boast (Rom 4:2). There is no room for any boasting before God, because the Christian has received his whole existence in Christ from God (1 Cor 1:30; cf. Rom 11:36; Eph 2:8).

Through our baptismal incorporation into his body, Christ Jesus has become "wisdom for us" (1 Cor 1:30). All the treasures of divine wisdom and knowledge, so highly praised in the OT (e.g., Proverbs 8–9; Job 28) are bound up in Christ (Col 2:3) and now are on display in the "foolish" and "weak" act of his crucifixion and the "foolishness" of preaching about it. In Christ, all "the depth of the riches and wisdom and knowledge of God" (Rom 11:33) is now accredited to us and bestowed as a gift "from God" (1 Cor 1:30).

Paul then explains what this wisdom-treasure consists of: "righteousness and sanctification and redemption" (1:30). The first part of the wisdom gift comes to us in the form of Christ's righteousness. In ourselves, of course, we are sinners, but the righteousness of the Christ has been imputed to us and covers our sins: "[God] made him who knew no sin to be sin for us, that in him we might become the righteousness of God" (2 Cor 5:21; cf. Phil 3:9).

The second part of the gift is "sanctification" or holiness (1 Cor 1:30; cf. 6:11, where again sanctification is linked to justification). Sinful humans cannot stand in God's holy presence. But in his suprahuman love (Hos 11:8–9), God graciously provided the means—the covenant and sacrifices of the OT, and the perfect sacrifice of Christ—by which our guilt is taken away and our sin atoned for (Is 6:1–7). Holy Baptism (1 Cor 12:13) is now one of the most important means by which Christ's holiness (1:30) is conveyed to us, for it is by the washing of water in the Word that he sanctifies the church (Eph 5:26). We are then called to live as saints.

Third, these gifts of righteousness and sanctification could not come to us without the gift of "redemption" (1 Cor 1:30; see also Rom 3:24). Just as Israel was redeemed from slavery and death in Egypt by the sprinkled blood of the Passover lamb, so we have been redeemed by "Christ our Passover" (1 Cor 5:7), by the "sprinkling of the blood of Jesus Christ" (1 Pet 1:2). "You were bought with a price" (1 Cor 6:20; 7:23; 1 Pet 1:18–19). Again, Paul has in mind "the word of the cross" (1 Cor 1:18).

Thus, instead of boasting of his own wisdom, his own intellectual or rhetorical attainments, the Christian is directed away from himself to the wisdom of another, the Lord Jesus Christ. Only by being in Christ and having that alien wisdom conferred on him as a cover for his own foolishness and sin, does the Christian gain the wisdom that is pleasing to God. According to the divine master plan, all the wisdom God displayed throughout the OT in granting righteousness, holiness, and redemption to his sinful and needy people, has now culminated in the perfect gift of Christ. Thus, in this verse we find one of the great points of confluence in biblical theology.

Paul clinches his argument with support from the OT Scriptures: "[Christ became wisdom for us, 1 Cor 1:30] to bring about what has been written, 'Let the one who boasts boast in the Lord'" (1:31). The quotation is based on Jer 9:23–24:

> Thus says the Lord: "Let not the wise man boast in his wisdom, let not the mighty man boast in his might, let not the rich man boast in his riches; but let him who boasts boast in this, that he understands and knows me, that I am the Lord, who practices steadfast love and justice and righteousness on the earth, because in these I delight."

As Paul had heard it from Chloe's people, the sin of the Corinthians is that each of them is boasting of his own wisdom in attaching himself to Paul or Apollos or Cephas or Christ. The words from Jeremiah strike at the roots of this factionalism, urging the Corinthians to stop boasting in human beings (1 Cor 3:23) and lift their sights and start boasting only in "Jesus Christ and him crucified" (2:2), as should be characteristic of each Christian.

1 CORINTHIANS 2:1–5

GOD'S ELECTION OF AN UNSOPHISTICATED PREACHER

TRANSLATION

2 [1]And I, when I came to you, brothers, I did not
come with superior eloquence or wisdom as I
proclaimed to you the mystery of God. [2]For I
resolved not to know anything among you except
Jesus Christ and him crucified. [3]And I came to you
in weakness and fear and much trembling, [4]and my
speaking and my preaching were not in persuasive
words of wisdom, but in a demonstration of the
Spirit and power, [5]so that your trust might not
be in human wisdom but in the power of God.

COMMENTARY

God's decision to save the world through the lowly message of the cross (1:18–25) had been illustrated by his calling so many lowly people to form the Corinthian church (1:26–31). With the words "and I," Paul now introduces a second illustration: himself. The "weak" and "foolish" nature of the Gospel had also been illustrated by the lack of showiness in his own preaching (2:1–2) and personal bearing (2:3) in the early days of his ministry among the Corinthians.

In contrast to most Greek orators and philosophers, Paul declined to show off his skill as a speaker or debater. He had not come to Corinth "with superior eloquence or wisdom" (2:1). The words "eloquence" and "wisdom" echo 1:17, where Paul said Christ had not sent him to preach the Gospel with sophisticated eloquence. Unlike the rhetoricians of his day, the sophists, Paul refused to rely on rhetorical technique or any other worldly strategy for making an impression. To the extent he relied on such human things to "carry the day," he would be hiding the weakness and offensiveness of the cross—which *is* its power! Thus, he did not mind if, by his opponents' standards, he lacked rhetorical skill (2 Cor 11:6), for it was his consistent goal to present the Gospel mystery in a simple, sincere, and straightforward manner which would commend its truth to everyone's conscience (2 Cor 1:12; 4:2; 1 Thess 2:1–12).

This does not mean that Paul was totally lacking in rhetorical and debating ability. As a writer, he was a stylist of note. It would seem, however, that this was not matched by his ability as a speaker, a deficiency which seemed all the greater in comparison with the eloquence of Apollos. Paul's critics, at least, considered him a poor speaker, claiming that while "his letters are weighty and strong, . . . his bodily presence is *weak* and his speech *contemptible*" (2 Cor 10:10; cf. 2 Cor 11:6). In conceding his deficiencies as a speaker, Paul's concern is clearly not to depreciate these gifts; they have their proper place in helping the preacher convey his message persuasively. But the preacher must resist the urge to draw his hearers' attention to himself. Paul's passion throughout his ministry, including the eighteen months in Corinth, had been to help his audience concentrate on the message of "Jesus Christ and him crucified" (1 Cor 2:2). Nothing could be allowed to overshadow or distract from that Gospel.

Paul's policy statement is a powerful corrective to any tendency which displaces Christ and his Gospel from the center of Christian faith and witness. All programs and methods focused primarily on human efforts to impress are hereby called into question. The Gospel, as Paul proclaimed it, directs us away from ourselves: it is the Gospel concerning God's Son (Rom 1:1–3). To proclaim Christ is the church's only essential task (Col 1:28).

Some have suggested that as he reflected on his earlier ministry in Athens (Acts 17:16–34), Paul concluded that his outreach there had been unsuccessful because he had relied too much on his knowledge of Greek philosophers and poets. There are, however, no indications in Luke's account of the Athenian ministry that Paul's strategy had been ill-advised. Rather, Luke's extensive report of the Areopagus sermon suggests he saw it as a model for missionary proclamation to pagans, just as the Pisidian Antioch sermon is a model sermon to Jews (Acts 13:16–41).

Jesus Christ had been crucified "in weakness" (2 Cor 13:4). In solidarity with his Lord, Paul, too, had carried out his ministry in suffering and weakness (1 Cor 2:3; Phil 3:10). Not only was Paul's presence as a public speaker unimpressive (2 Cor 10:10), but he suffered recurrent attacks of a debilitating malady (Gal 4:13; cf. 2 Cor 12:7). A further difficulty for him in Corinth was that he had come to the city in "fear and in much trembling" (1 Cor 2:3). He still had vivid memories of a beating and imprisonment in Philippi, rioting and a nighttime escape from Thessalonica, another hasty withdrawal from Beroea, and cool indifference in Athens (Acts 16:16–17:34). As he arrived in cosmopolitan Corinth, with its dubious reputation, he naturally felt trepidation about what might await him. Thus, he needed the assurance the Lord would bring him in a nighttime vision: "Do not fear, but speak and do not be silent. For I am with you and no one will set upon you to harm you. For I have many people in this city" (Acts 18:9–10).

Despite his weakness and lack of eloquence, the effectiveness of the apostle's message should not be underestimated, for it was "a demonstration of the Spirit and power" (2:4). Through the powerful, Spirit-filled word of the cross, God had planted his church among the Corinthians.

Moreover, as was true of Paul's ministry everywhere in the Mediterranean region, Christ had worked through him "in word and deed, in the power of signs and wonders, in the power of the Spirit of God" (Rom 15:18–19). "The signs of an apostle"—"signs and wonders and miracles" (2 Cor 12:12; see also Heb 2:4)—always accompanied Paul's preaching, providing divine attestation to the lowly word of the cross. Thus, the Corinthians should place their confidence where it rightly belonged—not in the cleverness of any human speaker, but in the power of God (1 Cor 2:5; cf. 1:18).

1 CORINTHIANS 2:6–9

The Cross Is God's Wisdom for Mature, Spiritual People

TRANSLATION

2 [6]Wisdom, however, is what we speak among
the mature, but not a wisdom of this age nor of
the rulers of this age, who are being reduced to
nothing. [7]No, we speak God's wisdom in [the
form of] a mystery, the hidden [wisdom] which
God foreordained before the ages for our glory,
[8]which none of the rulers of this age recognized.
For if they had recognized [it], they would not have
crucified the Lord of glory. [9]But as it is written:

> **What things an eye has not seen and an ear has not heard,**
> **and upon a human heart have not arisen,**
> **what things God has prepared**
> **for those who love him.**

COMMENTARY

WE PREACH *GOD'S* WISDOM (2:6)

Up to this point, Paul has been warning the Corinthians that to rely on human wisdom is incompatible with preaching the "foolish" message of Christ crucified (see 1:18–25). But now, to ward off the possible misunderstanding that he is opposed to wisdom in any form, as if Christianity had *no* wisdom to offer, he adds this: "*Wisdom,* however, is what we speak" (2:6). In the Greek text, "wisdom" is placed first for emphasis. Wisdom, true wisdom, was indeed to be found in the preaching of Paul and his associates. Christ himself is the wisdom from God, wisdom that brings righteousness, sanctification, and redemption (1:30).

With a touch of irony, Paul adds that this true Christian wisdom is spoken "among the mature" (2:6); "the mature" appreciate it. At this point, some of his proud readers may have congratulated themselves, "He's speaking of us; we are certainly mature!" not realizing that Paul is preparing the way for his remonstrance in 3:1: "Brothers, I was not able to speak to you as spiritual people but as fleshly people, as babies in Christ." Consequently, he had fed them with milk, not solid food (3:1–3). Exactly what was on the menu for the more mature we do not know, but for such a diet the Corinthians were not yet ready. Thus, Paul will shame his hearers for their lack of maturity, but only in order to encourage them to strive for greater maturity, as he does in other epistles, for example, in Eph 4:13–14, where he says this: "until we all attain the unity of the faith and the knowledge of the Son of God and become mature [as in 1 Cor 2:6] . . . that we may no longer be babies [as in 1 Cor 3:1; 13:11]" (cf. Phil 3:15; Col 1:28; 4:12).

Paul quickly adds that the wisdom the apostles offer to the mature is not "a wisdom of this age" (1 Cor 2:6; cf. 1:20), nor "of the rulers of this age, who are being reduced to nothing" (2:6). The Jerusalem authorities in the AD 30s—"wise by human standards," "powerful," and "noble" (1:26) men like Herod Antipas, Pontius Pilate, and Caiaphas—were steeped in the culture and wisdom of their day. But with all their sophisticated knowledge, they failed to recognize Jesus as the Messiah and executed him (Acts 4:26–28; 13:27). These rulers, however, are "being reduced to nothing" (1 Cor 2:6). Like all people who belong to "this age" (2:6), their power and influence is transitory and in the process of fading from the scene.

GOD'S WISDOM WAS HIDDEN IN THE FORM OF A MYSTERY (2:7–9)

In contrast to the wisdom of this age (2:6), the apostolic message has permanent value, for unlike the wisdom of this age and of its rulers, the apostolic message conveys *God's* wisdom. In the Greek of 2:7, "God's" is placed before "wisdom" for emphasis. The apostolic preaching is not a human message and cannot be evaluated by human criteria. It is "God's wisdom in [the form of] a mystery, the hidden [wisdom] which God foreordained before the ages for our glory" (2:7). Jesus had praised the Father for concealing the mystery of the Gospel from the wise and understanding, and revealing it to babies (Mt 11:25; Lk 10:21). In Romans, Paul, too, breaks out in doxology for the proclamation of the Gospel, "according to the revelation of the mystery that was kept secret for long ages but is now disclosed" (Rom 16:25–26). Foreshadowed in the OT from Gen 3:15 on, the full light of the Gospel, eagerly anticipated by many prophets and righteous people (1 Pet 1:10–12), had burst on the world in the incarnation and ministry of Jesus (Mt 13:16–17; cf. also Col 1:26) and was being revealed in the apostolic preaching.

God had foreordained this wisdom before the ages (2:7; cf. Rev 13:8; 14:6; Eph 1:4–11). This eternal Gospel God had predestined "for our glory" (1 Cor 2:7). 1 Cor 2:7b has a sweep that encompasses not only eternity past, but also eternity future: God's age-old Gospel plan, which already casts a bright light into our lives, will lead ultimately to our final glorification—our entry into the glorious inheritance "God has prepared for those who love him" (2:9). Thus, the believer's life is illuminated—and ultimately will be fully lit up—by "the Lord of glory" (2:8). Through faith in him, we are being transformed from one degree of glory to another (2 Cor 3:18; 4:17; Phil 3:20–21), in contrast to the rulers of this world, who are fading from the scene (1 Cor 2:6).

"None of the rulers of this age recognized" the wisdom of the Gospel (2:8). During the crucifixion, Jesus had prayed for them, "Father, forgive them, for they know not what they do" (Lk 23:34). According to Paul's sermon in Pisidian Antioch, it was because the residents of Jerusalem and their rulers did not recognize him or understand the words of the prophets that they fulfilled those words by condemning him (Acts 13:27; cf. Peter's words in Acts 3:17). Thus, Jesus, Peter, and Paul all acknowledge that the rulers acted in ignorance.

Again, Paul returns to the theme of the crucifixion (1 Cor 2:8; cf. 1:13, 18, 23; 2:2). If the rulers had known who Jesus was, "they would not have crucified the Lord of glory" (2:8). Thus, Paul reflects on the enormity of what these petty princes had perpetrated. Admittedly they were acting in ignorance, but they had subjected the glorious Lord of the universe to the most ignominious death of all, the shame of the cross (Heb 12:2). The contrast between Christ's majesty and the shameful treatment meted out to him is graphically portrayed.

The Crucifixion of "the Lord of Glory"

How was it possible for the "Lord of glory" (1 Cor 2:8), the Son of God, to die on a cross as a human being? On the basis of texts like 1 Cor 2:8, church fathers spoke of the remarkable union and communion of Christ's divine and human natures in one person. Although one would assume that since God is immortal, the divine nature cannot die, nonetheless, the person who died on the cross was not merely a man, but "a man whose human nature has such a profound and ineffable union and communion with the Son of God that it has become one person with him" (FC Ep VIII 13; cf. FC Ep VIII 14; Chemnitz, *The Two Natures in Christ*, 210–211; *LSB* 448:2).

The word of the cross is a wisdom surpassing all human understanding (1 Cor 2:9). Human wisdom, with its predilection for spectacular signs and impressive philosophies, had failed to recognize the Lord of glory in the weak, contradicted, and crucified Jesus. Indeed, no human being would ever have conceived or predicted that God would bring his salvation in this way. But, Paul insists, that way should not be surprising; it is thoroughly in keeping with OT prophecy, where Isaiah foretold that the God whose thoughts and ways are higher than human thoughts and ways (Is 55:8–9) would bring about "new things," "hidden things that you have not known" and have "never heard" (Is 48:6–8; cf. Is 43:19; 44:7). The composite quotation of Is 64:4 and Is 65:16 in 1 Cor 2:9 gathers up and summarizes these and other texts which look forward to God's incredible new plans to redeem his people through the sufferings of the Servant (see especially Is 52:13–53:12).

It is significant that Paul adds that these are plans God has prepared "for those who *love* him" (1 Cor 2:9). We do not please him by displaying our knowledge and wisdom, but by showing him our love (cf. Rom 8:28).

EXCURSUS

Christian Maturity

Several times in 1 Corinthians, and in some of his other epistles, Paul distinguishes between those who, in their Christian faith, are like a "baby" (1 Cor 3:1; Eph 4:14) or a "child" (1 Cor 14:20) and thus, are more prone to "fleshly, carnal" (1 Cor 3:1) passions and perspectives, and others who are more "mature" (1 Cor 2:6; 14:20; Col 4:12), "spiritual" (1 Cor 2:13, 15; 3:1; Gal 6:1), "tried and tested" (1 Cor 11:19; 2 Cor 10:18; 2 Tim 2:15). We may compare those Pauline passages to the epistle to the Hebrews, where the author shames his hearers for becoming dull in understanding (Heb 5:11), needing someone to teach them again the fundamentals of the faith. They still need milk, not solid food, like infants "unskilled in the word of righteousness," for solid food is for the "mature" (as in 1 Cor 2:6; 14:20), who have been trained to distinguish good from evil (Heb 5:13–14).

Paul's concern is that many Christians in Corinth were still thinking and living on the basis of the world's kind of wisdom, not on the basis of the word of the cross, which is God's wisdom. That worldly wisdom results in worldly thinking and worldly living. Recent converts to the faith bring along considerable baggage from their former way of life and must learn, step by step, how to walk in the Spirit.

In calling the Corinthians to become more mature, Paul is aware of the danger posed by complacency and the allure of the world's wisdom, which would pull them back into their former way of life. It would be an abuse of Paul's message to suggest that because the immature and carnal Christians in Corinth were still under grace, immaturity and sin pose no threat to a Christian's salvation. In the case of the incestuous man in 1 Corinthians 5, Paul commands the church to excommunicate him (5:5, 7). The apostle's directive "to hand this one over to Satan" (5:5) is a declaration that the man has fallen from grace. "Those who walk according to the flesh can retain neither faith nor righteousness" (Ap IV 348).

While Paul urges all Christians to *pursue* maturity (Eph 4:13–14; Phil 3:12–16; cf. also Heb 6:1), and in 1 Corinthians 2–3 Paul leads the Corinthians toward greater maturity, none can claim to have already *attained* "full maturity" or "perfection" in Christ (Eph 4:13; Col 1:28). The Christian is called to live in repentance, confessing his sin and seeking, by the power of the Spirit, to grow into the fullness of the new life in Christ that will be completed only in the resurrection. Even Paul had to confess that throughout his Christian life as a baptized believer, he constantly had to battle his old, sinful nature, and so in that sense he remained "fleshly, carnal" (Rom 7:14). He looked forward to the day when he would be delivered from his sinful nature once and for all (Rom 7:24–25). But in his earthly life he had to admit, "Not that I have already obtained this or have already reached the goal" (Phil 3:12).

An important part of Christian maturity is coming to the sober recognition that on this side of eternity, we will always remain both saint and sinner (Rom 7:14–25). In fact, a sign of real maturity—in contrast to the supreme self-confidence of the Corinthians—is the capacity to confess with Paul, "I am the chief of sinners" (1 Tim 1:15).

At the same time, Christian maturation is also an upward growth in ever-increasing appreciation for the plenary forgiveness of sins won by Christ on the cross, and increasingly joyful hope in the life of the world to come, secured for us by Christ's resurrection (1 Corinthians 15).

The maturing Christian will also recognize the fluctuations in the Christian life. At times, our outlook is more mature according to God's wisdom; at other times, we lapse into an outlook that is more secular and immature. According to the Formula of Concord (FC SD II 68)

> in this life we have received only the first fruits of the Spirit, and regeneration is not as yet perfect but has only been begun in us, [and therefore] the conflict and warfare of the flesh against the Spirit continues also in the elect and truly reborn. Again, there is not only a great difference between Christians, one being weak and the other strong in the Spirit, but even the individual Christian in his own life discovers that at one moment he is joyful in the Spirit and at another moment fearful and terrified, at one time ardent in love, strong in faith and in hope, and at another time cold and weak.

Because of those fluctuations and all the other trials of life in this fallen world, the maturing Christian prays more earnestly, "Maranatha" (1 Cor 16:22), that is, "Come, Lord Jesus" (Rev 22:20).

1 CORINTHIANS 2:10–16

God Has Revealed the Mystery to Us through the Spirit

TRANSLATION

2 [10]To us, however, God has revealed [these things]
through his Spirit. For the Spirit searches out
everything, including the deep things of God. [11]For
what human being knows what is going on inside a
person except the person's spirit, which is in him?
Likewise also, no one understands the things of
God but the Spirit of God. [12]Now we ourselves did
not receive the spirit of the world but the Spirit
which is from God, so that we might know the
things graciously given to us by God. [13]We also
speak about these things not in words taught by
human wisdom but in [words] taught by the Spirit,
explaining spiritual things to spiritual people. [14]But
the unspiritual person does not receive the things
of the Spirit of God, for they are foolishness to him;
indeed, he cannot understand [them], because they
are spiritually discerned. [15]But the spiritual person
discerns everything, while he himself is discerned by
no one. [16]For "who has known the mind of the Lord,
so as to advise him?" But we have the mind of Christ.

COMMENTARY

GOD'S SPIRIT TEACHES SPIRITUAL THINGS TO SPIRITUAL PEOPLE (2:10–13)

What the human eye, ear, and heart failed to discern (2:9) God has revealed to us through the Spirit (2:10). In Greek "to us" is placed first in 2:10 for emphasis. Rack their brains as they might, the worldly wise could not understand God and his mysterious wisdom. To these people everything remained a closed book. But "to us" as Christian people, however lowly our status, God has bared his heart, granting us the high privilege of being made privy to his glorious plan of salvation.

This revelation has taken place "through his [God's] Spirit" (2:10). The operation of God's Spirit is not to be understood as some generic spirituality into which a person may get caught up, a spirituality akin to that of the Stoics or devotees of the mystery religions or the modern New Age movement. Rather, the Spirit is the agent through whom we receive the special gift of divine revelation and are thus, able to appreciate the things of God. Since the Spirit is given in Baptism (e.g., Acts 2:38–39; 1 Cor 12:13), this divine revelation occurred in Baptism.

The Spirit is able to reveal these divine mysteries, for he searches out everything, including the deep things of God. According to Daniel 2, "there is a God in heaven who reveals mysteries" (Dan 2:28), a God who "gives wisdom to the wise and knowledge to those who have understanding," who "reveals deep and mysterious things" (Dan 2:21–22). Paul now ascribes to the Holy Spirit this same power to reveal divine mysteries. The great "mystery" is the Gospel of Jesus Christ (1 Cor 2:1, 7; cf. in 4:1; 13:2; 14:2; 15:51). Having plumbed "the depth of the riches and wisdom and knowledge of God" (Rom 11:33), the Spirit is able to display to us God's wonderful gifts.

Paul illustrates the Spirit's deep knowledge of God by an analogy from human experience. No one knows precisely what is going on inside another person's heart except the spirit of the person himself (2:11). In the same way, no one understands the mind of God except the Spirit of God himself.

But when we became Christians through "the hearing of faith" (Gal 3:2) and through Baptism (Gal 3:27), what we received was not "the spirit of the world" (1 Cor 2:12), which is estranged from God and totally blind and deaf to the things of the Spirit. Puffed up with pride in its own cultural and philosophical accomplishments, its own religiosity and "spirituality"—indeed, its own popular personalities—this secular spirit is always trying to make the church conform to its own agenda rather than letting the church be conformed to the mind of Christ (2:16; cf. Rom 12:1–2). This spirit of secularism seeks to negate special revelation graciously bestowed by God.

In contrast, "the Spirit which is from God" (1 Cor 2:12) gives God's children a childlike appreciation of his rich grace and profound wisdom freely given us in the word of the cross. God's purpose was that we might be aware of "the things graciously given to us by God" (2:12). In the words "the things graciously given" we hear the word "grace." These things graciously given include grace and peace from God our Father and the Lord Jesus Christ (1:3), together with all the gifts of grace, the miraculous gifts bestowed on the congregation (1:4–7) and, in Paul's case, the grace which had called him to be an apostle and enabled him to labor so fruitfully (3:10; 15:10).

The apostles' preaching sets before the hearers a table laden with these gifts. The apostles speak of the gifts in a straightforward manner, without resorting to "words taught by human wisdom" (2:13; see the commentary on 2:1). Rather, the words they use are "taught by the Spirit" (2:13), in keeping with Jesus' promise to his disciples: "The Comforter, the Holy Spirit, whom the Father will send in my name, he will *teach* you all things and remind you of everything I said to you" (Jn 14:26).

Here in 1 Cor 2:13, we find, in its briefest form, the doctrine of verbal inspiration. The apostles preached, taught, and wrote "not the word of human beings but . . . the word of God" (1 Thess 2:13). The very words in Scripture, while not mechanically dictated, were inspired—"taught by the Spirit" (1 Cor 2:13). Those divine words demonstrate God's Spirit and power (2:4).

Only spiritual people welcome these Spirit-taught words. In Greek Paul places "to spiritual people" at the beginning of the last phrase in 2:13 for emphasis: "*to spiritual people* explaining spiritual things." Thus, he is setting the Corinthians up for the blow that is coming in 3:1: "Brothers, I was not able to speak to you as spiritual people."

The second Greek word in the last phrase of 2:13, "spiritual things," is a neuter plural corresponding to "the deep things of God" (2:10), "the things of God" (2:11), and "the things graciously given" (2:12). It comprehends all the spiritual things the apostles had sown among the Corinthians—the Spirit-inspired teaching, with its center in the word of the cross.

It was the apostles' task to explain these spiritual matters to spiritual people (2:13). By so doing, they were following in the footsteps of Joseph (Genesis 40–41) and Daniel (Dan 5:7–30), who by divine inspiration were able to explain mysterious dreams. Just as these men of the OT were inspired by the Spirit of God, so Paul and his associates explained God's revelation "in [words] taught by the Spirit" (1 Cor 2:13).

THE UNSPIRITUAL PERSON IS DEAF TO THE THINGS OF THE SPIRIT (2:14)

On the basis of 2:14 and related texts (cf. 12:3; Ephesians 2), Lutheran theology teaches that without Christ and the Spirit whom Christ sends, the natural state of a human being is completely unspiritual, dead in sin and thus, totally unable to contribute toward his conversion. Luther's explanation of the Third Article of the Apostles' Creed, the article on the Holy Spirit, states the following: "I believe that by my own reason or strength I cannot believe in Jesus Christ, my Lord, or come to him. But the Holy Spirit has called me through the Gospel, enlightened me with his gifts" (SC II 6).

Similarly, the Formula of Concord's article on free will denies that our conversion and rebirth may be ascribed in any way "to the human powers of the natural free will, be it entirely or one-half or the least and tiniest part, but altogether and alone to the divine operation and the Holy Spirit" (FC SD II 25). The Formula cites a sermon of Luther: "In spiritual and divine things . . . which concern the salvation of his soul, man is like a pillar of salt, like Lot's wife, yes, like a log or a stone, like a lifeless statue" (SD II 20). The Formula continues: "He is worse than a block because he is resistant and hostile to the will of God" (SD II 24). Our conversion, our rebirth takes place "out of pure grace through the gracious and efficacious working of the Holy Spirit" (SD II 22). All glory for our conversion belongs to God alone.

THE SPIRITUAL PERSON DISCERNS EVERYTHING (2:15–16)

Whereas the unspiritual person is deaf in spiritual matters, the spiritual person is able to exercise good judgment in all things (1 Cor 2:15), both secular and sacred. His judgment is informed by the Word and Spirit of God. The Word and Spirit go together; the way to discern whether a person is in accord with the Spirit is by whether he is in accord with God's Word, through which the Spirit works. However, Paul writes that the spiritual person himself "is discerned by no one" (2:15). In this context, "no one" probably means no natural, Spirit-less man, no one who is purely "fleshly" (1 Cor 3:1, 3) and purely "human" (3:3, 4), that is, an unbeliever, unbaptized, and not indwelt by the Holy Spirit. To such a person, the Christian remains an enigma; the non-Christian cannot make him out or comprehend the reason for his words and actions.

Once again, Paul rounds off and underscores his argument with a quotation from the OT Scriptures (as also in 1:19, 31; 2:9). No one with an attentive ear to the OT prophets would be surprised that the unspiritual person has no capacity in spiritual matters, while the spiritual person has discernment, since Isaiah had posed the question: "For who has fathomed the Spirit of the Lord and is a man of his [the Lord's] counsel who can make known to him [to the Lord]?" (Is 40:13). The context in Isaiah 40 speaks of the Lord's incomparable greatness as the powerful and all-wise Creator of the ends of the earth (Is 40:28). He is the God "who has measured the waters in the hollow of his hand" and has no need to consult anyone for his enlightenment (Is 40:12, 14). Thus, when he formed his plan to save the world through Jesus Christ and him crucified, he had no need to run this by any human adviser (cf. 1 Cor 1:25).

However, in his gracious condescension he has poured out his Spirit to create spiritual people who can discern and trust his plan. Consequently, they no longer see things from a worldly point of view (2 Cor 5:16); they are in the privileged position of knowing the mind of the Lord, for they have "the mind of Christ" (1 Cor 2:16). But lest this privilege tempt them to become puffed up, they should remember that having the mind of Christ encompasses the humility of the cross (cf. Phil. 2:2, 3, 5, 8).

In 1 Cor 2:10–16, Paul speaks in absolute terms as if Christians are always completely "spiritual people" (2:13, 15) in contrast to unbelievers, who alone are "unspiritual" people (2:14). However, he modifies the picture in 3:1–4, where he rebukes the Corinthian Christians as "fleshly" (3:1, 3) and "human" (3:3–4), even though they are baptized believers "in Christ" (3:1). Thus, 2:10–16 paints the portrait of the Christian as the "spiritual" person he *should* be now and ultimately *will* be after the resurrection (15:44–46), while 3:1–4 depicts how the Christian actually *is now,* as the Spirit and his new "spiritual" nature struggle against his old, "fleshly" and "human" nature.

1 CORINTHIANS 3:1–4

Your Divisions Are a Sign of Spiritual Immaturity

TRANSLATION

3 [1]For my part, brothers, I was not able to speak
to you as spiritual people but as fleshly people,
as babies in Christ. [2]Milk was what I gave you to
drink, not solid food, for you were not yet able.
But you are not yet able even now, [3]for you are
still fleshly. For where there is jealousy and strife
among you, are you not fleshly and are you not
walking in a human way? [4]For when someone
says, "I myself belong to Paul," and another, "I
belong to Apollos," are you not human beings?

COMMENTARY

Paul seems to have gone far afield since he began to address the problem of the Corinthians' divisions (1:10–17). His extensive discussion of the wisdom of the cross (1:18–2:16), however, was not a digression; it penetrated to the heart of the matter. The Corinthians' divisions were not only threatening the church's unity but, more importantly, they were violating and endangering the Gospel on which that unity was based. As long as a theology of glory led them to vie with each other in running after brilliant rhetoric and sophisticated argument, the message of the cross was being stripped of its power.

Having clearly enunciated the Gospel (1:18–31) and shown that its wisdom is only accessible to those with the Spirit (2:10–16), Paul comes back to the Corinthians themselves. With the gentle and affectionate word "brothers" (3:1), he addresses them as a pastor. Then he refers again to his early preaching among them: "I was not able to speak to you as spiritual people" (3:1; cf. 2:1–5). He had not been able to treat them like the discerning "spiritual person(s)" he described in 2:13, 15. Paul's sharp words are intended to shame them and call on them to live up to what they really are—people sanctified by the Holy Spirit (1:2). Indeed, they did possess the Spirit, for otherwise they would not be Christians (Rom 8:9). But they had not been living up to their high calling. Although they had come to faith and spiritual life by the Spirit, they were not "walking" (1 Cor 3:3) by the

Spirit (Gal 5:25), but according to the spirit of the world (1 Cor 2:12). Thus, Paul could only speak to them as "babies in Christ" (3:1). Their squabbling showed a lack of love, which was a sure sign of immaturity (13:11).

As their spiritual father (4:15), Paul had fed these babies in Christ milk, not solid food (cf. Heb 5:12–14; 1 Pet 2:2). That was appropriate as long as they were still beginners in the faith. But milk should not remain the regular diet for those beyond infancy. Some four or five years had elapsed since Paul first planted the church in Corinth. By now, they should have developed the capacity for solid food. There is a strong reproach in the words: "But you are not yet able even now" (3:2). Paul calls them to spiritual maturity.

The Corinthians were still unable to digest solid food, for they were still "fleshly" (3:1), that is, acting as natural children of Adam, who plunged the human race into sin and death. Paul finds proof for this strong assertion in the presence of "jealousy and strife" among them (3:3). Now, he is returning to the original concern brought to him in the report from Chloe's people, the presence of "factions" (1:10) and "quarrels" (1:11). Both "jealousy" and "strife" figure in Paul's list of the works of the flesh in Gal 5:19–21 (cf. James 3:14). In the face of such reports, there is no way the Corinthians can deny that they are "fleshly" (3:1, 3) and that their behavior (their "walking," 3:3) as Christians is typical of a fallen "human" (3:3, 4) rather than a "spiritual" person (2:13, 15; 3:1).

Paul presses his point home by reminding the Corinthians of what he had heard from Chloe's people: one person was saying, "I myself belong to Paul"; another, "I belong to Apollos" (3:4; cf. 1:12). Such self-assertion over and against one another was a sure sign that the Corinthians were conducting themselves like Spirit-less human beings. As he would later write to them in 2 Corinthians: "When [people] measure themselves by one another, and compare themselves with one another, they do not show good sense" (2 Cor 10:12 NRSV).

It is noteworthy that now Paul only mentions two of the four factions he described in 1:12; the "Cephas" and "Christ" factions have dropped from view. Probably the "Paul" and "Apollos" parties were the largest and most vocal.

After excoriating the Corinthians for their unregenerate and carnal ways, Paul will now address them as Christians who still do, by God's grace, possess the Spirit and the manifold gifts graciously given them by God (2:12). They still remain God's field, building, and temple (3:5–17).

1 CORINTHIANS 3:5–9
God's Field

TRANSLATION

**3 [5]What, after all, is Apollos? What is Paul? Servants
through whom you came to faith, and as the Lord
assigned to each: [6]I planted, Apollos watered, but
God was giving the growth. [7]So neither the planter
is anything nor the waterer, but only God, who
does the growing. [8]Moreover the planter and the
waterer are one, but each will receive his own reward
according to his own work. [9]For we are God's co-
workers, you are God's field, God's building.**

COMMENTARY

The Corinthians had been making far too much of their teachers (1:10–15). Their fawning, immature attachment to one or the other cried out for some reality therapy from the apostle. Paul's abrupt questions are designed to draw their attention away from the person to his office. Thus, he asks not "who?" but "what?": "What, after all, is Apollos? What is Paul?" (3:5). Apollos he places first as a mark of respect. This further underlines that Paul does not consider his own person a matter of primary importance. No worker is to be put on a pedestal as a lord to whom God's people must pay homage.

Apollos and Paul are simply servants of Christ and his people (3:22; 4:1). Their ministry is modeled on that of Jesus, who came not to lord it over others but to wait on them, not to be served but to serve (Mk 10:41–45; Lk 22:25–27). Through the ministry of Paul and Apollos, the Corinthians had come to faith. Paul carefully chooses his words in 3:5: "*through* whom you came to faith." The missionaries were merely instruments through whom God had called the Corinthians to faith. They were not to become objects of faith.

Apollos and Paul were totally dependent on their Lord. Without him they could have accomplished nothing (Jn 15:5). Thus, he alone could properly claim the Corinthians' faith and allegiance. He had assigned Apollos and Paul their respective roles in Corinth, and it was under his oversight and by his gracious provision ("as the Lord assigned to each," 1 Cor 3:5) that their labors had led to the establishment of the church.

Paul now describes his and Apollos' different roles using an analogy from agriculture. Paul had planted the seed of the Word (Lk 8:11) during his eighteen months in the city, when he became the young church's first spiritual father (Acts

18:1–18; 1 Cor 4:15). Then, Apollos watered the sprouts Paul had sown (Acts 18:24–19:1). He had helped the church by preaching eloquently and proving through the Scriptures that Jesus is the Christ (Acts 18:28).

However, as everyone knows from agriculture, no gardener or farmer actually causes plants to grow; all he does is provide the conditions under which growth can take place by the blessing and power of God. To God alone belongs the credit for producing the growth. As Paul turns from considering the labor of Apollos and his own activity to the activity of God, there is a significant change in tense. Whereas Paul's church-planting ministry was limited to an eighteen-month period, and Apollos was engaged in watering for a limited time, throughout the whole period of their activity and beyond, whether they were awake or asleep (cf. Mk 4:26–29), God was continually at work, causing the Word to keep growing and thriving ("was giving;" ongoing action) among them (3:6).

Because it is God who keeps giving the growth, "neither the planter is anything nor the waterer, but only God, who does the growing" (3:7). Back in 3:5, Paul had asked: "What, after all, is Apollos? What is Paul?" Now he answers, saying in essence, "We are nothing!" (cf. 2 Cor 12:11; Gal 6:3). Paul was keenly aware that the church lived totally by the grace of God, each church worker being totally dependent on God for any fruit in his ministry. Luther's words apply to all ministers of the Gospel: "We are beggars. That is true" (AE 54:476). All glory for a fruitful ministry must be given to God alone. Whereas Paul and Apollos are nothing, God is everything. To emphasize this, Paul places "God" last in 3:7.

But while Paul and Apollos are "nothing," they are "one thing" in a vitally important ministry that will be rewarded by God. God has chosen to grow his church from the seed planted and watered by servants called to a single task. Anyone who watches a gardener or farmer at work sees that planting and watering serve a common goal. Thus, Apollos and Paul did not work independently of each other; they formed a harmonious unit, one in purpose, one in fellowship (Gal 2:9).

Moreover, what matters most is not how much the Corinthians make of Paul or Apollos, but how God assesses their work. Again, Paul is emphasizing that he and Apollos are servants, working for a master who will allot each of them his pay ("reward") in keeping with his productivity ("work," 3:8). The pay will, indeed, vary according to each one's faithfulness in service. But what each will receive will only be disclosed on the Last Day, when everyone receives his recognition from God (4:5). Paul's "crown of boasting" on that day would be the presence there of his children in the faith (Phil 2:16; 1 Thess 2:19–20). With the resurrection on the Last Day in view, Paul would encourage fellow church servants as he encourages all Christians: "Be steadfast, immovable, always abounding in the work of the Lord, knowing that your labor is not in vain in the Lord" (1 Cor 15:58). 1 Cor 3:8b anticipates the argument of 3:12–15, where Paul will have more to say about the reward coming to the faithful worker on Judgment Day.

This reward will come to each worker from God, for each belongs to God. As Paul stated in 3:5, he and Apollos are God's "servants." Neither of them is an independent operator, seeking a following and plaudits for himself. The church in Corinth does not belong to Paul or Apollos; it is "the church of God" (1:2). And under God, Paul and Apollos work together as a closely knit unit in a common ministry, a ministry that belongs to God and is answerable above all to him.

But the Corinthians had been leaving God out of the picture. Their factious fighting had led them to focus myopically on human beings ("I belong to Paul" and so on, 1:12) and forget the great overarching truth that all church workers and church members belong to God.

The picture of the church as "God's field" (3:9) recalls the parable of the sower, where God is represented as sowing the good seed of the Word in a field (Mt 13:3–9; cf. also Jn 15:1–8, where the Father is depicted as a farmer).

While the picture of the field sums up Paul's imagery in 1 Cor 3:6–9, the image of the building will be expanded in 3:10–17.

1 CORINTHIANS 3:10–17
GOD'S BUILDING: THE TEMPLE

TRANSLATION

**3 10According to the grace of God which was given
me, as a wise master builder I laid a foundation,
and another builds on it. But let each one watch
how he builds on [it]. 11For no one can lay any other
foundation than the one that is laid, which is Jesus
Christ. 12If anyone builds on the foundation [with]
gold, silver, precious stones, woods, hay, straw, 13each
one's work will become evident. For the Day will
make it evident, because it is revealed by fire, and
the fire will test of what sort each person's work was.
14If the work someone has built on [the foundation]
survives, he will receive a reward. 15If someone's
work is consumed, he will suffer loss, though he
himself will be saved, but only as through fire.**

**16Don't you know that you are the temple of God and
God's Spirit is dwelling in you? 17If anyone destroys
God's temple, God will destroy him. For God's
temple is holy, and you yourselves are that temple.**

COMMENTARY

All is of God. The term "of God" in 3:10 echoes the three uses of "God's" in 3:9. Paul never forgets that he owes everything to God, even though he is about to speak of his own contribution in building up the church. It was by the grace and mercy of God that he, "the least of the apostles" (1 Cor 15:9), had initially been called to the priestly service of the Gospel (Rom 15:15–16; Eph 3:8). By that same grace, he had labored in Corinth (1 Cor 15:10), where he says, "as a wise master builder I laid a foundation" (3:10). God had supplied him with the wisdom of Christ crucified, which is foolishness to the world but is wiser than any worldly wisdom (1:18–25). This wisdom he passed on to the Corinthians (2:6–7)—the basic tenets of the Gospel of Christ crucified (15:1–4)—and thus, Paul laid the church's foundation. This was consistent with his ambition to preach the Gospel only in places where Christ had not already been named, lest he build on another's foundation (Rom 15:20).

With the foundation in place, "another builds on it" (1 Cor 3:10). He lays the foundation, then another—a preacher he has appointed (Acts 14:23)—continues the building. The word "another" followed by the present tense "builds" (1 Cor 3:10) is sufficiently general to include Apollos as the one who had originally watered the church but also (since Apollos was not at present in Corinth, 16:12) whoever was currently engaged in ministering to the people.

To all current and future builders of the Corinthian church, Paul adds the warning: "Let each one watch how he builds on [it]" (3:10). The builders need to watch out to ensure two things: (1) that they do not lay a different foundation, but build on the one already in place (3:11); (2) that they use only precious and enduring materials (3:12–15).

After the slab for a house has been poured, it would be ridiculous for the builders to ignore it and proceed to pour another slab beside it. Paul had laid the foundation for the Corinthian church by preaching "Jesus Christ and him crucified" (2:2). No doctrine was to be preached in Corinth that did not have this Gospel as its base (cf. 15:1–4; Gal 1:6–9). All teaching and practice is to be in harmony with what the founding father has put in place.

Every minister is responsible for the quality of the materials he uses in building the superstructure. The materials listed, "gold, silver, precious stones, woods, hay, straw" (1 Cor 3:12) are arranged in descending order of value. But more importantly, they fall into two groups of three. Gold, silver, and precious stones clearly possess greater value than the items in the second group. In addition (and this is most important in the context), these three more valuable items are noncombustible, whereas the materials in the second group are all combustible.

The precious, noncombustible materials represent preaching, teaching, and pastoral care that rest upon the Gospel. The combustible items signify teaching and methods motivated by human "wisdom" (1:17–22; 2:1–5, 13; 3:19) and therefore at odds with God's "wisdom" (1:24, 30; 2:6–7)—the doctrine of Christ. The OT refers to gold, silver, and precious stones as building materials used in the tabernacle and the temple (e.g., Ex 26; 1 Ki 6). Thus, Paul anticipates the temple imagery of 3:16–17.

The quality of each minister's work "will become evident" in due course, "for the Day will make it evident" (3:13). It is accordingly premature for the Corinthians to play off one pastor against another (1:10–12; cf. 4:5). The only evaluation that counts is what will happen in the light of "the Day." The Day is Judgment Day, known in both the OT and NT as "the day of the Lord" and in the NT more fully as "the day of our Lord Jesus Christ."

The next clause adds "because it is revealed by fire" (1 Cor 3:13; cf. 2 Thess 1:8). As much as some Christians love to pass judgment on their pastors, and as much as some pastors love to judge other pastors, no one is in the position to lay bare the whole story of another's life and ministry and make a fair and comprehensive appraisal. But the fire of the Last Day will uncover everything and show it in its proper light. Only when that day comes, "burning like an oven" (Mal 4:1), will the true quality of each church servant's contribution come to light, for then each person's work will be assayed by the God who judges impartially "according to each one's work" (1 Pet 1:17). More than any human assessment, this final assessment should make stewards of God's mysteries aware that they must be "found faithful" (1 Cor 4:1–2), proclaiming the scriptural Gospel and properly administering the Sacraments (1:13–17; 11:23–24) to create and build up believers in the faith.

Paul concludes this part of his argument with two conditional clauses. On the one hand, "If the work someone has built on [the foundation] survives, he will receive a reward" (1 Cor 3:14). Pastors whose work is shown to consist of fireproof gold, silver, and precious stones will hear God's commendation, "Well done, good and faithful servant" (Mt 25:21)! They "shall shine . . . like the stars for ever and ever" (Dan 12:3). On the other hand, "If someone's work is consumed, he will suffer loss, though he himself will be saved, but only as through fire" (1 Cor 3:15). On Judgment Day, workers who have used wood, hay, and straw will have to look on while their shoddy efforts—oriented to results in this age—are incinerated. However, this tragic loss will not extend to the minister's own person. "He himself will be saved" (1 Cor 3:15). But he will pass through the refiner's fire, becoming "like a brand plucked from the burning" (Zech 3:2; cf. Jude 23). He will be like a person whose car is totally destroyed in an accident, but who walks away from the wreckage physically unharmed.

Does Paul have in mind only the work of the preacher of the Gospel, or does the text apply, as some scholars think, to all believers? In other words, how broadly should the indefinite pronouns "anyone" (1 Cor 3:12), "someone," and "someone's" (3:14–15) be understood? In the light of the preceding verses, where Paul has been speaking of his own labors as a church planter and master builder and of Apollos' contribution as church "waterer" and construction worker (3:4–11), he is thinking mainly of the church's pastors and teachers, who have a special responsibility to ensure that the church is solidly built on the Word of Christ. Undoubtedly, though, what he says of pastors applies to all: being saved through the refiner's fire is the only way anyone is saved, and the Last Day will reveal the true quality of each person's activities in life (Mt 25:31–46).

Thus, 1 Cor 3:12–15 is a solemn warning to all Christians that proper construction of the church is a project precious to God; he will not tolerate workmanship that does not serve the Gospel and thereby promote the church's integrity and unity.

1 Cor 3:15 has often been used in support of the doctrine of purgatory. However, the text does not speak of a slow process but of the instantaneous purgation and transformation which takes place at Christ's return, when what

is mortal puts on immortality (15:54). At the same time, the text is remarkably emphatic that "he himself will be saved" (3:15). A Christian's salvation depends not at all on his works or deeds, not even on his most important actions in the building of God's kingdom. His portion in the life to come is secured solely and completely by the accomplished work of Christ on the cross (1:18–23; 2:8–9).

After picturing the Corinthian church as God's field (3:6–9) and God's building (3:10–15), Paul now specifies what *kind* of building the Corinthians are. Gently, he shames them a little for their lack of self-awareness: "Don't you know that you are the temple of God?" (3:16). Like the temple of the OT, constructed with gold, silver, and precious stones, they are a precious, divine sanctuary. Just as the glory of God dwelt in the OT tabernacle (Ex 40:34–35) and temple (1 Ki 8:11), so for Paul, the church is now the place where God's glory dwells (2 Cor 6:16; Eph 2:21; cf. Ps 26:8). Indeed, although the second temple, magnificently refurbished by Herod the Great, was still functioning in Jerusalem at the time of Paul's writing, the church had rendered it obsolete. Consequently, God's sanctuary was no longer a structure made of stones; it was a spiritual house inhabited by the Spirit of God. If the Corinthians would only be conscious of their significance as God's sanctuary, the dwelling place of his Spirit, they would want to adorn and build it up with their finest contributions (Is 60:3–11; 66:18–23; Rev 21:24, 26) rather than tearing it apart (1 Cor 1:10; 3:1, 3–4).

For many of Paul's listeners, the expression "God's temple" would have recalled not only the Jerusalem temple but also the many pagan temples in Corinth. Later, Paul will address the problem of those who were asserting that they had a right to continue to frequent those temples (chapters 8–10). But Paul is reminding them that just as there is only one true God, so there can be only one true temple in Corinth: the temple of God. No longer should they seek God's presence in the Jerusalem temple or a pagan building; *they* were his temple, each of them a living stone in that temple (1 Pet 2:5).

Thus, anyone tearing apart the fabric of the church is no better than the Babylonians who burned the Solomonic temple and the Seleucids who defiled the second temple and its worship and thereby assaulted the God of Israel. 1 Cor 3:17 is Paul's solemn warning not only to the Corinthians but to the church of all ages. The statement is entirely general, applying to anyone who would destroy the church by whatever means—false teaching or destructive practices. With respect to his immediate audience in Corinth, Paul's warning applies especially to anyone who foments factions by his boasting in human beings and their wisdom (1:10–17; 3:21). The punishment will fit the crime: "If anyone destroys God's temple, God will destroy him" (3:17). God will condemn him to eternal destruction.

God's retaliation will be so severe because the church is his special possession, the apple of his eye (Zech 2:8). "For God's temple is holy, and you yourselves are that temple" (1 Cor 3:17). God's holy church in Corinth may not be desecrated by unholy human rivalry. And that holy church is "you yourselves." The Greek pronoun ("you yourselves"), which ends 3:17 and the paragraph, echoes and balances the rhetorical question with which 3:16 began: "Don't you know?" Paul is accenting the pronoun to bring home to his hearers their solemn responsibility toward one another within the holy temple.

1 CORINTHIANS 3:18–23

No Boasting in Human Wisdom

TRANSLATION

3 18 **Let no one keep on deceiving himself. If anyone**
thinks he is wise among you in this age, let him
become a fool, so that he may become wise. 19 **For**
the wisdom of this world is foolishness in the
sight of God. For it is written: "He traps the wise
in their craftiness," 20 **and again, "The Lord knows**
the thoughts of the wise, that they are futile." 21 **So**
let no one continue to boast in human beings. For
all things are yours—22 **whether Paul or Apollos**
or Cephas, or the world or life or death, or things
present or things to come—all things are yours,
23 **but you are Christ's, and Christ is God's.**

COMMENTARY

WORLDLY WISDOM IS FOOLISHNESS TO GOD (3:18–20)

Paul follows up the sharp warning of 3:17 with the exhortation, "Let no one keep on deceiving himself" (3:18). In their fascination with communication skills and philosophy, the Corinthians have lost their perspective. Their values are upside down. This self-deluded complacency is placing them in serious spiritual danger. Paul calls for radical repentance: "If anyone thinks he is wise among you in this age, [if anyone thinks he is so astute at assessing the church's servants,] let him become a fool, so that he may become wise" (3:18). The call is for a 180-degree turn. Anyone who has a high opinion of his intellectual ability and judgment in comparison with his fellow Christians needs to rethink his attitude, despair of himself, and be willing to become and be called a fool. Only by this route will he gain real spiritual understanding—the childlike wisdom in Christ which the Scriptures so highly commend.

In calling for radical repentance, Paul is following Jesus' call for people to die to themselves, to their own egos, and to all personal concern for status (Jn 12:24–25) and find true life through faith in the Son of God (Rom 14:7–8;

2 Cor 5:15; Gal 2:19–20). God overturns this age's values and standards. "He has put down the mighty from their thrones and exalted the humble" (Lk 1:52).

Paul grounds ("for," 3:19) his call for repentance by repeating in essence what he had said in 1:20: "Has not God made foolish the wisdom of the world?" As the apostle made plain (1:18–25), the word of the cross is foolishness to the worldly wise. But by the same token, "the wisdom of this world is foolishness in the sight of God" (3:19). God's standards are totally at odds with the world's. The two are opposed, even hostile toward each other.

Paul supplies scriptural support from two texts, Job 5:13 and Ps 94:11, both of which speak of God's dealings with the wise. The first text is one of the few formal quotations from the book of Job in the NT. Eliphaz the Temanite, one of Job's "miserable comforters" (Job 16:2), is the speaker. But on this occasion, Eliphaz tells the truth about God: like a hunter trapping his prey, God "traps the wise in their craftiness" (Job 5:13). He turns the tables on his clever opponents. A noted OT example is the Persian official Haman, who was hanged on the gallows he had prepared for Mordecai the Judean (Esth 6:10).

Paul's second text, Ps 94:11, is from one of the imprecatory psalms. The psalmist prays that the "God of vengeance" will "shine forth" (Ps 94:1) against the proud evildoers who crush his people. The proud, who think they can get away with their schemes, are "brutish, beastly, stupid" (Ps 94:8) and "fools" (Ps 94:8). From God's perspective, all the thoughts and schemes of these "wise" people are futile. He knows what they are up to; he has the measure of all the worldly wise.

It is noteworthy that in both of the OT quotations, the Lord God is the subject of the sentence. Human beings in their "wisdom" may delude themselves into thinking they are autonomous, but in reality God is the one in charge.

ALL BELONGS TO GOD (3:21–23)

Paul has already declared that the Christian should only boast in the Lord (1 Cor 1:31). Now he states the same truth negatively: since Scripture (Job 5:13 and Ps 94:11, quoted in 1 Cor 3:19–20) shows the futility of human craftiness and scheming, "let no one continue to boast in human beings" (3:21). Not only is such boasting misdirected, but as Paul goes on to explain, it greatly limits the Christian's horizons. Anyone who thinks he is beholden solely to one particular teacher of the faith is in danger of cutting himself off from the spiritual wisdom others may have to offer. Rather than enriching himself, he is impoverishing himself, missing out on the opportunity to benefit from other faithful pastors and teachers. Paul is, of course, speaking of other leaders who are indeed faithful to the Gospel; he names Apollos and Cephas and would not name others who might be compromising or distorting the Gospel.

Paul explains, "all things are yours" (3:21). The apostle may be citing a favorite slogan of the spiritual elite in the Corinthian church (the "wise"). But Paul uses the slogan to turn the tables on the "wise": "If your slogan is true, then you should no longer be boasting in any human leader. Rather, if 'all things are yours,' then you should be expanding your horizons to admit that Paul *and* Apollos *and* Cephas are yours. These men are all your servants on behalf of the same God (cf. 3:5), not leaders of narrow factions. They all proclaim the same Gospel, not different gospels. How foolish to restrict yourselves to what you can learn from one of the three!"

"Moreover," Paul in effect continues, "not only do all your instructors in the faith belong to you, so do 'all things,' both the things of this world and those of the life to come" (3:22–23). In fact, the whole created order (3:22) is the Corinthians' as the spiritual children of Abraham, "the heir of the world" (Rom 4:13). As God's child and heir (Rom 8:17), the Christian sees everywhere and in everything the signs of his Creator and Redeemer's bounty and beneficence toward him (cf. Rom 8:28, 32).

As Paul will later assure the Romans, spelling it out in more detail, nothing in this world could separate the Christians from God's love for them in Christ (Rom 8:35–39). Here in Corinthians, Paul states it positively and more briefly: Everything "life" (1 Cor 3:22) brings the Christians' way will be for their good, for they have found that faith in Christ is the secret to life (cf. Jn 14:6: "I am . . . the life"; Col 3:4: "Christ . . . our life"). "Death" (1 Cor 3:22), too, is no longer a cruel master, but the servant of Christians, ushering them into eternal life (cf. Phil 1:21: "For me, to live is Christ and to die is gain;" also 1 Cor 15:55–57). The list of the Christians' possessions goes on. "Things present" (1 Cor 3:22), everything that makes up the rich tapestry of our daily lives, are all God's gift to us. The final gift is "things to come" (3:22; cf. Rom 8:38). Nothing in the present and nothing that comes our way in the future can ultimately do us harm—all comes from the hand of our gracious God who ordains everything for our good. Paul rounds off the section with another summary: "All things are yours" (1 Cor 3:22).

But while Paul freely grants that all things belong to the Christian, he must add an important qualification. If those in Corinth who boast of superior wisdom want to become really wise, then they must renounce any notions of being the center of the universe. As Christians, they can no longer think of themselves as autonomous; they belong to Christ (1 Cor 3:23)—to the one who loved them and gave himself for them (Gal 2:20; see also 1 Cor 6:20; 7:23). Paul says this applies to the whole congregation, not just the faction that boasted "I belong to Christ" (1:12). Paul would later write to the Romans (14:8), "Whether we live or die, we are the Lord's" (cf. Gal 3:29).

As the Christian is Christ's, so "Christ is God's" (1 Cor 3:23). The Son's subjection to the Father will be brought out in two more places in the epistle, 11:3 and 15:24–28. Paul is not denying or detracting from the fact that the Son is "of one essence with the Father" (Nicene Creed). What he has in mind is Christ's saving work. When the Father sent him to deliver the human race, he humbled himself and took a place among humanity. In that respect, he subordinated himself to the Father, who in turn exalted him over all (Phil 2:9–10).

1 CORINTHIANS 4:1–5

Apostles Are Stewards of God's Mysteries

TRANSLATION

4 [1]This is how a person must regard us, as servants
of Christ and stewards of the mysteries of God.
[2]Now what is looked for in stewards is that a
person be found faithful. [3]For me, then, it is quite
insignificant that I am investigated by you or by a
human day, but I do not even investigate myself.
[4]For I have nothing on my conscience, but that does
not make me innocent; the one who investigates me
is the Lord. [5]Consequently, stop judging anything
before the time, until the Lord comes, who will
both bring to light the secret things of darkness
and manifest the motives of the hearts. Then the
approval will come to each person from God.

COMMENTARY

CHRIST'S SERVANTS AND STEWARDS OF GOD'S MYSTERIES (4:1)

Commentators have noted that 4:1 begins without a word like "for" or "therefore" binding it to the previous sentence. After the almost doxological passage that brings chapter 3 to a close, Paul's argument is taking a new turn. Whereas his focus in 3:16–23 was on the Corinthians—on *"you"* (plural) being God's temple (3:16–17), on *your* self-deception and boasting, and finally on *your* riches in Christ ("all things are yours," 3:21), the new chapter turns (or rather returns; cf. 3:5–15) to *"us"*—to *"us"* apostles and church servants and how a person should properly evaluate *"us."*

We must be regarded, Paul begins, above all as "servants of Christ" (4:1; cf. 3:6). While the Corinthians could say that Paul, Apollos, and Cephas belonged to them (3:22), since the labors of these men had been devoted to their personal benefit, they needed to recognize that the ministers of the Gospel are ultimately accountable only to their Lord (4:5). Consequently, they are not concerned with personal popularity. Rather, as the personal aides of Christ they possess a high dignity—and high responsibility. Just as the whole congregation is "Christ's" (3:23), so—no less—are Paul, Apollos, and Cephas.

Paul proceeds to elucidate more precisely the responsibilities of Christ's servants: they are "stewards of the mysteries of God" (4:1). A steward often was a slave but one in charge of his master's entire household and property. Moses was God's steward, trustworthy in all his house (Num 12:7; Heb 3:5; see Heb 3:1–6). Jesus refers to "the faithful and prudent steward whom his master will put in charge of his slaves, to give them their allowance of food at the proper time" (Lk 12:42; cf. Mt 24:45). Jesus continues: "Blessed is that slave whom his master will find doing that when he arrives" (Lk 12:43). Paul understood his and his co-workers' responsibility for faithful stewardship in the light of Christ's instructions.

Paul and his colleagues were entrusted with management of "the mysteries of God" (4:1). Understanding "the mysteries of the kingdom of heaven" was Jesus' gift to his disciples (Mt 13:11). These mysteries are not accessible to human wisdom (1 Cor 2:14; see 1 Cor 2:6–16). The mystery of the Gospel of Christ had been hidden throughout the ages and generations (1 Cor 2:7–9; see also Rom 16:25; Eph 3:4, 9; Col 1:26) and continues to be hidden from the wise and understanding (1 Cor 1:18–25; see also Mt 11:25). But now it had been revealed "to his holy apostles and prophets in the Spirit" (Eph 3:5; that was Paul's theme in 1 Cor 2:10–16). As the Gospel mysteries were a gift that had been revealed to them, not knowledge acquired by their own brilliance, Paul, Apollos, and Cephas—and faithful Christian pastors in any age—can only be regarded as stewards of a sacred trust.

Paul speaks of the divine "mystery" or "mysteries" four times in 1 Corinthians (1 Cor 2:1, 7; 4:1; 15:51). In 2:1, 7, the "mystery" is the Gospel itself, which is a "mystery" because it is hidden from the world in the "foolish" word of the cross. Paul preached the mystery of Christ crucified and risen from the dead without employing human eloquence or wisdom (2:1–2). The mystery of this Gospel was ordained by God in eternity to bring Christians into glory (2:7). But the worldly rulers failed to comprehend the person of Jesus Christ and so crucified him (2:8–9). In the same way the worldly wise have failed to comprehend the wisdom of God hidden in the Gospel mystery. Therefore, "mystery" sums up the plan of God to save sinners through the "foolishness" and "weakness" of Christ crucified, which is the Gospel Paul preaches (1:18–25; 2:6–16), and the same Gospel preached by faithful pastors throughout the ages.

The "mystery" will be consummated when the risen Christ returns and all Christians are changed (1 Cor 15:51). At the resurrection, the mystery will be revealed to all. At that time too, each pastor's stewardship of the mysteries will be revealed and evaluated by God (4:1, 5). That stewardship encompasses the entire Gospel ministry, all the avenues through which the Gospel of Christ crucified and the hope of resurrection in him is proclaimed.

Some dismiss the suggestion that "the mysteries" (4:1) means the Sacraments. But the suggestion is not totally wrong; it is simply too narrow. Part of the pastor's stewardship of the Gospel *is* the proper administration of the Sacraments. The Gospel mystery of incorporation into Christ's crucifixion and resurrection for the forgiveness of sins is hidden in Baptism (1 Cor 12:13; see also, e.g., Acts 2:38–39; Rom 6:1–4; Col 2:11–13) and the Lord's Supper (e.g., 1 Cor 11:23–26). Through the Sacraments, God bestows the gift of grace and the promise of resurrection—the consummation of the mystery (1 Cor 15:51). But "the mysteries of God" (4:1) include much more: they embrace all the articles of evangelical doctrine, of which the Sacraments are an important part. This comprehensive Gospel teaching is the "allowance of food" (Lk 12:42) which Paul and his colleagues are to pass on to God's people (cf. Mt 28:20: "teaching them to keep *all* that I commanded you").

It is helpful to recognize that in the history of the church the word "sacraments" has sometimes been understood in a broader sense that corresponds to Paul's use of the term "mysteries." For example, the work "De sacramentis" by Hugo of St. Victor (died 1141) deals with matters such as the Trinity and the Incarnation.

The Lutheran Confessions use the term "mystery" to refer to various doctrinal truths of the Christian faith, including the Holy Trinity, which is called the highest mystery (FC Ep VIII 18; FC SD VIII 33), the personal union of the divine and human natures in Christ, which is called the next highest mystery after that of the Trinity (preface to the *Book of Concord;* FC Ep VIII 18; FC SD VIII 22, 33–34, 96), the doctrine of election and God's foreknowledge (FC Ep XI 11; FC SD XI 26, 43, 52, 55, 64), and the bodily presence of Christ in the Lord's Supper (FC Ep VII 42). The Lutheran attitude toward the mysteries of God is summed up in FC Ep VII 42, which refers to the eating of Christ's body and the drinking of Christ's blood in the Sacrament of Holy Communion, but which well describes the proper response to all of God's mysteries: "Here we take our intellect captive in obedience to Christ, as we do in other articles also, and accept this mystery in no other way than by faith and as it is revealed in the Word."

LEAVE THE JUDGMENT OF STEWARDS TO THE LORD (4:2–5)

Since a steward was often left unsupervised for long periods, the most important quality looked for in such men was faithfulness (cf. Lk 12:42). A number of Jesus' parables teach the need for faithfulness during the absence of the master, who upon his return will demand a strict accounting (Mt 25:14–30; Lk 19:11–27; cf. Mk 13:34). Similarly, "the Lord of hosts" had spoken through Jeremiah, "Let him who has my word speak my word faithfully" (Jer 23:28). Paul himself had faithfully discharged his responsibility to transmit the Gospel tradition he had received (1 Cor 15:1–11).

Thus, any assessment of his ministry by human beings was "quite insignificant" (4:3). While the Corinthians were making much of their own assessments of their teachers (1:12), in Paul's scheme of things it all counted for very little. In Greek "for me" is placed first for emphasis (4:3). Paul is contrasting his own attitude with that of the Corinthians. Any preliminary evaluation of his ministry by them or anyone else is beside the point. The only day that counts is the great day of the Lord referred to in 3:13 (cf. 3:8). Paul is reminding the Corinthians again of the importance of the eschatological perspective.

In the light of his anticipation of the Day, Paul adds "I do not even investigate myself" (4:3). Such self-evaluation would also be inappropriate and irrelevant. (Later, Paul will affirm the necessity of proper self-examination before the Lord's Supper [11:28]).

Having asserted that his ministry was not subject to human scrutiny (4:3), Paul realizes he could easily be misunderstood. His opponents could charge that there were good reasons for his not wanting an investigation of his ministry. To scotch such suggestions, he adds: "I have nothing on my conscience" (4:4). Indeed, he has lived up to his own requirement that a pastor be above reproach (1 Tim 3:2; cf. his self-assessment in 2 Tim 4:6–8).

However, his own assessment could not be the final word: "but that does not make me innocent" (1 Cor 4:4). The Lord Jesus, "the just Judge" (2 Tim 4:8), is his true examiner. Ever since his experience on the Damascus road, his one ambition has been to please his Lord (2 Cor 5:9; cf. 1 Thess 2:4). He knew that as long as he aimed to please people, he would not be a servant of Christ (Gal 1:10).

On the basis of his argument in this paragraph ("consequently," 1 Cor 4:5), Paul urges the Corinthians to stop passing judgment on his ministry and that of his co-workers. His injunction against such premature judgments ("stop judging anything before the time," 4:5) reflects Jesus' words in Mt 7:1 ("judge not!"). The proper time for judgment will be the Last Day, when the person to make the assessment will be the returning Lord himself (cf. 2 Cor 5:10). On that day, he "will both bring to light the secret things of darkness and manifest the motives of the hearts" (1 Cor 4:5). He alone understands all the hidden counsels of the human heart (1 Sam 16:7; Ps 139:1; Rom 2:16; 8:27); thus, he alone will be able to make a true assessment.

APPLICATION TO THE CONTEMPORARY CHURCH

Paul's words in 1 Cor 4:1–5 apply directly to congregations today. While Paul considers any investigation of his ministry by the congregation in Corinth to be "insignificant" (4:3) and commands them to "stop judging" (4:5), he is not saying that he and other ministers of the Gospel are not to be held accountable by the congregations of which they are stewards. These are statements by an apostle who can say "I have nothing on my conscience" (4:4). It would be a rare pastor who could honestly make a similar claim of complete innocence regarding his ministry.

Those who preach and teach are under trust. Ministers are accountable to God (4:4–5) and are to be judged by the standard of fidelity (4:2). They are "servants" and "stewards" (4:1), not lords or despots. A Christian congregation has the right, and indeed the responsibility, to protest if its minister is not faithful to the Word of God. That requires that the members of a church have a sufficient knowledge of the Scriptures to be able to discern truth and distinguish it from error.

In addition to false doctrine, pastors are to be removed should they lead a scandalous life. Not only must they teach what befits sound doctrine (Titus 1:9; 2:1), their conduct should meet the standards Paul lays down in the Pastoral Epistles (1 Tim 3:1–7; Titus 1:5–9).

On the other hand, the main thrust of 1 Cor 4:1–5 is that congregations should not criticize—much less attempt to remove—their pastors for petty reasons. A "hire and fire" mentality should have no place in the church.

Congregations must treat their ministers with the respect and forbearance due their holy calling (4:1). This also requires an eschatological view. Parishioners and pastors need to learn how to hold their tongues "until the Lord comes" (4:5). Only at that time "the approval will come to each person from God" (4:5; cf. Rom 2:29). Once God has pronounced over a minister's life, "Well done, good and faithful servant" (Mt 25:21, 23), no human being or devil will be able to challenge God's verdict.

1 CORINTHIANS 4:6–7
LEARN NOT TO GO BEYOND SCRIPTURE

TRANSLATION

4 [6]These illustrations, brothers, I applied to myself
and Apollos for your sake, in order that you might
learn through us [the true meaning of] "not beyond
what stands written," that no one be puffed up in
favor of the one against the other. [7]Who concedes
you any superiority? What do you have that you
did not receive? But if indeed you received it, why
are you boasting as if you did not receive [it]?

COMMENTARY

Paul had been speaking in 4:1–5 of the high regard in which apostles and teachers must be held as Christ's "servants" and "stewards of the mysteries of God." First person pronouns predominated, as Paul ("I") spelled out how the Corinthians should regard him and his co-workers ("me" or "us"). But now in 4:6–7, he focuses on the implications for "you" (plural in Greek)—the saints in Corinth: "What lessons do you need to draw from what has just been said about the servant role of your ministers?"

Paul had described his and Apollos' role in terms of metaphors drawn from farming (3:5–9), building (3:10–17), and household management (4:1–5). These three metaphors, "these illustrations" (4:6, literally, "these things"), he had applied to himself and to Apollos for the Corinthians' benefit ("for your sake," 4:6). Paul's aim in all this was to teach them. They were to imitate his and Apollos' example in not going beyond what had been written.

With the cryptic "not beyond what stands written" (4:6), we come to a particularly difficult crux for commentators. Some suggest Paul is quoting a proverbial saying from the political arena (like "keep within the rules") which the apostle has adopted for his purposes.

The simplest solution, however, is to see the phrase as Paul's own reference to the authority of Scripture. He has already employed the "it is written" formula four times in this epistle (1:19, 31; 2:9; 3:19–20), and in each case Paul used it to introduce a quotation from the OT Scriptures. Moreover, he will use the same formula or its variants another seven times in this letter (9:9, 10; 10:7, 11; 14:21; 15:45, 54), each time in reference to the OT Scriptures. In the present context, he is speaking about boasting and has used biblical texts in support of his theme: "Let the one who boasts boast [only] in the Lord" (1:31; see also 3:19–21). In order to check the tendency of some in Corinth to get carried away with enthusiasm for human leaders (1:10–17) and think more highly of themselves than they ought, becoming "puffed up" (4:6), like the unrighteous man in Hab 2:4, Paul reminds them that they must learn to submit humbly and soberly to the Scriptures. The Corinthians should take the Scriptures to heart, regard them as the voice of God, and recognize their supreme value in providing instruction and encouragement from him whose ways and thoughts are higher than ours (Is 55:8–9; Rom 15:4; 1 Cor 10:11).

If they would learn from Paul and Apollos and submit to Scripture, they would not "be puffed up in favor of the one against the other" (4:6). They would stop championing Paul at Apollos' expense, or vice versa (1:12; 3:4–6, 22). The verb "puff up" colorfully expresses the Corinthians' tendency to become inflated with pride because of their spiritual and intellectual gifts. None of the other churches Paul founded seems to have been as prone to inflated pride as Corinth.

To deflate their pride, Paul asks three rhetorical questions. The first question, "Who concedes you any superiority?" (4:7), probably means, "Who has made you so distinguished?" Obviously the answer is "no one." No one has conferred on any Christian so distinguished a status that he has a vantage point for invidiously comparing one servant of Christ with another.

But not only are the Corinthians being presumptuous. The second question, "What do you have that you did not receive?" (4:7), reminds them that they are also being ungrateful. They should have recognized that all their spiritual gifts, all their endowments of speech and knowledge, have come to them from the rich grace of God (cf. 1:4–7). It was that question which made an impression on St. Augustine, as he was led during the controversy with Pelagius to a deeper appreciation of the grace of God (cf. FC SD II 26–27).

Under these circumstances, there is no room for boasting (cf. 1:29–31). Thanksgiving is the only appropriate response to God's grace.

1 CORINTHIANS 4:8–13
Fools for Christ

TRANSLATION

4 [8]Already you are satiated! Already you have begun
to be rich! Without us you have begun your reign!
And how I wish you had begun your reign; then we
too could share your reign with you! [9]For I think
God has put us apostles on display as those who
are last, like those condemned to death, because
we have become a spectacle to the world—both
to angels and human beings. [10]We are fools on
account of Christ, but you are wise in Christ. We
are weak, but you are strong. You are honored, but
we are dishonored. [11]To the present hour we are
also hungry and thirsty and naked and roughly
treated and homeless [12]and toiling hard, working
with our own hands. While we are being slandered,
we bless; while we are being persecuted, we put up
with it; [13]while we are being defamed, we answer
in a kind manner. We have become like the scum
of the earth, the dirt of all—until the present.

COMMENTARY

Paul's argument in chapters 1–4 reaches its high point and conclusion in 4:8–13. This is the peroration of his argument against the Corinthians' propensity to boast "in human beings" (3:21; cf. 1:29, 31; 3:18–20; 4:6).

Three brief sentences, ascending to a climax, flesh out Paul's charge that the Corinthians are "puffed up" (4:6): "Already you are satiated! Already you have begun to be rich! Without us you have begun your reign!" (4:8). Paul's words are charged with heavy irony. Whereas he and his fellow apostles are engaged in an arduous struggle "to the present hour" (4:11; cf. 4:13), the Corinthians, in their own estimation, have *already* attained full spiritual maturity. Not for them is the attitude of the beggar, "the poor in spirit" who still "hunger and thirst for righteousness" (Mt 5:3, 6). Not for them is the pressure of having to live between the times, in the tension between the now and the not yet of the Christian's eschatological existence. They are already satiated with spiritual food. There is little to look forward to because they believe that they have already received and attained everything.

Paul continues his ironic indictment: "Already you have begun to be rich!" (1 Cor 4:8). Like the self-satisfied church in Laodicea, they are saying: "I am rich, I have prospered, and I need nothing," while failing to recognize that they really are "wretched, pitiable, poor, blind, and naked" (Rev 3:17). Although Paul has thankfully acknowledged that the Corinthians have been greatly enriched in Christ (1 Cor 1:4), this did not mean they needed no more spiritual supply.

The Corinthians have gone ahead, leaving Paul and his co-workers far behind. "Without us" Paul adds, coming to the climax, "without our having a share in it, you have begun your reign" (1 Cor 4:8). While Paul and Apollos are still embattled, the Corinthians are like emperors taking pleasure in a triumph. But they had failed to take note of the other side of the coin. On the one hand, God's kingdom had indeed been inaugurated among them. They had received God's grace in Jesus Christ, and *in that way* they "were enriched" in him (1 Cor 1:5) and so lacked no spiritual gift (1:7). However, on the other hand, they had failed to grasp that the kingdom had not yet reached its consummation, that its manifestation in this world would always be coupled with "tribulation" and "patient endurance" (Rev 1:9), that indeed, as Paul would later write to Timothy, only "if we endure with him, will we also reign with him" (2 Tim 2:12). Paul had assured the Corinthians that God would preserve them in Christ "until the end" (1 Cor 1:8), but that "end" still lay in the future.

On the great "Day" of the kingdom's consummation (3:13; 4:5), Christ will most assuredly share his royal dignity with his people. In Rev 3:21, he promises: "The one who conquers, I will grant to him to sit with me on my throne, as I myself conquered and sat down with my Father on his throne." This royal rule is the ultimate destiny of those who are in Christ (cf. Rev 4:4).

As he contemplates this prospect, Paul gives vent to the wretchedness he and his co-workers experience as they struggle to fulfill their vocation and long for the glory that will at last be revealed (Rom 7:24; 8:18, 23): "How I wish you had begun your reign!" (1 Cor 4:8). If it were true that the Corinthians had begun their reign in glory, that would mean the apostles could share it with them; their sufferings would be over.

But the apostles' current experience presents a totally different picture (1 Cor 4:9). Far from being able to share the Corinthians' triumphalism, Paul could only think of his ever-present weakness and suffering. Fresh in his mind were memories of the riot in Ephesus, when his travel companions, Gaius and Aristarchus, had been dragged into the theater, and his friends, fearing for his life, had forbidden him from following (Acts 19:28–31). Paul and the others thought they had received the sentence of death (2 Cor 1:8–9). Probably this riot at the theater is part of what prompted the imagery of this verse. The threat of arrest and imprisonment was constantly hanging over the apostles' heads (cf. Acts 4:3;

20:22–24). By contrast with the Corinthians, who are riding high, Paul thinks "God has put us apostles on display as those who are last, like those condemned to death" (1 Cor 4:9). The Corinthians were first in line, but the apostles were last (cf. Mt 19:30; 20:16).

Above all, Paul's imagery is drawn from the well-known scene of a victorious Roman general celebrating a triumph. At the rear of the procession would be the captives condemned to die in the arena. This striking image compares God with the general, and Paul and his fellow apostles with the captives who must bow to the general's will. In 2 Cor 2:14, we find the same picture. Paul thanks God, "who always leads us in triumph in Christ and spreads the fragrance of the knowledge of him through us in every place." He is grateful to God for the privilege of following Christ always and everywhere, his every thought captive to the obedience of Christ (2 Cor 10:5).

In his infinite wisdom, God has put the apostles on display on a vast stage—the whole universe, embracing both angels and human beings (1 Cor 4:9; cf 1 Pet 1:12). In this great theater, a life-and-death struggle is being played out. On the surface, the drama seems to portray the apostles and the saints as simply "sheep for the slaughter" (Rom 8:36, quoting Ps 44:22), a sorry spectacle before a derisive world. But in reality, those doomed to death are "more than conquerors" (Rom 8:37), and the eternal welfare of each person in the audience hangs on how he regards these "fools on account of Christ" (1 Cor 4:10) and their message.

Just as the world regards the word of the cross as "foolishness" (1:18) and "weakness" (1:25), so it regards the bearers of that word as "weak" and insignificant men, as "fools on account of Christ" (4:10; cf. 3:18). Paul is closing out the argument of chapters 1–4 and anticipating his second epistle's catalogues of the apostles' sufferings (2 Cor 4:7–12; 6:4–10; 11:23–29). The word of the cross, which they preach, has been imprinted on their lives, as they follow their Savior in the way of the cross "like those condemned to death" (1 Cor 4:9).

The Corinthians, on the other hand, had done all they could to maintain their intellectual respectability. They were "wise in Christ" (1 Cor 4:10; see also 2 Cor 11:19), or so they thought; the real situation was that they were wise in their own eyes (Prov 3:7). Moreover, where the apostles were "weak," the Corinthians were "strong" in Christ (1 Cor 4:10) and self-assured to the point of conceit (Col 2:18). Then, reversing the order, Paul adds: "You are honored, but we are dishonored" (1 Cor 4:10; cf. 2 Cor 11:24–29). The change in the order makes for a smooth transition to 1 Cor 4:11–13, which spells out how the apostles are dishonored.

We may compare the catalogue of sufferings in 4:11–13 with similar lists in 2 Cor 4:7–10; 6:4–10; 11:23–29. In these hardships, Paul saw the divine purpose at work, enabling him to be in communion with Christ's suffering, to conform to Christ's death, and thus to attain the resurrection of the dead (Phil 3:10). In fact, he rejoiced in his sufferings, because thereby he was filling up what was remaining in Christ's afflictions (Col 1:24).

The list of sufferings begins with the hunger and thirst (1 Cor 4:11) he would have suffered during long journeys by land and sea, and particularly during imprisonment (cf. 2 Cor 6:5; 11:27). Thus, he was conformed to Christ, who suffered hunger in the wilderness (Mt 4:2) and thirst on the cross (Jn 19:28). Nakedness was an indignity to which Paul and others had been subjected on at least one occasion during their journeys. Acts 16:22–23 records how Paul and Silas were attacked in Philippi, where the magistrates tore off their clothing and ordered them to be beaten with rods (cf. 2 Cor 11:27, and for Jesus' experience, Jn 19:23–24 and parallels). The incident in Philippi was only one of many occasions when Paul suffered a beating (cf. Acts 23:2; 2 Cor 6:5; 11:23). Again, this brought him into conformity with Christ: the verb "to beat" is used to describe the beating Jesus received (Mt 26:67; Mk 14:65; cf. Jn 18:22; 19:3).

Another hardship of Paul's life as a missionary was the need to be constantly on the move. Unlike the local "elders" whom he had appointed in every church (Acts 14:23), men who had roots in the community and could continue to live there, Paul could rarely settle for long in one place; like his Lord, he had "no place to lay his head" (Mt 8:20). As men who were essentially homeless (1 Cor 4:11), the apostles declared they had no permanent city in this world (Heb 11:13–16; 13:14).

Hard work with their own hands was another feature of the apostles' labors (1 Cor 4:12). The Greeks (probably including many members of the Corinthian congregation) traditionally despised manual labor, thinking it was fit only for slaves. On the other hand, Jews insisted that every boy learn a trade. Jesus became a mason-carpenter (Mk 6:3), like his stepfather, Joseph (Mt 13:55). John, James, Simon, and Andrew were fishermen, and Paul was a tentmaker and repairer. Paul, Aquila, Priscilla (Acts 18:1–3), and other like-minded Jewish Christians would have stood out in Corinth for their willingness to get their hands dirty. Thus, they modeled Paul's admonition that Christians should not be lazy but work for their living (Eph 4:28; 1 Thess 2:9; 2 Thess 3:8).

But it was not only his Jewish appreciation for manual labor that led Paul to pursue his tentmaking. He was also concerned to present the Gospel of God's free grace free of charge to his hearers and, in the process, to set an example as one who willingly gives up his rights for the sake of others (cf. Acts 20:33–35; 1 Cor 9:6–18).

Paul's words in 1 Cor 4:12b–13a closely echo his Master in the Sermon on the Mount. Again, Paul shows his hearers the way of the cross, which to the world seems utter foolishness. Worldly people tend to live by principles of self-assertion and "getting even." But the apostles, following their master's example, bless and pray for those who harm them, seeking to overcome evil with good (Mt 5:44; Acts 7:60; Rom 12:14, 17–21; 1 Pet 3:9). Despite insults, persecution, and slander, their consistent response is prayer, patience, and conciliation. Indeed, the present participles in 1 Cor 4:12–13 indicate that such Christlike behavior takes place even as the abuse is occurring!

With another "we have become" (4:13; also in 4:9), Paul rounds off his description of the apostles' sufferings: "We have become like the scum of the earth, the dirt of all—until the present." Paul seems to have derived the words "scum" and "dirt" from Lam 3:45: "You have placed us as offscouring and refuse among the nations." Just as ancient Jerusalem had been destroyed by Babylon and her inhabitants sent into exile, the apostles had been treated like the scum of the earth by the enemies of the Gospel (cf. 1 Cor 4:9–13a). With this allusion, Paul may be suggesting not only the pillaging of Jerusalem, but also the ministry and sufferings of Jeremiah (the author of Lamentations) as a prophetic model of the life and sufferings of the faithful apostles—and of faithful pastors throughout the church's history.

1 CORINTHIANS 4:14–21

Paul's Fatherly Appeal for Unity

TRANSLATION

**4 [14]I am not writing this to make you ashamed, but
to admonish you as my beloved children. [15]For even
if you should have countless tutors in Christ, you
certainly do not have many fathers. For in Christ
Jesus, through the Gospel, I myself begot you. [16]I
encourage you, therefore, become imitators of
me. [17]For this reason I have sent to you Timothy,
who is my beloved and faithful child in the Lord,
who will remind you of my ways in Christ Jesus,
as I am teaching everywhere in every church.**

**[18]Some have become puffed up, as if I were not
coming to you. [19]But I will come to you quickly if
the Lord wills, and I will ascertain not the talk of
those who are puffed up but the power. [20]For the
kingdom of God does not consist in talk but in
power. [21]What do you wish? Am I to come to you
with a stick, or in love and a spirit of gentleness?**

COMMENTARY

Paul's tone suddenly becomes more tender. Such changes of tone are understandable in a personal letter. He now assures the Corinthians that his intention was not to put them to shame. Although his pointed comparisons between their complacency and the apostles' hardships could hardly have failed to embarrass them, that was not his ultimate goal. When he felt it was called for, of course, he would not hesitate to say "shame on you" (6:5; 15:34). But now his overriding concern is to restore his fatherly relationship with his children and to lead them to a more humble, repentant attitude (cf. 2 Cor 7:8–10). Thus, he insists, he is simply appealing to them, trying to reach the hearts of his "beloved children" (1 Cor 4:14).

Paul's understanding of himself as father of the Corinthians has already been anticipated by earlier references to his unique contribution as planter and master builder (3:6–10). Now, in calling the saints in Corinth "my beloved children" (4:14), he is reminding them of his special relationship to them (cf. similar designations in 2 Cor 6:13; 12:14; Gal 4:19; 1 Thess 2:7, 11; he also frequently calls an individual he has converted "my child" (1 Tim 1:2, 18; 2 Tim 1:2; 2:1; Titus 1:4; Philemon 10).

The noun "admonition," which is related to "admonish," (6:14), is found in Eph 6:4, where Paul urges fathers to bring up their children "in the nurture and admonition of the Lord" (KJV). Pastors are to be like fathers to their flock, admonishing them (Titus 3:10; Acts 20:31; Col 1:28; 1 Thess 5:12) and also encouraging them to admonish one another (Rom 15:14; Col 3:16; 1 Thess 5:14; 2 Thess 3:15). Paul himself modeled this fatherly approach.

As valuable as the services of Apollos, Peter, and others may have been, no one could replace Paul as the Corinthians' father (1 Cor 4:15). Apollos (and possibly Peter) had served as "tutors" (4:15) in the past; others were serving in that capacity now. In Roman society, a "tutor" was a superior slave who supervised a boy's education. Tutors could be replaced, but no one could replace a father. Paul does not want to put Apollos and the others down. They too instructed the Corinthians "in Christ" (4:15). But they were not the father.

The Greek word order in the next sentence in 4:15 is important: "For in Christ Jesus, through the Gospel, I myself begot you." Paul is careful not to overstate what he has been claiming for his own role. All glory for what had happened in Corinth belonged to Christ. Paul's mission had been carried on in Christ's name, and its success was solely due to the regenerative power of the Gospel—the word of the cross. With the word "Gospel," now used for the first time in this epistle, the argument returns full circle to where it began in 1:17 with the verb "preach the Gospel" (also in 9:16, 18; 15:1, 2).

As the Corinthians' father in Christ, Paul has a right to encourage his children to imitate him (4:16). Both in his teaching and in his conduct he sees himself as an example (2 Thess 3:9) for them to follow. In the immediate context (cf. 4:9–13), imitating the apostle would involve adopting his humble attitude, his willingness to suffer for the Gospel, his refusal to boast except in weakness and in Christ (in contrast to the factiousness of some), and his understanding of the centrality of Christ crucified. By imitating Paul, the Corinthians would at the same time be imitating Christ, to whose image the apostle had been and was being conformed (11:1).

To make it easier for them to remember him and thus imitate him, Paul had sent Timothy to them (4:17). Whether Timothy ever reached Corinth we do not know. Paul was clearly concerned that some of the Corinthians might not welcome a visit from the young pastor and could even treat him with contempt (16:10–11). He therefore stresses Timothy's close relationship to himself as "my beloved and faithful child in the Lord" (4:17). It was Timothy's task to remind the Corinthians of Paul's "ways in Christ Jesus, as I am teaching everywhere in every church" (4:17). The expression "ways" includes Paul's preaching and his example—his preaching the message of the cross, and his way of life under that cross. He modeled the "way of peace" (Rom 3:17), the "more excellent way" (1 Cor 12:31), and the way of "love" (1 Corinthians 13). Paul adds that what he expected of the Corinthians in terms of their concord with apostolic teaching, and their practice of Christian love and humility was by no means exceptional; it was his standard expectation for the church of God throughout the world (cf. 7:17; 14:33). The Corinthians should not think they were on a higher spiritual plane that exempted them from the way of the cross.

The word "some," which in Greek comes at the end of 4:18, receives some emphasis. Although Paul has been addressing the whole congregation, he is aware that only "some" of its members have been puffed up with arrogance. As a good pastor, he is careful not to castigate the whole congregation when only "some" are to blame.

Nonetheless, the problem had to be laid on everyone's heart, for "a little leaven leavens the whole batch" (5:6). Paul's self-important opponents (cf. 4:6) were apparently seeking to persuade everyone that the apostle was just another traveling sophist, another "fly by night" operator whom they would never see again. Since they were confident he would not be returning, they felt free to say what they liked about him. Meanwhile, they may have invited Apollos to return and keenly anticipated another opportunity to revel in his eloquence (cf. 16:12).

But Paul declares his firm intention of returning to Corinth as soon as possible (4:19). His "child" (4:17) Timothy's impending visit would be a prelude and preparation for a visit from their father in the faith (4:15). Soon after Timothy's visit, Paul would come to them quickly (4:19). Definite plans for this visit are, indeed, already in place, and will be spelled out in 16:5–7. Paul adds the proviso "if the Lord wills" (4:19). As the Lord's servant, he lived by the prayer "Thy will be done" (Mt 6:10). Often he was taught that his travel schedules could only be provisional; it was the Lord who made the final decisions (Acts 16:6–7; 18:21; Rom 1:10; 15:32; 1 Cor 16:7).

The book of Acts informs us that Paul was able to carry out his plans. Some months later, he spent three months in Greece, most of it presumably in Corinth (Acts 20:2–3). Before this extended stay, he may have paid a brief "painful visit" (2 Cor 2:1; cf. "with a stick" in 1 Cor 4:21) to the city.

While his opponents were impressed by anyone with "the gift of the gab" (cf. 1 Cor 2:1, 4), the apostle was more interested in whether they were upholding the word of the cross, with its power to save and to build up the church (4:20; see also 1:18; 3:9–17). "For," he explains, "the kingdom of God does not consist in talk but in power" (4:20). Paul uses "word, talk" in two opposing senses, just as he does "wisdom," which can denote either the world's futile "wisdom" (1:17, 19–22; 2:1, 4–5, 13; 3:19) or God's "wisdom" in Christ (1:21, 24, 30; 2: 6–7; 12:8). So too "word, talk" can denote the word of the cross, which conveys God's wisdom (1:5,

18; 2:4; 12:8; 14:36), or a Christ-less word expressing worldly wisdom (1:17; 2:1, 13; 4:20). It is in that latter sense, then, that Paul contrasts the "word, talk" of those who are puffed up to their "power" (4:19). The Christ-less "word" has no divine "power," though it may persuade some. In 1 Corinthians "power" mostly refers to God's saving power in the crucified and risen Christ (1:18, 24; 2: 4–5; 4:20; 5:4; 6:14: 12:10, 28–29; 15:43), a "power" which those who are puffed up lack (4:19).

Although the theme of the "kingdom of God" (4:20) is not as pervasive in Paul's letters as it is in the gospels, he does refer to it in eight epistles, and most frequently in 1 Corinthians (4:20; 6:9–10; 15:24, 50). The kingdom which the Corinthians have entered is not constituted and upheld by the empty words, wisdom, gossip, or rhetoric of human beings. It is the kingdom of the powerful God and of his beloved Son (Col 1:13). God's wisdom in Christ bestows the divine gifts of "righteousness and sanctification and redemption—to bring about what has been written: 'Let the one who boasts boast in the Lord'" (1 Cor 1:30–31). By this criterion, Paul will judge the contribution to the kingdom of heaven of those who think they already have begun to reign (4:8). With two sharp questions, Paul concludes his extensive rebuttal of the theology of glory: "What do you wish? Am I to come to you with a stick, or in love and a spirit of gentleness?" (4:21). The Corinthians have a choice. They can persist in arrogant opposition to their father in Christ and to the word of the cross he preaches. But if they do so, he warns, they can expect his anger and public rebuke when he comes. Or, moved by the Spirit's power, they can allow the word of the cross to perform its Gospel work in them (1:30–31), so that they mend their ways, and can look forward to being treated "in love and a spirit of gentleness" (1 Cor 4:21). Either way—whether Paul comes with a stick or in love—he will be doing his duty as a father. Scripture accepts that a father may carry the rod of correction (2 Sam 7:14; Prov 22:15; 23:13; 29:15; cf. Is 22:15; Lam 3:1). At the same time, Paul's preference—and God's preference—is for them to repent so that Paul could come "in love and a spirit of gentleness" (1 Cor 4:21), in keeping with the meekness and gentleness of Christ (Mt 11:29; 21:5; 2 Cor 10:2).

1 CORINTHIANS 5:1–7:40

THE WORD OF THE CROSS IS THE BASIS FOR THE CHURCH'S HOLINESS

5:1–13

A Case of Incest

1 CORINTHIANS 5:1–5

Paul's Verdict Against Puffed Up Tolerance

TRANSLATION

**5 [1]It is commonly reported that there is sexual
immorality among you, and the kind of immorality
that is not even among the pagans, with the result
that someone has his father's wife. [2]And you are
puffed up, and shouldn't you rather have gone into
mourning so that the one who did this deed would be
removed from among you? [3]For I on my part, being
absent in body but present in spirit, have already
passed judgment as one who is present on the man
who has done this: [4]In the name of our Lord Jesus,
when you and my spirit have assembled together
with the power of our Lord Jesus, [5]to hand over such
a fellow to Satan for the destruction of the flesh, so
that the spirit may be saved on the day of the Lord.**

COMMENTARY

After his critique of factionalism (chapters 1–4), Paul seems at first sight to be making an abrupt transition to an entirely new problem, a case of sexual immorality. However, there is a close link between the Corinthians' factionalism and their tolerance of immorality, as two Greek words help make plain. The first is "you are puffed up" in 5:2. Just as the root of the faction-fighting lay in their tendency to boast in people (3:21) and become "puffed up" (4:6, 18, 19), so this extraordinary case of immorality had flared up and continued to fester because of the same tendency. It cried out for the application of the fatherly rod (4:21). Again, as Paul had said about factionalism in chapters 1–4, healing could come only through the word of the cross (5:7b).

The second linking word is "power" in 5:4. Paul had chided the Corinthians for their love of empty talk, and their failure to live by the power of the Gospel. The kingdom of God is characterized by power, not talk. Now he calls on them to let "the *power* of our Lord Jesus" be demonstrated in their midst (5:4) through the proper exercise of church discipline.

Whether the apostle's impending visit to Corinth will be with a stick or with love (4:21) will depend in part on the Corinthians' response to his demand for appropriate action. It seems he has already written to them about their associations with immoral people (5:9), so it is high time they responded in "obedience of faith" (Rom 1:5; 16:26; cf. 2 Cor 7:15; 10:5–6) with actions befitting those who had been "sanctified in Christ Jesus" (1 Cor 1:2).

The case of the incestuous man may have been brought to Paul's attention by Chloe's people, who were the source of his information about the factions (1:11). But if so, it is unlikely they were his only informants; the case seems to have become notorious, even in a culture accustomed to rampant immorality.

It is noteworthy that Paul does not begin by excoriating the offender. What concerns him even more than the individual's sin is the congregation's attitude to it. Thus, he indicts the congregation as a whole: "It is commonly reported that there is sexual immorality among *you*" (plural, 5:1) and *you*, instead of acting to stop this cancer from spreading, are "puffed up" (5:2) and boastful (5:6). His chief concern, clearly, is for the whole body of Christ in Corinth. If all parts of the body had shown proper concern for one another (12:25), they would not have let this matter fester.

The sexual immorality which had now come "inside" the congregation was, of course, endemic in the Greco-Roman world "outside." (Paul will have more to say on the subject in 1 Cor 6:9–20.) Demosthenes (*Orations*, 59.122) could say, "Mistresses we keep for the sake of pleasure, concubines for the daily care of the body, but wives to bear us legitimate children." In Greek, "sexual immorality" (5:1) included all kinds of extramarital sins, including homosexuality. "Sexual immorality," is the first among "the works of the flesh" listed in Gal 5:19–21, not because Paul was obsessed with the sexual problems in the churches, but because those problems were so endemic. Our epistle testifies that, in Corinth, the believers had come out of a pagan background characterized by "sexual immorality" and that many were tempted to revert to former patterns.

But as accustomed as they were to sexual transgressions, even pagans would have been horrified by the kind of sin being perpetrated in Corinth. The Roman statesman Cicero (*Pro Cluentio 6)* described the marriage of a woman with her son-in-law as "unheard of in all experience save for this single instance!" Greco-Roman law as laid down in the Institutes of Gaius (1.63) stipulated: "Neither can I marry her who has aforetime been my mother-in-law or step-mother, or daughter-in-law or step-daughter." The standard punishment was banishment.

The Corinthian case involved a member of the congregation who was living with a woman who apparently was his stepmother. He may have been a man of high social status, which made the congregation hesitant to correct him. Whether he was seducing her under his father's nose, or whether the father was dead or divorced, is not known to us. Presumably the woman was not a Christian, or Paul would have commanded her expulsion as well. This is apparent from chapter 7, where his instructions on marriage matters are given to men and women alike.

Paul sharply rebukes the church for tolerating the incestuous relationship. "And you are puffed up!" he exclaims (5:2). It seems the Corinthians were priding themselves on their openness, broadmindedness, and tolerance (their "inclusiveness," in modern parlance), and specifically with regard to this case. They thought they were practicing and celebrating their Christian freedom in the Spirit; after all, they reasoned, "all things are in my power" (6:12).

But the Corinthians' behavior was totally inappropriate. Rather than being puffed up, this sorry development should have sent them into mourning (5:2). Rather than taking the attitude that the man's sin was within Christian liberty, or was his private business, they should have called for congregation-wide contrition and confession, along the lines of the prayers of national confession in Ezra 9, Nehemiah 9, and Daniel 9. It was as if one of their number had died. His faith had suffered a complete shipwreck, and the congregation should mourn his loss and their shared responsibility for his loss.

Furthermore, their grief should have led to their removing the man from their fellowship. But the congregation had succumbed to a superficial, secular view of the Christian faith, without a sufficient sense of the enormity of sin, the need for repentance, and the holiness of God. They had failed to grasp that the Gospel of Christ's crucifixion for their sins teaches Christians to crucify their proud egos (Gal 5:24), leave behind their former way of life, and, as people "sanctified in Christ Jesus" (1 Cor 1:2), follow him in the way of the cross.

With an emphatic *"I,"* Paul contrasts himself with the Corinthians—*"you"* who are "puffed up" (5:2). "Regardless of your attitude," he is saying, "it is obvious to me that the incestuous man should have been removed." Although physically absent from Corinth, their spiritual father (4:14–15) is still present among them in spirit and demands a hearing (cf. Col 2:5). In saying he is present in spirit, Paul does not mean merely that his thoughts are with them. Rather, in the power of the Spirit he is actually present among them (see further below). And, "as one who is present" (1 Cor 5:3), he has already rendered his decision concerning the guilty man.

The apostle states his verdict: "In the name of our Lord Jesus . . . to hand over such a fellow to Satan" (5:4–5). The phrase "in the name of our Lord Jesus" is linked grammatically to the infinitive at the beginning of 5:5a, "to hand over." The congregation will be taking a powerful step, not by any arbitrary exercise of authority, but in the name of the Lord of the church, who is present among them (Mt 18:15–20; cf. Titus 3:10).

Paul now sets out the circumstances under which this step is to be taken: the congregation is to assemble, and Paul's spirit will be with them together with the power of the Lord Jesus. All this is to take place "in the name of our Lord Jesus" (1 Cor 5:4a). While this prepositional phrase may not seem to have a direct grammatical link with the rest of 5:4, by virtue of its position it indicates that everything which follows—their assembling, the presence of Paul's spirit with the power of Jesus, and the decision to hand the man over to Satan—will happen in Jesus' name.

As the authorized representative of the Lord Jesus, and on the basis of the OT Scriptures, Paul has already made his pastoral decision. But he does not proceed unilaterally; he enlists the full participation and cooperation of the local church. The congregation is to be fully instructed and of one mind with the apostle so as to carry out his decision. Thus, pastor and people are to act in concert.

Presiding in the congregational gathering will be Paul's own spirit "with the power of our Lord Jesus" (5:4). Paul's spirit is now under the powerful influence of the Spirit of Jesus. The Holy Spirit inspired the OT Scriptures, and that same Spirit is now inspiring Paul as he follows the OT Scriptures and composes a book of the NT Scriptures. The directive he is writing to the Corinthians is not just his own opinion; it is the will of God. When his epistle is read to the assembled congregation, the Spirit, who inspired Paul's writing, will be at work "with the power of our Lord Jesus" (5:4; cf. Rom 1:1–5, which connects the sacred Scriptures, the resurrection of Jesus Christ, the power of the Spirit, and the apostle's ministry). Paul would, of course, expect his whole letter to be read to the congregation in due course. But on the day they assembled to hear this case, he probably deemed it sufficient for the lector to read chapter 5. Thus, they would be hearing Paul's voice. His spirit would truly be present with them, speaking with the apostolic authority the Lord Jesus had vested in him. The power of the risen Lord Jesus will be brought to bear on the congregation and its problem through the reading of the dominical and apostolic Word.

Paul's verdict is that the man should be delivered to Satan (cf. 1 Tim 1:20). Since the man's attitude has been thoroughly worldly, it is only fitting that he return to the world, which lies in the grip of the evil one (1 Jn 5:19; cf. Eph 2:12; Col 1:13). He will not be permitted to mingle with the saints, eat with them, or receive the Lord's Supper with them (see the commentary on 5: 9–13).

By this drastic measure, the apostle hopes to bring about "the destruction of the flesh" (5:5). Appealing to passages such as Acts 5:5–10 (Ananias and Sapphira) and 1 Cor 11:29–32 (where some of the Corinthians suffered sickness and even death because of their failure to discern the Lord's body in the Lord's Supper), many scholars have understood this "destruction" as some form of physical punishment.

However, it is by no means obvious that Paul has physical punishment in mind. The Ananias and Sapphira story can hardly be relevant. If the incestuous man were to die suddenly, that would preclude any opportunity for him to be led to repentance and salvation, which is the apostle's ultimate purpose. The afflictions of those who despised the Lord's Supper (1 Cor 11:29–32) may, at first glance, seem to be a closer parallel. But one significant difference is that Paul deals with the incestuous man as an unbeliever, while the Corinthians who partook of the Lord's Supper were Christians who needed to examine themselves, but who were not to be excluded from the Supper. Another difference is that whereas the case of the incestuous man concerns future congregational action, in the case of the Lord's Supper Paul is analyzing the Lord's judgments that had already taken place.

More important, in interpreting Paul's theology, one is not bound to interpret the word "flesh" in physical terms in every instance. Especially in Paul's thought, the "flesh" denotes mankind's sinful nature and inclination. Our flesh has its "works," the first being "sexual immorality," then "impurity, licentiousness, idolatry, sorcery, enmity, strife, jealousy, anger, selfishness, dissension, party spirit, envy, drunkenness, carousing, and the like" (Gal 5:19–21). Christian people are expected to "crucify the flesh with its passions and desires" (Gal 5:24). This was what the incestuous man had not done. Paul hoped that the man's expulsion from the community would be such a shock to his fleshly pride (1 Cor 5:2; cf. 2 Thess 3:14) that, like the prodigal son (Lk 15:11–32), he would come to his senses and seek God's grace and forgiveness. Then the apostle's purpose would have been achieved: the man's spirit would be saved on the Last Day. This restoration of the sinner will always be the chief purpose of the evangelical practice of church discipline.

1 CORINTHIANS 5:6–8

The Paschal Lamb Has Been Sacrificed

TRANSLATION

5 6Your boast is not good. Don't you know that a
little leaven leavens the whole batch of dough?
7Clean out the old leaven, so that you may be a
new batch, just as you are unleavened. For Christ,
our Passover Lamb, has been sacrificed. 8So let
us continue to celebrate, not with old leaven, nor
with leaven of malice and wickedness, but with
unleavened breads of sincerity and truth.

COMMENTARY

The congregation should have been ashamed of the incestuous relationship in their midst (1 Cor 5:1), instead of crowing about it. Their pride in their openness and tolerance was "not good" (5:6). It was not edifying or constructive, not conducive to the church's welfare. Proud as they were of their knowledge, they should have known better. They needed to be reminded of the proverb, "a little leaven leavens the whole batch" (5:6). In Galatians (5:9) Paul uses the same proverb to warn a church that has been infiltrated by the leaven of the Judaizers that a little legalism can completely overthrow the Gospel. Here his concern again is with a failure to understand the Gospel of Christ crucified and with the arrogance to which such ignorance leads. Allowing this man to continue in the congregation's midst was like allowing a boil or ulcer to keep festering and poisoning the body. Later, Paul will quote the poet Menander, "Evil associations corrupt good habits" (15:33). The congregation needs to come to its senses. Its present conduct indicates a lack of knowledge of God (15:34).

In a culture in which bread was the staple food, everyone knew how a little leaven (fermented dough, "sourdough") would permeate a batch of flour, causing it to swell and rise, ready for baking (cf. Mt 13:33). At the same time, this powerful ingredient, so useful in baking, also came to symbolize evils which had the power to spread. Jesus used the word "leaven" to characterize the teaching and practices of Pharisees, Sadducees, and Herod Antipas, which threatened to corrupt the body of believers (Mt 16:6, 11–12; Mk 8:15). It is this negative sense that the term carries in the present context. Perhaps there is a connection between Paul's accusation that some in the church had become "puffed up" (1 Cor

4:6, 18–19; 5:2) and the image of bread rising and expanding as it fills with small bubbles.

The symbol of leaven as infectious evil probably is rooted in the exodus deliverance of Israel from Egypt, when the Israelites ate unleavened bread by necessity (Ex 12:34–39). God commanded that they celebrate their redemption by eating only unleavened bread at the Passover meal. They were to throw out all leaven, so that no leaven could be found in their houses during the time of the Passover and the seven days of the Feast of Unleavened Bread (Ex 12:8–20; 13:3–7; Deut 16:3–4). This was such a vital part of membership in the people of God that disobedience would lead a person to be "cut off" from Israel (Ex 12:15, 19). Paul's command to expel the immoral man from God's people and hand him over to Satan (1 Cor 5:5) should be understood with that OT background.

Paul moves naturally from the proverb about leaven to imagery from Israel's great Passover history. The imperative "clean out" (1 Cor 5:7) emphasizes the need for decisive action in removing every last bit of the old leaven of sin from the community, just as the Israelites cleansed their homes of leaven on Passover Eve. Failure to obey the injunction to clean out the leaven carried the penalty of excommunication (Ex 12:15, 19).

Removal of the old leaven will make it possible for the Corinthians to be a fresh, new batch of dough. Paul's call for renewal of the congregation has parallels in his appeal to Christians to put off the old man and, by the renewal of their minds (Rom 12:1–2), to put on the new (2 Cor 5:17; Eph 4:22–24). In other words, he is instructing the Corinthian church: "Manifest the holiness of your new life in Christ! As people living under the cross, don't shrink from the painful task of drawing a line of separation between yourselves and someone hardened in unrepentance! Clean out from your fellowship this man who refuses to grieve over—and turn from—his sin!" The imperative and the following subjunctive ("*Clean out* the old leaven, so that *you may be* a new batch") rest on the Gospel indicative "just as *you are* unleavened" (1 Cor 5:7). Certainly, the Christian, insofar as he is a new person in Christ, is led by the Spirit to do what is right. But he remains *simul justus et peccator*, "simultaneously saint and sinner," and his sinful nature still needs to hear the imperative. Also, the new person in Christ needs the instruction of the Word to be led by the Spirit, since the Spirit works through the Word to guide the Christian's life. To that one may add that it is precisely through God's power in his Word (and Sacraments; see 1 Corinthians 10–11; 12:13) that God makes the church what he calls her to be.

Complacency about sin is incompatible with the Gospel. The purity of the Corinthian community in the future, as in the past, results from the work of God, whose commands and promises lead to repentance, faith in the forgiveness of sins, and the new life in Christ. The immoral man cannot be part of God's community until he is led to repentance, faith, and new life. By a deeper appreciation of what God has done for them in Christ, making them "unleavened" (5:7) by the power of the Gospel, they will recognize that "leaven" (5:6–7) is foreign to them and must be expelled. Their community life will be renewed "by the power of our Lord Jesus" (5:4), and their walk and ways (cf. 4:16–17) will better reflect who they *are* by grace: "God's saints," his holy temple, the dwelling place of his Spirit (1:2; 3:16–17; 6:11).

Paul proceeds to lay out the Gospel basis for their standing as a new community, cleansed from "the old leaven" (5:7). This came about as a result of God fulfilling his promise to send Jesus, the Passover Lamb, to be sacrificed on Calvary. The NT portrays Jesus as "the Lamb of God, who takes away the sin of the world" (Jn 1:29, 36; see also the "Lamb having been slain" in Rev 5:6, 12; 13:8). In a similar fashion to Paul, Peter in his first epistle grounds an appeal to "be holy in all your conduct" on the Gospel of redemption "by the precious blood of Christ, as of a lamb without blemish or spot" (1 Pet 1:14–19). Trust in "Jesus Christ and him crucified" (1 Cor 2:2; see also 1:23) had made the Corinthians a community of repentant sinners who lived under the cross. They had "washed their robes and made them white in the blood of the lamb" (Rev 7:14). Such a community could not tolerate in its fellowship an arrogant person who showed open contempt for the Gospel by his unwillingness to repent and look for forgiveness to Christ crucified. The man's "puffed up" (1 Cor 5:2) indifference to the gravity of his offense and its effect on the community was incompatible with his status as a new man in Christ.

Paul draws his conclusion (5:8). He exhorts the Corinthians to keep celebrating the fulfilled Passover inaugurated by Christ's crucifixion. Every day is now an Easter! The best commentary comes from *Chrysostom (Homilies on First Corinthians*, 15): "It is festival, therefore, the whole time in which we live. . . . [Paul is] pointing out that the whole of time is a festival unto Christians, because of the excellency of the good things which have been given." With heartfelt thankfulness we will continually celebrate God's forgiveness and respond to his grace by holy living.

As it celebrates the new life in Christ, the church should no longer be infected by "the old leaven" (5:7–8) of arrogance. Nor should it feature "malice and wickedness" (5:8), two generic words for all kinds of sin, including sexual immorality, greed, idolatry, and the other sins listed in 5:10–11. Rather, the new life in Christ should feature the fresh, unleavened bread "of sincerity and truth" (5:8). For the Corinthians, this would mean not only a greater appreciation for sincere and truthful preaching and teaching, rather than being impressed by style (a major issue in chapters 1–4), but also a greater concern for sincere and truthful living—the chief issue here.

1 CORINTHIANS 5:9–13
REMOVE THE WICKED MAN

TRANSLATION

5 [9]I wrote to you in the letter not to associate with
sexually immoral people. [10]By no means [was I
referring] to the sexually immoral people of this
world or to the greedy and rapacious or to idolaters—
for otherwise you would have to go out of the world.
[11]But now I wrote to you not to associate if anyone
called a "brother" should be sexually immoral or
covetous or idolatrous or abusive or a drunkard or a
swindler—not even to eat with such a person. [12]For
what business of mine is it to judge those outside?
But isn't it for you to judge those on the inside?
[13]Those on the outside God will judge. "Remove
the wicked person from among yourselves!"

COMMENTARY

Paul refers to a previous letter in which he had warned the congregation against Christian fellowship with sexually immoral people (5:9). The manner in which Paul now explains his earlier injunction has much to say about church fellowship issues.

Concerning the contents of the previous letter, all we can say with reasonable assurance is that it contained at least the words "not to associate with sexually immoral people" or words to that effect. Warnings against sexual immorality and idolatry are likewise contained in the circular letter issued by the great council meeting in Jerusalem (Acts 15:29). It seems "brothers from the Gentiles" (Acts 15:23) were especially in need of such admonition. Jewish Christians would have been familiar with the OT Scriptures, including the Decalogue and other expressions of God's Law; but Gentiles may have been ignorant about God's will and would have been influenced by the widespread acceptance of immorality and vices by Greek and Roman society.

Paul hastens to add some clarification (5:10). It is not unlikely that the Corinthians had disregarded or misinterpreted the instructions of the previous epistle. When something is stated briefly in a letter, there is always the danger of misinterpretation, especially when the recipients are not well-disposed toward the writer. In this case, we can imagine that the Corinthians argued that Paul's directions were unrealistic: "How can we live in the real world and not have anything to do with sexually immoral people? How can we avoid them altogether in the marketplace, the workshop, and the sports arena?" Paul explains that "by no means" (5:10) was it his intention to forbid Christians from *all* contact and associations with the sexually immoral people *in this world*—nor, for that matter, "the greedy and rapacious" nor the "idolaters" (5:10) in this world. Of course he understood that it was impossible in a fallen world to avoid associating with such people. When he wrote that previous epistle, it was not at all his intention to urge withdrawal into a ghetto or hermitage. He realized that if the Corinthians were not to associate *at all* with sexually immoral, greedy, and idolatrous people, they "would have *to go out of the world*" (5:10). Rather, his stricture applies to fellowship *within the church.* People whose public lifestyles are contrary to the will of God are to be removed from the church's fellowship.

In 5:9–11, Paul is concerned first of all with sexual immorality. As he will explain in 6:18, sexual sins are especially serious because they involve one's own body in such an intimate way. For that reason, sexual sins are sins against one's own body (6:18). A person thereby degrades and defiles himself. Paul states in the strongest possible terms that the sexually immoral, including adulterers and homosexuals, simply will not inherit the kingdom of God (6:9–11; see further the commentary there). Sexual promiscuity and perversion constitute spiritual harlotry, and a person who persists in defiling himself or herself in this manner cannot remain part of the church, which is the pure, virgin bride of Christ. Such a person is "outside" the kingdom (5:12–13; see further below).

By "the greedy," Paul means those who are covetous, who continually want to have more than they have. Jesus had warned his disciples to beware of all covetousness (Lk 12:15). Covetousness was and is one of the main characteristics of the pagan world (Rom 1:29; 1 Cor 6:10; Eph 4:19; 5:5). Likewise, "the rapacious" (or "swindlers") belonged together with the "unrighteous" and the "adulterous" people of this world (Lk 18:11); they would not inherit God's kingdom (1 Cor 6:10). Jesus called false prophets "rapacious" wolves (Mt 7:15).

Finally, Paul mentions "the idolaters" (1 Cor 5:10), with whom this world is filled. These, too, will not inherit the kingdom (6:9). This reference to idolaters prepares the way for the detailed discussion of idolatry and idol-food in chapters 8–10 and the Lord's Supper in chapters 10–11.

We may note that these three kinds of sins (sexual immorality, greed/rapaciousness, and idolatry) are to some extent related to one another. The first on the list, sexual immorality, is a form of the second sin, greed/rapaciousness/covetousness. Sexual immorality involves a lack of contentment with one's sexual state, which leads to cheating or robbing another person by taking what is not rightfully yours. Compare the Tenth Commandment, which includes the words "You shall not covet your neighbor's wife" (Ex 20:17; Deut 5:21). Then the sin of greed, in its turn, is associated a number of times with idolatry (Eph 5:5; Col

3:5: "covetousness, which is idolatry"). Covetousness involves misplaced trust in money and possessions rather than in the true God. However, Paul's concept of idolatry at this point should be understood broadly to include all forms of false worship.

What Paul would have the Corinthians learn was to live among these people—in the world—without becoming "of the world" (Jn 17:14–16). But as long as they continued to be puffed up (1 Cor 5:2) and entangled in fellowship with a man who would not repent, they were in danger of succumbing themselves to "the spirit of the world" (1 Cor 2:12).

To leave no further room for misunderstanding, Paul clarifies what he meant in his previous letter. His strictures against mixing with immoral people were not meant to forbid the Christians in Corinth from any secular contact with the immoral people of this world (5:10). What he specifically had in mind was to warn them against associating *in Christian fellowship* with "anyone called a 'brother'" (5:11) who persisted in the unrighteousness characteristic of an unbeliever. Such a person's profession of faith was belied by his behavior—his arrogant refusal to let his life be one of repentance and trust in Christ crucified. In a similar manner, both Jesus and Paul censure those who profess to be Christians but are not (Jn 8: 30–47; 1 Cor 6: 9–10; Gal 5:21).

The apostle proceeds to list six lifestyles which are incompatible with the Christian faith (1 Cor 5:11). Four of them—sexual immorality, greed, idolatry, rapaciousness—were mentioned in 5:10. Now he adds two more. "Abusive" refers to someone given to various forms of verbal abuse, a slanderer. Scripture often warns against the propensity of slanderous tongues to wreak havoc (e.g., Col 3:8). A "drunkard" is someone enslaved to alcohol.

Any Christian may on occasion fall prey to these sins, and then admit his sin, grieve over it, and seek, by the power of the Spirit, to amend his life and avoid that sin in the future. Paul is concerned here with those who surrender themselves to sin as a way of life. In other words, they "let sin *rule*" over themselves (Rom 6:12). In Romans 7, for example, Paul portrays the drama of his own personal struggle against sin. His old sinful nature wars against the new person in Christ. Sometimes he succumbs (Rom 7:19). But he continues the fight, by the power of the Spirit, to put to death the deeds of the flesh. The person in 1 Corinthians 5 whom Paul commands the church to expel has given up that battle; he has laid down his weapons and has surrendered to the enemy. Although he goes by the name of a Christian "brother," he has instead earned for himself the reputation of one characterized by a particular sin. He now carries the designation *"sexually immoral"* (5:11).

With such a hypocritical "brother" the Christian should not even eat. The congregation is to make a radical break with him. There can be little doubt Paul has in mind both the sharing of ordinary meals (cf. 2 Jn 10) and—a fortiori—participation in the Lord's Supper. In other words, the man is to be excommunicated.

For many Christians in the twenty-first century, the word "excommunication" sounds intolerably punitive. The spirit of the age urges toleration, compromise, and permissiveness. But Paul saw excommunication as an action to be carried out in loving concern for the sinner's ultimate salvation. The person to be excommunicated is to be handed over to Satan, with the goal that he repent and his soul be saved on the Lord's Day (5:5). The evil, influential yeast must not be allowed to permeate God's loaf (5:6–8).

Moreover, the proper evangelical guidelines are laid down by the Scriptures themselves: "If anyone does not obey our word through the epistle [2 Thessalonians], mark this person so as not to associate [as in 1 Cor 5:9] with him, that he may be ashamed" (2 Thess 3:14). Paul establishes the Scriptures as the basis for church fellowship. If a person or group refuses to comply with God's Word, fellowship is to be terminated.

Two rhetorical questions and two short statements conclude the argument. The first question picks up the Corinthians' misinterpretation of Paul's previous letter to mean that the apostle was forbidding *any* contact with immoral people. Paul says it is none of his business "to judge those outside" (1 Cor 5:12). The expression "those outside" derives from the OT. In Israel's communal life, persons who became unclean were expelled "outside the camp" until such time as they might be cleansed, and then they could return (Lev 13:46; 14:3, 8; Num 12:14–15). Compare also Lev 24:14, 23; Num 15:35–36, where those who violated the Torah were put to death "outside the camp." Jesus also distinguished his disciples, who had access to the mysteries of the kingdom, from those "outside" (Mk 4:11; cf. Col 4:5; 1 Thess 4:12; 1 Tim 3:7). The book of Revelation (22:15) also uses the word "outside" to refer to the eternal abode of the ungodly.

That God will judge the whole world, believers and unbelievers, living and dead, is axiomatic in Scripture (Gen 18:25; Pss 9:8; 67:4; 82:8; 94:2; 96:13; 98:9; Is 66:16; Joel 3:12). Paul could be provoked to anger when confronted by the world's gross idolatry (Acts 17:16), but it was not his mission to engage in a crusade against unbelievers, nor to pronounce judgment "before the time" (1 Cor 4:5).

With the second rhetorical question, Paul reminds the Corinthians of their responsibilities: "But isn't it for *you* to judge those on *the inside?*" (5:12). It may be asked how Paul's question comports with our Lord's command: "Judge not, that you be not judged" (Mt 7:1). Torn from its context (e.g., Mt 7:15!), Mt 7:1 has been misused in modern churches in the interests of an "anything goes" attitude which tolerates blatant sin and false teaching. Jesus' words, however, apply to a carping, censorious spirit which delights in finding fault with other people and ignores one's own sin. Paul was on the receiving end of such treatment from some of the Corinthians (1 Cor 4:3). But the apostle's present concern is the church's toleration of persistent immorality in its midst, and how that toleration erodes its confession of Christ and the Gospel.

Having said in 5:12a that it is none of his business to judge those outside the church, Paul states in 5:13a whose business it is: "Those on the outside *God* will judge." Then, with a quotation from Deuteronomy (17:7; also 22:22, 24), he wraps up his argument: "Remove the wicked person from among yourselves!" (1 Cor 5:13). Thus, the excommunicated man is to become an "outsider," someone the community regards as "a Gentile and a tax collector" (Mt 18:17). This means he is facing God's eternal wrath and, like all "outsiders," stands in need of the church's prayer, testimony, and love.

The judgment Paul has now pronounced is not a matter of personal vagary; it is a decision taken in his capacity as an apostle and ambassador of the Lord Jesus, supported by his power (5:4) and backed by the testimony of God in the OT Scriptures. Thus, the judgment begins with God and is conveyed through his apostle to his community—and must be completed by their action.

There may, indeed, be evidence in Paul's second letter to the Corinthians that the congregation did take the appropriate action and that this action bore good fruit. Paul writes:

> If anyone has caused grief, he caused it not to me, but in part—so that I do not exaggerate—to all of you. This punishment by most [of you] is sufficient for such a person; so now instead you should forgive and console him, so that he may not be overwhelmed by excessive grief. Therefore I urge you to reaffirm your love for him. I wrote for this reason: that I might know your testedness, whether you are obedient in everything. Anyone whom you forgive, I also forgive. What I have forgiven, if I have forgiven anything, has been for your sake in the presence of Christ. And we do this so that we may not be outwitted by Satan; for we are not ignorant of his intentions. (2 Cor 2:5–11)

Whether Paul is speaking of the restoration of the incestuous man or of another person, this text is a powerful reminder of the pastor's and congregation's duty to forgive and restore the repentant sinner. That restoration is the ultimate goal of all church discipline.

1 CORINTHIANS 6:1–8

Lawsuits among Brothers

TRANSLATION

**6 1How dare anyone of you, who has a case against
the other, go to law before the unrighteous people
and not before the saints! 2Or don't you know that
the saints will judge the world? And if the world is
judged by you, are you unworthy [to settle] trivial
cases? 3Don't you know that we will judge angels,
not to mention things of this life? 4If then, you have
disputes about the things of this life, do you set [as
judges] those with no standing in the church? 5I say
this to your shame. Is it so—that there is no wise man
among you who will be able to arbitrate between his
brother [and another brother]? 6But does brother go
to court with brother, and this before unbelievers?**

**7As it is, it is an utter failure for you that you have
lawsuits with yourselves. Why don't you rather let
yourselves suffer injustice? Why don't you rather let
yourselves be defrauded? 8But you commit injustice
and defraud, and [you do] this to brothers.**

COMMENTARY

In this new chapter, the apostle may seem to move abruptly to a completely new topic. On closer inspection, however, one finds an intimate connection between the Corinthians' refusal to take action in the case of the immoral man (chapter 5) and their litigation before pagan courts. What links the two cases is an acceptance of and participation in the world's way, an unwillingness to condemn and restrain their own sin, to die to self, and thus, to go the way of the cross, a failure to exercise church discipline and spiritual judgment in matters tearing their community apart. A key verb in Paul's treatment of both cases is "to judge" (5:3, 12–13; 6:1, 2, 3, 6). More specifically, we see that 5:12b ("Isn't it for you to judge those on the inside?") leads directly into the issue addressed in 6:1–8, the need for the Corinthians themselves to judge among brothers with regard to everyday matters and to avoid public lawsuits, which sully the name of Christ.

We should not diminish the forcefulness of the verb "dare" with which Paul introduces his argument. The Greek words with which 6:1 begins have their closest natural English equivalent in the exclamation "How dare you!" Paul is not merely frowning on the practice of Christians pursuing lawsuits against one another; with the full weight of his apostolic authority he is expressing his outrage.

Greed, one of the sins denounced in 5:11, seems to have been the main factor in the Corinthians' lawsuits (cf. 6:7–8). Recent studies of the Roman Empire's legal system have shown that most civil cases were brought by the wealthy against those of lesser means. Because of their social status, the well-to-do could usually count on the judges' support against the "have nots." It is likely, then, that the wealthier members of the congregation were still affected by this cultural tendency, and were exercising their legal clout at the expense of poorer members. If this analysis is correct, then the way the rich despised the poor at the congregation's communal meals presents a parallel situation (1 Cor 11:22).

For the first of six times in this chapter (6:2; also 6:3, 9, 15, 16, 19), Paul asks them, "Don't you know?" His aim is to put them to shame (6:5) and thus bring them to their senses. A church so gifted with knowledge (1:5) should know better! Have the Corinthians forgotten that, just as the saints will sit on Christ's throne and reign with him as kings, so they shall sit with him as judges of the world (cf. Matt. 19:28, Luke 22:30)? Following the principle "greater to less," Paul argues that if the saints are to be entrusted with that weighty responsibility, surely they can handle a far lighter task. Again, we see the apostle's high regard for the church in Corinth—for all their aberrations, they are still God's "called saints" (1:2). As such, they need a long-range view of what that means; they need to see their calling in eschatological perspective, with all the responsibility that will entail. By comparison with the judicial task awaiting them on the Last Day, these cases in Corinth are "trivial" (5:2).

On that day, Paul continues, all of us will participate with God in judging the angels (5:3). Fallen angels will be condemned (2 Pet 2:4; Jude 6), while holy angels will continue in their service. As those whom the exalted Christ calls his "brothers," God's children are superior to angels, who are "ministering spirits sent to serve" the heirs of salvation (Ps 8:5; Heb 1:14; 2:5–11). Reasoning once more from the greater to the less, Paul concludes that Christians, who hold such an exalted rank, surely are worthy and competent to handle "things of this life" (1 Cor 6:3).

But what should Christians do when they cannot agree about worldly matters (6:4)? The second clause in 6:4, which answers this concern, is best understood as a question: "Do you entrust jurisdiction to people with no standing in the church?" In favor of taking it as a question is the context. That, precisely, has been the apostle's concern—that they should not take their cases before outsiders, before those "of no standing in the church" (6:1; cf. "outside" in 5:12–13). Paul's intention is not to belittle non-Christians in high offices. In other contexts, he insists that Christians pay all authorities (heathen or Christian) their proper honor in matters that lie under their jurisdiction (Rom 13:1–7; cf. 1 Pet 2:13–17). His point here, however, is that they cannot be called on to settle disputes between believers, within the body of Christ, which is God's holy temple (1 Cor 3:16–17).

Then in 6:5, in contrast to his more gentle tone in 4:14, Paul declares that he is deliberately setting out to put them to shame (cf. 15:34). Is he to draw the conclusion that among this large congregation, so richly endowed with wisdom and knowledge and so proud of its gifts, there is not one person wise enough to arbitrate a property dispute between Christian brothers? Divine wisdom and knowledge was the topic of 1:5, 18–25; 2:6–7; 3:18–23. The use of the word "brother," both in 6:5 and in 6:6, is highly pointed. It is completely antithetical to the meaning of Christian brotherhood that members of the church fight over earthly property and other legal matters.

It is unclear whether one should understand 6:5 as an exclamatory statement or another question. Either way, it makes little difference to the sense. Paul is horrified at what is happening. Instead of airing their dirty linen "before unbelievers" (6:6; "the unrighteous people," 6:1), Christians must make every effort to maintain a good reputation and not cause offense to Christ, whose name they bear.

Now, Paul continues (6:7), the fact that you have any lawsuits among you at all is a sign that your sinful passions have utterly gotten the better of you. That in itself would serve to indict you, even if you did not go the extra step and bring your cases before pagan judges. Then, with two sharp questions, the apostle cuts off all possible protests. It is futile to argue, "But you don't know what he did to me" or "Just imagine the consequences if we allowed him to get away with this." Any such protests arise from a lack of faith that God can and will set things right in his own good time. He does not need our court cases to bring about justice.

But more important, such behavior demonstrates a failure to live according to the "grace" and "peace" God has shown us in Christ (1:3). Thus, Paul reminds the Corinthians of the way of the cross, challenging them to endure mistreatment uncomplainingly in keeping with the Lord's Sermon on the Mount: "Don't resist one who is evil. . . . Turn the other cheek" (Mt 5:38–40). The Christian way of meekness which Jesus and Paul set forth is the opposite of all human self-assertion. We see Jesus' influence on Paul's teaching in this regard also in Rom 12:17; 1 Cor 4:12–17; 1 Thess 5:15.

Rather than following their Lord and his apostle (1 Cor 4:12–13) in the way of suffering, the Corinthians actually inflict suffering on others, even their Christian brothers (6:8). Paul is not saying it is all right to inflict suffering on non-Christians. His point is that while they are supposed to do good to all people, honor all, and live at peace with all (cf. Rom 12:18; 1 Pet 2:17), they have special obligations to fellow members of the household of faith (Gal 6:10). It strikes Paul as incredible that it is especially their brothers in the faith who are suffering mistreatment at their hands. Their attacks on one another contradict the fellowship in Christ into which they were called (1 Cor 1:9).

The principle Paul will later affirm regarding meat sacrificed to idols applies equally to lawsuits: "By your knowledge, the weak person, the brother for whom Christ died, is being destroyed. So by sinning against your brothers and striking their weak conscience, *you are sinning against Christ.* Therefore, if food [one could also say 'a lawsuit'] causes my brother to fall, I will never eat meat to eternity, lest I cause my brother to fall" (8:11–13; see also 10:32–33).

THE CHRISTIAN AND COURTS OF LAW

Paul's sharp denunciation of Christians who take one another to court may lead us to ask whether secular courts are to be totally shunned by the Christian. To this the apostle would certainly answer no. On a number of occasions Paul himself appealed to Roman law to come to his defense and the defense of the Christian "way" (Acts 9:2) in the face of unjust treatment at the hands of non-Christians (Acts 16:37; 22:25; 25:11). He regarded the Roman authorities as "ordained of God" and accountable to God (Rom 13:1); thus, it was incumbent upon Christians to obey them and proper for him to appeal to them. The NT never suggests that the offices of the civil ruler, the magistrate, the tax official, or the soldier are in themselves displeasing to God. Thus, the Christian may properly serve in these offices.

Under what circumstances, then, may a Christian or a congregation resort to the civil court? Here the first questions to be asked may be these: Who are the parties involved? Is it a case of Christian brothers going to law against one another instead of letting the problem be solved by a competent person within the church? Is it a quest for revenge instead of forgiving the brother? Or is it a case of a Christian or a church, in their capacity as responsible citizens, taking a case to court out of concern for the neighbor? Much depends on the cause and the motive. Is the purpose to harm and defraud one's neighbor, to "get back at him"? Or does the plaintiff bring his suit with no selfish motives, but simply in order to defend the church and her mission against attacks from those outside the church, or to protect others and promote the welfare of society (cf. AE 21:108–111)?

It is proper for Christians to serve as judges or lawyers, and it is proper, under some circumstances, for Christians to bring a lawsuit. Examples would be when a church presents a brief as a "friend of the court" in order to forbid abortion or support similar initiatives which promote human welfare and the sanctity of human life, or when a Christian or church appeals to a court to seek protection from violence or criminal acts, or to defend the right to proclaim the Gospel or lead a Christian life.

But it is never proper for a Christian or a church to take fellow Christians or church leaders to a secular court, or to do anything which arises out of selfish motives or ecclesiastical divisions (1:10–17). The church should never wash its dirty linen in public. The proper place for hearing such disputes is before an ecclesiastical judge—someone within the Christian community who is "wise" (6:5).

1 CORINTHIANS 6:9–11
You Were Cleansed of All Unrighteousness

TRANSLATION

6 [9]Or don't you know that unrighteous people will not
inherit God's kingdom? Stop deceiving yourselves:
neither the sexually immoral nor idolaters nor
adulterers nor catamites nor sodomites [10]nor thieves
nor greedy people, not drunkards, not abusive people,
not swindlers will inherit the kingdom of God. [11]And
such were some of you. But you were washed, but you
were sanctified, but you were justified in the name of
the Lord Jesus Christ and by the Spirit of our God.

COMMENTARY

"UNRIGHTEOUS PEOPLE WILL NOT INHERIT GOD'S KINGDOM" (6:9–10)

We should not overlook the close link between 6:1–8 and what follows; the particle "or" serves as a link between the paragraphs. The apostle has just been rebuking the Corinthians for bringing lawsuits against brother Christians before "unrighteous" judges (6:1) and for their injustice toward their brothers (6:8). It would be better for them to suffer unrighteous treatment (6:7) than to inflict it upon others. Now he warns: "Or don't you know that unrighteous people will not inherit God's kingdom?" (6:9).

The word "unrighteous" is a broad, general term. It is a synonym of "unbeliever(s)" (6:6; also 7:12–15; 10:27; 14:22–24) and an antonym of a "brother" Christian (6:5, 6, 8). The unrighteous lack faith in Christ and thus stand outside God's covenant relationship with his people. Unrighteous people are characterized by "unrighteousness" (Rom 1:18, 29) and do not know the grace of God. Their wickedness manifests itself in the lifestyles listed in 1 Cor 6:9b–10. The righteous person (Rom 1:17; Gal 3:11), on the other hand, stands in the right relationship with God through faith in Christ. Only the righteous have fellowship with the righteous God and inherit his kingdom.

This is not the only place where Paul categorically denies that wicked people will inherit eternal life. Similar stern warnings are found in Eph 5:5 and Gal 5:21.

An inheritance is conferred by a father on his children. "If we are children, then we are heirs" (Rom 8:17). Children receive their inheritance simply by virtue of their birth into the father's household. According to the NT, those who are born again by water and the Spirit (Jn 3:5) can look forward to an "imperishable and undefiled and unfading" inheritance in heaven (1 Pet 1:4; cf. Titus 3:7). But this inheritance is conferred on those who are righteous through faith (Rom 4:13). Those who wantonly persist in wicked behavior testify that they are not God's children; they have no claim to the heavenly inheritance.

Paul appeals to the Corinthians: "Stop deceiving yourselves!" (6:9). Congregational members living in wickedness should not think that "God will forgive me, that's his business!" (Heinrich Heine). Writing in a similar vein to the Galatians, Paul warns, "Stop deceiving yourselves! God is not mocked. Whatever a person sows, this he will also reap. For he who sows to his flesh will from the flesh reap corruption, but he who sows to the Spirit will from the Spirit reap eternal life" (Gal 6:7–8). We may also compare Paul's use of "Stop deceiving yourselves!" in a similar context in 1 Cor 15:33, where he warns the congregation of the damage done by associating with evildoers: "evil associations corrupt good habits." If the Corinthians persist in playing with fire, they will be burned! Again, Paul is reminding them of the need for a proper eschatological perspective. Christians must exercise judgment and discernment *now* regarding their own behavior and that of brother Christians, because God's judgment is coming (6:1–8; cf. also 11:27–32).

The apostle proceeds to spell out categories of "unrighteous people" (6:9) who will not inherit the kingdom. Six of these he already mentioned in 5:10–11; now he will add four more. In chapter 5, he warned the Corinthians not to have fellowship with anyone who calls himself a "brother" (Christian) but who is sexually immoral or who has fallen into other gross sins (5:9–11). The present chapter opened with some sharp words regarding the unsuitability of the unrighteous to hear lawsuits between Christians, and a reminder that one day the tables will be turned, with the saints sitting in judgment on the whole world, including unrighteous judges (6:1–2). Whereas the Corinthians have been blurring the distinction between the righteous and the wicked (cf. Mal 3:18), Paul calls on them to keep things straight. Now he depicts the gulf between God's kingdom and people who practice various forms of unrighteousness.

The first two categories on Paul's list (the "sexually immoral" and the "idolaters") are the same as in 5:11. His reason for placing idolatry in the midst of various sexual sins may be that the two often went together and that immorality deifies personal pleasure above obedience to the true God. The third category, "adulterers," needs no explanation beyond that given by the Lord himself (Mt 5:27–32). Two more sexual offenders follow, "catamites" and "sodomites," reflecting another vice common in the Greco-Roman world, a vice for which the Greeks were especially notorious. Paul's comments specify the passive and active partners (respectively) in acts of male homosexuality. In his epistle to the Romans (1:26–27), Paul includes lesbianism with male homosexuality as perversions which subject those who practice them to the wrath of God.

Sadly, the church today needs to be reminded of the obvious implications. In light of the apostle's warning that practicing homosexuals will not inherit the kingdom, it is obvious that they must not be ordained in the church of God. They are to be treated as unbelievers, who need to be brought to repentance and Christian faith (Mt 18:17), in the same way that the church reaches out with Law and Gospel to those in bondage to other forms of sexual immorality, to idolaters, and to the others on Paul's list.

It is significant that Paul emphasizes sexual sins as prime examples of unrighteousness. In 6:18 he will state why: sexual sins are committed with and against one's own body. Sexual immorality and spiritual apostasy go together (e.g., Jeremiah 2–4; Ezekiel 16; 18; Hosea). Sexual immorality is a kind of idolatry. A person cannot engage in sexual sins and remain part of the body of Christ (see also, e.g., Rev 21:8, 27; 22:15).

Paul now turns from sexual sins to list an assortment of aberrations that pertain to property and to physical and verbal abuse. Of the five categories listed in 6:10, the only new one is "thieves," a word which covers all kinds of theft and exploitation. The others were listed in 5:10–11.

None of these persons, Paul reiterates, will inherit God's kingdom. The repetition of that fact in both 6:9 and 6:10 serves to underline the gravity of the issue. These sins cannot be condoned or ignored by the church. Those who habitually practice them will not be saved.

It should be noted that Paul does not mean that a person who has at some time or another fallen into any of these sins will never inherit the kingdom. Scripture depicts murderers, prostitutes, adulterers, and thieves who repented and who did enter God's kingdom, and Paul considers himself to be in that category (1 Tim 1:13–16). What the apostle is stating—and that with great emphasis—is that persistence in such practices is rebellion against God and a rejection of God's kingdom. It signals a wrong relationship with God, which spurns his grace and so debars a person from eternal life.

The Righteous and the Wicked in Paul

Paul's clear distinction between the righteous and the wicked runs counter to an age-old tendency to blur the distinction. The prophet Malachi looked forward to the day when God's people would once more "distinguish between the righteous and the wicked, between one who serves God and one who does not serve him" (Mal 3:18). At the start of the third millennium, many people have been affected by the dominant spirit of universalism, tolerance, and inclusiveness—the spirit that says it is wrong to condemn other people's lifestyles and that God ultimately will accept all people.

To arrive at a fair understanding of the biblical distinction between the righteous and the wicked, it is important to remember that when the Scriptures speak of the righteous, they do not mean the self-righteous. Rather, the opposite is the case: the righteous are those who humbly repent of their sins and "hunger and thirst" for the righteousness which God confers on them by his grace alone (Mt 5:6; 6:33). The wicked, on the other hand, are those who repudiate repentance and spurn God's grace.

The abominable practices named in 1 Cor 5:9–11 and 6:9–10 had characterized some of the Corinthians in the past (6:11). Paul often distinguishes between the dark days of his readers' former lives, what they had been before conversion ("once"), and what, by God's grace, they had become "now." We may compare Eph 5:8 ("For you were *once* darkness, but *now* [you are] light in the Lord") and Titus 3:3 ("For we also were *once* foolish"). In Corinth, only some of the people had sunk as low as the groups mentioned in 1 Cor 6:9–10. For them, too, that belonged to their former life; an enormous change in their spiritual state had taken place.

Those who condone and those who practice sins such as Paul lists in 6:9–11 may offer a variety of explanations in order to excuse such behavior. Among those explanations are ones that claim that certain people have an innate predisposition toward certain sins. That predisposition may be attributable to genetic factors or other inherited traits, or to the environment in which a person was raised. Homosexuality and alcoholism are two sins regarding which researchers have looked for, and some have claimed to have found, genetic factors.

But Paul's statement in 6:11 ("such *were* some of you. But you were washed . . . sanctified . . . justified") implies that the grace of God has the power to overcome all sins. Regardless of what factors may be involved, God's grace "in the name of the Lord Jesus Christ" and "the Spirit of our God" (6:11) are able to defeat those sins. The Christian, by the power of the Spirit, can and must put to death the deeds of the sinful flesh, and daily rise to new life by virtue of Baptism into Christ's death and resurrection (Romans 6; 1 Cor 12:13). "Now having been set free from sin, and having become servants of God, you have your fruit unto sanctification, with the end result of eternal life" (Rom 6:22). "If you live according to the flesh, you are going to die. But if by the Spirit you put to death the deeds of the body, you will live" (Rom 8:13).

WASHED, SANCTIFIED, JUSTIFIED (6:11)

Paul's statement "but you were washed, but you were sanctified, but you were justified" (6:11) functions in a similar way to the indicative of 5:7, "Christ, our Passover Lamb, has been sacrificed." There the consequential imperative "clean out the old leaven" (5:7) rested on the indicative of the Gospel; here, too, in 6:9–11 Paul's warnings are intended to prevent the congregation from falling away from God's gracious work in Christ Jesus.

In 6:11, Paul describes what God has done for the Corinthians with three verbs in the simple past tense, all of which point to different facets of their conversion. The order he follows is a logical one that suits the context, rather than a theological order. It is logical to mention first that they "were *washed.*" The apostle is pointing to the washing away of sin in Baptism, the "washing of water in the Word" (Eph 5:26), the "washing of regeneration" (Titus 3:5). The only other time the same verb for wash is used in the NT is in Acts 22:16, where Baptism is explicitly in view: "Arise and *be baptized* and *wash away your sins.*" When we couple Acts 22:16 to Eph 5:26 and Titus 3:5, in which Paul uses the related noun "washing" in connection with Baptism (especially indisputable in Eph 5:26), the impression that Baptism is in view here also in 1 Cor 6:11 becomes overwhelming.

In connection with that washing, they "were *sanctified*" in Christ Jesus (6:11; similarly, Paul, in his opening greeting, described them as "having been sanctified," 1:2). By faith in Christ's atoning blood their hearts had been cleansed and sanctified, so that they had become people dedicated to God. Now they were "called saints" (1 Cor 1:2) who enjoyed fellowship with Jesus Christ and had begun to walk in his marvelous light. What they had become by faith—holy, sanctified people—they should become in practice and living.

From another angle, their transformation from what they were "once" (Titus 3:3) to what (by God's mercy) they are now, can be viewed as their *justification.* As the last of the three verbs, "you were justified/declared *righteous*" nicely rounds off the unit, which began with the warning to the *"unrighteous"* in 1 Cor 6:9. Having been pronounced justified, free from sin's guilt and its consequence, death, the Corinthians must see that persistence in unrighteousness is incompatible with faith and life in Christ.

The two prepositional phrases which conclude this section ("in the name of the Lord Jesus Christ and by the [Holy] Spirit of our God") and which identify the source of the Corinthians' washing, their sanctification, and their justification (6:11), recall the Trinitarian formula of Baptism in Mt 28:19 ("in the name of the Father and of the Son and of the Holy Spirit."). In confirmation of this observation, it may be noted that sometimes the NT, using only the words of the first of these two phrases at the end of 1 Cor 6:11 as a shorthand version of the Trinitarian formula, refers to Baptism "in the name of Jesus Christ" (Acts 2:38; 10:48) or "in the name of the Lord Jesus" (Acts 8:16; 19:5). Through faith and Baptism in the name of Jesus, the Corinthians had been granted spiritual wholeness (Acts 3:16); through the power of "the Spirit of our God" (1 Cor 6:11), they had been regenerated and made a spiritual temple (3:16–17). In Baptism they were given the Holy Spirit to drink (1 Cor 12:13). That the Spirit now dwells in their bodies has profound implications for their Christian life, and to that subject Paul now turns (6:12–20).

EXCURSUS
HOMOSEXUALITY

In discussing the biblical and Pauline attitude toward homosexuality, it will be helpful to distinguish between homosexual desires or inclinations, and homosexual practice or behavior. That a person may sometimes be overtaken by homosexual thoughts does not justify indulging those thoughts and acting on them. By way of comparison, we may consider the more common human propensity toward adulterous desires. These desires are condemned by Jesus as sinful in themselves (Mt 5:28). But to indulge them to the point of physical adultery involves the person in far more serious spiritual bondage and social damage, both to himself ("the one fornicating sins against his own body," 1 Cor 6:18) and to others. The biblical condemnations of homosexuality focus their spotlight on indulgence in homosexual *behavior.* There is a distinction between temptation and acting on that temptation.

From beginning to end, the Bible condemns the practice of homosexuality as an unnatural perversion. The Creator's original design for human sexual relations, a design affirmed by Jesus and the apostles, is the union of one male and one female in lifelong marriage (Gen 1:26–28; 2:18–25; Mt 19:1–9; Eph 5:22–33). When the men of Sodom and Gomorrah perverted that design, committing "grievous sin" (Gen 18:20), eventually divine judgment in the form of sulfur and fire fell on them from heaven (Gen 19:24–29). The nature of that sin becomes evident when the men of Sodom, young and old, surround Lot's house and demand, "Where are the men who came to you tonight? Bring them out to us so that we may know them" (Gen 19:5).

In Israel, the Mosaic Law decreed about "a man who lies with a male as one would lie with a woman" that "the two of them have committed an abomination" (Lev 20:13). Both men were to be put to death (Lev 20:13). Lev 18:22 also calls homosexuality an "abomination." Thus, homosexuality takes its place alongside other capital offenses like murder, sacrificing a child to Molech, consulting a medium, cursing a parent, incest, bestiality, and adultery (Lev 20:1–27). The Israelites were to be a unique and holy people, who refused to follow the practices of their Canaanite environment (Lev 20:22–24). Should they fail to heed the divine warnings, the land would "vomit" them out (Lev 20:22).

When the men of the Benjamite city Gibeah degenerated to the point of repeating Sodom's sin, the other eleven tribes carried out the Lord's judgment (Judges 19–20). Narrated toward the end of the book of Judges, the episode represents the darkest period of Israel's Dark Ages—the chaotic period when "there was no king in Israel; each person did what was right in his own eyes" (Judg 21:25).

The NT's testimony against homosexual practice is fully consonant with that of the OT. In Romans 1, Paul condemns homosexual practice as the prime example of the "ungodliness" and "unrighteousness" (Rom 1:18) which call down God's anger from heaven (Rom 1:18–27). Lesbianism is listed first as an especially egregious and unnatural offense (Rom 1:26), followed by male homosexuality, which the apostle excoriates as an unnatural forsaking of the natural use of the female and a shameful perversion for which the males receive their due penalty (Rom 1:27). See the commentary on 1 Cor 6:9–10 regarding Paul's warning that practicing homosexuals will not inherit God's kingdom.

The emphasis in 1 Cor 6:9–10 (and also in Rom 1:18–32 and similar passages) is on the practices and actual deeds that are part of a person's way of life. Therefore, the passage is best interpreted as referring to *practicing* homosexuals, *practicing* adulterers, and so on, rather than to all persons who have immoral *thoughts*—which would include *all* people! Rom 8:13 supports this interpretation: "If you live according to the flesh, you are going to die. But if by the Spirit you put to death the deeds of the body, you will live." The Christian has sinful desires, as does the non-Christian. But the Christian is called to kill those desires by the power of the Spirit; that is, with God's help he must not actually carry out those desires. Instead, he is to confess them and be absolved from them.

If a person succumbs to the desires of the sinful flesh and commits a homosexual sin (or any of the other sinful behaviors listed in 1 Cor 6:9–10), forgiveness is available in Christ: "If we confess our sins, he [God] is faithful and righteous and will forgive to us our sins and cleanse us from all unrighteousness" (1 Jn 1:9). But God's offer of forgiveness in Christ must never be twisted into a license to sin or to excuse the sin of others (cf. Rom 6:1–2). Nor may it be allowed to rob the scriptural word of its force: those who do such things will not "inherit the kingdom of God" (1 Cor 6:9–10).

Eph 5:5 has a similar list of persons who have no inheritance in God's kingdom, including the "sexually immoral person" and the "unclean person;" both Greek terms apply to the homosexual. 1 Tim 1:10 lists male homosexuals (the second term for male homosexuals in 1 Cor 6:9) among the "ungodly people and sinners" (1 Tim 1:9) against whom God's Law is directed, and who are also opposed to the "salutary doctrine" of "the Gospel of glory of the blessed God" (1 Tim 1:10–11). Significantly, Paul says there that homosexuals (and other "sinners," 1 Tim 1:9) are antithetical (1 Tim 1:10) to the very "Gospel" itself (1 Tim 1:11), not just to God's "Law" (1 Tim 1:8–9).

Finally, in a manner consistent with 1 Cor 6:9–10, there are two passages in the last book of the Bible which apparently include homosexuals among those excluded from the holy city and condemned for eternity to the lake of fire. The first passage, Rev 21:8, lists those who are "detestable." That word is a cognate of the word which is applied specifically to homosexuality in the Greek translation of Lev 18:22 and Lev 20:13.

The other passage, Rev 22:15, places "the dogs" at the head of the list of people "outside" the heavenly city. Dogs were generally despised in Israel. In Deut 23:17–18 God commands, "There shall not be a female sacral prostitute from the daughters of Israel, and there shall not be a male sacral prostitute from the sons of Israel. You shall not bring a female prostitute's price, or the hire of a dog, into the house of the Lord your God for any vow, because indeed both of them are an abomination to the Lord." In those verses, the persons described stand in Hebrew parallelism: the "female sacral prostitute" (Deut 23:17) is the same person as the "female prostitute" (Deut 23:18), and the "male sacral prostitute" (Deut 23:17) is the same person described as the "dog" (Deut 23:18).

In light of this OT background and the abhorrence of homosexuality elsewhere in Scripture, there are grounds for inferring that "the dogs" in Rev 22:15 probably denotes practicing homosexuals.

All of the above seems intolerably harsh to our modern culture. Attempts to promote "gay" and lesbian "rights" have persuaded many, even in the Christian church, that the homosexual lifestyle is a culturally acceptable alternative to heterosexual relationships. The movement has been fueled by the rise of negative critical attitudes toward the Scriptures.

In response to modern rejection of the biblical word on homosexuality, this excursus has focused on the need to take the divine Word at face value. However, none of the above justifies the abuse of homosexuals and "gay bashing," let alone murder. Rather, our awareness of the way the Scriptures expose the spiritual danger in which the homosexual stands should lead us to adopt a pastoral approach. The last thing the suffering homosexual may need is any further application of the Law; often he will already be painfully aware of his sin. Sensitive pastoral care will involve assuring the homosexual person of love and acceptance (but not approval), avoiding anything that smacks of pharisaic condemnations, keeping lines of communication open for Law/Gospel ministry, opening opportunities for confession and absolution, and above all, keeping the understanding reception of the Gospel as the goal.

A distinctive contribution of 1 Cor 6:9–11. To this discussion is that after the list that includes "catamites" and "sodomites" (6:9), Paul includes the phrase *"and such were some of you"* (6:11). Apparently, some of the Corinthian Christians had been practicing homosexuals before their conversion, before they were "washed . . . sanctified . . . justified" (6:11). In the modern era, some have argued that it is not possible to truly change one's sexual orientation, perhaps even because of a genetically determined predisposition. But Paul's statement implies that a true transformation did take place; those who had been homosexuals were so no longer. Paul does not say whether this means they no longer had any homosexual thoughts or desires, but their actual behavior no longer included any homosexual activity. One might speculate that the former "adulterers" (6:9) may still have had adulterous desires, even as former "thieves" (6:10) might still have suffered from avarice. Sinful inclinations and desires will remain part of human existence as long as we remain in this fallen state (cf. Romans 7).

But the Gospel provides God's resurrection power to live a new kind of life. Baptized into Christ's death and resurrection, the Christian is called to put to death the old Adam so that the new person of faith may come forth and govern his daily life as a member of the body of Christ (Romans 6; 1 Cor 12:13). The Christians in Corinth who had been homosexuals but were so no longer stand as examples of the Gospel's power to change lives.

1 CORINTHIANS 6:12–20

Our Bodies Belong to the Lord

TRANSLATION

**6 12“All things are in my power,” but not all things are
beneficial. “All things are in my power,” but I for one
will not be overpowered by anything. 13“Foods are
for the stomach, and the stomach is for foods, and
God will destroy both it and them.” But the body
is not for sexual immorality, but for the Lord, and
the Lord is for the body. 14And God both raised the
Lord and will raise us through his power. 15Don’t
you know that your bodies are members of Christ?
So am I to take away the members of Christ and
make them members of a prostitute? By no means!
16Or don’t you know that the man who joins himself
with the prostitute is one body [with her]? For it says,
“The two will become one flesh.” 17But the one who
joins himself with the Lord is one spirit [with him].**

**18Flee from sexual immorality! Every [other] sin
which a person may commit is outside the body.
But the one fornicating sins against his own body.
19Or don’t you know that your body is the temple
of the Holy Spirit in you, which you have from
God, and you are not your own? 20For you were
bought for a price. So glorify God in your body!**

COMMENTARY

Paul has just warned the Corinthians that living in sin is incompatible with the Christian faith; no one who does so will inherit God’s kingdom (1 Cor 6:9–10). Now Paul turns to another issue in which the Corinthians were failing to show proper judgment and spiritual discernment and so were jeopardizing their salvation. In chapter 5, he dealt with their failure to judge a man who was guilty of a form of sexual immorality not even found among pagans. In 6:1–11, he expressed his concern that the Corinthians seemed incapable of judging and settling disputes among themselves. Now he addresses their lack of discernment regarding a form of sexual immorality which was very much to be found—even taken for granted—among pagans, and which apparently persisted among some recent converts from paganism.

Not only was prostitution legal in Paul's day, but it was socially acceptable for men to have sexual relations both with boys and with prostitutes. Paul included two terms for homosexuals among those who will not enter God's kingdom (6:9). Some of the Corinthian Christians seem to have defended their right to continue consorting with prostitutes. "After all," they may have argued in the Stoic-Cynic fashion, "we are 'wise;' we are 'free to do anything.' We now move on a higher plane; what we do with our bodies does not affect our new spiritual existence." Concerned at this perversion of Christian freedom, Paul warns the church that resorting to prostitutes definitely comes under his condemnation of sexual immorality (6:13, 18). Such behavior excludes a person from God's kingdom (6:9–10). The remedy—Christian marriage—is set forth in chapter 7.

Paul's response to the Corinthians' sinful laxity falls into three parts: (1) In 6:12–14, he quotes the slogans they used to justify visiting prostitutes, and adds some correctives. He also tries to instill a proper respect for the body as belonging to the Lord. (2) In 6:15–17, he argues specifically against prostitution, showing the incompatibility of union with a prostitute and union with Christ. (3) Finally (6:18–20), in case they still haven't been persuaded, he specifically forbids sexual immorality with a direct command.

"NOT ALL THINGS ARE BENEFICIAL" (6:12–14)

The slogan "all things are in my power" (6:12) seems to have arisen from pagan Greek philosophy. The Corinthians may have tried to justify their behavior by appealing to their newly found freedom and spiritual power in Christ. As Christians, each of them was "a perfectly free lord of all, subject to none" (Luther, AE 31:344). But they failed to understand that Christian freedom from sin and the Law's condemnation is *not* freedom *to sin,* but instead is freedom to live by the power of the Spirit in accord with God's Law (e.g., Romans 6; 13:10). Christians must keep in mind the other part of the paradox: a Christian is also "a perfectly dutiful servant of all, subject to all" (AE 31:344). To that end, Paul supplies the necessary corrective: "Not all things are beneficial" (1 Cor 6:12; cf. 7:35). The verb "are beneficial" is synonymous with "build up" in the parallel passage in 10:23 ("not all things build up"; cf. also 12:7). The Corinthians have been thinking only of themselves, rejoicing in their spiritual privileges, without giving sufficient thought to what benefits the whole body of Christ. They are causing offense to the Gospel and are defaming their Lord.

As they sin, they are remaining enslaved to the passions of their sinful nature, which must be crucified and die (e.g., Rom 6:6–11). Scripture sometimes personifies sin as a tyrant, which tries to overpower its devotees and keep them subject to its authority (Gen 4:7; Rom 6:12–16). Like the ancient serpent (Gen 3:5) and the false prophets castigated in 2 Peter, sin promises freedom, but fails to deliver; its subjects find themselves caught in a cycle of bondage and corruption that leads to death and hell.

Paul cites another of the Corinthians' slogans, "The foods are for the stomach, and the stomach is for the foods, and God will destroy both it and them" (1 Cor 6:13). It was the Christian position that all foods were clean (Mk 7:19; Acts 10:9–15) and could be eaten freely. But the Corinthians seem to have drawn an analogy between the need to satisfy one's hunger with all kinds of food, and an (alleged) need to satisfy one's sexual appetite, even if it meant resorting to prostitutes. Thus, they apparently claimed, sexual indulgence is as natural as eating. Besides, what one does with one's physical body is unimportant; God will one day destroy it just as he will destroy the foods that sustain it. So a person may just as well "eat and drink [and fornicate!], for tomorrow we die" (1 Cor 15:32).

But Paul rejects the analogy between eating and sexual sins. To be sure, foods belong to this passing age, as do our bellies with their digestive functions. True, marriage and reproduction will not continue in heaven (Mt 22:30). All these belong to "the form of this world" that "is passing away" (1 Cor 7:31), the corruptible "flesh and blood" which cannot inherit the kingdom of God (15:50). But Paul distinguishes bellies from bodies. The belly, representing digestion as a process necessary to sustain life, may pass away, but the body will be raised. Plato and other Greek philosophers had a low view of the body. But the biblical view is that the body, as the physical aspect of a person and an essential part of human beings, created by God, is to be honored. A Christian's body is God's property, an integral part of a person he has redeemed and claimed for the resurrection. At the resurrection, our bodies will be transformed to be like Christ's glorious body (Phil 3:21; cf. Mt 22:20; 1 Cor 15:44, 51). With this glorious destiny ahead of us, God's will for our bodies is not immorality, but sanctification and unhindered devotion to the Lord Jesus (1 Cor 7:35; 1 Thess 4:3). Compare Rom 14:7–8: "For none of us lives to himself and no one dies to himself. For if we live, we live to the Lord, and if we die, we die to the Lord. Therefore, whether we live or whether we die, we are the Lord's."

A major reason for ascribing such dignity to the body is God's promise of the bodily resurrection. Paul's argument against the Corinthians degrading of the body by sexual sinning continues with an appeal to this fundamental doctrine. Just as God raised the Lord Jesus' body from the grave (15:4, 15, 20; see also Rom 8:11), so he "will raise us" (1 Cor 6:14). God will achieve this great result of resurrection "through his power" (1 Cor 6:14). According to the parallel in Rom 8:11, God's powerful instrument for raising our mortal bodies will be "his Spirit, who dwells in us" (see Mk 12:24 and 2 Cor 13:4 on the resurrection as a display of God's power).

Here in 1 Cor 6:14, Paul is stating briefly what he will spell out at length in chapter 15. The doctrine of the bodily resurrection has important ethical implications for the Christian life. In chapter 15, the apostle speaks in general of the way our resurrection hope should dispel the frivolous attitudes of those who say, "Let us eat and drink, for tomorrow we die" (15:32). In our present text, his specific concern is to show the folly of associating with prostitutes in light of the glorious destiny God has in store for our bodies. The Christian's body belongs to Christ, the Lord (6:13), and so the Christian must not defile Christ's possession by sexual immorality.

In this connection, Baptism and the Lord's Supper pertain to the Christian's proper use of his body. In Baptism, the body is washed (Eph 5:26; Titus 3:5–7) and the name of the Lord Jesus is applied (1 Cor 1:9–16). The baptized believer, body and soul, belongs to the Lord. In Baptism, a person is made a member of Christ's body (1 Cor 12:13). The Lord's Supper is a communion in the body and blood of Christ (10:16), which the communicant receives into his body orally (11:23–32). The Christian must recognize and discern Christ's body (11:29), lest he sin against the body and blood of Christ (11:27). Since the Christian is a member of Christ's body and has received Christ's body and blood, his body must be kept pure "for the Lord" (6:13).

"YOUR BODIES ARE MEMBERS OF CHRIST" (6:15–17)

For the fourth time in this chapter, Paul asks, "Don't you know?" (6:15; also 6:2, 3, 9). This is the first occurrence in his epistles of the analogy of Christ's body and its members. It will recur in 1 Cor 12:12–31 and Rom 12:4–8. This analogy probably was part of Paul's fundamental instruction to the Corinthian converts. The imagery seems to have arisen from the connection Paul draws between the communion with Christ's body in the Lord's Supper and the church thereby being built up as "one body" (1 Cor 10:16–17). Part of the background may also be found in the apostle's experience on the Damascus Road, when the Lord asked him, "Saul, Saul, why do you persecute me?" In persecuting the members of the church, Paul was persecuting the head to whom they belonged and with whom they were organically joined. Christ is the head of his church and of each believer (11:3).

Against this background, the apostle is understandably horrified at the idea that some of Christ's members were being removed from their intimate connection with their head and made members of a prostitute. Paul's abhorrence is expressed in the words "By no means/"God forbid!" (6:15). We find this expression in passages where Paul finds himself in fundamental opposition to views that would destroy the essentials of the faith (Rom 3:4, 6, 31; 6:2, 15; 7:7, 13; 9:14; 11:1, 11; Gal 3:21; 6:14).

With another "don't you know?" (6:16), Paul addresses the issue of the close intimacy between a man and a prostitute. The phrase "who joins himself" comes from a verb which in classical Greek meant "to glue, cement." But the close bonding that takes place when two pieces of paper are glued together, or when one pane of glass is laid on top of another, are inadequate analogies to describe the fusion of two persons into one physical entity in the act of sexual intercourse. In a mysterious way, the two become one (Eph 5:32). God intended this to happen only within the covenant of marriage, which is the lifelong union of one man and one woman (Mt 19:3–6). However, Paul warns, even in the gross caricature that takes place when a man consorts with a prostitute, he becomes one body with her.

Paul now adds the scriptural basis. While the Creator's words in Gen 2:24 describe and undergird the institution of marriage (Mt 19:5; Eph 5:31), they also describe the relationship that develops when a man visits a prostitute. They, too, are no longer two, but "one flesh" (1 Cor 6:16). But unlike a man and woman joined in holy matrimony, unmarried sexual partners are bonded together in an unholy union. Desecration is the result not only of prostitution, but also of unmarried heterosexual lovers, and of all homosexual and lesbian relationships.

This "one flesh" bonding with anyone other than the lawfully wedded spouse is simply incompatible with the believer's union with the Lord (cf. Deut 10:20; Ps 73:28; 1 Ki 11:2). As Paul warned in 6:9–10, those who do such things will not inherit the kingdom of God.

But the person who is united with the Lord "is one spirit [with him]" (1 Cor 6:17). His union with the Lord was effected through the indwelling presence of the Holy Spirit, the Spirit of Jesus, poured out in Baptism and operative through God's faith-generating Word (1 Cor 12:13). When the words of Christ, which are Spirit and life, dwell in his heart, he enjoys a spiritual, mystical union with his Lord, even as a bride enjoys union with her bridegroom.

"FLEE FROM SEXUAL IMMORALITY!" (6:18–20)

Finally, the apostle pleads, "Flee from sexual immorality!" (6:18). Christians must run away from sexual temptations, as Joseph fled from Potiphar's wife (Gen 39:12). Christians should not dally with temptation, but "flee youthful passions and pursue righteousness, faith, love, peace" (2 Tim 2:22; cf. 1 Cor 10:8; 1 Tim 6:11).

It is most likely that 1 Cor 6:18b is part of Paul's own argument and not another Corinthian slogan in defense of the Corinthians' view that their sexual sins did not threaten their salvation. Assuming all of the words in 6:18 are Paul's words, the meaning must be that sexual sins harm the body and personality like no other sins. All other sins, by contrast, are "outside the body." What this means has been subject to debate. Other sins, too, like drunkenness and gluttony, have their grim effects on the body. However, those sins involve the abuse of things which come from outside the body; sexual immorality involves the direct misuse of the body itself. The ravages of sexually transmitted diseases tend to confirm that assessment. Later, in his epistle to the Romans, Paul will refer to the bodily harm suffered by the sexually immoral. God gives them over to "the degrading of their bodies with one another" (Rom 1:24). This is "the due penalty for their perversion" (Rom 1:27, specifically about homosexuality and lesbianism; cf. 1 Cor 6:9).

Thus, Paul has argued, not only does the sexually immoral person sin against the church and her spiritual union with the Lord (6:15–17), but he also defiles his own body. This body, which has been consecrated by God as a temple of his Holy Spirit (3:16–17), which has been bought for a price, and which is destined for resurrection, has now been torn from its spiritual union with Christ and joined in an unholy union. Again, that desecration takes place in all sinful liaisons—in any sexual act besides that between husband and wife.

A sixth and final "don't you know?" (6:19) shows Paul's agitation over what seems to have been a widespread problem. Now he reminds the Corinthians of the high honor God has bestowed on their bodies in making them temples of the Holy Spirit, whom they had received from him. The bright cloud of God's glorious presence had filled the tabernacle and then the temple which replaced it (Ex 40:34–38; 1 Ki 8:10–11). Those structures had been superseded by the greater temple, the body of the Lord Jesus himself (Jn 2:21). Each believer in Christ serves as a "living stone," a mini-temple of the Spirit within the great "spiritual house" of the new aeon (1 Pet 2:4–5).

Back in 1 Cor 3:16–17, Paul had spoken of the whole congregation as God's temple. There his concern was the sins of jealousy, strife, and pride, which were tearing the congregation apart. Now, in ascribing the glorious designation "temple" to each believer (6:19), he wishes to impress on the Corinthians that abusing their bodies by sinning sexually violates the very holiness and presence of God. Since the Holy Spirit had taken up residence in their bodies through Baptism (12:13), they should take care not to grieve their divine guest (Eph 4:30; 1 Thess 5:19).

Now that their bodies had become the Spirit's residence, the Corinthians could no longer live for themselves (see Rom 14:7). "You are not your own," Paul writes (1 Cor 6:19). Earlier he had reminded them whose they really were: "You are Christ's" (3:23)—and God's.

Living for themselves as if they were autonomous, "free," and "in control" was no longer possible, "for you were bought for a price" (6:20). No other NT saying brings together in such compact form both the essence of the Gospel and its implications for the Christian life. So powerful is this idea that Paul repeats it in 7:23. On the one hand, the Gospel shines forth brilliantly, pointing to God's once-for-all action on Calvary as an accomplished fact. On Calvary, the ransom price was paid, "not with silver or gold . . . but with the precious blood of Christ as of a lamb without blemish or spot" (1 Pet 1:18–19; cf. Acts 20:28). God's grace did not come cheaply! It was a costly ransom from slavery, from captivity to the power of sin (Rom 6:18, 22). Like the rest of the NT, 1 Corinthians is rich in metaphors describing God's acquisition of the sinner and the sinner's liberation from the hands of his tyrannical masters, using terms like "redemption" (1 Cor 1:30; also Rom 3:24; Eph 1:7; cf. Gal 4:5) and "acquire, win" (Paul acquires or wins people for God, 1 Cor 9:19–22). Again, Paul's theology of the cross comes to the fore in a succinct and powerful way.

At the same time, God's purchase of the sinner from slavery does not mean he is now free to go his own way. Rather, through that purchase he comes under new ownership. Implicit in the Gospel, while it retains its character as a free expression of God's grace, is the understanding that the believer now has a new Lord. At the same time he rejoices both in his freedom and also that he has become a slave of Christ (7:22). This "slavery" is perfect freedom because it frees a person to serve God in holiness and righteousness, as God originally intended for his creatures. Christ's yoke is easy, and his burden is light (Mt 11:30).

So, having opened the final paragraph of the chapter with the negative command "flee from sexual immorality!" (6:18), Paul closes it with the positive exhortation "glorify God in your body!" (6:20). The apostle expects the Corinthians to follow his example (4:16; 11:1) so that their entire life magnifies Christ (Phil 1:20). His appeal to them as God's temple is similar to the great introduction to Romans 12: "I urge you, therefore, brothers, by the mercies of God, to present your bodies as a sacrifice that is living, holy, acceptable to God" (Rom 12:1).

Introduction to Chapter 7

Some commentators and English versions see 7:1 as introducing a major new division of the epistle. Here we find the first occurrence of the formula "now concerning . . ." (the formula occurs again in 7:25; 8:1; 12:1; 16:1, 12). From this point on, Paul will be responding to questions from Corinth, conveyed in a letter which had probably been handed to him by Stephanas, Fortunatus, and Achaicus (16:17).

But while 7:1 begins this new section of the letter, there is a close connection between Paul's warnings and commands about sexual immorality in chapters 5 and 6 and his positive efforts in chapter 7 to form healthy attitudes toward marriage and sex. The close link between the chapters is evident from the term "sexual immorality" in 5:1; 6:13, 18; and now in 7:2, where Paul says, "Because of the [temptation to] sexual immoralities, each man must have his own wife, and each woman must have her own husband." Relevant, too, are Paul's prior commands about sexually immoral people (5:9–11; 6:9, 15–16, 18 and also 10:8). Now he commands husbands and wives not to deny one another, but show full mutuality in satisfying the other's sexual need.

These commands enunciated in 7:2–5 show a totally different Paul from the picture of the ideal celibate painted by Jerome and Roman Catholic tradition on the one hand, and on the other hand the similar view, widespread in liberal Protestantism, that Paul was a misogynist who thought sex was degrading. Such snap judgments fail to consider the full range of Paul's statements. Could a misogynist have penned the moving admonition to husbands that they should love their wives in the manner of Christ's self-sacrificing love for his bride, the church (Eph 5:21–33)? Nor was Paul by any means a grim ascetic; indeed, in Col 2:20–21 and 1 Tim 4:3 he condemns asceticism. The way he balances his statements, saying exactly the same things to husbands as to wives (e.g., 7:2–4) reveals an egalitarian view of the sexes that leaves no room for misogyny.

At the same time, faithful exegesis needs to acknowledge that in this chapter Paul does call celibacy (albeit *voluntary* celibacy) a "good" thing—even a "better" thing (7:38)—for those endowed with the requisite charisma (7:1, 7a, 8, 26). He never suggests, however, that celibacy is a more meritorious state, a state in which it is easier to attain Christian perfection, or one that makes someone more sacred than ordinary Christians. Just as a Christian family with children is no more meritorious than a Christian couple without children, so celibacy is no more meritorious than marriage. Whether a Christian is celibate or married is entirely a matter of Christian freedom. What really counts in God's sight is the calling to be a Christian, and the keeping of God's commandments (7:19)—living the life of obedience, faith, and love.

The one advantage of celibacy—a great advantage—is that the unmarried person can serve God and neighbor with fewer distractions. For that reason Paul wishes all Christians could be celibate like himself. But he is utterly realistic: the celibate life is not for everyone; not all have the gift (cf. Mt 19:11–12). It is far better to marry than to burn with sexual desire (1 Cor 7:9). And to live the married life well, sustaining its burdens and anxieties, is also a noble thing in God's sight and requires his special grace.

The interpreter's orientation to chapter 7 depends to no small degree on how he understands 7:1. It has long been debated whether the words "it is good for a man not to touch a woman" were coined by *Paul* and thus express his own negative view of the marital relationship, or whether they actually stemmed from *the Corinthians,* whose letter to Paul may have expressed their reservations about marriage in this catchy manner (cf. similar slogans of the Corinthians in 6:12, 13).

The perspective of this commentary is that 7:1b is the *Corinthians'* slogan. Paul agrees there is some truth in their slogan, but he is quick to qualify it with the positive advice that, in order to avoid immorality, each believer should be married (7:2). If 7:1 were an expression of Paul's own view, it is difficult to explain how he could go on to commend marriage as the remedy for immorality (7:2) and to command those who are married to remain in that state (7:10–11, 27) and to satisfy one's spouse (7:3). Thus, the central emphasis of the opening paragraph falls on what Paul thinks should be the normal situation: that everyone will marry and meet his or her partner's sexual need (7:2–5). This paragraph, then, sets the tone for the rest of the chapter.

Thus, in counseling the Corinthians in sexual matters, Paul has to contend on two fronts. In chapters 5 and 6, his concern is an antinomian libertinism which condoned immorality, including adultery, homosexuality, and liaisons with prostitutes (5:9–11; 6:9–20). Now, in chapter 7, he begins by countering an ascetic overreaction on the part of others which frowned on marriage and sexual relations within marriage as not befitting a Christian's new spiritual existence.

Asceticism of this kind was a widespread feature of Greco-Roman religion and philosophy during the first century AD. Religious ascetics believed their self-discipline gave them additional spiritual power and holiness. The traditional religion of Rome had its Vestal Virgins; the priestesses of the Delphic oracle were also virgins. The Stoics and Cynics debated whether the married or the unmarried state was preferable. Monastic movements, like the Essenes and the Therapeutae, also arose in late Judaism. Some of the Corinthian ascetics may have found justification in Jesus' words regarding the coming age, when there will be no marriage but everyone will be like the angels (Lk 20:34–36), or in Paul's own example. That Paul had to contend with asceticism in other congregations is evident from Col 2:20–23, where false teachers were saying "Do not handle, do not taste, do not touch," and 1 Tim 4:3, where he opposes the hypocrisy of some who were forbidding marriage.

Throughout Paul's counsel in chapter 7, there runs a consistent thread which is summarized in the central paragraph (7:17–24): "Let each person remain in the state in which he was called" (7:24). Those who were already married when God's call came should stay married; those who were unmarried should not seek a spouse (7:27). But Paul never applies this pattern of advice rigidly. He does not bind consciences where he has no specific command from the Lord, leaving each Christian free to determine how best he can serve.

The chapter responds to the following issues:

- Mutuality in marriage (7:1–7)
- Widowers and widows (7:8–9)
- To the married: no divorce! (7:10–11)
- Mixed marriages (7:12–16)
- General advice: remain as you were when called (7:17–24)
- Those never married may remain single (7:25–28)
- Living as those whose time is short (7:29–31)
- Service without anxiety (7:32–35)
- To marry—or not to marry—one's virgin (7:36–38)
- A widow may remarry—a Christian (7:39–40)

A word of explanation is needed about the translation. Throughout chapter 7, when Paul is giving an authoritative and permanent directive for the church, this commentary will render the third person imperatives with the word "must," as in 7:3, "The husband *must* give his wife her marital due." Similarly, most of the third person prohibitions are also translated with "must," as in 7:12–13, "He *must not* divorce her. . . . She *must not* divorce her husband." The reason for this translation practice is that the force of the Greek is stronger than is reflected in the common English renderings with "let," as in the KJV, "*Let* the husband render unto the wife due benevolence" (7:3), and "*Let* him not put her away. . . . *Let* her not leave him" (7:12–13).

Some of the other constructions, such as the infinitives in 7:10–11, are also translated with "must" because they are part of authoritative commands. The stronger translations with "must" are also supported by Paul's statement in 7:25, "Now concerning the virgins, I do not have a command of the Lord," which implies that Paul's earlier pronouncements *are* commands from the Lord. Paul refers explicitly to "the commandments of God" in 7:19 (and "the Lord's command" in 14:37). God's commands are not optional for the Christian; they are normative and *must* govern the life of the church.

1 CORINTHIANS 7:1–7
MUTUALITY IN MARRIAGE

TRANSLATION

7 [1]Now concerning the things you wrote: "It is good
for a man not to touch a woman." [2]But because of the
sexual immoralities, each man must have his own
wife, and each woman must have her own husband.
[3]The husband must give his wife her marital due,
and likewise also the wife to her husband. [4]The wife
does not have authority over her own body, but her
husband [does], and likewise also the husband does
not have authority over his own body, but his wife
[does]. [5]Stop depriving one another, unless perhaps
it be by mutual agreement for a period, in order to
give your time to prayer and then to come together
again, so that Satan may not tempt you because
of your lack of self-control. [6]But I say this as a
concession, not as a command. [7]To be sure, I want all
people to be like myself. But each has his own gift of
grace from God, one of this kind, another of that.

COMMENTARY

1 Cor 7:1b ("it is good for a man not to touch a woman") has often been seen as Paul's opening programmatic statement that colors the whole chapter. However, it seems more likely that these were not Paul's own words but a quotation or summation of what the Corinthians had written to him on the topic of marriage. Then the apostle appears in a very different light as a strong advocate of mutual sexual satisfaction within Christian marriage. Whether 7:1b is understood as a slogan or not, it must certainly be seen in the closest connection with the qualification that follows in 7:2.

Indeed, it is in 7:2 that we find the center of gravity: "Because of the sexual immoralities, each man must have his own wife, and each woman must have her own husband." Marriage is to be the general rule. Celibacy, while it can be "good" (7:1, 8), is to be the exception. A similar pattern appears a number of times in the chapter. In 7:7, for example, Paul begins by granting that there is some validity to the ascetic point of view ("I want all people to be like myself"), but quickly adds: "Each has his own gift of grace." Similarly in 7:8–9, he first agrees that it is "good" for the unmarried to stay unmarried but adds that those who lack self-control should marry. The pattern emerges again in 7:25–28, where Paul emphasizes with a twice-repeated "good" that it is good for virgins to stay that way, but he adds that it is not sinful for them to marry (cf. 7:38).

The normal practice should be that every Christian is married. The imperatives in 7:2 ("must have . . . must have") should be noted. In a matter of fact manner, he advocates marriage "because of the sexual immoralities" (7:2), which in this context may be specifically liaisons with prostitutes. At this point, some commentators are at pains to insist that Paul does not here lay down the general ground of marriage as a remedy against sin. But we should not detract from Paul's sober and realistic statement. While marriage was instituted to provide companionship (Gen 2:18), procreation (Gen 1:28), and so on, one of its important functions is to provide the proper place for the expression of human sexuality, and thus serve as a remedy for sin, a buffer against Satan's temptations (1 Cor 7:5).

On a basis of full reciprocity, both the husband and the wife are to fulfill their sexual obligations to one another. The context, which speaks of power over one another's bodies and of not depriving one another (7:4–5), indicates that by "marital due" Paul has the sexual act in mind. He emphasizes the importance of unselfish giving in the sexual relationship ("must give," 7:3) rather than a self-centered seeking to get the best out of the relationship for oneself. Paul's stress on unselfish love and consideration for the needs of one's spouse is in harmony with the great discourse on love in chapter 13. It is in striking contrast with the modern emphasis on self-fulfillment and the individual's sexual autonomy.

It also stands in contrast with the rabbinic Judaism of Paul's background. Specifically mentioning periods ranging from one week to thirty days, the rabbis did not object if a man vowed unilaterally to abstain from intercourse with his wife (*Mishnah*, Ketuboth, 5.6). Compare Paul's insistence that any such abstinence from intercourse for a religious purpose must be "by *mutual* agreement" (7:5). Finally, it is noteworthy that Paul's only guideline for the frequency of intercourse is the spouse's need.

"You are not your own," Paul insisted in the previous chapter (6:19). Christians belong first to the Lord who bought them, and then to one another. Thus, the wife does not have the right to do what she likes with her body, depriving her husband of his marital due, nor does the husband have the right to deprive his wife. Paul first insists that Christian women should give themselves sexually to their husbands, and then he gives equal weight to the requirement that husbands must not deprive their wives. In contrast to pagan cultures, where sex is commonly viewed one-sidedly as the man's privilege and prerogative, with the woman at his beck and call, Paul stresses the need for total mutuality in the marriage relationship.

Thus, the Corinthians should desist from depriving one another. The verb "depriving" (literally, "defrauding") in 7:5 was used in 6:7 with reference to the practice of some Christians defrauding each other in property cases. To deprive one's spouse of sexual relations is to rob the other of what rightfully belongs to him or her (cf. the use of the same verb in James 5:4).

Only under exceptional circumstances should there be abstinence from sexual relations between husband and wife. Paul spells out three conditions: (1) that it be by mutual agreement; (2) that it be temporary; (3) that it be for the purpose of prayer. There may be times of crisis which call for special prayer, but then couples should resume sexual intimacy as soon as possible. Otherwise the tempter could seize this opportunity to draw them into sin. The marital relationship serves as a protective shield against the devil's cunning.

The demonstrative pronoun "this" in "I say this" (7:6) must refer to the concession Paul has just made in 7:5 ("unless perhaps it be by mutual agreement for a period, in order to give your time to prayer"). The apostle is conceding, not commanding, temporary abstinence with the consent of both husband and wife. Within the wider context (7:2–5), the passage can hardly be interpreted to mean that Paul's concession is that the Corinthians may marry. After all, Paul has commanded marriage, using four imperatives to insist that each person take a spouse and then fulfill his or her conjugal duties (7:2, 3, 5). Then he concedes that there may be circumstances which call for a brief abstinence for the sake of prayer.

"To be sure," he continues, "I want all people to be like myself," that is, unmarried (7:7). Whether Paul had ever been married will be discussed in connection with 7:8. At the time of writing, however, he was celibate. Thus, he was free from the restraints and obligations of marriage and able to devote himself single-mindedly to Christ's mission (cf. 7:35). Such undistracted devotion to the Lord's service was his ideal for all Christian people.

Although Paul would like everyone to follow his example and remain unmarried, he realizes he cannot require this of anyone. The gracious gift of remaining not only celibate but also free from burning sexual desire is not given to everyone (cf. Mt 19:11; 1 Cor 7:9). Whether the Christian is called to a chaste celibacy or to marriage, his vocation is God's gracious gift. Both celibacy and marriage are God's good gifts to be received with thanksgiving (1 Tim 4:4). Both vocations can only be lived out in a God-pleasing manner under the blessing of God's continual grace.

1 CORINTHIANS 7:8–9
Widowers and Widows

TRANSLATION

7 [8]I say to the widowers and to the widows, it is good for them if they remain as I do. [9]But if they do not have self-control, they must marry. For it is better to marry than to burn.

COMMENTARY

At the time of writing, the apostle was not married (7:7–8). Such undistracted devotion to the Lord's service was his ideal for all Christian people. But this does not mean that Paul had never been married. He may have been a widower. Another possibility is that his wife had left him, perhaps as a result of his conversion. Either of those two situations would be in harmony with the Lord's commands and Paul's advice in 1 Corinthians 7. The question is this: to what degree of detail should Paul's comparison in 7:8 be pressed? His counsel for widowers and widows to remain "as I" could imply that he, too, was a widower. Or the comparison could be simply on the basis that he now has no wife, without offering any details about his past circumstances. His wish in 7:7 for "all people to be like myself" is probably best understood as referring simply to his lack of a spouse at the present time.

Among Paul's fellow Jews, marriage was the norm, to which celibacy was the very rare exception. Especially was this the case with men who were devoted to the study of the Law and were thus expected to set an example. Acts 26:20, where Paul speaks of his functions as a judge, points to him being such a one set aside for the study of the Law. This greatly increases the likelihood that he had been married.

Further items may be advanced in support of the translation "widowers," instead of "those who have never been married": First, most ancient cultures had a word for widows, since their problems were conspicuous, but many cultures lacked a word for their male counterparts. Greek speakers could have used the masculine form of the usual term for a "widow;" it is found in classical Greek but not in the Greek Scriptures. During the NT period, "unmarried" (as in 7:8) served in its place. Second, it may be observed that throughout chapter 7 Paul deals with men and women in mutuality (twelve times altogether), and it would be natural to see the same pattern here. He speaks the same message to both "widowers" and "widows" (7:8), just as he gave the same instructions to both husbands and wives (7:2–4). Third, the use of "unmarried" at other points in chapter 7 (especially in 7:11 of a divorced woman, and in 7:34 of a currently unmarried woman in contrast to a virgin) indicates that it regularly denotes those who were married but are not now, rather than unmarried people in general.

Thus, Paul grants that it is "good" if widowers and widows follow his lead and refrain from remarrying (7:8). Up to a point, he concurs with the sentiments of the Corinthians' letter to him, which apparently contained the slogan in 7:1: "It is good for a man not to touch a woman." He will have further advice for widows in 7:39–40.

The apostle insists, however, that an exception must be made to his advice that widowers and widows remain as he does. If they lack self-control and are tempted to visit prostitutes (cf. 7:2) or indulge in extramarital affairs, then the remedy is that they must marry. "For," Paul says, "it is better to marry than to burn" with sexual passion (7:9). Again, he is almost certainly countering an ascetic group which sought to forbid the remarriage of widowers and widows. Paul, on the other hand, consistently maintained that the death of a spouse left the surviving partner free to remarry (7:39; see also Rom 7:2–3).

1 CORINTHIANS 7:10–11

To the Married: No Divorce!

TRANSLATION

**7 [10]To the married I command—not I, but the
Lord—that a wife must not separate from her
husband. [11]But if she separates, she must remain
unmarried or be reconciled to her husband.
And a husband must not divorce his wife.**

COMMENTARY

Paul now turns to married people in situations where both partners are Christians. He states categorically that they are not to divorce. His authority for this ruling is not his own, although elsewhere he will express his counsel as a faithful apostle (e.g., 7:25, 40). Rather, in this case Paul has a specific word from the Lord Jesus himself, just as he has other specific words when he later reminds the Corinthians of the Lord's command that those who preach the Gospel should live from the Gospel (1 Cor 9:14; see Lk 10:7), when he passes on the tradition concerning the Lord's Supper (1 Cor 11:23–26), and when he addresses the role of women in worship (14:37). Jesus had specifically forbidden divorce as contrary to the Creator's design and will (Mt 5:32; 19:9; Mk 10:9; Lk 16:18), thus putting himself at odds with the liberal views of Rabbi Hillel and his followers (Mishnah, *Gittin*, 9.10), and with the prevailing ethos in Greco-Roman society.

It is remarkable that Paul first forbids wives from initiating divorce proceedings against their husbands. In Judaism, it was generally not permissible for a woman unilaterally to file for divorce. But Greco-Roman society was different. In communities like Corinth, there were no legal obstacles to a woman taking such an initiative. It seems some highly "spiritual" Corinthian women, who were drawn to an ascetic understanding of Christianity and rejected sexual relations with their husbands, may have been taking the further step and divorcing their husbands. Paul tells them that in so doing they are contravening the Lord's command.

However, if the unthinkable should happen and the wife in fact leaves, she should not seek a new husband. Only two options are open to her as a Christian: to remain unmarried or be reconciled to her husband. This apostolic word reflects the NT view that marriage is indissoluble: the two have become one flesh and will always remain so. Only death can dissolve a marriage (Rom 7:2; 1 Cor 7:39). Note how in both 7:10 and 7:11 the weight falls on what in Greek is the final clause: "a wife from her husband *must not separate*" (7:10) and "a husband his wife *must not divorce*" (7:11). The Scriptures take a stern and uncompromising stand against divorce; "'I hate divorce,' says the Lord" (Mal 2:16).

Finally, Paul adds that a husband must not divorce (literally "send away") his wife (1 Cor 7:11). Although men had this legal prerogative both in Jewish and Greco-Roman society, the apostle does not take his standards from the culture but from the word of his Lord.

1 CORINTHIANS 7:12–16
Mixed Marriages

TRANSLATION

7 12To the rest of you I say (I myself, not the Lord): If
any brother has an unbelieving wife and she agrees
to live with him, he must not divorce her. 13And if
any wife has an unbelieving husband and he agrees
to live with her, she must not divorce her husband.
14For the unbelieving husband has been sanctified
by his wife, and the unbelieving wife has been
sanctified by her husband. Otherwise, your children
would be unclean, but as it is, they are holy. 15But if
the unbelieving partner wants to separate, let him
separate; the brother or the sister is not bound in such
cases, and God has called us in peace. 16For how do
you know, wife, if you will save your husband? Or how
do you know, husband, if you will save your wife?

COMMENTARY

Paul has discussed conjugal relations within marriage (7:1–7). He provided counsel to widowers and widows (7:8–9) and to married people in situations where both partners are Christians (7:10–11). Paul now turns to "the rest" (7:12)—believers who are married to unbelievers. Mixed marriages were forbidden in the OT, and Jesus had not left a specific word on the issue, so Paul speaks to it on the basis of his apostolic authority. By no means were all Christians in the fortunate situation of Lydia, the Philippian jailer, or Stephanas, who had been converted and were baptized together with their entire households (Acts 16:15, 33; 1 Cor 16:15). In Gentile areas newly penetrated by the Gospel, mixed marriages were common. Timothy's mother was a Jewish Christian, while his father was a pagan Greek (Acts 16:1). Peter, too, offers detailed advice to Christian women married to pagans (1 Pet 3:1–6).

Paul's advice to Christians in a mixed relationship is consistent with his earlier word to Christian couples (1 Cor 7:10–11): remain as you are! If the unbelieving spouse is content to be married to a Christian, then the Christian partner should not dissolve the marriage.

While we cannot reconstruct with certainty the situation into which Paul is speaking, it seems a reasonable suggestion that he was concerned to calm the fears of some that their marriage to a non-Christian could rob them of their holiness. After all, hadn't the apostle in a previous letter, and now again in the present epistle, warned them against associating with the immoral (5:9–13)? Didn't he command them to expel an evildoer from their midst (5:13)? Moreover, the ascetic group in the congregation may have been arguing that marriage to a pagan defiled the Christian partner. Paul now assures the church that the opposite is the case: the believer is not besmirched by the unbeliever; rather, the unbeliever is sanctified through association with the believer (7:14).

To say that the unbelieving spouse "has been sanctified" (7:14) does not necessarily mean that he or she will be saved. As much as the believing spouse may desire and pray for the partner's salvation and proclaim the Gospel, the unbeliever may continue to reject the Gospel. However, the unbelieving spouse does come under the holy influence of the Christian, whose faith and moral purity set an example and have a significant impact on the tone of the whole household. The atmosphere in the home is constantly sanctified by the Word of God and prayer (1 Tim 4:5).

The holy influence of the Christian spouse also extends to the children: "otherwise, your children would be unclean, but as it is, they are holy" (1 Cor 7:14). If the Christian parent were the father, he would certainly have the authority to raise the child as a Christian from an early age. And in cases where the Christian parent is the mother, she would be determined to do all in her power to see that her child is raised in the faith. Timothy's mother, Eunice, and his grandmother Lois saw to it that the boy was subject to the sanctifying influence of the holy Scriptures from early childhood (2 Tim 3:15). Timothy's Greek father may have been indifferent to what the women were doing; he may even have been opposed, but for the sake of the child, the women feared and obeyed God rather than a man (as did the midwives in Ex 1:15–21; see also Acts 5:29). It would be reasonable to assume that cases like Timothy's were common in Paul's day. We may compare recent church history, where, for example, the Russian babushkas (grandmothers) often undertook the Christian instruction of their grandchildren when the parents were unwilling or unable.

While we cannot deduce from this text with certainty the further implication that the children of mixed marriages were holy because they had been baptized, the adjective "holy" does tell in its favor. The apostle is assuring the Christian already married—and probably it was mostly wives who needed this reassurance—that continuing the union with the spouse, far from being displeasing to God, was indeed hallowed, and that their children (despite the non-Christian parent) were now holy (7:14; cf. 1:2; 6:11). In 12:13, Paul will state that those who are baptized (with no restriction stated as to age) are given the Holy Spirit to drink.

The next situation Paul describes (7:15) probably was common in the early church. Many non-Christians would have found their spouse's new religion strange and embarrassing, with the result that they wished to opt out of the relationship. Under these circumstances, Paul says—and only under these—may the marriage be dissolved. "Let him (or her) go," he writes. "Don't try desperately to save the marriage." It would have been understandable if Christian women in particular fought to preserve their marriages, for a deserted wife could find herself in severe financial straits. She would also be aware of the divine injunctions against divorce. Another factor would be her hope that her husband would eventually be won to the faith. But Paul states that the Christian brother or sister "is not bound" (7:15) when the non-Christian partner wants to end the relationship. Since the responsibility for the marriage breaking up rests with the unbeliever, the Christian should not let it burden his or her conscience. Rather than trying to force the unbeliever to maintain the marriage, and thus destroying whatever "peace" (7:15) was left in the home, the Christian should let the separation occur as peacefully as possible. The Christian is called to a life of peace (Rom 12:18; 14:19; 1 Cor 14:33; 2 Tim 2:22).

It is much debated whether 1 Cor 7:16 should be understood "optimistically" or "pessimistically." According to the optimistic view, Paul is encouraging believers to maintain the marriage if possible in the hope of saving the spouse, because the unbeliever eventually may be brought to the faith and so be saved. But a comparison of similar rhetorical questions in the OT (1 Sam 12:22; Esth 4:14; Eccl 2:19; 3:21; Joel 2:14; Jonah 3:9) leaves it open whether to interpret 1 Cor 7:16 optimistically or pessimistically, and the context favors the pessimistic view. The Christian does not know whether the unbeliever would ever be converted, so the Christian should not force the unbeliever to stay on the assumption that the unbeliever's conversion is a certainty if the marriage continues. The apostle understands, and speaks tenderly to, the deep desire of the Christian spouse to save the partner. This is what makes it so hard for the spouse to let the marriage break up. But to cling to the marriage when the partner is determined to leave would only lead to frustration and hostility. The guiding principle must be "peace" (7:15).

1 CORINTHIANS 7:17–24
Remain as You Were When Called

TRANSLATION

7 [17]Only as the Lord has assigned to each person, as God has called each person, so he must walk. And I order thus in all the churches. [18]If someone was called after being circumcised, he must not remove the marks of circumcision. If someone was called as an uncircumcised person, he must not be circumcised. [19]Circumcision is nothing, and uncircumcision is nothing, but [what counts is] keeping the commandments of God. [20]Let each person remain in the state in which he was called. [21]If you were called as a slave, don't let it worry you. But if indeed you are able to become free, by all means make use of [the opportunity]. [22]For he who is called in the Lord as a slave is the Lord's freedman; likewise, he who is called as a free man is Christ's slave. [23]You were bought for a price; do not become slaves of human masters. [24]Brothers, let each person remain in the state in which he was called, in the presence of God.

COMMENTARY

Paul's paragraph on the Christian's calling (7:17–24) is a digression from the various marital topics that dominate this chapter. But it enunciates a principle which should govern the congregation's whole approach to marriage issues, the principle that unless there are good reasons to the contrary, a Christian should be content with whatever his marital status happened to be at conversion. Paul states this principle three times (7:17, 20, 24), drawing parallels with circumcision and uncircumcision, then freedom and slavery.

In these verses we find the verb "I call" eight times, the noun "calling" once. The noun in 7:20 refers to one's role or station in life (and is translated above as "state"). But the verb denotes God's call to faith in Christ. Paul is not thinking of calling primarily in the sense of one's vocation, that position in life to which one is called, but of the condition in which God finds a person when he first calls him into the fellowship of his Son (1:9).

Back in 7:7, Paul established that whether a person was single or married, his marital status was a personal gift from God. Now he urges everyone to be content in that status. The particular circumstances in which someone was called to the Christian faith—whether as a male or as a female, single or married, or (as Paul will soon add) circumcised or uncircumcised, slave or free, rich or poor—have no bearing on his standing in God's sight. Paul's argument here parallels his baptismal catechesis in Gal 3:28: "There is no longer Jew or Greek, there is no longer slave or free, there is no longer male or female; for you are all one in Christ Jesus" (cf. 1 Cor 12:13). Thus, the Gospel does not prescribe what the Christian's social situation ought to be: no one can claim he is a better Christian because of his higher place in society. Even slaves could enjoy the high dignity of the call to eternal life in Christ Jesus (Phil 3:14), and indeed, in the early church, great numbers of slaves became believers. In contrast to modern "prosperity doctrine," which sees affluence as a sign of God's call and blessing, Paul stresses contentment whatever one's lot (Phil 4:11–13). All sorts and conditions of people may live (literally "walk," 7:17) the Christian life with a good conscience, knowing that they are serving their Lord.

Paul now adds (7:17) that his instructions on marriage matters, and the illustrations he is about to paint regarding circumcision and uncircumcision, slavery and freedom, are consistent with his advice to churches everywhere (cf. 4:17; 11:16; 14:33).

His constant advice is that people should remain as they are (7:18–19). If someone was called to the faith as a circumcised person, he should not have an operation to conceal his circumcision. Such operations had become popular as Israel was subjected to cultural pressure from its Greek-speaking environment, and Jewish men wished to compete in the gymnasium without embarrassment. Paul condemns the practice. Rather, the Jewish Christian should follow Paul's example and remain "a Jew to the Jews" (9:20). For that reason he had Timothy circumcised (Acts 16:3). As the son of a Jewish woman, Timothy was regarded as a Jew anyway, and once he was circumcised, he would be able to witness more effectively to fellow Jews. But the apostle steadfastly refused to circumcise Titus, who was a Greek (Gal 2:3). As Titus had been called in uncircumcision, it was not right to demand circumcision of him or other Gentiles. After the advent of Christ and his fulfillment of the Torah, whether a man was circumcised or uncircumcised became ultimately irrelevant. That is Paul's great argument in the epistle to the Galatians. What really matters is not an external operation on the body, but "keeping the commandments of God" (1 Cor 7:19).

What does Paul mean by "commandments of God" (1 Cor 7:19)? A helpful non-Pauline starting place is the succinct definition in 1 Jn 3:23: "And this is his commandment, that we believe in the name of his Son Jesus Christ, and love one another, as he has commanded us." This Johannine definition corresponds closely to Paul's pronouncement to the Galatians: "In Christ Jesus neither circumcision nor uncircumcision means anything, but faith working through love" (Gal 5:6). Here we find the core of Paul's theology. Of paramount importance is "the obedience of faith" (Rom 1:5; 16:26). While we are justified by faith alone, this faith is never alone; it is "a living, busy, active, mighty thing" (AE 35:370), constantly serving the neighbor in loving obedience to the Ten Commandments (Rom 13:8–10).

This definition of what Paul means by God's commandments lies at the heart of his conception, as is demonstrated especially by Gal 5:6. But in our present context, we need to add that he also works with a broader definition, which understands God's commandments to embrace the whole deposit of divine revelation handed down in the OT and the sayings of the Lord. This revelation constitutes the divine mandates which the Christian is to honor and observe. It is in this sense that the only other occurrence of "commandment" in 1 Corinthians (14:37) should be taken.

In 7:20, Paul reiterates the principle of 7:17. The Christian should remain in the "state" or "calling" in which God's call first found him. The noun "state" (7:20) here approaches the sense of our term "vocation" (the vocation to be married or unmarried, the vocation to live as a circumcised or uncircumcised person). But the verb in the context ("in which he was called") refers to the divine call to be a Christian, which happens to find a person in a particular social setting.

Taking his second illustration from the practice of slavery (7:21), Paul encourages the many slaves in the congregation not to let their social condition bother them. They may still live out the Christian life under those circumstances. What matters above all is that they are free of worry (see 7:32), allow their calling in Christ to transform them, and glorify Christ as they carry out their roles in life.

However, should their master offer them their freedom, they should seize the opportunity (7:21). In support of this positive interpretation of the text are the following considerations: (1) Paul has just been speaking of freedom in the "if" clause of this conditional sentence. Therefore, it is much more likely that the unexpressed object of the verb "make use of" is "freedom" than that we should supply "slavery" from further afield. (2) The verb "make use of" in the Corinthian letters regularly means "take advantage of an opportunity" (1 Cor 7:31; 9:12, 15; 2 Cor 1:17; 3:12; 13:10) (3) Finally, it is highly unlikely that Paul would have taken any other view. On a number of occasions he appealed to his Roman citizenship in order to gain freedom to further Christ's mission (Acts 16:37; 22:25). He certainly did not regard imprisonment or slavery as desirable states.

1 Cor 7:22a answers to 7:21a and explains why the person called as a slave should not be concerned about his social circumstances. His calling to be in Christ has conferred on him the glorious liberty of being one of God's children, set free from bondage to sin (Rom 8:21). But this does not mean that

the Christian is now at liberty to be his own master. Rather, his emancipation in Christ has resulted in transference of ownership. He has come under new management: from now on, he will be a willing slave of his Lord Jesus. Paul served as a pattern in this regard. Although he was a free Roman citizen, he often introduced himself to his readers as a slave of Christ Jesus (Rom 1:1; 2 Cor 4:5; Gal 1:10; Phil 1:1; Titus 1:1). As slaves of Christ, Christians should not curry favor with people but do God's will wholeheartedly (Eph 6:6).

Paul's paradoxical teaching on the Christian life as the way of glorious freedom coupled with devoted service has found one of its finest expositions in Luther's 1520 treatise "The Freedom of a Christian." Here (AE 31:344), Luther sets forth two theses that "seem to contradict each other": "A Christian is a perfectly free lord of all, subject to none. A Christian is a perfectly dutiful servant of all, subject to all." This teaching he derives first of all from Paul, beginning with 1 Cor 9:19: "For although I am free of all people, I have made myself a slave to all."

The Corinthians' status as freedmen had come at a price—the precious blood of Christ (1 Pet 1:18–19; Rev 5:9). The axiom "you were bought for a price" (1 Cor 7:23) is repeated from 1 Cor 6:20. In that context, Paul's concern was that the Corinthians glorify God with their redeemed bodies, and not sin sexually. In the present context, he is urging them to appreciate their newly won freedom, and not become enslaved to the false asceticism which seems to have been promoted especially by the "spiritual" women, nor sacrifice their freedom by following factional leaders (1:12; 3:4, 21; cf. 2 Cor 11:20) or anyone else who might take them captive through human philosophy and speculation (Col 2:8, 20).

Paul concludes his digression by repeating in 1 Cor 7:24 his thesis that, unless there are good reasons to the contrary, everyone should continue in the situation in which he was called (cf. 1 Cor 7:17, 20). The call to be a Christian sanctifies and ennobles all stations in life.

Whatever his station, the Christian has the assurance that he is not alone. He can live out his calling in God's presence (7:24), confident that God is with him and will never leave him (cf. Deut 31:6; Josh 1:5; Heb 1:5).

1 CORINTHIANS 7:25–28

THOSE NEVER MARRIED MAY REMAIN SINGLE

TRANSLATION

7 [25]Now concerning the virgins, I do not have a
command of the Lord, but I give my opinion as one
who by the Lord's mercy is trustworthy. [26]I think
that this is good in view of the present distress—that
it is good for a person to continue as he is. [27]If you
are bound to a wife, do not seek a dissolution; if you
are free from a wife, do not seek a wife. [28]But if you
do marry, you have not sinned, and if the virgin
marries, she has not sinned. But such people will
have worldly trouble, and I would like to spare you.

COMMENTARY

Paul has now given his apostolic counsel to widowers and widows, to married couples in general, and to couples in mixed marriages. There remains one large group whose situation he has not addressed: the "virgins," who have never married. To this group, he devotes much of the second half of the chapter (7:25–38).

With the phrase "now concerning" (7:25), Paul signals that he is taking up a fresh topic from the Corinthians' letter to him. Whereas he had a definite command from the Lord in the case of married people (7:10), he has to use his own pastoral judgment in the case of virgins. Nonetheless, the Corinthians could have confidence that he gives his opinion not as a harsh lawmaker, but as one whose whole life was under the impress of the Lord's mercy and compassion. The Corinthians could be sure that he had their best interests at heart.

Paul's advice is that he thinks it is good for female virgins and their male counterparts to remain unmarried "in view of the present distress" (1 Cor 7:26). With these words, Paul may be alluding to the end of the world (thus NRSV: "impending crisis"). Here an appeal can be made to the context, where he says the time is short (7:29) and the form of this world is passing away (7:31). See also 7:32–35. Both the words "distress" (7:26) and "trouble" (7:28) are used in the NT of the woes preceding Christ's second coming. While this may be part of the reason, Paul may have had in mind an additional specific cause of distress for the people in Corinth at that time.

Numerous Greek states were affected by food shortages in the AD 40s and 50s. If the citizens of Corinth, especially the poor, were suffering from famine, Paul's advice to people not to marry becomes more understandable. It is easier for an unmarried person to cope with hardship than for parents who have to provide for their children. The famine crisis may also lie behind the apostle's concern for those who were going hungry at the communal meals which accompanied the Lord's Supper (11:21, 34). That Paul has current food shortages in mind is not at all incompatible with the suggestion that "distress" has to do with the end times, for Jesus lists "famine" as part of the "distress" of those times (Lk 21:11, 23).

1 Cor 7:26 may be compared to Jer 16:1–4, where God commands the prophet—and only the prophet—not to marry and father children. The reason is the imminent fall of Jerusalem to the Babylonians. God tells Jeremiah that parents and children in Jerusalem will die from sickness, famine, and the sword. This comparison may support the view that a local famine or other hardship could be a reason for celibacy in Corinth too.

Since the destruction of Jerusalem because of her sins was a prefiguration of Judgment Day upon Christ's return, this comparison may support the interpretation that "the present distress" (1 Cor 7:26) also has in view Christ's parousia and the world's end. The eschatological perspective of passages such as Matthew 24 suggests that many earthly hardships (e.g., wars, famines, earthquakes, persecution, false christs) should be seen as signs of Christ's return and the world's end. That time may come at any moment, and certainly it is closer now for us than it was for Paul and the Corinthians.

Paul had learned to be content in whatever state he was in (Phil 4:11). Now he again commends the wisdom of this policy to the congregation. The married man should be content with his situation and not seek a divorce (1 Cor 7:27a). Thus, Paul reiterates the injunctions of 7:10–13. On the other hand, the man who was not legally bound to a woman (because he was divorced or a widower or a bachelor) should not seek a wife (7:27b; cf. 7:8).

However, if an unmarried person disregards the apostle's advice and decides to marry, he may be assured that this is not a sin (7:28). These words at first sight seem strange, coming from a Jewish man for whom marriage was the norm. As noted above, some have suggested that Paul is countering ascetic slogans which promoted the single life as being more "spiritual" than marriage. More likely, however, he is simply assuring young Christians who held the founder of their church in the highest regard that it was fine if they did not follow him in his preference for celibacy. After all, he had no command from the Lord on this topic (7:25). His advice was simply advice; to disregard it did not imperil anyone's spiritual welfare. Moreover, his words of reassurance here for those who wish to marry are consonant with 7:2 ("Each man must have his own wife, and each woman must have her own husband") and 7:9 ("If they do not have self-control, they must marry").

Paul adds a warning that the married person will have "worldly trouble" (7:28, literally, "trouble for the flesh"; for similar language see 2 Cor 12:7). Probably Paul is thinking in general terms of the worldly anxieties that afflict the married person in trying to please his or her spouse (7:32–34). These normal anxieties seem to have been accentuated in Corinth by famine (see above on 7:26). Unless they are under necessity to marry, the apostle would like to spare the Corinthians these worries.

1 CORINTHIANS 7:29–31

Living as Those Whose Time Is Short

TRANSLATION

7 [29]This is what I mean, brothers: the time has been shortened, so that from now on those who have wives should live as if they had none, [30]those weeping as if they were not weeping, those rejoicing as if they were not rejoicing, those buying as if they didn't own anything, [31]and those using the world as not abusing it. For the form of this world is passing away.

COMMENTARY

Paul now speaks with pastoral affection to the whole church, calling the Corinthians "brothers" (7:29). He reminds them that they live in the last days. "The Lord is at hand" (Phil 4:5); their salvation is nearer than when they first believed (Rom 13:11); the days have been shortened (Mt 24:22). Thus, they should live "eschatologically"—as people who are always aware they may have to leave this world at any moment. This heightened awareness of our transience has been well illustrated by the analogy to the terminally ill. The person who knows his remaining time is limited has a changed perspective. He sees, hears, and values everything in a new way.

During the time that remains to them in this world, believers should focus on eternal matters. This does not mean they should cultivate a stoic aloofness and detachment from the concerns of the present age. But they should not let their lives be dominated by the world and its values. They should not become too preoccupied, too absorbed, too engrossed in this transient existence. Their true citizenship is in heaven (Phil 3:20; cf. Heb 13:14; 1 Pet 1:4). Thus, in the middle of all these legitimate earthly concerns, they should always have the attitude of someone who can do without the things this world has to offer (cf. Lk 14:26).

Here Paul becomes poetic, employing five well-balanced lines, each featuring the words "as if . . . not" (1 Cor 7:29–31):

> Those who have wives should live *as if* they had none,
> those weeping *as if* they were not weeping,
> those rejoicing *as if* they were not rejoicing,
> those buying *as if* they didn't own anything,
> and those using the world *as* not abusing it.

A similar passage is found in 2 Cor 6:10: "as sorrowing but always rejoicing, as poor but making many rich, as having nothing and possessing everything."

Paul grounds his appeal to the church to keep her heavenly focus with an affirmation that rounds off the argument of 1 Cor 7:29–31: "For the form of this world is passing away" (7:31). These words form a framework with 7:29a, "the time has been shortened." Paul has in mind the Last Day (cf. 1 Jn 2:17–18), when the form (1 Cor 7:31) of this present creation will pass away and be superseded by a new heaven and a new earth (Revelation 21–22), just as the form of our lowly body will then be transformed (Phil 3:21) so that it conforms to Christ's glorious body (1 Cor 15:35–58).

1 CORINTHIANS 7:32–35
Service without Anxiety

TRANSLATION

7 [32]So I want you to be unconcerned. The unmarried
man is concerned about the things of the Lord, how
he may please the Lord. [33]But the married man is
concerned about the things of the world, how he
may please his wife, [34]and he is divided. And the
unmarried woman and the virgin are concerned
about the things of the Lord, to be holy, both in body
and spirit. But the married woman is concerned
about the things of the world, how she may please
her husband. [35]I am saying this for your benefit,
not to throw a noose on you but to promote proper
conduct and devotion to the Lord undistractedly.

COMMENTARY

Paul now expresses his wish that the whole congregation be as free as possible from burdensome cares (1 Cor 7:32). This was his underlying concern in the previous admonition to live in this world as citizens of heaven, who did not become too engrossed in this world's affairs (7:31). As is evident from the context (7:33–34), freedom from care should be understood in a broad sense to include freedom from the worldly anxieties attendant on marriage and raising a family (cf. Mt 6:25–34; Phil 4:6; 1 Pet 5:7). In contrast to the married person, an unmarried man (like the apostle himself) is able to devote all his time and attention to serving and pleasing his Lord. Paul constantly encouraged Christian people not to be self-centered and please themselves, but to live for the Lord who had died for them and make it their goal to please him and their fellow human beings in everything (Rom 8:8; 15:1–3; 1 Cor 10:33; Gal 1:10; Col 3: 22–24; 1 Thess 2:4, 15; 4:1; 2 Tim 2:4). Compare also Luther's Morning Prayer: "that all my doings and life may please You" (SC VII 2). This desire to please the Lord should be the Christian's overriding concern whether married or single.

Nowhere in this chapter does Paul argue that it is wrong for a person to marry and assume the duties of married life. Elsewhere he maintains that "if anyone does not provide for his relatives, and especially for his immediate family, he has denied the faith and is worse than an unbeliever" (1 Tim 5:8). The married Christian must not shirk these responsibilities. At the same time, with sober realism, the apostle points out that the mundane cares of maintaining a household and trying to please one's wife do limit the time available to a married man who wants to devote himself to the Lord. He has divided loyalties (7:33–34).

By the same token, unmarried women are free to consecrate themselves ("be holy," 7:34) in body and soul to the Lord. By "holy," Paul does not mean that they are holier than other Christians, but they can serve their Lord with single-minded devotion. Like the faithful widows referred to in 1 Tim 5:5, they are able to continue in supplications and prayers night and day (cf. Anna, Lk 2:37).

Paul has been speaking eloquently of the advantages of remaining unmarried in terms of Christian service. No doubt this is the voice of experience: he knows how freedom from family ties and concerns has enabled him to be totally at his Master's service, providing him with freedom to travel and work long hours in fulfilling his ministry as apostle to the Gentiles throughout the Mediterranean world. What benefits, he argues, would accrue to the church if more Christian people could share his freedom and flexibility!

THE OUTSTANDING SERVICE OF SINGLE AND CHILDLESS CHRISTIANS IN "THE THINGS OF THE LORD"

Through the centuries, the church and her missions have continued to benefit from the outstanding services of many devoted single people. Another group which has rendered sterling service is the so-called "married singles," married couples who have not been blessed with children and have thus been able to contribute more of their time to church service or remain longer on the world's mission fields, while those with children have had to return home for the sake of their children's education and acculturation.

On the other hand, we need to recognize that Paul's advice is influenced by the special needs of his day, "the present distress" (7:26). There will be other times and places where a person with a family can minister more effectively, for example, in family counseling.

While Paul speaks highly of the single-minded service and freedom from distraction of the single person, he is careful not to make a rule of celibacy. At no point does he say that the marital state is displeasing to God. In no way does he wish to put a "noose" (7:35) on anyone's neck, or burden anyone's conscience. Not everyone has the gift (7:7) of remaining single; many are gifted with the grace of caring for spouse and family, and strive to please the Lord within that state. Of course, it may not be as easy for them to focus on single-minded service and to find time for the Word which sanctifies "in body and spirit" (7:34; cf. 1 Tim 4:3–5). But one does not have to run off to a monastery or mission field or spend one's whole day at church in order to be holy. The mother who has her hands full with small children is sanctified by the same Word as the single woman. What matters is that she "not despise preaching and [God's] Word, but hold it sacred and gladly hear and learn it" (SC I 6). Whether single or married, we should follow Mary in choosing "the better part," and not allow ourselves, like Martha, to be excessively distracted with "much serving" (Lk 10:38–42).

1 CORINTHIANS 7:36–38
To Marry—or Not to Marry—One's Virgin

TRANSLATION

7 36 If anyone thinks he is conducting himself
improperly toward his virgin, if his passions are
strong and it has to be, let him do what he wishes.
He is not sinning; let them marry. 37 But he who
stands firm in his heart, not having necessity, and
has control over his own will and has decided in his
own heart to keep his own virgin, he will do well.
38 So he who marries his own virgin does well,

COMMENTARY

These verses provide the interpreter with the challenge of identifying the "anyone" who thinks he is acting improperly, and then identifying the "virgin" who is being subjected to his improper behavior. Three views have gained prominence among scholars:

1. "Anyone" refers to the girl's father or guardian, who has acted improperly in not providing for her marriage. It is suggested he may have been motivated by ascetic ideals or concern over the current distress (7:26). On this view, the reference to "strong passions" must apply instead to the girl and mean something like "past the flower of youth." The further explanation, "and it has to be," would mean she does not have the gift of contentment in celibacy. The chief consideration in favor of this view is the verb translated above as "marry," which normally in the NT means "to give someone to someone else in marriage." On the other hand, the expression "his virgin" would be unusual for "his daughter." Another difficulty in seeing the father as the key figure is the exhortation in 7:36, "let them marry," which is strange when (in this view) the fiancé has not yet been introduced.

2. A second view is that Paul has in mind "spiritual marriages," where an ascetic couple lived together as brother and sister in Christ, abstaining from sexual intercourse. In this view, the reference to "strong passions" applies to the man. The chief objections to this view are (a) the lack of first-century evidence for such "spiritual marriages" and (b) Paul's specific injunction to married couples not to cease sexual relations (7:3–5), which makes it most unlikely he would approve of a "marital" situation where the sex act was routinely avoided.

3. The view adopted in this commentary is that Paul is concerned for engaged or betrothed couples who were postponing marriage because of economic pressures or their expectation of the Lord's imminent return. Under these circumstances, some of the men found the lengthy abstinence difficult and thought it was dishonorable to keep their fiancées in suspense. Paul assures them there is nothing sinful about finding a remedy in marriage. Such men will be doing well (7:38a). The apostle's advice is reminiscent of his word to widowers and widows in 7:8–9: "It is good for them if they remain as I do. But if they do not have self-control, they must marry. For it is better to marry than to burn."

On the other hand, there may be some men who have the gift to prolong the engagement indefinitely. Such men are under no necessity to marry; they can control their sexual desire and have made a decision to continue the present circumscribed relationship with their fiancées (7:37). Presumably this is because they wish to give themselves fully to the service of the Lord, who could return at any moment (7:29–35). These men will do even better (7:38b).

1 CORINTHIANS 7:39–40
A WIDOW MAY REMARRY—A CHRISTIAN

TRANSLATION

7 [39]A woman is bound as long as her husband is alive.
But if the husband should fall asleep, she is free to
marry whomever she wants, only in the Lord. [40]But
she is more blessed if she remains as she is, in my
opinion. And I think I have the Spirit of God.

COMMENTARY

Earlier in this chapter, Paul dealt in a comprehensive way with the situation of widowers and widows, married and divorced people, those in mixed marriages, and those who had never married. Although he has already had a pastoral word for widows in 7:8–9, that was a general word that applied equally to widowers, encouraging them all to be content with their situation, but to marry if they found the single life intolerable. It was natural for Paul to begin with that group, for he may have belonged to it as a widower, and he was able to use his own situation as a model for the principle he wished to articulate from the outset: remain as you are (7:8, 17, 20, 24). But now, as he concludes the chapter, he adds a special word for widows, a group which often experienced great distress and needed special pastoral support (e.g., Acts 6:1–4).

In 7:39, Paul reiterates the Lord's command that marriage is for life (7:10–11, 13); a woman is bound to her husband as long as he lives (see also Rom 7:2; 1 Cor 7:27). However, if her husband is laid to rest (literally, "should fall asleep"), she is free to remarry. Paul adds a qualification: she should remarry "only in the Lord" (7:39). Undoubtedly this means that her new husband should be a Christian. In 9:5, Paul will say the same thing about himself and the other apostles: they have the right to take a Christian sister as a wife (implying that they should not take an unbeliever as a wife). This principle probably applies to *all* the unmarried Christians Paul addresses throughout chapter 7. Most likely he assumed that his readers would take for granted that marriage should be "in the Lord" (7:39). In his later epistle to the Corinthians, he states the principle in general terms that apply to a wide variety of relationships, including marriage: "Do not become unequally yoked to unbelievers" (2 Cor 6:14).

Paul allows that a widow has every right to remarry, and that there is absolutely nothing sinful about doing so. However, his personal opinion is that she would be more blessed if she remained single (7:40). The reasons for this, in terms of worldly troubles and distractions, have been spelled out earlier in the chapter (7:32–35). His opinion is given as a Spirit-filled apostle, who is in no way inferior to anyone else in Corinth claiming the gift of the Spirit: "I think I have the Spirit of God" (7:40).

Throughout the chapter, Paul has been arguing against the apparent exaltation of celibacy and asceticism by some members of the Corinthian church. On the one hand, he agrees that for those gifted to cope with it, the single life spares a person many worldly anxieties and leaves him or her free to serve the Lord without distractions. On the other hand, Paul affirms marriage as a God-pleasing institution and forbids married people to deny one another their marital rights. To cope with marriage and its responsibilities also requires a special gift of God's grace. Both ways of life are pleasing to God and valid options for the Christian. Marriage is good, and "for those to whom it has been given" (Mt 19:11), the single life is even better.

1 CORINTHIANS 8:1–11:1

THE WORD OF THE CROSS IS THE BASIS FOR THE CHURCH'S FREEDOM

Introduction to Chapter 8

8:1–13 Foods Sacrificed to Idols

8:1–3	Knowledge Puffs Up, Love Builds Up
8:4–6	One God and One Lord
8:7–13	Love for the Weak Brother

9:1–27 The Apostolic Example of Lovingly Renouncing Rights

9:1–2	A Free Apostle
9:3–14	Four Proofs of the Apostles' Right to Support
9:15–18	Paul's Decision Not to Exercise His Rights
9:19–23	All Things to All People
9:24–27	Self-discipline to Win an Imperishable Prize

10:1–11:1 Conclusions about Idol-foods

10:1–13	Warnings against Spiritual Complacency
10:1–5	*Our Fathers in the Wilderness*
10:6–13	*Patterns in the Pentateuch for Our Instruction*
10:14–22	The Lord's Table and the Table of Demons
10:23–11:1	Consideration for Others to the Glory of God

Introduction to Chapter 8

Paul now turns to another question from the Corinthians' letter to him: What should their attitude be to food that has been offered to idols? It seems the "wise" in Corinth were arguing the case for a more liberal attitude than had been customary in the church since the decree of the Jerusalem council (Acts 15:19–20, 29). That decree, issued to facilitate relationships between Jewish and Gentile Christians in Syria and Cilicia, called on Gentile Christians to abstain from food sacrificed to idols, as well as blood, strangled animals, and sexual immorality. Those Gentiles were among the firstfruits of Paul and Barnabas' Gentile mission. At that time, the main issue was whether or not these newcomers to the church should be circumcised. Under these circumstances, the church's decision not to insist on circumcision, but simply to ask Gentiles to refrain from idol-meat, blood, strangled animals, and sexual sins, would not have seemed a harsh imposition.

In Corinth, however, some members of the Gentile Christian community could not see why they should give up idol-meat at all. Paul's response in chapters 8 and 10 carefully distinguishes three different issues: (1) the primary issue for Paul and the Corinthians—whether they could recline at table and eat sacrificial food in an idol's temple (8:1–10:24); (2) whether they could eat in their homes food purchased at the food market (10:25–26); (3) how they should conduct themselves as guests in non-Christian homes (10:27–30).

The nature of the idolatrous worship practiced in Corinth during Paul's day has been considerably illuminated by archaeology and by studies of contemporary literature. Most notable are the recently excavated sanctuary of the two goddesses Demeter and Kore on the Acrocorinth citadel, and the sanctuary of Asklepios 500 meters north of the agora (the city square). The rites of Demeter and Kore were linked to the agricultural calendar and were intended to promote fertility and prosperity. The sanctuary was on three levels: a lower terrace close to the road, with at least forty dining rooms which seem to have been accessible to the public; a middle terrace with a theatrical area probably used to celebrate the mysteries, and open only to initiates; and the highest terrace with buildings displaying the cult images. Among the debris have been found statues of Demeter, votive pits into which were thrown votive offerings (crude representations of cakes and fruits, of the female figure, and of animals), cooking ware, much ash, and the bones of young pigs. Clearly the eating of sacrificed pigs and of dedicated cereals and fruits was an important part of the Demeter cult.

In preparation for initiation, temple patrons would honor Demeter by drinking a cup of a prepared beverage. They would also eat from a platter, which had sections for foods. Paul will later insist (10:19–22) that for a Christian such drinking or eating is unthinkable; it is playing with fire.

A more ambiguous situation was provided by the great courtyard surrounding the fountain of Lerna, a pleasant place for relaxation attached to the sanctuary of Asklepios. Under the sanctuary's main building have been found three dining rooms opening onto the courtyard. Because Lerna was such a desirable public place, it is likely that some Christians in Corinth would have defended their right to eat there, whether of their own accord or in response to an invitation.

As in the case of those initiating lawsuits against their less privileged "brothers" (1 Cor 6:1–8), it may have been the more affluent members of the congregation for whom the Lerna restaurant presented a special temptation. They would have been invited to meals in such places for birthdays, weddings, or other important occasions. Such events would have been a virtual obligation of their social and professional lives. The poor, on the other hand, probably had access to meat only at public religious festivals where meat was distributed to everyone. For them, the eating of meat may have taken on connotations of pagan worship.

Finally, we need to mention the dilemma facing the Christian who was invited to a meal in the home of a non-Christian. While it appears that many meals in pagan homes were not accompanied by religious rites, it was particularly at special celebrations like feasts in honor of the gods, weddings, birthdays, days of thanksgiving, funerals, and some lesser celebrations that sacrifice was likely to be offered. For the Christian to avoid all such social events, or to refuse the food offered on such occasions, could have serious consequences. It could destroy opportunities for friendship and social advancement. The apostle's wise counsel was needed to enable the Corinthian church to enjoy (as far as possible) normal social intercourse without compromising the faith. Paul advocates a middle course between the overly scrupulous attitudes of traditional Judaism and some Jewish Christians, and the tendency of Gentile Christians (and perhaps some "enlightened" Jewish Christians) not only to cause offense but also to endanger their salvation by their associations with heathen temples.

Paul's language differentiates between the Christian with "knowledge" (8:1, 7, 10, 11) and the "weak" Christian (8:7, 9, 10). All Christians are wise in the sense of knowing the Gospel, the word of the cross (1:18–25, 30; 2:6–7). Paul's use of these terms in chapter 8 seems to refer not to the strength of one's faith but to how easily a Christian is offended. The Christian with "knowledge" knows that false gods do not exist and cannot exert any power. But the "weak" Christian is more easily offended by any participation in anything associated with paganism. Paul's concern is not so much to try to educate the "weak" so that they have "knowledge," but rather that all Christians—especially those who consider themselves wise or strong—act in *love,* a love that *builds up* others in Christ.

An important issue in the interpretation of 8:1–11:1 is the relationship of chapter 8 to chapter 10. Paul is aware that he cannot address everything at once;

as a good pastor, he first offers one general argument, then another more specific discussion. In chapter 8, his primary concern is that reclining in an idol's temple will harm *one's brother* (8:11). In chapter 10, he will argue at length that flirting with idols (instead of fleeing them) will harm *oneself* (10:1–22).

8:1–13

Foods Sacrificed to Idols

1 CORINTHIANS 8:1–3

Knowledge Puffs Up, Love Builds Up

TRANSLATION

8 [1]Now concerning meat sacrificed to idols, we
know "we all have knowledge." Knowledge puffs
up, but love builds up. [2]If anyone thinks he knows
something, he does not yet know as he ought to know.
[3]But if anyone loves God, he is known by him.

COMMENTARY

Appealing to the slogan, "we all have knowledge," some of the Corinthians had taken a broad view of their entitlement to eat food that had been offered to idols. Apparently they felt they could eat such food with impunity on a variety of social occasions, and even recline at table in dining rooms such as those near the Lerna fountain, since (so they might argue) these had only a loose connection with the temple of Asklepios. Whether some also had the temerity to drink the cup or eat from the dish in the dining rooms on the lower terrace of Demeter's sanctuary is difficult to say. But the wording of 10:19–22 suggests that some may not have had scruples about going this far, reasoning that the cup and dish were not part of the cult that was practiced on the middle terrace. From their catechetical instruction, the saints in Corinth had learned not to fear idols nor the so-called deities behind them. Thus, the more sophisticated members of the congregation seem to have operated with a broad interpretation of the circumstances in which they thought they could eat idol-food.

In the face of this complacent attitude, Paul begins his pastoral response with this general truth: "knowledge puffs up" (8:1). The possession of a superior degree of religious knowledge did not guarantee that those who had it would take the right attitude toward the issue of idol-meat. The acquisition of expertise—be it religious, philosophical, or whatever—tends to inflate a person with a sense of superiority over others. This boasting in self, then, rather than in the Lord (cf. 1:31) puts him at odds with the Lord's purposes for his church. The Lord wants his church to be built up as a community, and that can only happen when its members display unselfish love for one another (cf. 10:23). This "love" is *not* "puffed up" (13:4).

The arrogant person (8:2), who is satisfied in his possession of a certain level of Christian knowledge, has not yet really comprehended the spirit of the

Christian faith. This is evident in Hab 2:4, which contrasts the righteous person, who lives by faith, with the "puffed up" person, who presumes that his accomplishments and virtues have elevated his status before God.

In contrast to the person who thinks he knows something, Paul sets the one who loves God (8:3). The logic of 8:3 is from evidence to inference. If someone loves God, it is because that person is known by God; God is the source of that person's love. Paul says something similar in Gal 4:9: "Now knowing God—or rather being known by God . . ." God's knowledge and election of a person come first and enable a person to then know and love God. While a person may think that he has learned about God and has chosen to believe in and love God, it actually was God's prior action of knowing him and revealing himself that results in the person knowing and loving God.

Such a person has been freed from self-centered pride in himself and what he knows. He no longer lives for himself, but for God, who has granted him salvation in Christ. In loving God, he will begin to love and build up God's people. When a person's focus is thus on God and others, he will no longer rejoice in his own knowledge but in God's gracious knowledge of him (cf. 1 Cor 13:12; Gal 4:9). His life will be characterized by humble gratitude (cf. 1 Cor 4:7).

1 CORINTHIANS 8:4–6

ONE GOD AND ONE LORD

TRANSLATION

8 [4]About the eating of meat sacrificed to idols,
then, we know "there is no idol in the world" and
"there is no God but one." [5]For even if there are
so-called "gods" either in heaven or upon earth,
just as there are many "gods" and many "lords,"
[6]for us there is one God, the Father,
from whom [are] all things and we [are] for him,
and one Lord Jesus Christ,
through whom [are] all things,
and we [are] through him.

COMMENTARY

1 Cor 8:1–3 laid the foundation for Paul's response to the question about idol-food. "Knowledge" and "love" (8:1) are the key terms. On the one hand, Paul concedes: "Yes, you and I know about idol-foods. We know that they are just food." On the other hand, Paul reminds the Corinthians that a self-centered knowledge without love has no value and does not build up the church (13:2).

What implications, then, must be drawn regarding the eating of idol-food? On the face of it, from the standpoint of Christian *knowledge* there should not be a problem. Again, Paul concedes that the Corinthians' slogans are true: "there is no idol in the world" and "there is no God but one" (8:4). After all, the first slogan was thoroughly consistent with the prophets and psalmists who mocked the lifeless idols of the heathen (e.g., Ps 115:3–8; Is 44:9–20). And the second slogan echoed Israel's foundational creed, the *Shema'* of Deut 6:4: "Hear, O Israel, the Lord our God, the Lord is one!" This creed was recited by the faithful Israelite every morning and afternoon. It also formed a key element in synagogue worship. It was, above all, this clear monotheistic affirmation that distinguished the Jewish people from the polytheistic cultures surrounding them. Paul here agrees with the testimony of the "wise" in Corinth to the continuity between Israel's ancient faith in the one true God and the monotheistic position of Christianity.

Paul continues to express his agreement with what the Corinthians had learned as part of their basic Christian knowledge. Israel's faith as expressed in the *Shema'* governed its attitude to the various gods and goddesses worshiped by neighboring peoples. Although Paul and the Corinthians knew that there were many of these—some with their primary abode in heaven, the usual dwelling place of the gods, others with their residence on earth—they were agreed that they were all merely "so-called 'gods'" (8:5); they had no real existence and no real power.

"Yes," Paul continues, "I acknowledge that there are many of these so-called 'gods' and 'lords.'" The term "lords" may include both the "lords" worshiped in the mystery cults and departed emperors who were worshiped as "lord and god." But the title was also given to the regular gods and goddesses like Isis and Serapis.

But no matter how dazzling was the array of so-called "gods" and "lords" offering themselves for allegiance, as far as Paul and the Corinthians are concerned, ("for us") there is only "one God, the Father" (8:6). This one God is no local deity with a circumscribed residence either in heaven or on earth. Rather, he is the almighty Creator and source of "all things" (1 Cor 8:6; cf. Gen 14:19, 22; Jonah 1:9). Christians live for their heavenly Father ("and we [are] *for* him," 8:6). In everything they are oriented toward him and strive to please him.

The Christian also knows only "one Lord Jesus Christ" (8:6; cf. Eph 4:5; 1 Tim 2:5). Echoing the church's confession, Paul makes bold to identify the "one Lord" of Israel's *Shema'* with the Lord Jesus. He senses no dissonance in attaching this affirmation to his declaration that there is only "one God," for he clearly regards the Father and the Son as distinct persons within the one Godhead. The Son is the eternal Word of God, affirmed also in Jn 1:3 and Heb 1:2 to be the agent through whom the Father made the whole created order (1 Cor 8:6). The believer knows that it is through Christ that he has both his physical and his spiritual existence.

1 CORINTHIANS 8:7–13
Love for the Weak Brother

TRANSLATION

**8 [7]But [this] knowledge is not in everyone. Some,
through being accustomed to idols until recently,
eat [the meat] as meat sacrificed to idols, and their
conscience, being weak, is defiled. [8]Food will not
present us to God. We are neither worse off if we do
not eat, nor are we better off if we eat. [9]But watch that
this authority of yours doesn't become a stumbling
block to the weak. [10]For if someone sees you, the
one having knowledge, reclining in an idol's temple,
won't his conscience, being weak, be built up to eat
meat sacrificed to idols? [11]For by your knowledge,
the weak person, the brother for whom Christ
died, is being destroyed. [12]So by sinning against
your brothers and striking their weak conscience,
you are sinning against Christ. [13]Therefore, if
food causes my brother to fall, I will never eat
meat to eternity, lest I cause my brother to fall.**

COMMENTARY

True faith in the Christian confession will always be active in love (Gal 5:6). Paul has established that he is at one with the more "enlightened" members of the church in the confidence and *knowledge* that idols represent gods that really do not exist, and the foods offered to them are just ordinary foods (8:4–6). But knowledge of the essentials of the faith merely puffs up if it is not applied in Christian *love*. Paul's loving pastoral concern for the whole congregation has made him aware that some of the Corinthians are not yet free from the emotional pull of their former attachment to idols. As soon as they give in to pressure from friends and join them for a meal in an idol's temple, the old associations begin to reassert themselves. They find they are not able to regard the meat simply as a gift from the Creator. The meat has been offered to idols. So their conscience is defiled; they eat and go home feeling guilty because they have participated, at least outwardly, in a ritual of worship of a false god (cf. Rom 14:23).

Preserving a good conscience is part of a Christian's high responsibility (Acts 23:1; 24:16; 1 Tim 1:5, 19; 3:9; Titus 1:15). Not only should each Christian strive to live before God and his neighbor with a good conscience, but he should also try to keep others in the congregation from the burden of a stained conscience.

The Corinthian situation may be compared with the mission field, where new converts often find it difficult to rid themselves entirely of their old fears of witchcraft and ancestral spirits. In countries like Papua New Guinea, the earliest converts often resisted suggestions from missionaries that they use traditional musical instruments like the kundu drum in their worship services. They explained that they could not hear these instruments without hearing the voice of the spirits. Later generations of Christians who never participated in the pagan practices were able to incorporate the drum in worship.

The words of 8:8a ("food will not present us to God") are in accord with Paul's position set forth elsewhere. He taught that "the kingdom of God is not food and drink, but righteousness and peace and joy in the Holy Spirit" (Rom 14:17). His attitude to rules about food and drink was similar to his stance on circumcision: for those in Christ Jesus it had become a matter of no importance. What really counted was "faith active in love" (Gal 5:6; cf. 1 Cor 7:19; Gal 6:15).

So if a Christian felt he must refrain from idol-food, Paul assured him he was at no disadvantage; he was not missing out on anything. By the same token, the Christian who participated in these meals should not think he was in any way superior.

The guiding principle is to be Christian love, which "builds up." Knowledge on the other hand, can puff up those who think they possess it (8:1). The apostle warns the Corinthians not to let their authority (8:9) as liberated Christian people go to their heads (cf. the slogan "all things are permissible" in 6:12; 10:23). They had become "puffed up" (4:19; 5:2) and arrogant in their newfound knowledge, as if in their sovereign freedom they could do anything they pleased. Paul wryly remarks that they had better watch that "this authority of yours doesn't become a stumbling block to the weak" (8:9), leading them into grave spiritual danger (8:10–13). True spiritual knowledge should always result in love for the Christian brother (Gal 5:13), especially the weak.

Paul now spells out his specific concern. Although many pagan Greeks and Romans no longer ascribed any significance to the old myths and deities, they continued to frequent the temples for social reasons. Once they became Christians, it was easy to rationalize that, after all, no divinities really inhabited these temples, the idols on show there were merely wood and stone, and the sacrificial food was merely food, a part of God's creation. Thus, (they would argue) they could continue to accept invitations to dine in these sanctuaries, even in the more overtly idolatrous context of the dining rooms of Demeter's sanctuary, thereby avoiding a painful breach with friends from their pagan past.

But Paul's question takes up the effect of this libertine attitude on the weaker brother. Far from being a support to the brother who still struggles with his conscience, far from building him up in the faith, "you" (8:11–12), by this public display of your rights and "Christian freedom," are only fortifying him to act against his conscience. To you, perhaps, the food is merely food, but to your brother it is still idol-food; he cannot rid his conscience of the thought that this food has been sacrificed to an idol. 1 Cor 8:10–13 is a stern condemnation of the loveless behavior of those who claimed to have superior knowledge.

While the self-confident Christian blithely goes ahead and parades his Christian "knowledge" and "freedom," he seems to be either unaware or completely careless of the effect his behavior is having on his weaker brother. Paul brings it home to every Christian that, in allowing himself to become puffed up with his knowledge, he has become *personally* responsible ("you" and "your" in 8:10–11) for jeopardizing his brother's salvation. This brother is being ruined spiritually (8:11; cf. 1:18; 10:9–10; 15:18). Four times in the last three verses of the chapter Paul reminds the Corinthian Christians that the weak Christian is their brother.

Paul's argument here, as throughout the final verses of the chapter, closely parallels his longer discourse in Romans 14 on the relationship between Christians. There his concern is twofold: that the weak should not judge the strong, and the strong should not despise the weak. Here his pastoral rebuke is directed only at the arrogance of those who sin against the "weak" and thereby sin against Christ (8:12), who had died for all, even the most fragile and despised (8:11; 2 Cor 11:14–15; Is 42:3).

PASTORAL IMPLICATIONS FOR TODAY

At first sight, the issue of idol-foods may seem to have little relevance today, since the eating of meat sacrificed to an idol is no longer an issue in Western Christianity. However, the principle of brotherly love which Paul enunciates does have broad application: "If food causes my brother to fall, I will never eat meat to eternity, lest I cause my brother to fall" (1 Cor 8:13). It is never appropriate to flaunt one's "Christian freedom" and thereby lead a vulnerable brother to do something against his conscience. To do so is to sin against Christ himself (8:12).

This will be true also regarding the Corinthians' abuses of the Lord's Supper. Because the body and blood of Christ are present with the bread and wine, the person who partakes unworthily sins against the Lord's body and blood (11:27–32). Such sins bring God's judgment (11:29–30). This requires the church, especially the pastor, to exercise discretion in the practice of Holy Communion (see the section "Closed Communion" at 11:27–34).

Moreover, while idol-meat has ceased to be an issue in the West, close parallels to the situation in Corinth may be found in countries newly opened up to Christianity, where the eating of food offered to ancestral spirits and the pouring of libations to invoke and appease them (not to mention other occult practices) are still live issues. In the West, comparable situations often arise. Many western Christians have been tempted to associate with pagan cults or to dabble in the occult (séances, Ouija boards, palmistry, astrology). Many more have been led astray by the multifaceted demonic temptations of a secular culture, for example, by certain forms of music and entertainment, or participation in certain clubs and fraternal orders like the Masons. In its broadest sense, idolatry includes every activity and thing in which people revel apart from God and his good gifts (e.g., materialism). As Luther said (LC I 21), "Idolatry does not consist merely of erecting an image and praying to it. It is primarily in the heart, which pursues other things and seeks help and consolation from creatures, saints, or devils."

The Christian faith, on the other hand, is opposed to all forms of idolatry and syncretism (cf. 1 Jn 5:20–21). Just as the OT prophets condemned Baal worship as incompatible with the biblical faith, so Paul would ask the Corinthians: "What accord has Christ with Belial? Or what part has a believer with an unbeliever? And what agreement has the temple of God with idols?" (2 Cor 6:15–16 NKJV). Thus, Christians may not enter into syncretistic associations with pagan cults.

Paul's concern that the brother not be destroyed may be applied even more broadly in areas of Christian ethics. How many Christians from cultures lacking a tradition of moderate drinking or how many recovered alcoholics or alcoholics' children have not been gravely offended by the flaunting of alcohol common in some Christian circles? Incitement to a gambling fling, or to other activities over which some Christians have scruples, or for which they have a weakness, also falls under the apostle's condemnation. It is one thing to thumb one's nose at pharisaical Christians; it is quite another thing when one's "Christian freedom" becomes the occasion of another's spiritual ruin.

Paul impresses on the Corinthian Christians that their conduct in the temples is not a sign of superior knowledge, nor the mark of free people; it is simply sinful. Far from helping and strengthening those with weak consciences, their brothers are hitting them when they are down. The verb "to strike, beat" in 8:12 is normally used in the NT for a physical blow (e.g., Acts 23:2), but here Paul uses it of a blow to a person's spirit.

In sinning against the least of Jesus' brothers, a Christian is sinning against Christ himself (1 Cor 8:12). Even the least important members of the church are temples of the Holy Spirit (3:16–17; 6:19) and vital parts of the body of Christ (6:15; 12:12–27).

In 1 Cor 8:13, Paul draws the conclusion to the first part of his argument concerning idol-meat. With a strong "therefore" (8:13), he informs the complacent Christians of the lengths to which he is prepared to go for the sake of his *brother.* If he became aware that something as peripheral to Christ's kingdom as food was ruining his brother, he would become a vegetarian for eternity. Twice in 8:13 Paul calls the "weak" Christian *"my brother."* Without question, his brother's eternal welfare is far more important than food.

This is not Paul's final word on meals in heathen temples. After what appears to be a long digression, he returns to the topic in 10:19–22 and absolutely forbids participation in pagan meals. His later discussion takes into account the Lord's Supper (10:16–17; 11:17–34), which is the Christian counterpart to pagan idol feasts. Thus, in chapter 8 Paul gives a preliminary response to the Corinthians' question. He admonishes them for being puffed up by their knowledge (8:1, 11) and for their abuse of Christian freedom, and he reminds them of the implications of the Gospel. If the Lord Jesus Christ had willingly sacrificed himself for the weakest brother (8:11), should they not also be willing to forego certain luxuries out of loving consideration for the brother?

9:1–27

The Apostolic Example of Lovingly Renouncing Rights

1 CORINTHIANS 9:1–2
A FREE APOSTLE

TRANSLATION

9 [1]Am I not free? Am I not an apostle? Have I not seen Jesus our Lord? Are you not my handiwork in the Lord? [2]If I am not an apostle to others, at least I am to you; for you are the seal of my apostleship in the Lord.

COMMENTARY

At first glance, chapter 9 may seem to interrupt the flow of Paul's discussion of idol-meat, which was the topic of chapter 8 and to which he will return in 10:14–11:1. Some have suggested that this discourse on his apostleship is a digression or an insertion from another letter. But closer study shows that the passage is integrally linked to the preceding argument. Paul has been chiding the believers who were puffed up with their knowledge (8:1) for their blithe disregard of the brother with a weak conscience (8:7–12). As we have seen, he concluded by changing the focus from the Corinthians ("you are sinning," 8:12) to himself, saying in essence: "If I saw that food was offending my brother, I would give up meat for good" (8:13).

Chapter 9, then, elaborates Paul's attitude as an apostle. He practices what he preaches. He is willing to give up his apostolic privileges, doing whatever it takes to win others to the Gospel. Of course, he has the right to eat and drink, to be married, and to receive support from the Corinthian congregation (9:4–7). But apparently his refusal to accept support struck the Corinthians as being particularly strange, accustomed as they were to their own philosophers and sophists, who thought it beneath their dignity to work with their hands. They were used to people in privileged positions exploiting their opportunities with no consideration for others. By renouncing his privileges, Paul is emphasizing that salvation is a free gift of God (Eph 2:8–9).

In the face of the Corinthians' misunderstanding of his motives, it is not surprising that Paul begins this new section of his argument with a series of sixteen rhetorical questions in the first fourteen verses.

At the outset, Paul asks four questions in rapid succession, all expecting the answer yes. The first asserts his Christian freedom: "Am I not free?" (9:1). Paul is saying: "I am not inferior to you. I share your knowledge that idols and idol-meat are nothing. Like you, my conscience allows me to eat all foods. I, too, am free in the Gospel."

"Indeed," he continues, "I possess even greater privileges. Am I not an apostle? Don't I possess all the knowledge and authority of an apostle and teacher of the church? And didn't I see Jesus our Lord with my own eyes on the Damascus road?" (cf. 1 Jn 1:1). Here Paul reminds them of the dramatic encounter which had transformed the persecutor into an apostle (Acts 9; 22; 26). Although he had not been associated with Jesus during his earthly ministry, ever since that day on the road to Damascus Paul possessed an apostle's most important qualification: he was "an eye-witness of his [Jesus'] resurrection" (Acts 1:22). Jesus had appeared to him "last of all, as to one prematurely born" (1 Cor 15:8). Paul never ceased to be amazed by the privilege so undeservedly bestowed on him. As he put it, the Lord appeared "even . . . to me" (15:8).

With the fourth question ("Are you not my handiwork in the Lord?" 9:1), Paul reminds them that they owed him their very existence as Christians. It was from his hand that they had received their freedom from the shackles of idolatry. He was their father in Christ (4:15). For a year and six months he had labored among them, and the Lord had blessed his planting of the Word (3:5–7; see also Acts 18:11). Now this congregation was a tribute to his skillful handiwork as master-builder in Corinth (1 Cor 3:10). The Corinthians were his pride and joy, his letter of recommendation (2 Cor 3:1–3; cf. 1 Thess 2:19–20).

Cephas, James, and John had concentrated on preaching to the Jews (Gal 2:9). Other apostles were laying the church's foundation (1 Cor 3:11) in other areas, and Paul had no wish to encroach on their territory (Rom 15:20–21). Paul recognizes that Christians in these regions owed allegiance to their own fathers in the faith rather than to himself. But it was otherwise in Corinth. He declares, "If I am not an apostle to others, at least I am to you; for you are the seal of my apostleship in the Lord" (1 Cor 9:2). It could not be denied that Paul had a special relationship to the Corinthian church. Indeed, the existence of that vibrant church was an outstanding recommendation of his apostolic ministry; it was a "letter . . . known and read by all people" (2 Cor 3:2; cf. Acts 18:7–11). Anyone who doubted the validity of his call need only look at the Corinthian church.

1 CORINTHIANS 9:3–14

Four Proofs of the Apostles' Right to Support

TRANSLATION

**9 [3]This is my defense to those who are putting me
under scrutiny: [4]Do we not have a right to eat and
drink? [5]Do we not have a right to take along a sister
as a wife, like the rest of the apostles and the Lord's
brothers and Cephas? [6]Or do only Barnabas and
I not have the right to refrain from working?**

**[7]Who ever serves as a soldier at his own expense?
Who plants a vineyard and does not eat its
fruit? Or who tends a flock and does not get
sustenance from the milk of the flock?**

**[8]Am I saying these things merely from a human point
of view? Does not the Law also say this? [9]For in the
Law of Moses it is written: "You shall not muzzle the
ox while it is threshing the grain." Does God care
about oxen? [10]Is he not speaking entirely for our
sake? Of course, it was written for our sake, because
the plowman should plow in hope, and the man who
threshes should do so in hope of a share in the crop.
[11]If we, for your benefit, sowed spiritual blessings, is
it [too] much [to expect] if we will reap your material
blessings? [12]If others share this authority over you,
do we not [have it] even more? But we did not take
advantage of this right. Rather, we endure everything,
lest we cause a hindrance to the Gospel of Christ. [13]Do
you not know that those who perform the sacred rites
receive their sustenance from the temple, that those
who serve at the altar receive a share with the altar?**

**[14]So the Lord commanded those who preach
the Gospel to live from the Gospel.**

COMMENTARY

APOSTOLIC PRACTICE (9:4–6)

Paul will now invoke four authorities to confirm his right to receive a living wage as compensation for his work as an apostle. The first is the conduct of the other apostles. Although it was obvious that the Lord had blessed Paul's ministry in Corinth, some of the factious members were questioning whether he was a genuine apostle. They argued that he had refused financial support because he knew he could not receive such support with a good conscience; he knew he had no apostolic "authority" or "right" (9:4–6, 12, 18) to it. It has been suggested that it was particularly the wealthier members of the church who had been hurt by his refusal of support and were now lobbying against him. Against such critics he now defends himself.

Paul is emphatic (9:4) that he and his co-workers (men like Barnabas, 9:6, and Timothy, 4:17) had every right to expect financial support from the Corinthians. As he will argue at length (9:4–14), the laborer is worthy of his hire (Lk 10:7; 1 Cor 9:14). Some Christians in Corinth had asserted their right to eat idol-meat in all kinds of situations (8:9–10). Paul responds: "We have rights, too, and totally legitimate rights. But (as he will argue later) we have renounced our rights for the sake of the Gospel and the brother."

A closely related question follows in 9:5. Does the missionary not also have the right to take a Christian woman (a "sister") along with him as his wife, and count on the church to maintain her as well? The Corinthians were aware that this was the general practice of the other apostles. The Lord's half brothers, James, Joseph, Simon, and Judas (Mt 13:55; Mk 6:3) were also in the habit of taking their wives along on their journeys for the Gospel (1 Cor 9:5). Finally, Paul mentions Cephas, the leader of the eleven original apostles (9:5). That Peter was a married man is well known from the gospel story of Jesus healing Peter's mother-in-law (Mt 8:14–15; Mk 1:29–31; Lk 4:38–39). This reference to Peter's married status, as if everyone in Corinth was familiar with it, has led many to think Peter must have visited Corinth. However, it is not necessary to assume this; the lives and activities of the apostles were of general interest to all Christians and would have been familiar to many who had never met them.

The Corinthians were also aware that most of the apostles devoted themselves to their ministry full time. Paul, Barnabas, and their companions stood out as exceptions. On his arrival in Corinth, Paul had stayed with Aquila and Priscilla "because they were of the same trade . . . and he [Paul] was working, for by trade they were tentmakers" (Acts 18:2–3). Although Barnabas and Paul had gone their separate ways since the end of the first missionary journey, it seems Barnabas had continued the habit of supporting himself, and this was well known to the Corinthians. As Greek intellectuals tended to despise manual labor, some members of the congregation may have been embarrassed that their leader and teacher demeaned himself in this manner. Paul's argument here follows a similar pattern to 2 Thess 3:8–9, where he counters a tendency to idleness. But while "tentmaking ministry" was his practice in Corinth, Paul insisted on his right to full support from the church.

CUSTOM (9:7)

By means of three rhetorical questions in 9:7, each beginning with the word "who," Paul argues from common custom that everyone considers to be only right and fair. In everyday life, it is considered proper that the laborer should receive sustenance on the basis of what his labor produces. Paul supplies examples from the life of a soldier, a vine grower, and a shepherd. It is noteworthy that Scripture often pictures God's people as an army, a vineyard, and a flock (e.g., Eph 6:10–17; Is 5:1–7; Ps 80:8–16; Ezek 34).

THE OLD TESTAMENT LAW (9:8–13)

Paul now asks (9:8) whether his use of human analogies in 9:7 suggests he is speaking from a merely human perspective. This rhetorical question expects the answer "of course not!" Rather, his line of argument has the support of divine Law as laid down in the OT.

Paul explains himself by pointing to the passage in the Pentateuch ("the Law of Moses," 9:9) where he finds the principle that the church worker should be maintained by the church. The passage is found in the fifth book of Moses, in Deut 25:4: "You shall not muzzle the ox while it is threshing the grain." Israel's farmers used oxen to pull a threshing sledge around a threshing floor until the kernels of grain were separated from the husks. The Mosaic Law prescribes that, while the ox is busy threshing, it should be permitted to eat some of the grain. This text is embedded in a context which inculcates fair treatment of one's fellow human beings, whether it be the poor neighbor, the poor and needy laborer, the alien, the orphan, the widow, or the condemned man (Deut 24:10–25:3). The God who cares even for the sparrow is laying down the principle that all have a right to payment for their services.

In this ancient text from the Mosaic Law, Paul maintains, God is speaking *"entirely for our sake"* (1 Cor 9:10). For the sake of all who sow spiritual things among you, so he argues, (9:11), this text was written, in order to assure us that the church is obliged to support her ministers.

Paul's insistence that God is speaking "entirely" for our sake (9:10), coupled with his denial that God is concerned for oxen (9:9), may be best understood as a Semitic manner of speech, where the lesser of two good things is regarded as subordinate and is denied altogether, as in Hos 6:6, where God says, "I desire mercy and not sacrifice," and Ezek 20:25, "I myself gave them statutes which were not good."

Many biblical passages reaffirm the Creator's compassionate concern for all his creatures (e.g., Ps 104:11; Mt 6:26). The rabbis took a great interest in Deut

25:4, interpreting it as an example of an argument from lesser to greater: "If God cares for oxen, how much more will he care for us!" We may compare Jesus' argument in Lk 12:6–7: "Are not five sparrows sold for two copper coins? And not one of them is forgotten before God. . . . Do not fear; you are of more value than many sparrows." Thus, Paul draws out the primary application of the Mosaic words. They apply even more to human beings than they do to oxen.

The phrase "it was written" in 1 Cor 9:10 harks back again to the quotation of Deut 25:4 in 1 Cor 9:9. Of course the Deuteronomy text was written for us, Paul continues, "because the plowman should plow in hope, and the man who threshes should do so in hope of a share in the crop" (9:10). The phrase "in hope" is in an emphatic position at the beginning of the first clause; it is then repeated in the clause about the one who threshes. The worker should live in confident expectation that his labors will be rewarded. Paul will use Deut 25:4 again in 1 Timothy (5:17–18) to undergird his insistence that pastors must be properly paid.

In 1 Cor 9:11, Paul continues with imagery from agriculture, but now it is not plowing and threshing but sowing. As the plowman and the thresher live in hope of a share in the harvest, so those who sow the seed may rightly anticipate their share in the crop. Back in 3:6, he said that he had "planted" the Corinthian church, and Apollos had "watered" it, though it was God who gave the growth. Under the plural "we sowed" in 9:11, Paul is probably including Silas and Timothy, who worked alongside him in Corinth (Acts 18:5). The if-clause is a condition of fact: Paul, Silas, and Timothy did in fact sow spiritual things (1 Cor 9:11) for the Corinthians' benefit. So it would not be extraordinary if they expected some material rewards in return; indeed, such compensation was *owed* to them. Paul presents a similar argument in Rom 15:27 to persuade his Gentile converts to support the collection for the poor saints in Jerusalem: "If the Gentiles have come to share in their spiritual blessings, they ought also to be of service to them in material things" (cf. also Gal 6:6).

Other sowers of the seed in Corinth had exercised their right to receive support from the believers (1 Cor 9:12). Presumably, Paul means Apollos and possibly Peter as well. Most likely, it was the contrast between their willingness to accept support and the refusal by Paul, Silas, and Timothy to follow suit that led some in Corinth to surmise that Paul and his colleagues felt they had no right to it. However, Paul continues, the very opposite was the case. As the founders of the church, Silas, Timothy, and he himself had an even greater right to support than Apollos and Peter. But, as Paul begins to explain, he and his fellow workers had not taken advantage of this right (see 9:15–18 for a fuller explanation). They were willing to put up with the hardship of "working two jobs"—working with their hands while making the most of every opportunity to preach the Gospel. This had been their normal practice ever since they began the mission in Thessalonica (1 Thess 2:9–10; 2 Thess 3:8).

As Paul will explain more fully in 1 Cor 9:15–18, his overriding concern had always been the advance of the Gospel. This was his consuming passion. Anything that stood in the way of the Gospel's free course had to be removed. While he does not spell out precisely what "hindrance" (9:12) he foresaw that could obstruct the Gospel in Corinth, it is reasonable to assume he wanted to make absolutely certain to the Corinthians that the free Gospel of God's grace was just that: it came to them totally free of charge; there was nothing they could do to earn it or buy it. Thus, Paul and his colleagues were careful to distance themselves from the itinerant philosophers and rhetoricians, the "wisdom" peddlers of their day, who provided their services for a fee (cf. 2 Cor 2:17; 1 Thess 2:5–10). The divine wisdom of the free Gospel is totally different from what the worldly wise have to offer (1 Cor 1:18–25); by dispensing with their right to remuneration, Paul and his team were trying to portray that message as graphically as possible.

Paul is not done establishing the church worker's right to support from his people. In 9:13–14, he offers two more pieces of evidence. First, he speaks of the common principle that those who officiated in the ancient temple could expect to be sustained by the gifts offered there. According to the OT, the priests were to be supported by those parts of the offerings that were kept from the fire, by the firstfruits of the harvest, and the meat of firstborn animals that were clean (Num 18:5–20; Deut 18:1–3). The Levites were to live from the tithes that the Israelites presented as their temple offerings (Num 18:21–32).

THE LORD'S COMMAND (9:14)

Paul has appealed to apostolic practice (9:4–6), to custom (9:7), and to the OT Law (9:8–13). The final piece of evidence which clinches the argument is a word from the Lord Jesus himself. Paul phrases Christ's command as a general principle: "Those who preach the Gospel [are] to live from the Gospel" (9:14). This principle may be gleaned from a number of passages in the gospels, especially from the practice of Jesus himself during the three years of his public ministry.

One statement of Christ that supports the principle Paul asserts is this: "The laborer is worthy of his wages" (Lk 10:7). Matthew's gospel also records this command (Mt 10:10). Originally this was spoken in the context of Jesus sending out the seventy-two with the command that they stay as guests in the houses of their receptive hearers, "eating and drinking whatever they give you" (Lk 10:7). Paul saw this command as having general application to all ministers of the Gospel: their claim to the church's support has the backing of a dominical decree. It is significant that this word of Jesus was directed to the full company of the seventy-two, not just the twelve apostles. Therefore, it has a wider application to all kinds of ministers of the Gospel in the church today.

THE SUPPORT OF MINISTERS TODAY

In 1 Cor 9:3–14, there is a message both for those who downplay the church's responsibility to support its workers, and on the other hand, for those church workers who demand lavish or burdensome support from their congregations. Normally, ministry is a full-time calling, and its demands require the full attention and energy of those called to minister. Those who overzealously or unfairly promote part-time ministry, expecting workers also to be engaged in another line of work, may cause the church to be short-changed. The tone of Paul's words would suggest that ministers have the right to be supported sufficiently to allow them to devote their undivided attention to the work of the Gospel. Support was freely given to the eleven apostles, with Paul and Barnabas as exceptions, not as the rule (9:6).

At the same time, Paul's example certainly stands as a testimony against any church workers who might think of the ministry as a for-profit commercial enterprise. Especially for missionaries and church planters, the Christians among whom they serve may be too few in number or too limited in financial resources to support them. Alternate sources of support may be necessary, such as the assistance of other congregations or the larger church body. The minister's priority must be the Gospel, not money or any other form of worldly gain, in accord with the apostle's eschatological outlook: "The time has been shortened, so that from now on those who [are] . . . buying [should live] as if they didn't own anything, and those using the world as not abusing it. For the form of this world is passing away" (7:29–31).

1 CORINTHIANS 9:15–18

Paul's Decision Not to Exercise His Rights

TRANSLATION

9 [15]**But I have not taken advantage of any of these**
[rights]. Nor am I writing these things in order that
this should happen in my case. For it is better for me
to die than—this boast of mine no one will nullify.
[16]**For if I preach the Gospel, that is nothing for me**
to boast about. For I am under compulsion; for woe
to me if I do not preach the Gospel. [17]**For if I am**
doing this voluntarily, I have a reward. But if [I do
it] involuntarily, I am entrusted with a stewardship.
[18]**What is my reward, then? That in preaching the**
Gospel I should offer the Gospel free of charge,
in order not to abuse my right in the Gospel.

COMMENTARY

Having thoroughly established his right to maintenance by the congregation in 9:3–14, Paul returns in 9:15 to the point he began to make in 9:12: "we did not take advantage of this right." But now he speaks only for himself. He can assure the Corinthians that in his ministry among them, *he himself* has never used any of the rights to material support articulated in 9:4–6. Nor should his detailed insistence on his right to such support be construed as if he were seeking to secure support in the future (9:15). For his practice of preaching the Gospel free of charge means so much to him that he would rather "die than—" (9:15). Here his emotions get the better of him, and he cannot complete his train of thought.

Throughout his ministry in Corinth, he has taken justifiable pride in being a "living paradigm" of the way the free Gospel comes to people "without price" (Is 55:1). And he is absolutely determined—so he finally continues—that no one will rob him of what he has taken so much pride in (see also 2 Cor 11:7–11).

Paul could not boast of his activity as a Gospel preacher, for he was under compulsion (1 Cor 9:16). That could be traced back to his divine call to be an apostle of Jesus Christ with a special commission to the Gentiles (Rom 11:13). His preaching of the Gospel, then, was simply discharging the debt that had been laid on him (Rom 1:14). There are two ways of incurring a debt. The first is when we borrow money from someone; the second is when someone entrusts us with money that he asks us to hand on to someone else. Until we actually hand it on, we stand indebted to the person for whom it is intended. Paul's debt was of this second kind. He had been entrusted with the Gospel and was obligated to preach it to others (cf. Jer 20:9). If he failed to discharge that debt, then "woe" (1 Cor 9:16) to him; he would have to face God's wrath.

Just as there are two ways of incurring a debt, so there are also two ways in which a person can carry out a task: either as a free person or as an involuntary conscript. If a person is free and does the work voluntarily, then he is entitled to a reward. But this is not the case with Paul. The first sentence in 1 Cor 9:17 merely sets up the contrast with 9:17b, which does apply to Paul: "but if [I do it] involuntarily, I am entrusted with a stewardship." Paul understood himself as a slave of Jesus Christ (Rom 1:1; Gal 1:10; Phil 1:1; Titus 1:1). He had no choice but to preach the Gospel. He was a "steward" entrusted with "the mysteries of God," and he was expected to carry out his commission faithfully (1 Cor 4:1–2; see also Eph 3:2).

Paul found enormous satisfaction in presenting the free Gospel free of charge (1 Cor 9:18). Consequently, no one could impugn the purity of his motives. Obviously he was not just another religious peddler, but a man of sincerity (2 Cor 2:17).

Our contemporary application of Paul's argument in 1 Cor 9:1–18 needs to be well balanced. There are two messages here, one for the church, the other for the minister. On the one hand, the principle that "the laborer is worthy of his wages" (Lk 10:7) certainly applies today. Churches must realize that ministers of the Gospel are entitled to their salary and benefits. The church benefits greatly when its ministers are sufficiently compensated so that they may devote themselves single-mindedly to the Gospel, free of worldly cares. Also, Paul freely chose not to accept what was owed him. The church did not pressure him to forego compensation; in fact, the pressure from the church seems to have been for him to accept pay.

On the other hand, concern for the Gospel itself must not be lost, nor should any "hindrance" (1 Cor 9:12) be put in the way of the Gospel. There may be circumstances today, also, when the church servant will decide to forgo some of his rights. Indeed, for the Gospel's sake—when the situation has called for it—many of God's servants have worked for minimal pay or even supported themselves from their own resources. The minister is given the model of Paul's selfless and sacrificial labor free of charge, which in turn imitates the ministry of Christ himself.

1 CORINTHIANS 9:19–23
All Things to All People

TRANSLATION

9 [19]For although I am free of all people, I have made
myself a slave to all, in order that I might win as many
as possible. [20]And to the Jews I became as a Jew, that
I might win Jews; to those under Law [I became] like
someone under Law (although I myself am not under
Law), that I might win those under Law; [21]to those
without Law [I became] like someone without Law
(although I am not without God's Law, but obedient
to the law of Christ), that I might win those without
Law. [22]To the weak I became weak, that I might win
the weak. To all people I have become all things, that
I might by all means save some. [23]I do it all for the
sake of the Gospel, that I might share in its blessings.

COMMENTARY

Paul has been defending his high calling and special standing in the church as a free apostle of the Lord Jesus (9:1–18). By maintaining his financial independence (9:15–18), he has made sure he is beholden to no one but his Lord. No one could manipulate him on the basis of favors rendered or owed.

Thus, in not seeking favors or financial privileges, even those he had a "right" to expect (9:4–6, 18), Paul had shown in every way the mind-set of a servant, in response to Jesus' challenge (Mt 20:26–28). Paul and his colleagues saw themselves as the Corinthians' slaves for Jesus' sake (2 Cor 4:5). By this humble approach, Paul aimed to win as many as possible for the Gospel. To be sure, the church would never be more than a minority in the community ("some," 1 Cor 9:22). But Paul had been assured that the Lord had "many people" in the city (Acts 18:10), and the apostle's ministry was designed to make good on that assurance by winning all he could for Christ.

Paul now gives four illustrations of how he had adapted his mission strategy to win different groups: (1) the Jews (9:20a); (2) those under Law (9:20b); (3) those without Law (9:21); (4) the weak (9:22).

His first concern was for his Jewish kinsmen. Although his calling was to be the apostle to the Gentiles (Rom 11:13; cf. 1 Tim 2:7), Paul still saw himself as under obligation to "the Jew first" (Rom 1:16). After all, the faith Paul preached was the fulfillment of Israel's ancient hope (Acts 26:6–7; 28:20). It was a constant source of sorrow to Paul that most of his fellow Jews had rejected the Gospel. That they might find salvation was the constant burden of his prayers (Rom 10:1) and a high priority in his ministry.

Thus, it was his policy in each town to begin his ministry in the synagogue, appealing to the Jews first. In fact, he did not hesitate to magnify his mission to Gentiles before Jewish audiences, in order to provoke his kinsmen to jealousy and thus save *some* of them (Rom 11:14).

To win the Jews, Paul knew he must become "as a Jew" (1 Cor 9:20). Accordingly, he was careful never to cause them unnecessary offense. He had Timothy circumcised "because of the Jews in those areas" (Acts 16:3). He also joined four Jewish men in the temple who were under a vow, purifying himself with them and paying their expenses (Acts 21:20–26).

The second part of 1 Cor 9:20, where Paul speaks of his eagerness to win "those under Law," is probably an expansion of 9:20a to include not only the Jews but also the numerous Gentile God-fearers who loved the Jewish people, attended synagogue, and willingly subjected themselves to many aspects of Jewish law. These people were attracted to Christianity in great numbers. Although Paul had turned his back on a punctilious observance of the OT ceremonial law and no longer saw himself as "under Law" but as "under grace" (Rom 6:14), he did not make an arrogant display of his new freedom but reached out to God-fearers in a sympathetic way, humbly identifying himself with them in order to win them for the Gospel.

Likewise Paul had become "to those without Law like someone without Law" (1 Cor 9:21). Gentile converts, he insisted, had no need to practice circumcision and observe the Jewish food laws, festivals, and Sabbath regulations (Col 2:16). The apostle was adamant that Titus, whose parents were both Gentile, must not be circumcised (Gal 2:3). As long as Gentiles believed the Gospel and were baptized, Paul was satisfied. After all, what mattered was not ceremonies but "faith active in love" (Gal 5:6).

When Paul calls the Gentiles "those without Law" and says that he, too, became as one "without Law" (1 Cor 9:21), he is not condoning immoral behavior. In 1 Corinthians 5, for example, Paul stated in the strongest terms that Gentile Christians must conform to God's moral Law. The expression in 1 Cor 9:21 refers to the Gentiles' status as people who lacked the Mosaic Law. To be sure, Gentiles had some sense for the requirements of natural law; "the work of the law" was written on their hearts (Rom 2:15). But the Jews had an advantage in that the divine law had been spelled out for them in a written code.

Lest his readers get the impression that Paul does not care about God's Law, he adds the qualification that he is "not without God's Law but obedient to the law of Christ" (1 Cor 9:21). By this he means he is subject to the pattern of self-sacrificing love which Jesus had inculcated and exemplified by his death on the cross. Paul bears the burdens of others and thus fulfills "the law of Christ" (Gal 6:2). In his outreach to Jews, God-fearers, Gentiles, and the weak, this law governs everything Paul does.

In 1 Cor 9:22, Paul now brings the argument full circle to his original concern for the weak Christians in Corinth (8:7–13). Although Paul himself had the "knowledge" that idols are nothing and that meat sacrificed to them is just meat (1 Cor 8:1–6), nevertheless he humbly identified with the weak and avoided anything that would give unnecessary offense (8:7–13). The expression "the weak" may have a twofold aspect—weak in the sense of vulnerable to peer pressure and more easily led into sin (8:10), and also weak in economic status. Most members of the congregation were not well educated, influential, or of noble birth (1:26–31). Many of them would have worked with their hands for a living. Paul had not held himself aloof from these humble people but had identified with them by taking up his tent-making trade. Thus, he exemplified his own maxim, "Do not be haughty, but associate with the lowly" (Rom 12:16 ESV). It is possible that those who were economically "weak" were more likely to be swayed by the actions of the affluent, while those who flaunted their supposed freedoms to indulge in sinful behavior were mostly the well-to-do.

Paul's flexibility in accommodating himself to all people was governed by one overriding purpose: "that I might by all means save some" (1 Cor 9:22). In this, he was modeling himself after his Master, who ate and drank with tax collector s and sinners (Mt 11:19), accepted water from a Samaritan woman and engaged in conversation with her (John 4), and healed the daughter of the Syro-Phoenician woman (Mk 7:24–30)—all for the great purpose of seeking and saving the lost (Lk 19:10). Just as Jesus had accommodated himself to those around him, without compromising his message, so Paul showed himself a model of missionary adaptability to the language and thought-forms of his hearers. In preaching to Jews, he made rich use of the OT (e.g., Acts 13:16–41). In addressing the Hellenistic Gentiles on the Areopagus in Athens, he drew instead on his knowledge of Greek poetry and philosophy (Acts 17:22–31). Fluent both in Greek and in Aramaic, he could switch from one to the other in order to captivate an audience (Acts 21:37–22:2). He was thoroughly conversant with both Jewish and Hellenistic culture (his familiarity with the latter will shortly become evident in the illustration drawn from the Isthmian Games in 1 Cor 9:24–27). But Paul carried his learning lightly; all was placed in the service of bringing salvation to the lost.

With all his concern to adapt himself to people, nowhere does Paul suggest the Gospel itself may be changed to suit people's religious or cultural tastes (cf. Gal 1:6–9). In 1 Cor 1:18–25, Paul described how God deliberately chose to save people through the preaching of a message that was "foolish" and "weak"—the very opposite of how people might expect God to save. But in the face of enormous pressure to conform his message to the world's wisdom, Paul was determined to know only Christ crucified (2:2). Through the Gospel, and only through the Gospel, do people find salvation. That is why it was so important that those entrusted with the Gospel "be unoffensive to Jews and to Greeks and to the church of God" (10:32). Paul had set the Corinthians a good example: "I please all people in all things, not seeking my own advantage, but that of the many, that they may be saved" (10:33).

In humbly serving the Gospel, Paul hoped that he would join fellow believers in enjoying the saving benefits of the Gospel (9:23). He was well aware of the possibility that he could fail to attain the salvation he proclaimed to others (9:27). Like every preacher of the Gospel, he must remain faithful until "the day of our Lord Jesus Christ" (1:8; see also 3:13; 5:5).

1 CORINTHIANS 9:24–27

SELF-DISCIPLINE TO WIN AN IMPERISHABLE PRIZE

TRANSLATION

9 24 Do you not know that those who run in the stadium
all run, but [only] one receives the prize? So run
that you may win! 25 Now every contestant exercises
self-control in all things. They do it that they may
receive a perishable wreath. But we [do it that we
may receive] an imperishable one. 26 So I do not run
aimlessly; I do not box like someone beating the air.
27 But I pommel my body and enslave [it], lest after
preaching to others I myself should be disqualified.

COMMENTARY

Paul proceeds to illustrate the need for self-discipline if he is to reach the goal of saving as many people as possible (9:22). As a resident of Corinth in AD 50–52, he had probably witnessed the Isthmian Games in the spring of AD 51. This prestigious event, second only to the Olympic Games, was celebrated every two years about ten miles from Corinth. The basic athletic events included racing, wrestling, jumping, boxing, hurling the javelin, and throwing the discus. Paul begins with an illustration from the footraces in the stadium. A number of runners competed in each event, but only one could win the prize. The analogy to the Christian life is, of course, imperfect, for in the Christian race all believers are prize winners. But Paul uses the analogy only to point to the exertion and self-discipline required of the successful runner. He challenges the Corinthians: "Run that you may win" (9:24).

Every entrant in the Olympic Games was required to devote ten months to strict training. Presumably the same rule applied to the games at Isthmia. As is well known from such contests both in ancient and modern times, the competitor must renounce not only bad habits, but give up many things that are fine in themselves, in order to focus totally on preparation for the goal. The theme of self-control applies equally to the Christian life (9:25). Self-control is one of the fruits of the Spirit that should be found in the lives of all Christians (Gal 5:23; 2 Pet 1:6). It is one of the qualities essential in a minister of the Gospel (Titus 1:8). Whereas contestants in the Isthmian Games exercised self-control in order to win a wreath of withered celery and some ephemeral honor and glory, it is infinitely more worthwhile for the Christian to practice self-control, for the crown awaiting him—if he completes the race—is the imperishable gift of eternal life (2 Tim 4:8; James 1:12; 1 Pet 5:4; Rev 2:10).

Paul now applies the imagery of the stadium to his own example as the Corinthians' apostle (1 Cor 9:26). It was not his practice to run the race of the Christian life aimlessly (2 Tim 4:7), like someone with no clear goal. Rather, he pressed on "toward the goal for the prize [same word as in 1 Cor 9:24] of the upward call of God in Christ Jesus" (Phil 3:14).

Likewise, in fighting "the good fight" (1 Tim 1:18; 6:12; 2 Tim 4:7), he did not behave like a boxer flailing the air and never landing a blow. We cannot be certain whether Paul has in mind the poor boxer who continually misses his opponent or the man who prefers shadowboxing at home or in the gymnasium and never steps into the ring. Paul could see no purpose in activities that did not serve the Gospel and the edification of the church. (In 1 Cor 14:9, Paul will tell those who speak in tongues without an interpreter, "you will be talking into the air.")

By contrast with such feeble efforts, his practice is to keep his body in check, so that it continually serves the great goal (cf. Heb 12:11–12). Paul is not here advocating asceticism or self-flagellation as a means to the individual's private spiritual ends. Rather, he is calling on Christians to give up whatever does not advance the cause of the Gospel. Paul himself gave up many things that he could have claimed a right to have (1 Cor 9:4–6, 11–12, 15, 18). He calls on Christians to avoid doing anything that offends others (8:9–13). Christians should forego their rights for the sake of winning others for the Gospel.

By thus disciplining himself, Paul's faith was active in loving service to all. If he were to live a life of self-indulgence, he would endanger not only the salvation of others, but also his own. The danger of being disqualified is real. Disqualification would mean nothing less than missing out on the crown of life, as the context makes clear (1 Cor 9:24–25). Paul has been devoting his life to commending the benefits of the Gospel to others. These benefits are worth having; Paul wants a share in them himself (9:23). What a tragedy it would be if, after preaching to others, he would be found to be no longer "in the faith" (2 Cor 13:5–6)! The implication for the Corinthians should be obvious: it would be a tragedy if they forfeited their salvation by ceasing to exercise self-control and thus relapsing into idolatry. Paul will now elaborate that message in 1 Corinthians 10. Christians must constantly exercise self-discipline, restraining their sinful nature and putting it to death by the power of the Spirit, so that they may live for God—now and in eternity (Rom 8:13).

10:1–11:1

Conclusions about Idol-foods

10:1–13

Warnings against Spiritual Complacency

1 CORINTHIANS 10:1–5

OUR FATHERS IN THE WILDERNESS

TRANSLATION

**10 [1]For I do not want you to be ignorant, brothers,
that our fathers were all under the cloud and all
passed through the sea, [2]and all were baptized
into Moses in the cloud and in the sea, [3]and all ate
the same spiritual food [4]and all drank the same
spiritual drink. For they were drinking from the
spiritual rock which followed them, and that rock
was Christ. [5]But with most of them God was not
pleased, for they were strewn in the wilderness.**

COMMENTARY

Paul is aware that complacency could cause him to forfeit the heavenly prize (1 Cor 9:23–27). Now he turns from himself to the Corinthians. For them, too, the danger of being "disqualified" (9:27) is real. Paul expresses his concern for them with these words: "I do not want you to be ignorant, brothers" (10:1), a formula he commonly uses to introduce important issues.

The imagery of the athletic games (9:24–27) is left behind, and the apostle turns to the OT, which provides instruction relevant for the church in the NT era (Rom 15:4; 1 Cor 10:6, 11). Although the Corinthian church consisted mainly of Gentile Christians, these had now been grafted into the vine of Israel and were as much entitled as any Jewish Christian to think of the fathers of the Jewish people as "our fathers" in faith (1 Cor 10:1; cf. Rom 4:11–12).

"All" of our fathers (1 Cor 10:1) experienced the exodus deliverance and God's sustenance in the wilderness. The word "all" occurs five times in 10:1–4 and receives emphasis throughout the section. The whole nation received God's grace. Paul first makes the point that *all* received these benefits *objectively*—all who passed through the sea and ate and drank in the wilderness. (Later, in 10:5–13, he will describe how *subjectively* many failed to receive and respond to God's gifts *in faith.*)

All were "under the cloud" (10:1) of God's glorious presence and power. The Lord went before them "in a pillar of cloud" (Ex 13:21), and at one point the cloud moved behind them to protect them (Ex 14:19). Other texts speak of the Lord spreading "a cloud for a covering" (Ps 105:39; cf. Wisdom 19:7).

As the Lord provided this protection, they "all passed through the sea" (1 Cor 10:1). The waters of the Red Sea became a protective "wall to them on their right hand and on their left" (Ex 14:22).

Israel's safe passing through the waters of the Red Sea prefigures and typifies the waters of Baptism. At the Red Sea, all the covenant people "were baptized into Moses" (1 Cor 10:2). They submitted to his leadership as he guided them through the waters, and when they saw what the Lord accomplished there, they "believed in the Lord and in his servant Moses" (Ex 14:31). Their salvation "in the cloud and in the sea" (1 Cor 10:2) led them to a trusting, personal relationship with the great mediator of the old covenant. (Later, Paul will describe how not all responded with or remained in this trusting faith.) Accordingly, Moses was a type of Jesus Christ, the greater mediator of the new covenant, into whom the Corinthian Christians had been baptized (1 Cor 1:13–17; 12:13).

Just as all the fathers of Israel received a type of Baptism, so they also received a type of the Lord's Supper. All of them were sustained by the manna, described by the psalmist as the "grain of heaven," the "bread of angels" (Ps 78:24–25), which the Lord "rained . . . on them to eat" (Ps 78:24; cf. Ex 16:4, 35). Its heavenly origin explains Paul's designation of the manna as "spiritual food" (1 Cor 10:3). It was superior to ordinary bread, just as the "spiritual body" with which the believer will be clothed in the resurrection is superior to the natural body (15:42–44).

Likewise, all the fathers received "the same spiritual drink" (10:4), which was water, but which also corresponds to the wine of the Lord's Supper. Both at the beginning and at the end of their wilderness wanderings, the Lord provided them with the miraculous water from the rock. Paul points to Christ as the true spiritual rock who accompanied Israel (10:4), ascribing to him the title "the rock," which the OT ascribes to the Lord (Yahweh) as Israel's great protector (cf. Deut 32). Paul's identification of the rock with Christ clearly implies Christ's preexistence" ("the rock *was* Christ," 1 Cor 10:4).

Five times in 1 Cor 10:1–4, the adjective "all" has introduced a statement about Israel's high privileges as God's covenant people. But now at the start of 10:5, with the strong adversative "but/ nevertheless," Paul reminds the Corinthians that most Israelites failed to reach the Promised Land. Of the hundreds of thousands of men who experienced the exodus (Num 1:46) only two, Joshua and Caleb, were able to enter Canaan. After the scouting report, only those two believed that Israel could conquer the Canaanites because the Lord was with them (Numbers 13–14). The others paid the penalty for their disbelief and murmuring. God swore that none of those men at least twenty years old who were counted in the census in Numbers 1 would enter the land (Num 14:20–35). Their corpses were strewn all over the wilderness (Num 14:16; 1 Cor 10:5).

THE SIGNIFICANCE OF 10:1–5 FOR THE CHURCH'S SACRAMENTAL THEOLOGY AND PRACTICE

Admittedly, the baptism into Moses and the spiritual eating and drinking in the wilderness were only shadows of the great sacraments of the NT era, Christian Baptism and the Lord's Supper. But it would be contrary to Paul's argument to claim that these OT types lacked any relationship to the NT sacraments. Paul clearly accords them significance as prefigurements of Baptism and the Lord's Supper. He draws a parallel between the Israelites, who were "baptized into Moses" (10:2) and ate the "spiritual food" and "spiritual drink" (10:3–4), and the Christians in Corinth. The Corinthians had received Christian Baptism: "we all were baptized with one Spirit into one body . . . and we all were given to drink one Spirit" (12:13). They also had partaken of Christ's body and blood in the Sacrament of the Lord's Supper (10:16–17; 11:23–34).

Paul's purpose in drawing the parallel is this: *just as many Israelites were disqualified because of their unfaithfulness and false worship, Christians, too, face the danger of being disqualified from salvation if they engage in false worship and fail to remain in repentance and faith worked by the Holy Spirit.*

In its attitude toward the sacraments, the church faces two equal and opposite temptations. One is the danger to which most of the Israelites and some of the Corinthians succumbed: the adoption of a complacent, "magical," view that there is spiritual benefit in simply "going through the motions," taking the sacraments for granted and forgetting that their purpose is to engender and strengthen faith. Faith should lead to godly lives and appropriate works. A Christian cannot participate in the sacraments and then blithely continue to live in sin. Paul stated categorically that unrighteous people will not inherit the kingdom of God (6:9–10; see also the excommunication of the immoral man in 1 Corinthians 5). The Corinthians may have felt that Baptism and the Lord's Supper made them immune to any harm from involvement with pagan worship. The Corinthians misunderstood Baptism and failed to grasp their baptismal unity in Christ (1:10–16). Some of them saw nothing wrong with dining in pagan temples (8:9–13; 10:14–31) and also partaking of the Lord's Supper (10:16–17, 21). The church as a whole abused the Supper (11:17–22).

The other danger is for the church to detract from the reality and power of the sacraments as true spiritual food and drink, and reduce them to mere symbols. This happens when Christians consider Baptism to be merely a human action—a demonstration of *our* faith, rather than an action of God which confers the forgiveness of sins, the Holy Spirit, life, and salvation, as Scripture affirms (e.g., Acts 2:38–39; 1 Pet 3:21). Regarding the Lord's Supper, this second danger occurs when Christians fail to discern the Lord's body and blood in the Sacrament, which give to the communicant the benefits earned by Christ when he gave his body and shed his blood on the cross.

Commenting on 1 Cor 10:3, Chemnitz (*The Lord's Supper*, 259) writes this:

> [I]n the New Testament debaucherers, fornicators, idolators, etc. [1 Cor 6:9–10], should not delude themselves because they have the same Baptism and the same Supper as the pious use. It is perfectly clear that Paul instituted and proposed this in order that he might take away from the Corinthians that false delusion that debauchery, whoring, communion with idols [1 Cor 10:16–21], etc., could not hurt them since they had been baptized and used the same Lord's Supper as did the truly pious.

The church's traditional understanding of 10:1–4 is finely preserved in the so-called "flood prayer" of Luther (*LSB*, 268–269):

> Almighty and eternal God, according to Your strict judgment You condemned the unbelieving world through the flood, yet according to Your great mercy You preserved believing Noah and his family, eight souls in all. *You drowned hard-hearted Pharaoh and all his host in the Red Sea, yet led Your people Israel through the water on dry ground, foreshadowing this washing of Your Holy Baptism.* Through the Baptism in the Jordan of Your beloved Son, our Lord Jesus Christ, You sanctified and instituted all waters to be a blessed flood and a lavish washing away of sin. We pray that You would behold *name(s)* according you Your boundless mercy and bless *him/her/them* with true faith.

1 CORINTHIANS 10:6–13

PATTERNS IN THE PENTATEUCH FOR OUR INSTRUCTION

TRANSLATION

**10 6Now these things happened as prefigurements of
us, to keep us from being cravers of evil things, as
also they craved. 7And do not be idolaters as some of
them [were], as it is written: "The people sat down
to eat and drink and rose up to play." 8Nor should
we indulge in sexual immorality, as some of them
were sexually immoral, and there fell on one day
23,000. 9Nor should we test Christ as some of them
tested [him], and were being destroyed by snakes.
10And do not grumble as some of them grumbled,
and were destroyed by the Destroyer. 11These things
kept happening to them as a prefigurement, and
they were written for our instruction, upon whom
the goals of the ages have come. 12So let him who
thinks he is standing watch that he doesn't fall. 13No
temptation has come upon you but what is common to
humanity. And God is faithful. He will not let you be
tempted beyond your capacity but will make with the
temptation also the way out so that you can bear it.**

COMMENTARY

The OT events Paul described in 1 Cor 10:1–5—God's gracious provision for Israel in the wilderness and his judgments on those who rebelled—depict for the Corinthians in a lively way that God has bestowed his grace on them, as he bestowed it on Israel, but if they succumb to the same sins, they will be punished just as Israel was punished. God's actions in the OT and NT eras are of one piece. His acts in OT times are "prefigurements" of the way he acts now in the fulfillment of the ages (10:11).

Using a series of five illustrations from the history of Israel, Paul now supplies specific reasons why the bodies of the Israelites "were strewn in the wilderness" (10:5). These illustrations all seem to have been chosen because of their relevance to the situation in Corinth: the Corinthians are prone to these sins, as Israel was.

The first illustration (10:6) refers to the incident that occurred immediately after Israel set out from Sinai. The rabble among them yielded to an intense craving for the meat and fresh vegetables that were plentiful in Egypt, and complained bitterly about the manna. In response, the Lord supplied them with quails but struck many of them with a plague (Num 11:4–5, 31–34).

The foods which were the objects of their craving were not "evil things" (1 Cor 10:6) in themselves, but they were evil because of their association with the idolatrous land of Egypt, and because the people preferred them over the manna, water, and other provisions God graciously gave them in the wilderness. In craving these things, the people were preferring slavery, idolatry, and impurity to the worship of the true God. Likewise, the Corinthians were tempted to crave the conviviality and the meat and other delicacies offered in idol temples. Paul addresses this issue at length in 1 Corinthians 8 and 10:14–33. Such coveting amounted to sin against the commandment, "You shall not covet" (Ex 20:17; Deut 5:21), and was in itself a form of idolatry, that is, a sin against the First Commandment (Eph 5:5; Col 3:5).

Coveting could also foster the grosser forms of idolatry. Paul's second illustration (1 Cor 10:7) refers to the golden calf Aaron fashioned from the people's earrings (Exodus 32), in defiance of the First Commandment's prohibition against the construction of images (Ex 20:4–6; Deut 5:8–10). Aaron built an altar before the calf and proclaimed a feast to the Lord. Then the Israelites "offered burnt offerings and brought peace offerings; and the people sat down to eat and drink and rose up to play" (Ex 32:6). The consequences were disastrous: the Lord came close to wiping out the whole nation in his anger but relented when Moses interceded for the people. However, "about three thousand men of the people fell that day" at the hands of the Levites (Ex 32:28).

Paul warns the Corinthians against falling into similar idolatry. Just as the Israelites had fallen into the temptation of sitting down and eating in honor of an idol, bringing the Lord's wrath on their heads, so some of the Corinthians were reclining and eating and drinking in an idol's temple (1 Cor 8:10; cf. 10:14–22). This could only have disastrous consequences.

In the case of the golden calf, the people's worship degenerated into sexual immorality: "they rose up to play" (Ex 32:6; 1 Cor 10:7). The verb has overtones of sexual play (cf. Gen 26:8; 39:14, 17). Breaking the First Commandment led them also to break the Sixth (Ex 20:14; Deut 5:18). The Corinthians, too, were guilty of sexual immorality, since they tolerated a gross form of incest in the midst of the congregation (1 Corinthians 5), and some were frequenting prostitutes (6:15–20). Paul had to warn them that the sexually immoral, including adulterers and homosexuals, will not inherit God's kingdom (6:9).

Paul then includes a third illustration, another example of sexual sin (10:8). Just as in the golden calf incident, Israel's self-indulgence led to idol worship and from there to fornication, so the pattern was repeated at Shittim in the plains of Moab. The Moabites invited the people to their fertility rites in honor of the Baal of Peor, which resulted in some of the Israelite men having intercourse with Moabite women. The Lord's anger was kindled. He gave instructions that the leaders of the people should be killed and exposed, and sent a plague that left 24,000 more corpses in the wilderness (Num 25:1–18). This incident at the very gates of the Promised Land is referred to a number of times in Scripture (Deut 4:3; Ps 106:28–29; Hos 9:10; cf. Num 31:16).

Paul is warning the Christians in Corinth not to fall into the same trap of idolatry and its attendant immorality. As the true temple of God, with the Spirit of God dwelling within them, their lives should be characterized by holiness (1 Cor 3:16–17; 6:19). Sexual sins are uniquely vile because they are sins against one's own body (6:18).

Many interpreters have been intrigued by the discrepancy between Num 25:9, which states that 24,000 died in the plague, and Paul's figure of 23,000 in 1 Cor 10:8. Among the various attempts at harmonization, the most common is to suggest that both the Numbers text and Paul used round numbers. Whatever the explanation may be, the discrepancy between the numbers does not detract from Paul's point: idolatry and immorality bring down God's judgment on a massive scale.

Paul's fourth illustration follows in 1 Cor 10:9. Paul has in mind when God sent "snakes" after Israel tested the Christ who followed them in the wilderness. As they made the long march around Edom, "the people became impatient on the way, and the people spoke against God and against Moses, 'Why have you brought us out of Egypt to die in this wilderness? For there is no food and no water, and we detest this accursed food.' Then the Lord sent the fiery serpents among them, and they bit the people, and many people from Israel died" (Num 21:4–6). Probably, it is significant that this example involves despising the "spiritual food" (1 Cor 10:3), the manna, and the water which God graciously provided them *in Christ* (10:4). It was a sin against Christ himself.

Finally, as his fifth illustration, Paul urges the Corinthians not to follow Israel's example in grumbling against the Lord and Moses (10:10). Grumbling is a recurrent theme in the wilderness accounts. But Paul has in mind a specific incident. The reference to "the Destroyer" (10:10) points to the Numbers 16 account of the earth swallowing up Korah and company. Again, this was in response to complaints against Moses and Aaron (Num 16:3, 41). Numbers 16 does not refer to the Destroyer, but in its recounting of the story, the book of Wisdom attributed the ensuing plague to "the Destroyer," the angel of destruction (Wisdom 18:25). If the Christians in Corinth persisted in grumbling against the apostolic authority of Paul and his colleagues, they ran the risk of suffering the same destruction.

For the church today, the equivalent grumbling would be to question and even to rebel against the authority of the sacred Scriptures, or against the church's ministers who faithfully proclaim and live by the Scriptures.

After recounting these five episodes from Israel's years in the wilderness (1 Cor 10:6–10) that resulted in the people's corpses littering the landscape (10:5), Paul sums up: All these disasters happened to Israelites "typologically," "as a prefigurement" (10:11) of the way God deals with his people in both judgment and salvation. These events were recorded not just for Israel's sake but "for our instruction" (10:11; cf. Rom 15:4). We now live "in the last days" (Acts 2:17), indeed "the last hour" of this world (1 Jn 2:18). All the "ages" of this universe, all the different epochs, have by God's gracious provision reached their common "goals" (1 Cor 10:11), their consummation in Jesus' death and resurrection (Heb 9:26), which inaugurated these last days so freighted with significance. Now we live constantly in the shadow of the last great day, the day of his final coming.

Mindful of this, the Corinthians should not be complacent and arrogant (1 Cor 10:12). Paul would later warn the Christians in Rome that since unbelief caused the natural branches (most Jewish people) to be broken off from the olive tree, how much more should Gentile Christians—wild branches grafted in—remain repentant, lest they, too, be broken off from the olive tree of the church. It was only by humble faith in Christ that they continued to stand. So he urges, "Do not be arrogant, but be afraid" (Rom 11:20 NIV). Paul's concern reflects the biblical maxim "pride goes before destruction, and a haughty spirit before a fall" (Prov 16:18 NIV). Likewise, those Corinthian Christians who prided themselves on their power and freedom in the Spirit should be careful not to fall from grace.

Having sounded a warning against the dangers of complacency and pride, the apostle hastens to add a corresponding word of encouragement. The Corinthians will not be tested beyond their God-given capacity. The temptations they will encounter are the trials "common to humanity" (1 Cor 10:13), trials to which all sinners are susceptible (cf. Gal 6:1). In each of Paul's five OT examples in 1 Cor 10:6–10, many Israelites fell, but God in his grace always kept some from falling, and God desired and tried hard to save all. Those who fell were the ones who spurned God's Word and promises, but nevertheless, God remains true to his promises (1 Cor 1:9). Faced with these trials, the Corinthians can count on God's faithfulness (1 Cor 10:13); he will keep them from falling (Jude 24). That God remains faithful to his covenant promises stands as an axiom of biblical theology (e.g., 1 Cor 1:9; 2 Cor 1:18). With every trial he will provide strength to endure, and he will also in his own good time create the specific "way out" (1 Cor 10:13) that finally brings the trial to an end. "Time passes and much change doth bring And sets a bound to everything" (*LSB* 750:5).

1 CORINTHIANS 10:14–22
THE LORD'S TABLE AND THE TABLE OF DEMONS

TRANSLATION

10 14 So then, my beloved ones, flee from idolatry. 15 I am
speaking as to sensible people: judge for yourselves
what I am saying. 16 The cup of blessing that we
bless, is it not a communion in the blood of Christ?
The bread that we break, is it not a communion in
the body of Christ? 17 Because there is one bread,
we the many are one body, for we all share in the
one bread. 18 Consider Israel according to the flesh:
are not those who eat the sacrifices communicants
in the altar? 19 Then what am I saying? That meat
sacrificed to idols has significance or that an idol
has significance? 20 No, but what they sacrifice "they
sacrifice to demons and not to God." I do not want
you to be communicants of the demons. 21 You cannot
drink the cup of the Lord and the cup of demons.
You cannot share in the Lord's Table and the table
of demons. 22 Or are we trying to provoke the Lord
to jealousy? Surely we are not stronger than he?

COMMENTARY

Paul closed the preceding pericope with a comforting promise (1 Cor 10:13). It needs to be added, however, that God's assurances apply only to those who seek "the *way out*" (10:13) of the everyday temptations of the Christian life. The assurances do not apply to those who, like the complacent Christians in Corinth, are ready to *walk right into* a situation fraught with temptation. When Paul introduced his discussion of the idol-meat issue (8:1–13), he asked the Corinthian Christians to consider that their self-indulgence in idol temples would lead their weaker brothers in Christ to join them in sinning and thereby perish (8:10–11). Now, he returns to the issue with a strong "so then" (10:14) and proceeds to draw the conclusion from the preceding warnings against following in the footsteps of disobedient Israel (10:1–12).

As in 4:14, he tempers a strong injunction with words of tender pastoral appeal. The Corinthians are Paul's "beloved" people (10:14). His great love for them prompts his warnings against idolatry. If they recline in an idol's temple, they have rushed headlong into idolatry. In a previous epistle, Paul had counseled them to have nothing to do with an idolatrous person who called himself a "brother" (5:9–11). Idolaters and other unrighteous people will not inherit the kingdom (6:9–10). Rather than dallying with this sin, the Corinthians must flee from it, as they must flee from sexual immorality (6:18; cf. Gen 39:12; 1 Jn 5:21).

There is probably some gentle irony in Paul's appeal to the Corinthians as "sensible people" (1 Cor 10:15). No doubt those in the "puffed up" segment of the congregation that prided itself on its "knowledge" (8:1, 7, 10, 11) thought they had a common-sense approach to idol-meats. If, then, they would maintain their claim to be "sensible" (10:15, as also in 4:10), they should be able to assess what Paul is saying about the dangers of idolatry.

The argument Paul proposes for the Corinthians' evaluation begins with two rhetorical questions in 10:16. "Is it not the case," he argues, "that your reception of the sacramental cup and bread establishes an intimate fellowship and communion with Christ? If so, how can this fellowship be compatible with participation in pagan festivals?"

The rhetorical questions of 10:16 are based on the Words of Institution of the Lord's Supper (11:23–25) and must be interpreted in that light. Paul is appealing to what they know from their Communion practice. Regarding the implications of 10:14–22 for the church's communion practice, see further the commentary on 11:27–34.

"The cup of blessing" (10:16) was the third cup of the Passover meal. Most likely it was this cup that Jesus used when he first instituted the Lord's Supper.

In 10:16, the phrase "that we bless" (or "for which we give thanks") marks this cup as something distinctive from all other cups. For this cup we are especially thankful, because through it we are blessed by receiving the blood of Christ.

It is the cup and the bread—not our faith—that constitutes "the communion in the body and blood of Christ. What is the nature of this communion? The word "communion" here in 10:16 bears its basic sense of "sharing." Together with their fellow believers, the Corinthians share in the gifts of the Lord's Supper. What is shared is a true communion in Christ's gifts. These gifts are the Lord's body and blood.

Paul does not mean that the believer merely realizes afresh the benefits of the Lord's sacrifice of his body and blood, as though the actual body and blood were far removed from us. Just as the very concrete gifts of charity for the poor saints in Jerusalem are designated by the same Greek word in Rom 15:26 and 2 Cor 8:4, so here Paul is not talking about fellowship as "warm fuzzy" feelings. Rather, *through the sacramental bread and wine there is direct oral reception of the Lord's crucified and glorified body and blood.*

Further evidence for this literal interpretation is furnished by Paul's use of the verb "to share/partake" as a parallel to "communion" and "communicant" in 10:16–21. Another parallel to "communion" and "to share/partake," is "to drink," which Paul employs in 10:21. This is literal language, not metaphorical.

Thus, the participation in Christ's body and blood takes place orally, by taking, eating, and drinking these holy things (10:17, 21). By this means, the Christian receives the benefits of the new covenant (11:25), namely, the forgiveness of sins—for which Christ gave his body and shed his blood—and life and salvation.

Because all Christians partake of one loaf, which conveys one sacramental body, "we the many" (10:17) are built up as the one mystical body of Christ, the Christian church. Indeed, through our physical reception of the Lord's crucified and risen body in his sacramental bread, we become one body with him and with one another in the communion of saints (10:17; cf. 6:15–17 and Eph 3:6). An early church order, the Didache, reflects Paul's words (9:4): "As this broken bread was scattered upon the hills, and was gathered together and made one, so let your Church be gathered together into your kingdom from the ends of the earth."

Using another imperative in 10:18, "consider" (cf. the imperatives in 10:14–15), Paul continues his diatribe against the Corinthians' flirtation with idolatry. He takes as his example "Israel according to the flesh," the Jewish nation as distinguished from spiritual Israel, the Christian church, consisting of both Jewish and Gentile believers (Rom 9:6; Gal 6:16; Phil 3:3). Anyone familiar with the OT sacrificial practices knew that those who ate the sacrifices were partners of the altar. When priests, Levites, and other Israelites consumed their allotted portions of the sacrificial animals, they entered into a close relationship with the altar and all it represented. The altar was the focal point for communion between God and people, and for the reception of divine gifts. In Mt 23:16–22, Jesus argues for the inseparable connection between the sanctified gifts on the altar, the altar itself, the temple, the throne of God, and the One seated on the throne. The vertical dimension is paramount. That the Corinthians' relationship to the supernatural—to demons and to God—is Paul's chief concern is spelled out by the succeeding verses (1 Cor 10:20–21). Above all, the Corinthians are not to tempt the Lord (10:22; cf. 10:9).

Paul hastens to correct a possible misunderstanding (10:19). In sounding these warnings against communion with idols, he is not retracting from his position that "there is no idol in the world" and "there is no God but one" (8:4). He maintains that there is no reality to an idol sacrifice—it is simply ordinary meat—and no reality to an idol constructed of wood or metal. Both are shams. However, as he will explain in 10:20, there is a sinister reality lurking behind them both.

The reality behind all pagan sacrifices lies in the realm of the demonic. Whether the participants are apostate Jews or pagan Greeks, their sacrifices are offered "to demons and not to God" (10:20). Paul primarily has pagan Greeks in mind, but he describes pagan worship in terms borrowed from the Song of Moses' indictment of Israel, whose later apostasy Moses foresaw (Deut 32:15–18): "He abandoned God who made him . . . They made him jealous with strange gods . . . They sacrificed to demons, not God, to deities they had never known." The application of this song to the Corinthian situation is pointed. The Christians in Corinth must not repeat Israel's mistake by forsaking the Rock that saved them and forging an alliance with demonic powers.

Paul then addresses them in a fatherly way: "I do not want you to be communicants of the demons" (1 Cor 10:20). Such an unholy communion is incompatible with their holy communion in Christ's body and blood (10:16). There is no room for neutrality. Association with evil spirits would be a renewed bondage robbing them of their newly found freedom in Christ (Gal 4:8–9).

Many Christians are in danger of overestimating their spiritual strength and capacity. Paul makes it clear that it is beyond the Corinthians' power to participate in the Lord's cup and Table as well as the cup and table of demons. Between the Christian celebration and demonic rites, there is no neutral, middle ground. Christian people cannot "have it both ways": participation in the Christian sacraments precludes participation in or compromise with any other religious rites or organizations. As Paul expresses it in 2 Corinthians:

> Do not be yoked together with unbelievers. For what do righteousness and wickedness have in common? Or what fellowship can light have with darkness? What harmony is there between Christ and Belial? What does a believer have in common with an unbeliever? What agreement is there between the temple of God and idols? (2 Cor 6:14–16 NIV)

As the OT prophets ruled out any compromising, syncretistic mix of the worship of Yahweh with the worship of Baal, so Paul lays it down for the Christian church that there is to be no syncretism, no toying with false religions and ideologies, no limping along with two different opinions. Nor should Christians tolerate any false teaching or teachers. Rather, Christians are to turn away from anything that is not in harmony with the Gospel faithfully passed down to them (cf. 1 Cor 11:23; 15:1–3) and shun any purveyors of false doctrine (cf. Rom 16:17–20). In contrast to the infinitely inclusive pantheon of Greco-Roman religion, the faith of the church, like the faith of ancient Israel, is fundamentally *exclusive.*

From 1 Cor 10:21, comes the designation of the Lord's Supper as "the Lord's Table" (see also Lk 22:30). The expression "the Lord's Table" has its roots in Mal 1:7, 12, where "my table" means the altar of Yahweh. See also Is 65:11; Ezek 41:22; 44:16.

For any Christian to imagine he can safely combine Christian worship with any form of idolatry is foolishness. No one should imagine he may provoke the Lord to anger with impunity. The Corinthians need to keep a proper perspective:

they are merely weak human beings; the Lord Jesus is the mighty God, whose jealous anger at idolatry is to be feared (see again the Song of Moses, Deut 32:16, 21). Paul's closing admonition in 1 Cor 10:22 prepares for his similar warning in 11:30–32, where he describes specific punishments that resulted from the abuse of the Lord's Supper.

1 CORINTHIANS 10:23–11:1

Consideration for Others to the Glory of God

TRANSLATION

10 23 “All things are in my power,” but not all things
are beneficial. “All things are in my power,” but
not all things build up. 24 Let no one seek his own
[advantage], but that of the other. 25 Everything
that is on sale in the food market eat without
asking questions for the sake of conscience; 26 for
the earth is the Lord’s and all that fills it. 27 If any
of the unbelievers invites you and you wish to
go, everything set before you eat without asking
questions for the sake of conscience. 28 But if someone
says to you, “this has been devoted in sacrifice,” do
not eat [it] for the sake of that person who informed
you, and for the sake of conscience—29 I do not
mean one’s own conscience, but that of the other
person. For why is my freedom judged by another
conscience? 30 If I partake with thanksgiving, why am
I criticized because of [food] for which I give thanks?

31 Therefore, whether you eat or drink or whatever
you do, do everything for the glory of God. 32 Be
unoffensive to Jews and to Greeks and to the
church of God, 33 just as I please all people in
all things, not seeking my own advantage, but
that of the many, that they may be saved.

11 1 Be imitators of me, as also I am of Christ.

COMMENTARY

CONSIDERATION FOR OTHERS IN THE MATTER OF IDOL-FOODS (10:23–30)

Paul has completed his polemic which he began in chapter 8 against the practice of reclining in pagan temples and eating idol-meat. This he has absolutely forbidden as gross idolatry and the worship of demons (1 Cor 10:20–22). But there are further issues on which the Corinthians need the apostle's guidance: (1) What about the meat on sale in the "food market"? Are they free to buy this and eat it at home? Paul gives his answer in 10:25–26. (2) What should they do when a non-Christian invites them to his home or a public area like the dining rooms near the Lerna fountain (see 10:27–30)?

The introduction to Paul's final wrapping up of his argument on idol-foods is almost identical to 6:12. There, too, in his argument against consorting with prostitutes and other sexual sins, he twice cites the slogan "all things are in my power." This slogan was, no doubt, asserted by the Christians who (as Paul would imply later) claimed to have superior "knowledge" (8:1, 7, 10, 11). And exactly as in 6:12, Paul's first qualification in 10:23 is this: "But not all things are beneficial." But whereas in 6:12 his second qualification reads "but I for one will not be overpowered by anything," now his second one is "but not all things *build up*." This echoes the maxim with which Paul opened his discussion of idol-foods: "Love builds up" (8:1). What it means to be engaged in the loving edification (building up) of the church he spells out in the next verse: "Let no one seek his own [advantage], but that of the other" (10:24). To say the least, eating idol-food in an idol-temple is neither beneficial nor constructive. Idols in themselves are merely wood or stone, and idol-food is merely food, but behind them lurk demons (10:19–21). Such unrestrained exercise of one's "authority, right" (8:9) and Christian "freedom" (10:29) is likely to be a serious stumbling block that causes weak Christians to trip and perish (chapter 8). Furthermore, as Paul has just demonstrated (10:14–22), it is idolatry, the same as Israel's idolatrous rebellion (10:1–13).

The guiding principle must always be what is beneficial to others and constructive, what promotes the congregation's progress and joy in the faith (Phil 1:25). No one should be selfishly preoccupied with his own rights, privileges, and personal satisfaction at the expense of others. Jesus himself had taught and modeled the way of loving service to others (Mt 22:39; Jn 13:1–17; Phil 2:4–11).

Paul now turns to another major issue for the young church in its attitude to food offered to idols: what should their policy be when shopping at the Corinthian food market? Should they pick and choose among the foods and only buy what had not been offered to idols?

Paul's reply is unambiguous: "You may buy and eat anything. And don't ask fussy questions!" In adopting this attitude, Christians were to be radically different from Jews, who were, indeed, permitted to buy from the food market, but only after they had investigated whether the food had been sacrificed to idols and whether it had been prepared in accord with the OT regulations about blood and other matters. Thus, the followers of "the Way," popularly considered a sect of Judaism (see, for example, Acts 24:14), were to be distinctive from Jews in their practice of Christian freedom. Their freedom was based on a clear recognition that there is no idol in the world, no God but the one Creator of all, and no Lord but Jesus, through whom all things exist (1 Cor 8:4–6). So they should have no scruples and raise no questions "for the sake of conscience" (10:25, 27), because no matter of conscience is involved.

Paul's attitude is consistent with Jesus, who exercised sovereign freedom toward the OT dietary laws, declaring all foods to be clean (Mk 7:19; cf. Rom 14:14; Gal 2:11–14). In Acts 10:15 and 11:9, the ascended Lord Jesus declared all foods and all peoples—the Gentiles—to be clean: "What God has cleansed, you must not call unclean" (see also Acts 10:28).

Paul grounds his counsel in the words of Ps 24:1: "The earth is the Lord's and all that fills it" (1 Cor 10:26). In Ps 50:10–12, we hear a similar affirmation that everything that fills the world—wild animals, cattle, birds, indeed all that moves—is the Lord's (see also Ps 89:11). Thus, Paul's strong theology of creation is deeply grounded in the OT. Later, it finds ringing reaffirmation in the first epistle to Timothy in connection with the gifts of marriage and food: "For everything created by God is good, and nothing is to be rejected if it is received with thanksgiving, for then it is consecrated by the Word of God and prayer" (1 Tim 4:4–5).

The great text from Psalm 24 ("the earth is the Lord's . . .") governs both what precedes and what follows in equal measure. On the strength of this word from the Lord, the Christian may eat "*everything* that is on sale in the food market *without asking questions for the sake of conscience*" (1 Cor 10:25). And on the strength of the same word, he may accept an invitation to a pagan home or dining room, and "*everything* set before you eat *without asking questions for the sake of conscience*" (10:27).

Such social invitations from pagans, however, could place the Christian in an ambiguous situation. While ordinary meals in a pagan home did not always involve food offered in sacrifice, food dedicated to a god was more likely to be served at special family celebrations, to which a Christian might be invited. How, then, should he conduct himself at the meal table? How could he avoid compromising his faith, on the one hand, and being too fussy on the other?

First, Paul reiterates in 10:27 that Christians are free; he implies that they are under no obligation to follow the OT ceremonial law or Jewish traditions. If they wish to accept a pagan's invitation, they are free to do so (cf. Acts 10:9–23; 11:2–3). And again in 1 Cor 10:27, as in 10:25, they are not bound to inquire about the origin of the food, "for the earth is the Lord's" (10:26).

However, the situation changes if someone points out that the food has been offered in sacrifice (10:28). Out of consideration for this informant and his conscience, the Christian should refrain from eating. Paul does not specify if the informant is the host (motivated either by thoughtful consideration or by a desire to embarrass his Christian guests), a non-Christian fellow guest, another Christian guest, or a Christian slave waiting on the table. Most likely the informant is a Christian, for in 10:25 and 10:27, as in chapter 8 and the parallel discussion in Romans 14, Paul speaks of the conscience of Christians. A Christian brother has somehow learned that the food has been offered to an idol. Out of deference to his host (and perhaps to pagan fellow guests) he refers to it as food "devoted in sacrifice" (1 Cor 10:28) instead of "meat sacrificed to idols" (8:1, 4, 7, 10; 10:19). But once he has drawn attention to the nature of the food, his Christian fellow guest cannot fail to observe the painful dilemma presented to his conscience.

Under these circumstances, the fellow Christian must leave his meat untouched (10:28). He should do this out of respect for the scruples of the informant, and for the sake of conscience (cf. 8:10–11). While Paul may envision the informant as being a Christian, his principle of making every effort to save as many as possible (9:19–23; 10:32–33) would dictate that the Christian must not eat if doing so would tarnish the Gospel or make it more difficult to gain and save anyone present. This would apply not just to foods, but also to a Christian's participation in anything that might sully his witness to Christ.

Paul now specifies in 10:29 that his concern for the conscience is not for one's own conscience, whether the apostle's own conscience or that of his Christian readers or hearers. They should not let a weak brother's overly zealous scruples give them a bad conscience about eating such food. Paul asks: "Why is my freedom judged by another conscience?" (10:29). Christians have no right to judge, nor to restrict the freedom of their brothers who can happily eat anything served up to them by a pagan. Paul's readers and hearers, for their part, need to be clear in their own minds that their only reason for abstaining is loving sympathy for a "weak" brother (8:7–12; 9:22; cf. Rom 14:22).

When a Christian receives the food that is set before him with thanksgiving, the food is "sanctified by the Word of God and prayer" (1 Tim 4:3–5; see also Rom 14:6). No one has the right to criticize a Christian for thankfully receiving the Creator's gifts. Paul's words here would have modern application not just to foods, but also to activities that may be condemned—without biblical warrant—by legalistic Christians.

ALL FOR THE GLORY OF GOD (10:31–11:1)

With the word "therefore" (1 Cor 10:31), Paul gathers up the discussion of the last three chapters on idol-meats. He has just shown that anyone who eats his meat thankfully should not be criticized (10:29–30). By partaking of food with thankfulness, he gives glory to God. Paul now extends this principle to the whole of the Christian life: everything—not only eating and drinking but every activity we engage in—is to glorify God and benefit the neighbor (cf. Col 3:17; 1 Pet 4:11).

In gratitude for God's mercy, the believer's whole self is to be a living sacrifice to God (Rom 12:1; 1 Cor 6:20).

When that is the Christian's chief concern, he will not cause offense to others. He will not tarnish the Christian faith. Paul specifies three groups: Jews, Greeks, and the church of God (10:32). The first two are non-Christian groups, "those outside" (5:12). Christians are to behave in a becoming fashion toward outsiders (1 Thess 4:12; cf. Col 4:5) in order not to alienate them further from Christianity and salvation. Jews could be alienated by an unseemly exhibition of Christian freedom, Gentiles by a display of legalistic rigor. In adding the third group, "the church of God" (1 Cor 10:32), Paul probably has in mind chiefly the weak brothers who could be led into sin and thereby perish because of the poor example set by other Christians (8:9–12).

Again (as in chapter 9), the apostle holds himself up as the proper pattern to follow (10:33–11:1). Like his Master, he is not engaged in this ministry in order to please himself. He is not motivated by selfish considerations, but by a concern to provide proper pastoral care and edification to others and to bear their burdens (cf. Rom 15:1–3; Phil 2:4). His sole concern is the salvation of others (see "save" in 1 Cor 5:5; 7:16; 9:22; 10:33; 15:2). Thus, he strives to please all people, not in the sense of currying favor with them (an idea he emphatically rejects in Gal 1:10 and 1 Thess 2:4), but in the sense of commending the Christian faith to them, profiting them spiritually (cf. his corrections of the Corinthians' slogan in 6:12 and 10:23). The wording "I please all people in all things" (10:33) echoes Paul's motto set forth in 9:20–22: "to all people I have become all things."

Paul rounds off his discussion by calling on the Corinthians to imitate him in loving self-sacrifice for the sake of their fellow Christians, a self-sacrifice modeled on Christ crucified (11:1; cf. Rom 15:3; 1 Cor 2:2; 2 Cor 4:11). Imitation of Paul and of the Lord necessarily involves walking in the way of love and the cross. By contrast, the self-indulgent trumpeters of Christian freedom "walk . . . as enemies of the cross of Christ" (Phil 3:17–19; cf. Eph 5:1–2; 1 Pet 2:21). Thus, Paul returns once again to the thesis of his epistle: the word of the cross is foolishness and a stumbling block to selfish, self-confident humanity, but it is God's hidden power and wisdom unto salvation (1 Cor 1:18–25). The only knowledge that avails before God is knowing Christ crucified (2:2; cf. 8:1), and that knowledge is communicated to others by living in imitation of him (11:1).

1 CORINTHIANS 11:2–14:40

THE WORD OF THE CROSS IS THE BASIS FOR THE CHURCH'S WORSHIP

14:13–19 **The Tongues-speaker Must Pray for the Gift of Interpretation**

14:20–25 **Tongues Serve as a Divine "Hardening Instrument"**

Excursus *Worship Practice Today*

14:26–33a **Guidelines for the Orderly Use of Tongues and Prophecy in Worship**

14:33b–40 The Lord's Command for Women to Be Silent in the Churches

Excursus *The Ordination of Women*

11:2–16

Women's Head-Coverings

1 CORINTHIANS 11:2–6
HEADSHIP AND HEAD-COVERINGS

TRANSLATION

11 [2]I praise you because you remember me in everything, and just as I handed over to you, you hold fast to the traditions. [3]But I want you to know that the head of every man is Christ, the head of the woman is the man, and the head of Christ is God. [4]Every man praying or prophesying with a head-covering dishonors his head. [5]But every woman praying or prophesying with her head uncovered dishonors her head; she is one and the same with her that is shaven. [6]For if a woman is not covered, let her be shaved. But if it is shameful for a woman to be shorn or shaved, let her be covered.

COMMENTARY

Paul has just appealed to the Corinthians to model themselves on him, just as he imitates Christ (1 Cor 11:1). Now, before he turns to the important issues which will engage his attention for the rest of the letter, he commends them because they do in fact keep his words and example constantly before their minds and retain the Gospel traditions he delivered to them (11:2). This is no empty compliment, merely to secure their goodwill. From the beginning of the epistle, he has expressed his gratitude for the way they have been enriched in Christ in all speech and knowledge and other gifts (1:4–7), and for their high calling in Christ (1:26–31). While there has been much for the apostle to correct in the young church, he has fond memories of their faithful adherence to the traditions he has handed on to them as their father in the faith (4:15). These traditions encompass not only worship practices, the Lord's Supper in particular (11:23–26), but also the basic and essential teachings of the Gospel itself (15:1–4).

However, while Paul is generally grateful for their adherence to the Gospel, he must still call them to account for deviating from the traditions in a number of areas: an attitude toward men's and women's head-coverings that may have been influenced by the pagan religious environment (11:3–16); a lax attitude toward the Lord's Supper (11:17–34); an unbalanced attitude toward spiritual gifts (12:1–14:33); the role of women in worship (14:34–40); and a failure to understand the implications of Christ's resurrection (15:1–58).

Paul turns first to the issue of men's and women's head-coverings. Part of the difficulty in interpreting this section of the epistle lies in our lack of precise knowledge of the customs in the first-century Mediterranean world. But there may be a partial parallel in the practices of modern Islam, where even moderate Muslim women cover their hair in public; it is unthinkable that a woman should enter a mosque and remove her head-covering. This modern practice has its roots in the same Middle Eastern and Mediterranean world which Paul is addressing.

From the outset, it should be noted that Paul does not wish to set in concrete a rule *about specific practices* for all places and all times regarding head-coverings. (When he does state a universal and permanent rule for practice, he often refers to a direct command from God, as in 14:37, or to the teaching or practice "in every church" or "in all the churches," as in 4:17; 7:17; 14:33.) Rather, he is establishing the *universal and permanent principle* that men and women at worship should conduct themselves modestly and sensibly (1 Tim 2:9; cf. 1 Pet 3:1–6), in keeping with whatever happen to be the *customs* of the time. In a similar way, Jesus laid down the permanent principle ("a new commandment") that his disciples should love one another (Jn 13:34) and, in keeping with the custom of his day, exemplified that principle by washing the disciples' feet (Jn 13:3–17), but Jesus did not command the specific *practice* of foot washing for all Christians of all times.

Apparently, some of the more "liberated" women in the congregation were abandoning the head-covering that both Jewish women and many Greco-Roman women traditionally wore in public in the first century. These women thought they could lay aside the markings of their womanhood and dress like men; they were not going to be bound by the conventions accepted as proper for the respective sexes. But Paul believes they have gone beyond the bounds of propriety and are acting immodestly. His concern is similar to Peter's in 1 Pet 3:1–6.

Paul begins to address the issue by laying down the principle of headship. He sets down three parallel clauses (1 Cor 11:3):

> The head of every man is Christ,
> the head of the woman is the man,
> and the head of Christ is God.

The parallelism requires that the three clauses be interpreted in a manner consistent with one another.

Before the modern debate on women's ordination, commentators never questioned that by "head of" Paul meant "authority over" ("the authority over every man is Christ," and so on). Recent commentators, however, have advanced the view that "head" means "source," as a river has its source in its headwaters. But while the word "head" may be *applied* or *refer* to a river's headwaters, that application does not necessarily mean that the word *means* "source," even when used of a river's headwaters. Nor is there any evidence that "head" cannot and does not signify "authority" in the texts under consideration. Suffice it to note here that Paul's discussion in 11:2–6 should be connected with the concept of subordination in this epistle's other key passage on the role of women in worship, 14:33b–38. Even more compelling is Eph 5:22–24, where Paul uses the same language of headship ("the husband is the *head* of the wife as also Christ is the *head* of the church") and immediately clarifies what he means in terms of subordination: "Just as the church is subject to Christ, so also [let] the wives [be subject] to their husbands in everything."

But we must immediately add that Paul never conceives of the man's authority in terms of a harsh subjugation of the woman to his will. The apostle is not granting to men the authority to wield autocratic power, but the responsibility for loving, self-sacrificing service. As soon as he has laid down in Ephesians that wives should be subject to their husbands, he adds that husbands are to love their wives as Christ loved the church and gave himself up to death for her (Eph 5:25). This is consistent with the whole NT witness concerning the exercise of authority among Christians. Unlike the Gentiles, they are not to lord it over one another, but be servants (Lk 22:24–27). Likewise, pastors are not to lord it over the flock, but be examples (1 Pet 5:3).

When Christian headship is exercised in a spirit of loving service, those Christians subject to such authority will not chafe under it or feel demeaned. Following the pattern of the apostle's argument, it must be conceded that it is no more demeaning for a woman to be subject to a man than it is for the man to be subject to Christ, and for Christ to be subject to God the Father. The argument must be taken as a whole. The parallel statements about Christ and God the Father also require this headship to be within a Christian context; Paul's words do not necessarily pertain to secular institutions or issues.

When Paul says that "the head of Christ is God" (1 Cor 11:3), he is not denying the full divinity of Christ, nor is he saying that God the Son is in any way inferior to God the Father because the Son willingly submitted himself to the Father's plan (Phil 2:5–11). For any team to function effectively, there must be a recognized leader and those who willingly follow that lead. The Christian members of a congregation, for example, are equals in God's sight with the pastor who, by God's will and call, leads them.

In 1 Cor 11:4–6, Paul now proceeds to spell out the implications of the headship principle for public worship in Corinth. Anyone who prays or prophesies should show proper deference to the one set over him or her as the immediate "head." In the case of a man, he should not cover his head, for as 11:7 explains, he is the direct "image and glory of God."

Is Paul speaking merely of a hypothetical case, or were some of the Corinthian men actually covering their heads as they prayed and prophesied? Parallels from Roman religious practices of the period suggest that some of the congregation's elite may have been pulling their togas up over their heads, in imitation of pagan priests who were normally members of the elite.

One important consequence of man being created in God's image is his commission to represent his Maker in *ruling* the creation (Gen 1:26–28; 2:15–24). Since he directly reflects the divine glory, it would not be proper for him to cover his head; this would dishonor Christ, his true head. Paul's argument is based on the order of creation. According to the order given in Genesis, "Adam was formed first, then Eve" (1 Tim 2:13; see also Gen 2:4–24). Thus, Adam was shaped directly as "the image and glory of God" (1 Cor 11:7), and then the woman was taken out of him and thus came after him, deriving her being from him according to that order (Gen 2:21–23).

On the other hand (1 Cor 11:5a), any woman who prays or prophesies with her head uncovered dishonors the man who is set in authority over her (her father or her husband, or perhaps the pastor or elder). There is ample testimony that, in general, it was customary in Paul's day for both Jewish and Greek women to wear head-coverings in public. Paul is clearly pressing for the maintenance of this general custom when Christians assemble for worship. He may also have wanted to avoid any suggestion that Christian women were imitating the devotees of the Dionysian mysteries, who participated in the rites with long, loose, uncovered hair.

If the women wish to flaunt their liberty by abandoning the customary head-covering, Paul says (11:5b–6) they should go the whole way and not just get their hair cut short like a man's, but be shorn like a sheep (11:6) or shaved bald (11:5–6). The pattern of Paul's argument is similar to Gal 5:12, where he expresses the wish that the Judaizing advocates of circumcision would go the whole way (actually, *far beyond* Jewish practice) and get themselves castrated. Likewise, he argues, the liberated women should be consistent. If they wish to blur the distinction between the sexes, they should be consistently masculine, leaving no one in doubt about their intentions. On the other hand, if it was considered disgraceful for a woman to have a masculine haircut or be completely shaved (and there is no doubt that the society of Paul's day considered that disgraceful), then she should accept and glory in her femininity (1 Cor 11:7) and wear a head-covering.

Paul's argument draws on the customs of his day. One may ask whether those customs are relevant for all peoples of all cultures. Paul seems to say in 11:13–16 that, to some extent at least, hairstyles may reflect natural law, the innate ordering which God built into creation (see commentary on 11:13–16).

1 CORINTHIANS 11:7–16

The Orders of Creation and Redemption

TRANSLATION

**11 [7]For a man should not have his head covered, being
the image and glory of God; but the woman is the
glory of man. [8]For man is not from woman but
woman from man; [9]and man was not created for the
sake of woman but woman for the sake of man. [10]For
this reason the woman should have [a symbol of]
authority on her head, for the sake of the angels.**

**[11]Nonetheless, in the Lord woman is not independent
of man, nor is man independent of woman; [12]for just
as the woman is from the man, so also the man is
through the woman; and all things are from God.**

**[13]Judge for yourselves: Is it proper for a woman
uncovered to pray to God? [14]Does not nature itself
teach you that if a man has long hair it is a disgrace
to him, [15]but if a woman has long hair it is glory to
her? Because the long hair has been given her as a
covering. [16]If anyone is disposed to be contentious,
we have no such custom, nor do the churches of God.**

COMMENTARY

THE ORDER OF CREATION (11:7–10)

Why is it disgraceful for a woman to discard her head-covering (1 Cor 11:2–6)? And why, on the other hand, should a man not cover his head (11:2–6)? The reason is to be found in the *order of creation* recorded in Genesis 1–2. The man should not have his head covered because he is "the image and glory of God" (1 Cor 11:7). When he worships, he should not be rude or disrespectful by failing to remove his head-covering in God's presence. It may be helpful to draw a comparison with the not too recent past, when men commonly wore hats. If a man did not remove his hat in church, he was considered rude. Likewise, a man or a boy would remove his cap or hat when he met a woman, spoke with someone of importance, said the pledge of allegiance, or sang the national anthem. To "doff your cap" was a sign of respect.

The expression "image of God" (Gen 1:27; 1 Cor 11:7) refers to man being the representative of God, particularly in his authority over the creation (Gen 1:28–30; 9:6–7). While the creation accounts do not refer to man as the "glory of God," similar expressions are found in the psalms, including Ps 8:5: "You [God] have crowned him with glory and honor."

On the other hand, the woman brings glory to the man (1 Cor 11:7). Paul is not denying that she, too, like the man, was created in God's image (Gen 1:27), but his focus at this point is on her relationship to the man as one who derives her being from him and exists to bring glory to him as her head. By attaching herself to him and being his helper, she honors her husband. See the parallels in 1 Cor 11:14–15, where "glory for/to her" (11:15) is in antithesis to "disgrace for/to him" (11:14).

1 Cor 11:7b is elliptical. Fully stated, it would read: "But the woman *should have her head covered because she* is the glory of man." By praying or prophesying with her head uncovered, she would bring shame on the one whose glory she ought to be.

In 11:8–9, Paul gives two reasons why the woman is man's glory. First in 11:8, he appeals to her origin, sculpted from one of Adam's ribs (Gen 2:22–23). The man is therefore her source, and she should honor the one from whom she came. Paul affirms this also in 1 Tim 2:13. A second reason why the woman is man's glory is that the man was not created for the woman, but she for him (1 Cor 11:9); she was formed for the purpose of providing Adam with a helper (Gen 2:18). This original ordering of the creation has ongoing significance for the relationship between the sexes. The man's priority in the order of creation lays on him the responsibility of leadership, while the woman is to be helpful (Gen 2:18), submissive, supportive, and complementary.

Paul began his argument from the order of creation by saying that a man ought not to cover his head (1 Cor 11:7). Now he rounds off the passage by saying that a woman ought to cover her head (11:10). Both commands are supported by the reasons given in 11:8–9.

In 11:10, the apostle simply calls the head-covering an "authority." Apparently, the shawl was a sign of womanly honor and dignity that provided both security and respect. Similarly (at least until recently in some cultural contexts), for a married woman to wear a wedding ring was a protection. It enabled her to do things she could otherwise not do and go places to which she would otherwise have no access. Her ring was a sign to the world that it was "hands off" with this woman; here was a woman to be respected.

Why does Paul now add in 11:10 that the woman should dress in a dignified manner "for the sake of the angels"? The best suggestion is that Paul refers to the holy angels present in Christian worship. The Corinthians knew from their Greek

Bibles that it was "before angels" that they sang their psalms (Ps 138:1; the Greek Bible renders the term for "gods" as "angels;" cf. Rev 5: 8–14). Likewise, Christians today confess in the liturgy that it is "with angels and archangels and with all the company of heaven" that "we laud and magnify your [God's] glorious name" (e.g., *LSB* 208). If the women of Corinth thought little of causing offense to the men, they should consider that their departure from the created order was also an offense to the angels, who never fail to carry out the role God assigns them for the benefit of his saints (Heb 1:14).

THE ORDER OF REDEMPTION "IN THE LORD" (11:11–12)

Paul now introduces an important qualification. The previous argument (1 Cor 11:3–10) in favor of the man's headship and the woman's submission should not be misunderstood as though the woman were an inferior creature. While the order of creation has led to their having distinctive roles, there is also interdependence and mutuality between the sexes. There is full equality "in the Lord" (11:11) created by the baptismal unity of male and female in Christ (Gal 3:28). Paul will say later in 1 Cor 12:13, "We all were baptized with one Spirit into one body, whether Jews or Greeks or slaves or free, and we all were given to drink one Spirit." To use the terminology of Christian dogmatics, while there are role differences according to the order of creation (11:3–10, 13–16), there is equality and unity according to the order of redemption (11:11–12).

Many modern interpreters try to set the order of redemption in opposition to the order of creation, and argue that the two are antithetical or incompatible. Often the claim is made that the order of redemption somehow trumps or renders obsolete the order of creation already now, in this life. But such a conflict is foreign to Paul's theology. Paul sees the two orders as complementary, and the Christian life is to be lived in obedience and harmony within both orders. Paul now illustrates that by means of a comparison that likens the order of redemption to an aspect of the order of creation. Although woman originally came from man, ever since then man comes into being "through the woman" (11:12). This observation from the course of human reproduction serves as a powerful analogy and testimony to the man and the woman's interdependence "in the Lord" (11:11). In Christ there is complete unity. Furthermore, both man and woman, indeed all created things, owe their existence to God (11:12). He is the ultimate source of everything and everyone. And his ultimate goal is for all creation to be united under his headship in Christ (Eph 1:10).

WHAT NATURE TEACHES (11:13–16)

Paul returns now to the order of creation (as in 1 Cor 11:7–10). He appeals to the Corinthians' sanctified common sense (cf. 10:15). By means of a rhetorical question which expects the answer no (11:13), he calls on them to exercise their sense for what is fitting and appropriate. Surely it cannot be right for a woman to participate in public worship without the appropriate head-covering. Normally, the verb "to pray" does not have an object. The addition of the words "to God" in 11:13 reminds the Corinthians of the solemn nature of worship. Here they approach the almighty and holy God, before whom the seraphim cover their faces and cry, "Holy, holy, holy is the Lord of hosts; the whole earth is full of his glory" (Is 6:2–3). In his presence the women should show due decorum.

By the expression "nature itself" (1 Cor 11:14), Paul means the instinctive sense of right and wrong. This sense has been implanted since creation, although it has become obscured and is not always reliable because of the fall into sin. Just as nature teaches (11:14) men instinctively to shrink away from doing what our culture labels as feminine, so it teaches women to dress and behave in distinctively feminine ways. The concept "nature" plays an important role in another Pauline discussion of human sexuality, Rom 1:26–27, where he condemns homosexuality as a practice that is likewise contrary to the divinely instilled sense of order and propriety. The fall into sin has led some to pervert God's order by doing what is grossly unnatural.

Paul's appeal to nature's teaching with respect to hair lengths probably means that (despite variations across the centuries and cultures) human beings generally have an instinctive sense that long hair makes a more glorious and fitting adornment on a woman than it does on a man, and that, conversely, short or closely cropped hair (not to mention baldness!) is more acceptable and "natural" for a man than for a woman. Normally—though with numerous exceptions—this instinctive sense of what accords with the created order has been reflected in hairstyles through the ages. From numerous paintings, statues, reliefs, and coins from the Greco-Roman era, we know that it was customary for Greek and Roman men to cut their hair short. The Spartans stood out as exceptions to the rule, drawing comment from Greek authors. According to the OT, Israelite men were not to trim the edges of their beards or the hair on the side of their temples (and that practice continues for the most pious Jews today), but that stipulation (Lev 19:27; cf. Lev 21:5) suggests that the rest of the hair probably was trimmed. The OT instruction for those who had taken a Nazirite vow stipulated that they were not to cut their hair until the vow was completed, but such a vow was an exception from the general norm for Israelite men (Num 6:1–21; Judges 13–16). From the NT Scriptures we know that Jewish men kept their hair trimmed, unless they were under a vow (Acts 18:18; 21:24).

Of course, Paul does not prescribe details of hair lengths and hairstyles which may vary in keeping with cultural fashions. But he makes it plain that a man who draws attention to himself by his abnormally long hair departs from the natural order and brings dishonor on himself. On the other hand, long hair is a woman's glory. It is given to her by God her Creator as a covering. By providing her with this glorious natural endowment, God is indicating that she should be appropriately covered at worship (see also 1 Cor 11:2–6).

Paul has concluded what he wants to say on the subject. He is not willing to enter into further argument. If anyone—whether a woman who wants to assert her "freedom," or a man who wants to spring to her defense against the apostle—would like to argue the point (literally, "is disposed to be a lover of arguing," 11:16), he or she should not bother Paul and his fellow apostles and pastors. For "we have no such custom, nor do the churches of God" (11:16). As he does elsewhere (4:17; 7:17; 14:33), Paul appeals here to the universal practice of the churches. And he reminds the Corinthians that these are the churches *of God.* Ultimately, anyone who wishes to defy apostolic practice and obscure the created distinctions between the sexes at worship is at loggerheads with God.

11:17–34

The Lord's Supper

1 CORINTHIANS 11:17–22

Abuses at the Communal Meal

TRANSLATION

**11 17 But in giving you this command I do not praise
[you], because your coming together does more
harm than good. 18 For first of all, when you come
together as a church, I hear that there are factions
among you, and to some extent I believe it. 19 For
there must be divisions among you, in order that
those who are genuine may be manifested among
you. 20 Accordingly, when you come together in the
same place, it is not to eat the Lord's Supper. 21 For
each one goes ahead with eating his own supper, and
one stays hungry while another gets drunk. 22 Don't
you have houses for eating and drinking? Or do you
despise the church of God and humiliate those who
do not have [anything]? What am I to say to you? Am
I to praise you? In this matter I do not praise you.**

COMMENTARY

Back in 1 Cor 11:2, Paul praised the Corinthians for retaining the Gospel traditions he had delivered to them. However, he immediately added a sober reminder that the women should not flaunt their freedom in Christ by abandoning their head-coverings at worship (11:3–16). Now, in moving to another issue, he must speak even more sternly. There is nothing praiseworthy about the Corinthians' conduct at the communal meals held in conjunction with the Lord's Supper. In fact, their coming together has a harmful effect on the congregation. So Paul must censure them and issue a command designed to correct the abuses. For the moment, we do not hear precisely what his directives will be. First, he must explain his concerns. But in 11:28, he directs, "Let a person examine himself. . . ." And then especially in 11:33–34 we hear these commands: "When you come together to eat, wait for one another. If anyone is hungry, let him eat at home."

Paul has heard reports that when the Corinthians come together as a congregation there are divisions among them (11:18). The divisions were probably of a different nature from those mentioned in 1:10–12, where people were egotistically aligning themselves with one church leader in opposition to another. There Paul spoke of four factions, whose politicking no doubt disrupted many aspects of the congregation's life. Now, in connection with the congregation's meals, he mentions only two groups, the "haves," who are prosperous and have plenty to eat, and the "have nots," who go away hungry (11:21).

Paul's first comment on the reports is cautious: "to some extent I believe it" (11:18). As an experienced pastor, he is aware that not everyone will have been guilty of arrogant behavior.

But Paul does believe the report, at least to a degree. His words in 11:19 parallel those of Jesus: "It is necessary that offenses come, but woe to the person through whom the offense comes" (Mt 18:7). Although Paul began the epistle deploring the existence of factions in Corinth and encouraging God's people to maintain their baptismal unity in the Spirit, at the same time he recognizes a certain sad inevitability about the rise of factions, stemming as they do from human self-centeredness and self-will.

But the almighty God can turn this evil to good (cf. Gen 50:20; Rom 8:28). As time goes by, it becomes apparent who are the tried and true believers, and who are the troublemakers, concerned chiefly with their own selfish interests. In his second epistle (2 Cor 13:5–7), Paul will appeal to the Corinthians:

> Test yourselves. Do you not realize that Jesus Christ is in you—unless, indeed, you fail to meet the test! I hope you will find out that we have not failed the test. But we pray to God that you may not do anything wrong—not that we may appear to have met the test, but that you may do what is right, though we may seem to have failed the test.

Behind this testing and sifting process there is a deeper, eschatological dimension: "Children, it is the last hour" (1 Jn 2:18). The present divisions, as painful and lamentable as they may be, are an inevitable part of the divine, eschatological drama going on in the congregation's midst, in which some are coming under God's judgment (1 Cor 11:29–30), while others are proving genuine and can hope to escape final condemnation (11:32). Earlier Paul spoke of such testing on the Last Day (3:12–15), but now he says that the process of testing has already started.

From these reports of disunity in the communal gatherings, Paul can only conclude that the Corinthians have completely lost sight of what it means that their gatherings are for the purpose of receiving the Lord's Supper (11:20). Their behavior is not at all in keeping with the Supper's significance as the Lord's sacred testament and gracious gift to all his people. After all, just as there is only one Baptism into one body and one Spirit (1:10–17; 12:13), so also there cannot be many suppers, a different one for each faction. There can only be the one Supper, which the one Master has instituted for all his servants.

But the Corinthians were destroying the holy character of the Supper by their selfishness and individualism. It was no longer "the *Lord's* Supper" (11:20) that was the highlight of their gatherings. Rather, each person's chief interest had become "*his own* supper" (11:21).

It seems that in the Corinthian church the celebration of the Lord's Supper accompanied a communal meal known as the "love feast" (cf. Jude 12 and some manuscripts of 2 Pet 2:13). While we cannot be certain of the order of events, it seems plausible that, just as the Lord originally instituted his Supper toward the end and as the climax of the Passover meal, so the early Christians began their gatherings with a common meal climaxing in the celebration of the Sacrament.

But the conduct of some of the Corinthians at the common meal was making a farce of the whole celebration (1 Cor 11:21). The wealthier members of the church, who provided most of the food, did not have the patience and courtesy to wait for the day laborers and slaves who would arrive later in the evening. Rather, they went ahead with their own meals. What could have been a marvelous opportunity for them to share with their less fortunate brothers and sisters was lost, as they freely indulged, in some cases to the point of drunkenness (11:21). By the time many of the poorer members arrived there was little or nothing left. The poor may thus have missed out on the Eucharist itself.

It is likely, too, that on these occasions the wealthy members were physically separated from the poor. They would dine with the host in the main dining room, the triclinium, where in a typical house there was space for about nine to twelve guests to recline at table. Here the host would entertain members of his own high social class. In plain view of the festivities in the triclinium, the other guests would be seated on couches in the atrium, a courtyard area with seating for about forty people. These lower-status guests were often served inferior food and wine. Thus, it seems that the culture of Roman Corinth was setting the agenda for the church's practice. The poor, who constituted the majority of the congregation (1:26–31), were being treated as second-class members of the church.

The time has come for those who had humiliated others to be humiliated themselves. With two rhetorical questions in 11:22, Paul addresses the rich as if to say: "Surely it's not the case that you rich people don't have private homes for your eating and drinking? Or do you look down your noses at the church of God and humiliate those who have nothing?" The apostle's sharp reproof needs to be given an attentive hearing again in our modern culture, where the influence of "prosperity doctrine" has led many Christians to regard the poor as "trash." Paul reminds the affluent of all ages that the church does not belong to them, but to God, who will always have a special place for the poorer saints, choosing them to be "rich in faith and heirs of the kingdom he has promised to those who love him" (James 2:5). Paul had begun his epistle on a similar note: "But God chose the foolish things of the world so that he might humiliate the wise people, and God chose the weak things of the world so that he might humiliate the strong things, and God chose the lowly things of the world and the despised things—the things that are not—so that he might reduce to nothing the things that exist, so that no one might boast in the presence of God" (1 Cor 1:27–29).

1 CORINTHIANS 11:23–26
The Words of Institution

TRANSLATION

11 [23]For I received from the Lord what I also handed
on to you, that the Lord Jesus in the night in which
he was being handed over took bread, [24]and having
given thanks he broke [it] and said: "This is my body,
which is for you; keep doing this in my memory." [25]In
the same way also the cup after the supper, saying:
"This cup is the new testament in my blood; keep
doing this, as often as you drink [it], in my memory."
[26]For as often as you eat this bread and drink the cup,
you proclaim the death of the Lord until he comes.

COMMENTARY

It is beyond the scope of this commentary to provide an extensive comparison of Paul's account of the Words of Institution of the Lord's Supper with the parallels in the synoptic gospels. It must suffice here to say this: (1) Despite some minor differences between the four accounts, they are very similar in the essentials. (2) Matthew and Mark represent one distinct form of the tradition, while Paul and Luke represent another. (3) The two most significant differences are as follows: First, in the cup saying, Matthew (26:28) and Mark (14:24) read "this is my blood of the testament," while Paul (1 Cor 11:25) and Luke (22:20) have "this cup is the new testament in my blood." Second, Paul (1 Cor 11:24, 25) and Luke (22:19) have the injunction "keep doing this in my memory." With regard to this injunction, whereas it appears only after the bread in Luke (22:19), Paul records it not only in connection with the bread but also with the cup (1 Cor 11:24, 25). Moreover, Paul adds 11:26 about how the communicants are to remember the Lord by proclaiming his death until he comes. Thus, Paul places special emphasis on the theme of the Lord's Supper as remembrance (11:24–25) of Christ.

THE LORD TOOK BREAD (11:23)

An emphatic "I" (1 Cor 11:23) introduces Paul's account of the Words of Institution of the Lord's Supper. In contrast to the Corinthians' misunderstandings and abuses, their father in the faith (4:15) is about to set out the directions for the Meal which he has personally received from the Lord.

Twice in 11:23, Paul reminds them with "the Lord" that it is not *their own* private meal they are celebrating, but the *Lord's* Supper (contrast 11:20–21). So the Lord's directions for its celebration must be accepted without question (see "the Lord" also in 11:26, 27 [twice], 32; and also see the Lord's commands in 7:10; 9:14; 14:37).

How had the Lord's directives been conveyed to Paul? Most commentators believe Paul received them from Christ indirectly, through the apostles who were in Christ before him. One opportunity for learning the Gospel traditions (11:2, 23; 15:3–4) would have been the fifteen days he spent with Peter in Jerusalem (Gal 1:18). But others hold that just as Paul received the Gospel itself directly from Christ through a revelation (Gal 1:12), so he received the important traditions integrally related to the Gospel, such as the Lord's Supper tradition, through a similar revelation. There were other occasions when Paul received direct revelations (Acts 18:9–10; 22:18; 27:23–25; 2 Cor 12:7; Gal 2:2).

What Paul had received concerned the Lord Jesus' actions "in the night in which he was being handed over" (1 Cor 11:23). Most readers are familiar with the traditional translation, "on the night when he was betrayed." That translation and interpretation are indeed possible. However, Paul's use of the same Greek verb in other places (e.g., Rom 4:25; 8:32) strongly suggests that the agent he has in mind is not Judas, but God himself. This usage reflects the Greek text of Is 53:6, "And the Lord handed him over for our sins," and Is 53:12b, "And he bore the sins of many, and because of their sins he was handed over."

The solemnity and poignancy of the events on that first Maundy Thursday evening stand in stark contrast to the Corinthians' irreverent celebrations.

In the midst of the Passover meal, the Lord took a loaf of unleavened bread, probably similar to what we know as "Peter bread" or Lebanese bread. This action and the subsequent actions of giving thanks, breaking, and distributing the bread remind us of the way he hosted the feeding of the five thousand (Mk 6:41).

"THIS IS MY BODY" (11:24)

Jesus' words over the bread are unambiguous: "This [bread] is my body, which is for you" (1 Cor 11:24). His words over the wine are equally simple (11:25). With the speaking of the powerful Words of Institution, the bread is no longer simply bread, the wine no longer simply wine. Rather, "it [the Sacrament of the Altar] is the true body and blood of our Lord Jesus Christ, under the bread and wine" (SC VI 2). Thus, these words may not be changed or trifled with. All attempts to avoid a realistic understanding by reinterpreting the verb "is" to mean "signify" or "represent," as if the Communion elements merely symbolized Christ's absent realities, fly in the face of the plain meaning. The Lord is identifying the bread as his body and the wine as his blood. He employs a figure of speech known as synecdoche, by which a part is put for the whole. "The cup" which Jesus blessed and which "he gave to them" (Mt 26:27; Mk 14:23) refers not only to the cup itself but especially to the wine it contains, which he identifies as his blood. A similar example of synecdoche is when a person shows a purse or wallet and says, "This is money." Although you only see a wallet or purse, it actually contains the person's money. More important than the purse is the money it contains. So with the Lord's Supper, the Lord's body, which is "in and under" (LC V 8) the bread, is the more important part of the whole (the bread and his body). Likewise with the cup that contains the wine that is Christ's blood, his blood is the most important part.

The sacramental bread conveys the Lord's body given in sacrifice "for you" (11:24). The preposition "for" is regularly used in contexts which speak of Christ's vicarious atonement (Rom 5:6, 8; 1 Cor 15:3; Gal 3:13). The Sacrament is a highly visible and tangible form of the Gospel. It confers on the believer the benefits of Christ's vicarious suffering and death.

Jesus then commands the disciples to continue celebrating the Sacrament: "Keep doing this" (11:24, 25). In this way, the church will have a perpetual memorial of her Savior. The annual Passover celebration in the first month of the year, with the slaughter of the lambs and all the attendant rituals, served as a powerful reminder to Israel of the Lord's redemption of his people from Egyptian bondage (Ex 12:14). By participating in the Passover meal, the people were made beneficiaries of the redemption event, and so even later generations could say that they celebrate the Passover because "the Lord brought *us* out of Egypt" (Ex 13:14, 16). Similarly, the repeated celebration of the Lord's Supper reminds the saints of the new and greater "exodus" their Savior had accomplished in Jerusalem (Lk 9:31). This remembering of the crucified and living Lord, who is physically present and whose body and blood truly are received orally in the Eucharist, is not merely a mental activity such as we engage in when we consider other historical figures. Rather, the crucified and living Christ truly comes to us here, presenting himself—his body and blood—in the bread and the wine. To remember him, then, does not primarily require mental effort, but God-given "wisdom," "fear of the Lord," "faith." That wisdom and faith rest upon the words of Jesus himself! And that faith can only be created and inspired by God, who makes "his wonderful deeds to be remembered" (Ps 111:4).

Paul began his epistle by saying that the Gospel itself is foolishness according to the world's way of thinking, but God's "foolishness" is wiser than the world's wisdom (1 Cor 1:18–25). So, too, the doctrine that Christ's body and blood are really present with the bread and wine may seem like foolishness to some, but Christ's words have the power to accomplish what they say. Like "the word of the cross," Christ's Words of Institution are "the power of God" to those "who are being saved" (1:18).

"IN MY MEMORY" (11:24, 25)

The background to the phrase "in my memory" (11:24, 25) is undoubtedly the original Passover account in Ex 12:14: "This day shall be for you *a memorial day*, and you shall celebrate it as a feast of the Lord throughout your generations;

you shall celebrate it as an ordinance forever" (cf. Ex 13:9). For the people of Israel, this remembering of the exodus and Passover was far more real and vivid than any merely mental recollection of events from an increasingly remote past. The first Passover may have happened "yesterday" or yesteryear, but for each new generation it was happening afresh "today." Here lies the Israelite sense of their nation as one corporate personality, with past, present, and future generations all bound together as one people sharing the same blessed redemption.

Especially does this become apparent in Deut 5:2–4: "The Lord our God made a covenant *with us* in Horeb. *Not with our fathers* did the Lord make this covenant, *but with us, who are, all of us, here alive this day.* The Lord spoke *with you* [plural] face-to-face at the mountain, out of the midst of the fire."

In the light of the OT background, the Lord's Supper is a "re-presentation" of the salvation event accomplished in Jerusalem. Like a prophetic sign in the OT (e.g., Jeremiah 19; Ezekiel 4 and 5; and the Passover itself), so Holy Communion is a sign that, by virtue of the powerful Words of Institution, makes the body and the blood of Christ real and effective *for you.*

THE LORD TOOK THE CUP (11:25)

Jesus' second action in instituting the Lord's Supper, the blessing and distribution of the cup (1 Cor 11:25), seems to have taken place at some interval after his action with the bread. In the meantime, the disciples would have eaten the sacramental bread and (in view of the phrase "after the supper" in 11:25) completed the remaining courses of the meal. Now, in the same manner as he took the bread and gave thanks, Jesus took the cup and gave thanks over it as well (Mt 26:27; Mk 14:23). This was probably the third cup of the Passover meal, the "cup of blessing" (1 Cor 10:16).

As has been noted, the Words of Institution at this point in Paul and Luke ("this cup is the new testament in my blood," 1 Cor 11:25 and Lk 22:20) vary from Matthew and Mark's "this is my blood of the testament which is poured out for many" (Mt 26:28; Mk 14:24; Matthew adds "for the forgiveness of sins"). But there is no substantial difference in meaning. Whereas the version in Matthew and Mark provides a neater parallel with the saying over the bread, Paul and Luke's version gives slightly greater prominence to the theme of the new testament which is sealed and ratified by the blood of Christ. This new testament supersedes the old testament, which God ratified with the Israelites by having Moses sprinkle them with the blood of oxen (Ex 24:8). Now the new testament is ratified, confirmed, and sealed by the blood of Christ. This blood confers on the believer the gift of the new testament, the forgiveness of sins (cf. Jer 31:31–34; Mt 26:28; Heb 8:12; 1 Jn 1:7).

"YOU PROCLAIM THE DEATH OF THE LORD UNTIL HE COMES" (11:26)

In view of the solemn circumstances under which the Lord instituted his Supper, and the precious gifts conferred through that meal, it is totally inappropriate for the Corinthians' churchly gatherings to be marked by reveling and drunkenness (1 Cor 11:21). Rather, whenever they gather to drink the Lord's cup, it should be with sober recollection of its original setting on the night when Jesus was handed over by his Father and with quiet thankfulness for the forgiveness of sins, which is conferred through his blood.

The Sacrament proclaims "the death of the Lord" (11:26). By their whole action in gathering for the Sacrament, hearing the Words of Institution, and eating and drinking the sacramental elements, members of the Christian community proclaim "Jesus Christ and him crucified" (2:2) for their sins (cf. 1:18; 15:3).

Not only does the Lord's Supper look back to the Lord's crucifixion, but it also looks forward to his final coming. The reveling Corinthians seem to have forgotten this eschatological aspect of the Supper. Thinking they had already arrived (4:8), they regarded Holy Communion as the heavenly feast to come. Throughout the epistle Paul must remind them of the interim character of the Christian life, which will always be lived in the tension between the now and the not yet. Indeed, the epistle is framed by this eschatological perspective: the introduction includes the reminder that we still "await the revelation of our Lord Jesus Christ" (1:7); the conclusion includes the prayer "marana tha," "our Lord, come" (16:22; cf. Mt 26:29; Rev 22:20).

Like the OT people of God, his saints in the NT era live as those who are "on the way." Redeemed from the Egypt of their sins, they walk with "loins girded" and "lamps burning," watching and praying as they await their Master's coming (Lk 12:35–36; cf. 1 Pet 1:13). As those who look forward to the parousia, they are challenged to be a different kind of people: "Since all these things will be dissolved, what kind of people should you be?" (2 Pet 3:11). Not only are they to appropriate the Sacrament in faith for their own benefit, but they should also let that faith express itself in loving service to others, particularly the church's needier members (1 Cor 11:21). That concern is expressed by the post-Communion prayer: "Strengthen us through the same in faith toward you, and in fervent love toward one another" (e.g., *LSB* 166).

1 CORINTHIANS 11:27–34
Unworthy Reception of the Sacrament

TRANSLATION

**11 27 So whoever eats the bread or drinks the cup of
the Lord in an unworthy manner will be guilty
of sinning against the body and the blood of the
Lord. 28 Then let a person examine himself and
so eat of the bread and drink of the cup. 29 For he
who eats and drinks eats and drinks judgment to
himself if he does not discern the body. 30 For this
reason many among you are weak and ill, and a
considerable number have fallen asleep. 31 But if
we were examining ourselves, we would not be
undergoing judgment. 32 However, while we are
being judged by the Lord, we are being disciplined
so that we will not be condemned with the world.**

**33 So, my brothers, when you come together to
eat, wait for one another. 34 If anyone is hungry,
let him eat at home, so that you don't come
together for judgment. I will give instructions
about the remaining matters when I come.**

COMMENTARY

The strong inferential conjunction "so" (1 Cor 11:27) links this paragraph tightly to the preceding account of the institution of the Lord's Supper (11:23–26). Everything Paul is about to say concerning the guilt of the Corinthians follows from the Words of Institution: "This is my body. . . . This cup is the new testament in my blood" (11:24–25).

EATING UNWORTHILY (11:27)

Paul proceeds to issue a solemn warning of the dire consequences of unworthy eating. By unworthy eating he has in mind the type of behavior described in 11:20–22 and 11:29–30. Many of the Corinthians were sinning against faith and love. They were sinning against faith by their failure to discern that, in the

Sacrament, they were receiving the body and blood of Christ (11:29–30). And they were sinning against love in not showing consideration for the poor and needy (11:20–22). What Paul said about the arrogant Christians in 8:12 is equally true here: by sinning against weak and lowly Christians, "you are sinning *against Christ.*" To eat the bread and drink the cup in this manner is to be unworthy of the food offered in the Supper.

The Corinthians' sin against the Lord's body and blood was tantamount to the sin of the soldiers, Pilate, Judas, and the Jewish leaders in murdering Jesus. In fact, those Corinthians were "crucifying the Son of God afresh" (Heb 6:6) by their unworthy eating and drinking (cf. Heb 10:29).

Flowing as it does from the Words of Institution, the final clause of 1 Cor 11:27 confirms that, by the very act of the eating of the bread and wine in the Lord's Supper, the communicant orally receives Christ's body and blood. The Lord's body and blood are bound up with the elements by virtue of the sacramental union.

Another implication must also be drawn: the unworthy eater, no less than the worthy recipient, actually receives Christ's body and blood. A person's lack of faith does not alter the fact that the gifts of Christ's body and blood are offered and received in the Sacrament. But a lack of faith or a failure to acknowledge that Christ's body and blood are present does prevent a *worthy* reception and draws down God's judgment (11:29–30). For the unbeliever as for the believer, the sacramental bread is the Lord's true body, and the cup is his true blood. The fact that Christ's body and blood are present rests entirely on the power of Christ's words; it does not depend on the pastor who distributes the Supper or on the person who receives it.

Closed Communion

> [Portions of this section and the following one are taken from Jeffrey A. Gibbs, "An Exegetical Case for Close(d) Communion: 1 Corinthians 10:14–22; 11:17–34," *Concordia Journal* 21, no. 2 (April 1995): 148–63 (hereafter cited as "Gibbs"); and The Lutheran Church—Missouri Synod Commission on Theology and Church Relations, *Admission to the Lord's Supper: Basics of Biblical and Confessional Teaching* (St. Louis: LCMS, 1999) (hereafter cited as "CTCR").]

Because the unworthy recipient actually receives Christ's body and blood to his harm (1 Cor 11:27–30), the church has traditionally recognized the need for pastors and congregations not to admit everyone indiscriminately to Holy Communion. Since this is "the *Lord's* Supper," it must be administered according to *his* institution and instructions. Whereas Christ delivered his word to the masses, he only celebrated the Sacrament with his closest disciples; following our Lord's practice, we are not to cast the Lord's Supper among a crowd. A careless "open Communion" policy should be avoided. The church should equally avoid an unloving rigor which denies the Sacrament to anyone to whom Christ wants it given.

A careful exegesis of 1 Cor 10:14–22 yields the following implications for the church's Communion practice (Gibbs, 152–53):

> 1. Christians . . . cannot and must not participate in non-Christian worship services.
>
> 2. By inference, non-Christians must not participate in the celebration of the Christian Lord's Supper.
>
> 3. The realities involved in the Eucharist are not created or altered by the attitude and/or faith of those who are eating and drinking. The cup and bread *are* the participation in the blood and body of Christ [1 Cor 10:16]. In a similar manner, when false gods are invoked, and sacrifice offered to them, the demons with their reality are present, even if an individual Christian is there as participant [10:20–21].
>
> 4. To speak of "individuals" communing with their Lord in the Eucharist can lead to a serious misunderstanding. For the participation in Christ's body and blood, through eating and drinking, necessarily involves the individual with those with whom he or she is communing [see especially 10:16–17].

Four additional exegetical conclusions may be drawn from 11:17–34. These are that (5) failure to discern the body is unworthy eating; (6) pastoral supervision is needed in determining who should be admitted to the Supper; (7) divisions within the local congregation may require that some Christians be excluded from the Supper; and (8) differences between denominations may require that some Christians be excluded from the Supper. These conclusions are discussed under the following four subheads.

Failure to "Discern the Body" Is Unworthy Eating (11:27, 29)

Christians should not commune if they would do so "in an unworthy manner" (11:27). Such unworthy communing calls down the judgment of God, which can result in various afflictions (11:29–30), even if those afflictions are to be seen as God's fatherly chastening, rather than as preludes to eternal condemnation (11:32).

> The key to communing in a worthy manner is the ability and willingness to "discern the body" [11:29]. . . . It consists of repentance and faith, and these move in two directions at the same time. Repentance applies to sin committed against God in general, the vertical dimension. But owing to the corporate character of the Sacrament, such repentance also applies specifically and especially to one's relationship to fellow communicants, the horizontal dimension. One who communes "worthily" acknowledges the importance of preserving a unity with

> fellow communicants and is willing to do what is needed to remove any fracture or division in that unity [CTCR, 20].

More specific aspects of communing "unworthily" are explained by Gibbs (161):

> Paul teaches that to commune unworthily means three things. First, unworthy communing takes place when Christians commune while abusing the horizontal relationship between Christians, or when that abuse is ignored and tolerated. Second, unworthy communing takes place when the Sacrament's very purpose—to sustain the unity of the members of the one body—is also ignored. Third, unworthy communing occurs when the reality of Christ's body and blood in the Sacrament is overtly or implicitly denied.

That third point rests on the interpretation that "body" in the phrase "discerning the body" (11:29) refers to the sacramental body of Christ, which is present with the bread that is eaten in the Lord's Supper. Several factors support that traditional interpretation. The only other occurrences of "the body" in the chapter are in references to Christ's sacramental body. The first occurrence in the context is in Christ's Words of Institution in 11:24, "this is *my body*." The second and only other occurrence of "body" in the chapter (besides its occurrence in 11:29) is in Paul's description of the main problem in the church in Corinth: many were "guilty of sinning against *the body and the blood* of the Lord" (11:27). The inclusion of the Lord's "blood" alongside of his "body" in 11:27 requires that "body" in 11:27 (as also in 11:24 and 11:29) must refer to the body of Christ given and eaten together with the bread in the Sacrament. If "body" in 11:27 were interpreted metaphorically to refer only to the church, to what could the Lord's "blood" refer? The church is never called Christ's blood.

There is a tight relationship between the three verses 11:27, 28, and 29. The problem is stated in 11:27; the remedy for the problem is found in the exhortation in 11:28; and 11:29 states the reason why Christians must heed the exhortation in 11:28 and so avoid committing the grievous sin described in 11:27. The cohesiveness of Paul's argumentation in 11:27–29 requires that "body" must refer to the sacramental body of Christ in 11:29 as well as in 11:27.

Pastoral Supervision

Pastors are to exercise oversight in the matter of determining who should be admitted to the Supper and who should not. To be sure, Paul does not issue an explicit command for the pastor(s) of the Corinthian congregation to determine who should commune and who should not. But "*the apostle himself is the one exercising pastoral oversight in the troubled situation.* He is their one 'father' in Christ (1 Cor. 4:15–16), and both of the canonical Corinthian epistles reflect the apostle's urgent need to call the Corinthians back to a joyful acknowledgment of and submission to Paul's own apostolic teaching and authority" (CTCR, 22).

Paul's apostolic example is to serve as a model for all pastors, who are "stewards of the mysteries of God" (1 Cor 4:1).

In 1 Corinthians 11, Paul does not forbid anyone from communing; rather, "Paul simply commands them to change. It is, however, a permissible logical step to move from 'before you continue communing change these sinful divisions among you' to 'don't commune if these divisions still exist'" (Gibbs, 161–62).

Divisions within the Local Congregation

Persons who may be excluded from the Lord's Supper can include those who are causing sinful divisions within the local congregation.

> Since the body and blood of Christ are for the oneness and unity of the body, those who commune must not perpetrate or ignore sinful disunity in their midst. . . . In 1 Corinthians the apostle is dealing, as it were, with members of his own congregation. He therefore addresses the immediate abuses regarding the Lord's Supper in chapter eleven, while pastorally, patiently, and firmly dealing with other doctrinal and moral aberrations throughout the remainder of the letter [CTCR, 21].

In 11:27–34, Paul is concerned about the relationships between members within one particular congregation.

> When bitter church fights are taking place, when resentful words and deeds are being hurled throughout a congregation and echoing round a sanctuary, what shall the believers and their pastor do? Shall they continue blissfully to commune together, leaving the divisions among them to wreak their spiritual havoc, and thus invite the judgment of God? Should the pastor not rather, in deep love and sorrow, propose that the factions refrain from participating in the Sacrament, until the differences and divisions be removed through repentance and mutual forgiveness [Gibbs, 162]?

Differences between Denominations

Paul's words to the particular congregation in Corinth also have wider application to the whole Christian church on earth throughout her history, including the present day. Doctrinal divisions between Christian denominations—the differences between the confessions of faith that define and delineate Christian church bodies—may also require that Christians from heterodox communions be excluded from the Lord's Supper.

> What about erroneous teaching that exists among those who still may be Christians? All error flows from Satan and from unbelief, and thus all error in itself is completely "non-Christian" or heretical. But false teaching can be confessed not only by unbelievers but also by believers, who by a felicitous inconsistency still cling in faith to Christ Jesus as Savior. This we call "heterodoxy" and the New Testament reveals the presence of heterodox teaching on the part of those who nevertheless may be in the church [CTCR, 26].

Examining the entirety of 1 Corinthians,

> one searches in vain for the attitude by which Paul would say, "You may think what you like about matters of morality (against 1 Corinthians 5), or pagan worship (against 1 Corinthians 8), or worship practices (against 1 Corinthians 11–14)." These [Christians in Corinth] are his members, and he exercises his oversight as steward of the mysteries [1 Cor 4:1]. It is inconceivable that Paul might say, "Think what you like about these issues. Disagree with me and still come to the Lord's Supper." Hardly. The apostle himself shows that his spiritual children are to follow in and confess his teaching . . . (1 Cor. 14:36–38) [CTCR, 28–29].

It is true that denominations as such did not exist in the NT era, and so Paul does not expressly say what should be done when an entire church body denies this or that biblical doctrine.

> But this much is clear. Paul did not tolerate doctrinal diversity. His teaching was that of one sent by Christ Himself and his hearers were to accept it as such. Moreover, the Eucharist was the congregation's sacrament of unity, and divisions were to be dealt with before mutual communing took place. The biblical evidence leads to this conclusion: unity in apostolic doctrine is appropriate and necessary among those who commune together at the Lord's Supper [CTCR, 30].

Gibbs (163) concludes: "It cannot be that sinful divisions be ignored among us, for in so doing, we would effectively deny, and thus sin against, the very Sacrament itself."

"LET A PERSON EXAMINE HIMSELF" (11:28)

In order not to incur this serious guilt, each believer should examine himself before he eats from the bread and drinks from the cup. To understand what Paul may have in mind by his call for self-examination, we may compare these passages: "Test yourselves to see whether you are in the faith. Examine yourselves" (2 Cor 13:5). And "let each person examine his own work" (Gal 6:4). The latter verse comes from a context which speaks of Christian love ("bear one another's burdens," Gal 6:2). Thus, Paul is calling on the Corinthians to check the sincerity of their faith and the depth of their love for one another, in light of the abuses that have come to his attention.

In its immediate context, the call for the Christian who would commune to "examine himself" (1 Cor 11:28) is intended to prevent the damage that is done to a Christian who eats and drinks judgment upon himself, sinning against the Lord's body and blood (11:27) because he fails to "discern the body" (11:29). The Christian who would commune must examine whether he discerns "the body" (11:29), since failure to discern the body is what incurs God's judgment. Based on a careful study of 11:28 in this context, three main dimensions of this self-examination seem to be required.

First, the communicant must examine himself by asking whether he believes that Christ's physical body and blood are present together with the bread and wine which he will eat and drink. Faith in this true presence rests on Christ's own words, "this is my body" (11:24) and "this . . . is . . . my blood" (11:25). An affirmation of this real presence is absolutely necessary for all discussion of Paul's theology and understanding of the Lord's Supper. Second, self-examination should discover faith in and desire for the benefits of the Lord's Supper, which are given according to the Lord's own promise. Chief among these benefits is "the forgiveness of sins" (Mt 26:28), and so self-examination should reveal an awareness of one's own sin and need for forgiveness. A third fruit of self-examination may be gleaned from Paul's emphasis in 1 Corinthians 10–11 on the unity of the body of Christ as the members of his body commune together, partaking of the one loaf (1 Cor 10:17). "All who commune must examine themselves and through repentance and faith they must find the divinely-created willingness to remove divisions and to preserve unity with fellow communicants" (CTCR, 19). This will include the resolve to amend one's own life for the sake of the church's unity and witness to Christ.

All three of those aspects of self-examination are intertwined. "A right perception of the presence of Christ's body and blood in the Eucharist will necessarily entail a right perception of one's relationship to fellow communicants" (CTCR, 19), and it will also entail a right perception of one's relationship to God through Christ's crucified body and his blood shed for the forgiveness of sins.

While self-examination should include these aspects, the apostle is not demanding perfection of believers before they come to Communion. It is regrettable that pietists have often understood 1 Cor 11:28–32 as if the purpose of self-examination would be to make it possible by one's own efforts to raise one's level of sanctification and thus become worthy of the Supper. On the contrary, the worthy recipient is the one who recognizes his unworthiness, his great deficiency in faith and love, and who thus hungers and thirsts for forgiveness, trusting Christ's promise (Mt 26:28) that the forgiveness of sins comes with the reception of Christ's body and blood in the Sacrament. The arrogant and skeptical Corinthians, on the other hand, were unworthy precisely because they were so full of themselves and their spiritual attainments.

Should the Sacrament Be Offered to Children?

The Lutheran church has traditionally used 1 Cor 11:28 ("let a person examine himself") as the basis for its practice of not offering Holy Communion to children. In recent years, however, the question of whether the Sacrament should be offered to children at an earlier age, and even to infants, has been the subject of vigorous debate.

Two observations may be made. First, the meaning of "examine" (11:28) cannot be reduced to merely the equivalent of "repent," or "believe, have faith." The verb "examine," in 1 Jn 4:1 involves the intellect, or theological acumen: "Examine the spirits, whether they are from God." Such testing or self-examination would not be possible for infants or very young children (or, for example, for an unconscious or comatose person). Second, while it may be possible to draw inferences from 1 Cor 11:27–32 regarding the communing of children, it needs to be recognized that this falls outside Paul's immediate purview.

Any changes to current practice should only be introduced on the basis of thorough study, with pastors and congregations taking care that "all things be done properly and in order" (1 Cor 14:40), and that any moves to commune younger children not be introduced at the expense of proper catechesis.

THE BODY AND THE CHURCH (11:29)

With the particle ("for," 11:29), Paul links the verse to the preceding context. Paul has asked the Corinthians to examine themselves (11:28) before eating and drinking the Sacrament because he does not want them to eat and drink judgment on themselves. And this will surely happen if one "does not discern the body" (11:29). These holy gifts are not to be despised or trifled with.

Some commentators deny that "body" in 11:29 refers to Christ's body in the Sacrament. They point instead to Paul's use of the term in 10:17 to designate Christ's mystical "body," the church. After all, they maintain, the overt sin in Corinth was the rift in the church between the prosperous and the poor in connection with the sacramental celebration. As has been argued above, the basic problem with a one-sided interpretation of "body" here as the mystical body, the church, is that it does not do justice to the immediate context, the Words of Institution, and the links which lead from those significant words to the text under consideration. A case can be made, however, that "body" in 11:29 may, in addition to its primary reference to Christ's physical body in the Sacrament, have an echo of its meaning further away in the wider context, where it refers to the church (10:17; 12:12–27).

MANY ARE ILL (11:30)

Paul now spells out the consequences of the Corinthians' abuse of the Sacrament for many in Corinth. As reported to him (possibly by the three-man delegation in 16:17 or by "Chloe's people," 1:11), an unusually large number of the Corinthians had fallen ill, and a considerable number had died. The spate of illnesses and deaths occurred despite the presence in the congregation of a number of people with gifts of healing (12:9). Paul interpreted the events as signs of a judgment from God on those who failed to discern the Lord's body in the Sacrament. The Lord's Supper is designed to serve "as a pure, wholesome, soothing medicine which aids and quickens us in both soul and body" (LC V 68). But this same wholesome medicine had instead proved harmful, even deadly, for those who despised it.

God's severe judgment on some of the Corinthians seems, indeed, to have been a special case, a timely warning to the Corinthians and to the young church at large. It does not mean there will always be similar physical consequences when the Sacrament is abused. At the same time, certainly it is a warning to the church of all ages that the Sacrament should not be taken lightly. To despise it brings God's judgment, even though the judgment may not manifest itself in the same way or come so quickly.

GOD'S DISCIPLINE "SO THAT WE WILL NOT BE CONDEMNED" (11:31–32)

Paul uses a softer tone in 11:31–32, speaking in the first person plural to include himself with the congregation. He first says, in effect, "None of these judgments would have happened to us if we had been examining ourselves" (see Paul's command in 11:28). But then he adds in 11:32 that when we are faced with the reality of such judgments, we should not despair of God's grace. Rather, we should look on the events as the Lord's fatherly discipline to bring us to our senses and keep us from finally being condemned with the unbelieving world (cf. Heb 12:5–7, 10).

CONCLUSION (11:33–34)

Addressing them pastorally again as "my brothers," Paul concludes his argument that the Sacrament should be held in proper reverence. There should be no more of the shameful scrambling at the agape meal, whereby each person went ahead with his own private meal without a thought for those who could not be present until later. This self-centered behavior was marring the whole evening, to the degree that the Lord's Supper held in conjunction with the meal was no longer worthy of the name (1 Cor 11:20); indeed, it was bringing the Lord's displeasure and judgment on the Corinthians (11:30–32). From now on, Paul says, they should wait for one another. Although the rich were the ones at fault, Paul delicately avoids mentioning anyone, but appeals to all. If anyone is so hungry that he cannot wait for others and share his food, then he should first satisfy his hunger at home. Thus, Paul implies that there must be a clear distinction between the fellowship meal and the Lord's Supper, a separation which became standard in the church.

Finally, he adds that he will attend to other matters during his next visit (11:34). While the reader can only guess what these other matters may have been, it seems reasonable to suppose they were less important details connected in some way to the Lord's Supper. At this stage he is unable to say precisely when that next visit will be, although he will discuss his future plans in more detail in 16:5–8.

12:1–31

SPIRITUAL GIFTS

1 CORINTHIANS 12:1–3

THE HOLY SPIRIT INSPIRES THE CONFESSION OF JESUS AS LORD

TRANSLATION

12 **[1]Now concerning the spiritual things, brothers,**
I do not want you to be ignorant. [2]You know that
when you were Gentiles you used to be carried away
to those dumb idols, however you may have been
led. [3]So I am informing you that no one speaking
by the Spirit of God says, "Jesus be cursed," and no
one can say, "Jesus is Lord" but by the Holy Spirit.

COMMENTARY

Paul presents the word of the cross as the basis for the church's worship in 1 Corinthians 11–14. In chapter 12, he deals with another problem affecting the congregation's worship: their ignorance concerning spiritual gifts. His efforts to correct their misguided thinking will occupy the next three chapters (12–14). Just as in his extensive discussion of idol-meat (chapters 8–10), where the critical issue, reclining in idol-temples, is only addressed directly (and forbidden) in chapter 10 after he has carefully prepared the groundwork, so the Corinthians' abuse of the gift of tongues will not be confronted directly until chapter 14, after he has prepared the way by presenting a broad theology of the role of spiritual gifts (chapter 12) and stressed the need to use each gift in love (chapter 13).

The formula "now concerning" indicates that, again, Paul takes up an item from the Corinthians' prior letter to him (see Introduction to Chapter 7). This time there is no quotation from their letter, so we can only guess the precise nature of what they may have said. But evidently Paul is concerned to correct some misunderstandings that have come to his attention about spiritual gifts.

From the outset, Paul had given thanks to God for the rich spiritual endowments God had bestowed on this church (1:4–7). There was not one gift of God's grace which they lacked (1:7). But a sense of proportion was missing. The congregation was infected by an all-too-human pride in its giftedness (cf. 4:6–8) and a tendency to exalt certain spectacular gifts rather than to cultivate those which best served their brothers and sisters in the faith. The very term "spiritual gifts" ("spiritual things," 12:1) should have been a reminder to them that the gifts came from God's Spirit; they were not the product of human effort.

Paul reminds the Corinthians of their recent experience as "Gentiles" (12:2). During those days, they were constantly being carried away to "dumb idols" (12:2), the lifeless and powerless representations of beings who were not really gods (Gal 4:8). The OT often refers to these idols as deaf and dumb, unable to lift a finger to help their devotees (Ps 115:5; Is 44: 9–20; Hab 2:18–19) in contrast to "the living and true God" (1 Thess 1:9) who acts with a powerful hand.

But although the idols were ineffective in themselves, behind them, as Paul demonstrated in 1 Cor 10:19–22, lay powerful demonic forces which sought to suck idol worshipers into their maw. In their pre-Christian days, the Corinthians were not strong, independent people freely following their choices. Devotees of ecstatic pagan cults, like the cult of Dionysus, for example, might persuade themselves that they had been filled with extraordinary spiritual power. In reality, however, they had been captured by forces far stronger than themselves. They had become the helpless victims of demonic powers which led them off to their fate as a prisoner is led away for execution. Paul does not name the agent who carried them away, but no doubt he primarily has in mind the devil.

Such mindless attraction to idols had been a feature of their heathen past. But now it is incompatible with their new life in the Spirit. Paul reminds them that "no one speaking by the Spirit of God says, 'Jesus be cursed'" (12:3). There are numerous suggestions about the specific situation Paul may be addressing. His words may be directed again to the "liberated" Corinthian Christians who thought they could flirt with idolatry by reclining in idol-temples and participating in the cup and the table of demons (8:10; 10:21). Like syncretistic Christians of all ages, they thought they could "have it both ways." It suited them on occasion to be indistinguishable from the world. And on those occasions they may even have thought it did not matter if they joined their heathen associates in cursing Jesus, either out loud or by actions that, in effect, denied that Jesus is the only Lord. It is conceivable that some of the overconfident Christians, carried away by their "liberty" in the Spirit, had given expression to blasphemous remarks, perhaps while under the influence of alcohol in an idol's temple.

Evidence from a later date shows that 12:3a (or at least the idea it expresses) quickly became known even to non-Christians. Christianity came under intense persecution in the second half of the first century and during the second century AD. In ca. AD 112, Pliny the Younger, the Roman governor of Bithynia, wrote to the emperor, Trajan, that in his investigation of those accused of being Christians, if a suspect would *curse Christ* and worship statues of gods and the emperor, he would let the suspect go because these were things "those who are really Christians cannot be made to do" (*Letters*, 10.96). Those who refused to curse Christ and worship the emperor were executed. Such a context of persecution, where confessing Christ as Lord or cursing him became a matter of (physical) life or death, reminds all Christians of just how weighty a matter it is to confess Christ and profess the Christian faith.

Where the Holy Spirit is present, Jesus will not be vilified. On the contrary, the Spirit's chief role is to glorify Jesus (Jn 16:14). Indeed, no one can glorify him and call him "Lord" but by the Spirit's power. Thus, the Corinthians should not conclude that so-and-so is a stranger to the Spirit because he or she lacks a certain gift. Here Paul reaffirms what he has stated at greater length in 1 Cor 2:10–14: the person who lacks the Holy Spirit is totally unable to understand and receive the things of God; he has no capacity at all in spiritual matters. Only the person who is reborn spiritually by baptismal water and the Spirit (Jn 3:5) is able to believe and confess Jesus as Lord and Christ (Rom 8:9; 10:9; 1 Jn 5:1). Luther (SC II 6) states this clearly: "I believe that I cannot by my own reason or strength believe in Jesus Christ, my Lord, or come to Him. But the Holy Spirit has called me by the Gospel. . . ."

The confession of Jesus' lordship is at the heart of the Christian confession of faith (see "marana tha," "our Lord, come!" in 1 Cor 16:22; cf. Rom 10:9; Phil 2:11). Thus, the first three verses of 1 Corinthians 12 provide the proper framework and perspective for the forthcoming discussion of spiritual gifts through chapter 14. Paul does not wish to talk about individual gifts until he has given due recognition to the Spirit's "inexpressible gift" (2 Cor 9:15) of the Lord Jesus himself.

1 CORINTHIANS 12:4–11

Varieties of Gifts from the One and the Same Spirit

TRANSLATION

12 [4]Now there are varieties of gifts of grace, but the
same Spirit. [5]And there are varieties of services, and
the same Lord. [6]And there are varieties of workings,
but the same God is the one who works all things
in all. [7]Now to each person the manifestation of the
Spirit is being given for the common good. [8]For to
one there is being given through the Spirit a word
of wisdom, and to another a word of knowledge
according to the same Spirit, [9]to another faith by the
same Spirit, and to another gracious gifts of healings
by that one Spirit, [10]and to another workings of
miraculous powers, to another prophecy, to another
discernings of spirits, to another kinds of tongues,
and to another the interpretation of tongues. [11]Now
all these things the one and the same Spirit works,
distributing to each one individually as he wishes.

COMMENTARY

In response to the Corinthians' enquiry about "spiritual things" (1 Cor 12:1), Paul begins to speak of the variety of "gifts of grace" (12:4) that have been poured out on the congregation. This is a gentle reminder to those who prided themselves on their possession of spiritual endowments that they possessed nothing which they had not received as a totally unmerited gift of God's grace (see 4:7). Here in 12:4 in this carefully chosen word, "gifts of grace," we find the heart of Paul's theology of grace, expressed as a loving and sobering pastoral corrective to Christians full of themselves ("puffed up," 4:6, 18–19; 5:2; 8:1) and their own giftedness.

God had graciously furthered the upbuilding of his church by pouring out a great variety of gifts, of which Paul's lists in 12:8–10, 28–30 are illustrative rather than exhaustive. Whereas the Corinthians seem to have been overly impressed by one or two spectacular gifts, like speaking in tongues, Paul corrects their myopia with his broader view. First, Paul had praised God that the church in Corinth did not lack *any* "gift of grace" (1:7). He uses the same Greek expression in a broad way in his other epistles too, for example, for the gift of salvation itself (Rom 5:15–16; 6:23; 11:29). He also uses it of some special gift of encouragement which he expected to come from his ministry in Rome (Rom 1:11). Even the capacity to live as a celibate or as a married person is a gift of grace (1 Cor 7:7). The term may also be used of the gift which helps a pastor to fulfill his office (1 Tim 4:14; 2 Tim 1:6). But all Christians, not just pastors, have gifts (1 Cor 1:7; cf. 1 Pet 4:10).

It may be debated whether Paul's emphasis falls on the variety of the gifts or on the fact that all gifts come from the same source: the one Spirit of the triune God. It seems evident that he is stressing both, but with the center of gravity falling each time on the second clause in 1 Cor 12:4–6: "the *same* Spirit," "the *same* Lord," "the *same* God." If this analysis is correct, there is a significant parallel in Eph 4:1–16. There Paul begins by urging the Ephesians "to preserve the unity of the Spirit in the bond of peace" (Eph 4:3), for there is one body, one Spirit, one hope, one Lord, one faith, one Baptism, and one God and Father. Then he goes on to mention various gifts of God's grace (Eph 4:7–11). But God gave these gifts, Paul concludes, with the purpose that "all of us come to the *unity* of the faith . . . and grow up . . . into him who is our head, into Christ," and be built up as one body "in love" (Eph 4:13–16).

No hard and fast distinction may be made between the contribution of each member of the Trinity, as if Paul meant to imply that the Holy Spirit only supplied "gifts of grace" (1 Cor 12:4), but not "services" (12:5) or "workings" (12:6, 10). Each of the three terms, "gifts of grace" (12:4), "services" (12:5), and "workings" (12:6, 10), should be understood as a comprehensive expression for the triune God giving to, serving through, and working through the believer. But it is fitting and in keeping with biblical usage that the Holy Spirit is seen as having a prominent role as the source of the spiritual *gifts*; that the Lord Jesus who came "not to be served but to serve" (Mk 10:45) is seen as the one who especially inspires Christian *service;* and that the Father who is unceasingly at work in sustaining his creation (Jn 5:17; cf. Gal 2:8) should be seen as the one who *works* "all things in all" (1 Cor 12:6). All glory for the congregation's giftedness belongs to the triune God alone.

There can be no doubt that Paul in 12:4–6 is giving expression to what later became known as the Christian doctrine of the Trinity: "Spirit . . . Lord . . . God." Other significant trinitarian passages in Paul are 2 Cor 13:14 and Eph 4:4–6, which mention the persons in the same order and with the same designations: "Spirit . . . Lord . . . God."

With his theological foundation in place—that the Holy Spirit's role is to glorify the Lord Jesus, and that all spiritual gifts ultimately come from the same triune God—Paul moves from these general principles to an extended discussion of specific gifts and their role within the body of Christ. But first he lays down his thesis in 1 Cor 12:7: *all these gifts, in their great variety, are given by and through the same Spirit, whose power and presence they manifest, and all are designed to serve the common good.* There is no room for the divisive spirit that jealously eyes others' gifts or looks down on what others have been given. After all, the gifts of the Spirit are precisely that: gifts, not personal accomplishments. Note the repeated use of the verb "is being given" in 12:7–8. As Paul had asked earlier: "What do you have that you have not received?" (4:7). All these gifts are to be used humbly for the edification of all (14:26).

It is not surprising that Paul mentions first in 12:8 "a word of wisdom" and then "a word of knowledge," for by the Gospel the Corinthians had been especially enriched with these gifts ("enriched . . . in all speech and all knowledge," 1:5). God's wisdom and knowledge are found in the Gospel of Christ crucified; that was Paul's theme in 1:18–2:16. The precise nature of these gifts in 12:8 is not easily determined. However, it seems reasonable to suppose that Paul begins with these two gifts because these were the ones most commonly found among those who had been led to the Spirit-inspired confession "Jesus is Lord" (12:3). The difference between "word of wisdom" and "word of knowledge" (1 Cor 12:8) is probably that the former involves the wise application of the Christian faith to another person's spiritual need, while the latter involves the gift of telling the basics of the Christian faith, which imparts knowledge of God (cf. Gal 4:9). What the gifts have in common is the ability through God's Word to offer the "counsel and help" of the Gospel "through the mutual conversation and consolation of brethren" (SA III IV).

The same Spirit had endowed another with a special gift of faith (1 Cor 12:9). This must be an addition to saving faith, for that trust in God's power displayed in the cross is bestowed on all Christians. In 12:9, Paul has in mind a greater measure of faith, as displayed, for example, by the Syro-Phoenician woman ("O woman, great is your faith," Mt 15:28) in contrast to the disciples, whose faith often was weak. Sometimes this greater measure of faith will manifest itself as a "heroic faith" which wrestles with God in prayer and moves mountains without doubting (Mt 21:21; 1 Cor 13:2), bringing about an extraordinary turn of events. Often, however, there may be nothing spectacular about this faith; it will simply take the form of a cheerful and steadfast trust and endurance in the middle of life's pain and difficulties. By their patience and their ability to see the hand of God in everything, people gifted with such faith are able to encourage others and build the congregation's morale.

To another is given "gracious gifts of healings" (12:9). The plurals could indicate that these gifts were not always of the same kind. Perhaps different ways of healing different kinds of infirmities are in view and were bestowed on some Christians from time to time at the Spirit's pleasure. Jesus' message was attested by miracles of healings as diverse as exorcisms and raising the dead. These were both expressions of his compassion (Mt 20:34; Mk 1:41; 9:22–27; Lk 7:13–15) and signs of the salvation in store for the believer in body and soul, to be fulfilled in the resurrection (1 Corinthians 15). So, too, the apostolic preaching was powerfully confirmed by gifts of healings (Acts 2:43; 3:1–9; 5:12, 15; 6:8; 8:6, 13; 9:34; 14:3; 15:12; 19:11–12; 28:8–9; 2 Cor 12:12).

It is debatable whether these "gracious gifts of healings" (1 Cor 12:9) are found in precisely the same form in the church today. Just as the gift of apostleship was an unrepeatable feature of the church's foundational period, and the writing of authoritative, inspired Scripture was completed with the book of Revelation (Rev 22:18–19), so it may be argued that prophecy and tongues were intended to be foundational gifts for the early church only, and that may apply also to gifts of healing. None of the so-called healing ministries in the church today exhibit the six traits of the healings performed by Jesus and the apostles: the ability to heal with a word or a touch, the ability to heal instantly, to heal totally, to heal anyone, to heal organic disease, and to raise the dead.

Just as speaking in tongues is found early in Acts and in 1 Corinthians, but not in 2 Corinthians or in other NT books, even in the NT we may perceive a fading of the healing gifts. For example, there is no mention that Paul exercised a healing gift (beyond the use of prayer) as part of the restoration of Epaphroditus' health (Phil 2:25–27). Similarly, we find Paul leaving his friend Trophimus sick at Miletus (2 Tim 4:20). Noteworthy, too, is the Lord's answer to Paul's thrice-repeated request to be relieved of his thorn in the flesh: "my grace is sufficient for you, for my power is made perfect in weakness" (2 Cor 12:9).

On the other hand, as countless Christians will attest, God often answers prayers for healing in a remarkable way, in keeping with John's assurance: "This is the confidence which we have in him, that if we ask anything according to his will, he hears us" (1 Jn 5:14; cf. Mt 8:2). Through his good Spirit, he also enhances the natural healing skills of a Christian doctor or nurse or parent. But such healings through means that are a natural part of the created order are of a different nature from the supernatural gifts of healing which characterized the ministry of Jesus, the apostles, and others in the early church.

In 1 Cor 12:10, Paul notes that the signs and wonders that attest the infant church's Gospel ministry (2 Cor 12:12; Gal 3:5) include more than miraculous healings. Some are endowed with "workings of miraculous powers." Included in this category would be exorcisms and other notable displays of spiritual power (e.g., Acts 13:9–11; 16:16–18). In the gospels, Jesus' miracles are sometimes called "powers" (e.g., Mt 11:20–23; Mk 6:2, 5, 14; see also Mk 5:30; Lk 4:36; 6:19; 9:1).

There is some overlap with these terms in 1 Cor 12:9–10; "healings" could also be called "miraculous powers," and exorcisms could be called "healings" (Mt 15:28; Lk 6:18; Acts 10:38). Also some of the Corinthians probably would have possessed more than one of the gifts.

Others were endowed with the gift of "prophecy" (1 Cor 12:10). See the excursus "Spiritual Gifts in 1 Corinthians" regarding the nature of this gift as the reception and imparting of special revelation. Prophecy is paired with the gift of "discernings of spirits" (12:10). That this means the ability to distinguish between true and false prophecies is demonstrated by 1 Jn 4:1–3. John urges all Christians to "test the spirits" because of the danger of being taken in by false prophets (see also Mt 7:15–23). The true prophet's confession of faith glorifies the Christ who has come in the flesh. In such prophets, the Spirit of God dwells, whereas it is the spirit of antichrist who dwells in the false prophet. The close link between John's use of the terms "false prophets" and "spirit/Spirit" coincides with Paul's terminology here in 1 Cor 12:1–11 (cf. 14:29; 1 Thess 5:21; Heb 5:14).

To yet another, Paul continues in 1 Cor 12:10, is given the gift of speaking in various kinds of tongues, while another is able to interpret or translate tongues-speaking. The precise nature of speaking in tongues—whether it consisted of the Spirit-inspired ability to speak in known languages (i.e., languages known to some people, though not to the speaker), as is the case in Acts 2, or whether it was "ecstatic utterance" not in any human language—is also discussed in the excursus "Spiritual Gifts in 1 Corinthians." At this point, however, it may be asked why Paul leaves this gift until last. Some commentators believe he does this to give it some prominence as the "problem" gift. But more likely, Paul lists it last in order to correct the Corinthians' tendency, in their overcharged emotional state, to place far too much value on it at the expense of more valuable gifts that edify the whole church. As chapter 14 makes plain, he certainly accords it lesser value than prophecy.

Whatever the gift may have been, it was necessary that there be an interpreter. Otherwise the church could not receive edification through it (14:5).

Now Paul rounds off the unit that began with 12:4. All these gifts derive from the same source—"the one and the same Spirit" (12:11). Thus, they are not intended to serve individual self-glorification nor the centrifugal forces in the church (cf. 1:10–15). Rather they are to serve the Spirit's edifying purposes. He remains sovereign, distributing the gifts to each person in keeping with his own free will. The Spirit "blows where he wills" (Jn 3:8; cf. Ps 135:6).

EXCURSUS

Spiritual Gifts in 1 Corinthians

From the outset of his epistle, Paul ties his discussion of spiritual gifts to the Gospel of God's grace in Jesus Christ. There is an intimate connection between the "grace" (1 Cor 1:3–4) bestowed on the Corinthians in the Gospel, and their rich endowment so that they "are not lacking in any gift of grace" (1:7), "in all speech and all knowledge" (1:5). Together with the grace of the Gospel, the church had been supplied with every gift needed for its well-being and upbuilding. While the Corinthians seem to have thought of themselves as "spiritual people" (3:1, though Paul's assessment was that they were still "fleshly") and they preferred to speak of their "spiritual gifts" (see the commentary on 12:1), Paul constantly reminds them that the Spirit's gifts are "gifts of grace" (1:7; 7:7; 12:4, 9, 28, 30, 31). "What do you have," he asks them, "that you did not receive? But if indeed you received it, why are you boasting as if you did not receive [it]?" (4:7).

The connection Paul draws between the "gifts of grace" and the "grace" is indeed so intimate and important that the gift is inseparable from the gracious power which bestows it. In other words, a gift of grace does not become the Christian's settled possession; it is constantly bestowed and manifested afresh by the gracious Spirit as the Spirit sees fit (cf. 12:7: "Now to each person the manifestation of the Spirit *is being given,*" and 12:11: "the same Spirit works, distributing to each one individually as he [the Spirit] wishes").

The close link between God's "grace" in the Gospel and the "gifts of grace" becomes evident again when we consider the work of the Holy Spirit. The same member of the Trinity who enables the heart and mouth to say "Jesus is Lord" (12:3) is the one who enlightens us with his gifts. Rather than glorifying himself and his dramatic performances, the Spirit's primary task is to glorify Jesus (Jn 16:14). As he thus points people to the Lord Jesus, focusing their attention on him, the one and the same Holy Spirit distributes to each individual those gifts which will best serve the common good of the body of Christ (12:7–11).

Every Christian, even the lowliest, has been endowed with the Holy Spirit in Baptism (1 Cor 12:13; cf. Acts 2:17–18) and is called to cultivate the fruit of the Spirit by the Spirit's power. Such fruit, all of which should be evident in the lives of all Christians, includes "love, joy, peace, patience, kindness, goodness, faith, humility, and self-control" (Gal 5:22–23).

In addition to those attributes of Christ himself, which are manifest in various degrees in all his saints, God has seen fit to bestow extraordinary gifts upon particular Christians. The biblical language suggests that every Christian may have at least one of these uncommon gifts. Both Paul and Peter speak of the

Spirit's endowment to "each" Christian (1 Cor 12:7, 11; 1 Pet 4:10). According to 1 Peter, each Christian should use the gift he has received in the service of others "as good stewards of God's multi-faceted grace." Peter places spiritual gifts in two categories: gifts of speech and gifts of service (1 Pet 4:10–11).

From another perspective, to be sure, gifts of speech are also (and essentially) gifts of service. No gift is given for the sake of the individual's self-indulgence or self-aggrandizement. There is no gift which does not bring with it a special responsibility for service to others.

In this epistle, one of Paul's favorite expressions for this work of Christian service is edification. The purpose of spiritual gifts is to enable each member of the body to serve, love, and encourage others, thus making a "constructive," "edifying" contribution to the upbuilding of the whole. Just as Jesus set before himself the goal of edifying (building) his church (Mt 16:18), so Paul saw his task to be the edification (not the tearing down) of the church (1 Cor 3:9; 2 Cor 10:8; 12:19; 13:10), and the Corinthians are urged, "Let all things be done for edification" (1 Cor 14:26).

Paul primarily uses the metaphor of building up or edifying the body of Christ as a plea for unity and harmony within the church, instead of the factionalism which threatened to tear it apart. But the expressions for edification refer in broad terms to the way the Word of God promotes and strengthens both the individual and the whole church in the life of faith. Where there is internal health and harmony, "when each part is working properly," external growth is more likely to occur (see Eph 4:16). Thus, the wholesome use of the edifying word of prophecy serves not only to strengthen believers but also to win the unbelieving outsider for Christ (1 Cor 14:24–25).

THE NATURE OF THE INDIVIDUAL GIFTS

God achieves his edifying purposes through a rich variety of gifts. The lists Paul provides in Romans 12, 1 Corinthians 12, and Ephesians 4 are illustrative rather than exhaustive. Some gifts may simply be a God-given talent enhanced by the Spirit to foster Christian service. Others are of a more spectacular character. Noteworthy, too, is the way Paul's lists include both abilities (e.g., "word of wisdom," "word of knowledge," 1 Cor 12:8) and persons (e.g. "apostles," "prophets," "teachers," 12:28).

TWO EXTRAORDINARY GIFTS: PROPHECY AND TONGUES

The nature of the less spectacular gifts (together with some spectacular gifts like healings and miraculous powers) is discussed in the commentary on 12:8–10 and 12:28. But the modern controversy regarding the nature of the remarkable gifts of prophecy and tongues and their place in the contemporary church warrants special comment.

Prophecy

A key text for understanding what Paul means by "prophecy" is 1 Cor 14:29–30: "As for prophets, let two or three speak and let the others evaluate. And if [a revelation] should be revealed to another while he is seated, let the first one be silent." This text makes it apparent that prophets derived their message from revelation. Just as the OT prophets were essentially "seers" who were given visions and taken up into God's council (Jer 23:18) to receive his word and then communicate it to the people, so the NT prophets were filled with the Spirit and given special revelation to proclaim (Lk 1:41, 67). Thus, the quintessential prophetical book in the NT is the book of Revelation, which the Spirit-filled seer calls "the words of the prophecy." In addition to John, other apostles also were given special revelations, including Paul himself.

Caught up into God's council, prophets were given a divine vista of the past, present, and future, enabling them to call God's people to repentance of past transgressions of the covenant, to apply the divine Word to the present situation, and to speak prophetically of the future. They were both "forth-tellers" and "foretellers." To say that they were foretellers does not mean they merely possessed some human facility to predict future events. Rather, they were entrusted with the powerful Word of God which creatively accomplishes what it says (Is 55:10–11). That this did encompass the future as well as the present is seen by the frequent NT use of the Greek preposition meaning "beforehand" with the verbs of the prophecy group (e.g., Rom 1:2).

Characteristically, the biblical prophets' forth-telling and foretelling had a Christ-centered focus. According to the NT, the OT prophets foretold what would be fulfilled in Christ, while the NT prophets and prophetesses hailed what God had set in train by the birth of the Messiah.

Stemming as it does from direct divine revelation, the phenomenon of biblical prophecy may not simply be equated with preaching. The distinction is that prophecy involved new revelations from God, while preaching was the proclamation and dissemination of the Gospel and other articles of the faith that had already been revealed. Thus, translating 1 Cor 11:4–5 as though it referred to ordinary proclamation confuses the issue of women's ordination by suggesting that, in Paul's day, women commonly preached in public worship. The text does imply that women were prophesying and speaking in tongues during worship, but there is no suggestion in the text that they also served as preachers.

The Fading of Prophecy in the Early Church

Paul wanted everyone in Corinth to be able to prophesy (1 Cor 14:5). But with the passing of the apostolic age and the decreasing need for this foundational gift (Eph 2:20), it gradually faded from the scene. In the OT, the prophets were not a continuous institution; God raised up prophets when and where he willed. Sometimes they abounded. At other times in Israel's history, prophecy was scarce (1 Sam 3:1).

Therefore, we should not be surprised if, in the NT period too, the gift of prophecy came and went in various places and times as the Lord saw fit. The chief reason for the decline of prophecy is that it was replaced by the written Word of God. Holy Scripture is even more reliable than firsthand experience. Peter, who witnessed the transfiguration of Jesus, says that in the Scriptures Christians have "the prophetic word made more certain" (2 Pet 1:19). (He then describes the inspiration of the prophetic Scriptures in 2 Pet 1:20–21. Also in 1 Pet 1:8–12, he explains how the Spirit inspired the prophecies of Christ, so that those Christians who do not see Christ nevertheless believe and hope in him.) The canonical epistles of Paul are part of the prophetic and apostolic Scriptures (2 Pet 3:15–16), which render further prophecies unnecessary. Scripture itself warns against those who may claim to receive additional revelations not in harmony with Scripture (e.g., Gal 1:6–12; 2 Tim 3:14–4:5; 2 Peter 2; 1 Jn 4:1–6). And the final book of the NT canon ends with a most severe censure against any who would presume to add or subtract anything from "this book of prophecy" (Rev 22:19), a warning that by extension applies to all of the Scriptures.

The Didache, an early catechetical treatise, still accords prophets high honor (Didache 13:1–7) but also gives detailed guidelines for unmasking false prophets (Didache 11:8–12). But in general, prophets became less prominent in the early post-apostolic period. Not only was the prophetic gift fading, but the increasing number of false prophets undermined the church's confidence in those who presumed to be prophets. Finally, the rise of the Montanist heresy (the "new prophecy") in the second century discredited prophecy to such a degree that it was no longer acceptable in the church. When their prophecies of wars and revolutions failed to eventuate, the movement was exposed as false.

Periodically throughout the history of the church, a "prophetic" spirit has found fresh expressions, down to the modern charismatic movement. Charismatics often try to bend others to their will by saying, "I have a 'word of knowledge' for you," or "the Lord told me to tell you. . . ." Such claims to continuous revelation contravene Paul's warning to the Corinthians not to go "beyond what stands written" (1 Cor 4:6). They belong to a type of which Montanism is the prototype.

Another characteristic of false prophecy is a loss of self-control, resulting in disorderly worship. Ancient Greek and Hellenistic prophecy, as well as some modern spiritual movements that claim to represent Christian prophecy, are manifested through ecstasy, a trance-like state, and dementia. But those features are contrary to the spiritual gift of Christian prophecy described by Paul. In calling for order, the apostle states, "spirits of prophets are subject to prophets. For God is not [a God] of disorder but of peace" (14:32–33a).

Tongues

The Nature and Function of the Gift of Tongues

"Let all things be done for edification" (1 Cor 14:26). According to this all-important criterion, Paul considers prophecy far more valuable to the church than tongues: "For the one who prophesies is greater than the one speaking in tongues" (14:5). Whereas many of the Corinthians were exaggerating the value of tongues, Paul places them at the bottom of his list of gifts (12:8–10, 28–30).

But this does not mean that Paul disparaged tongues altogether or thought they had no place in the church. He permitted two or three tongues-speakers to speak in the worship services, on the condition that an interpretation was provided; indeed, he insisted that tongues-speaking should not be forbidden (14:27, 39). Moreover, he permitted (even encouraged) the tongues-speaker to exercise his gift in private, praying and singing in the S/spirit "to himself and to God" (14:28). When Paul writes that the tongues-speaker merely edifies himself, in contrast to the prophet who edifies the whole church (14:4), he is not necessarily speaking pejoratively of tongues, as though this manner of edifying oneself in private was egotistical and wrong. Indeed, Paul himself thanked God that he could speak in tongues "more than you all." But it seems he preferred to use his gift in private (14:18–19).

The Nature and Purpose of Tongues in Acts

On Pentecost Day, the outpoured Spirit enabled the disciples "to speak in other tongues" (Acts 2:4). Thus, the Pentecost miracle was one by which "Parthians and Medes and Elamites" and others heard "each in his own language" the great things God had done in Christ (Acts 2:8–11). The Spirit's gift on that occasion was the ability to proclaim the Gospel *in known human languages.* The speaker may have had no natural facility in the language and perhaps did not understand what he was saying, but the hearers who had a natural competence in the language recognized the language as their native tongue and understood what was said.

The gift had a twofold purpose. On the one hand, it demonstrated that the Gospel of Christ crucified and risen was for "every nation and [all] tribes and peoples and tongues" (Rev 7:9). "The dividing wall of hostility" between Jews and Gentiles had been broken down (Eph 2:14), and the Gentiles had become "joint-heirs, joint-members of the body, and joint-participants in the promise" (Eph 3:6).

But the gift of tongues did not only signify that from Pentecost Day onward the Gospel would be proclaimed to all nations. The gift also had a negative purpose: it signified God's judgment on unbelievers (1 Cor 14:22–23). While salvation was "of the Jews" (Jn 4:22), the Pentecost miracle demonstrated that God's kingdom was being taken away from the Jews and given to a nation that would produce the fruits of the kingdom (Mt 21:43). Those who jeered on Pentecost morning that "these people are full of new wine" (Acts 2:13) were bringing that judgment on themselves.

The origin of the multiplicity of human languages lay in God's judgment against humanity's sin. All humanity spoke a common language when construction began on the tower of Babel. But to thwart humanity's arrogant ambitions,

God confounded human language, resulting in the great diversity of human languages, which makes universal communication impossible (Gen 11:1–9). But the Gospel reunites humanity—except for those who reject it.

The Nature and Purpose of Tongues in 1 Corinthians

The Corinthians' Gift Understood as Ecstatic Utterance. Since the 1970s, the dominant view in NT scholarship has been that the gift of tongues bestowed on the Corinthians was of a different nature from the gift described in Acts. Twenty-five years after Pentecost, the Spirit's gift to the church—in Corinth at least—was no longer the pouring out of the Spirit-given ability to speak foreign languages. It consisted, according to this view, in the ability to utter ecstatic speech. The chief text adduced in its favor is 1 Cor 14:2: "For the person who speaks in a tongue does not speak to human beings but to God; for no one understands, but by [his] spirit he speaks mysteries." On the face of it, Paul seems to be describing a different phenomenon from Pentecost, when people from all over the Mediterranean world heard tongues-speakers proclaiming the Gospel in the hearers' own native languages without the aid of translators or interpreters.

The Corinthians' Gift Understood as Speaking Foreign Languages. The two greatest obstacles standing in the way of the ecstatic-utterance view are the following. First, Paul uses the same terminology to describe the Corinthians' gift as Luke uses in Acts 2. In Acts and 1 Corinthians, the term used is "tongue, language" the common Greek term for a natural human language. The verb often rendered "to interpret" in 1 Cor 12:30; 14:5, 13, 27 is used in Acts 9:36 simply to mean "to translate" from one ordinary language into another (the Aramaic word "Tabitha" translates into Greek as "Dorcas," Acts 9:36). In 1 Cor 14:28, the Greek term could mean "translator" just as easily as "interpreter" (see also 1 Cor 12:10; 14:26; Jn 1:42; Heb 7:2). In particular, compare Acts 2:4, "they began to speak in foreign tongues," and 1 Cor 14:21, "by foreign tongues . . . I will speak to this people."

Second, in its original context, the text Paul adduces from Isaiah to describe the nature and purpose of the Corinthians' gift (Is 28:11, quoted in 1 Cor 14:21) can only be interpreted as a reference to foreign languages, particularly the language of Assyria, for foreign language as a sign of God's punishment lies behind Paul's use of Isaiah 28:11. Indeed, if Paul were to use the Greek word "tongue" to denote something other than known foreign languages, that would constitute a significant departure from a long-standing tradition in the OT and other Semitic literature. With the exception of the Montanist Tertullian, the church fathers understood the NT gift of tongues in the light of Acts 2 as speaking foreign languages. This interpretation continued through the Reformation.

A Supernatural Endowment with Facility in Foreign Languages. An important qualification must be added to the above analysis of the Corinthian gift of tongues as the gift of speaking genuine foreign languages. Paul leaves the reader in no doubt that he is not speaking of a *natural* facility in languages acquired through normal human contacts and study. The gift of tongues in Corinth is a *supernatural* gift bestowed by the Spirit of God for the promotion of the Gospel (1 Cor 12:4–11). Just as at Pentecost there was something amazing and inexplicable about the gift (Acts 2:12), so the gift poured out on Paul and others in Corinth transcended anything that could be explained in terms of normal learning processes. Unlike the bilingual or multilingual person whose mind is intensively engaged as he switches from language to language, the Corinthians were, in a sense, transported beyond themselves, ecstatic (though not in the sense of uncontrolled, irrational, or emotional frenzy), as they prayed in the Spirit while their minds (with their natural limitations) were in suspension (1 Cor 14:13–19). In this respect, the gift of tongues resembled the gift of prophecy whereby special revelation from God, transcending normal preaching and teaching, was conveyed to fellow Christians. Thus, the grace of God endowed tongues-speakers with a supernatural facility to convey to a multilingual city that the Gospel was for all people of all tongues. Consistent with the biblical pattern, the tongues served also as a negative sign pointing to divine judgment on those who reacted by saying in essence, "You are crazy" (14:23).

THE MODERN PRACTICE OF GLOSSOLALIA

If this analysis of tongues as a supernatural facility in normal human languages is correctly drawn from the Scriptures, then the modern tongues phenomenon—whatever it may be—is not the NT gift. The NT gift was evident in the infant church in Acts and is mentioned in 1 Corinthians, but never again in the NT. That could suggest that it faded already in the NT era.

SPIRITUAL GIFTS TODAY

The NT does not furnish a single definitive and comprehensive list of all of the gifts of the Spirit. Paul lists seven gifts in Rom 12:6–8, nine in 1 Cor 12:8–10, nine in 1 Cor 12:28–30, and four in Eph 4:11, while Peter summarizes all the gifts under two headings, speech and service (1 Pet 4:11). There is considerable variation in the items of each list, which suggests these are ad hoc rather than exhaustive, illustrating the variety of manifestations of the Spirit in NT times.

At least one of the gifts included on two of Paul's lists (1 Cor 12:28–29; Eph 4:11) is no longer available or necessary today: the gift of apostleship. The apostles' foundational work is done; their ministry was unique and unrepeatable (cf. Eph 2:20; Rev 21:14). The same may apply to some of the spectacular gifts like prophecy and tongues. If prophecy, like apostleship, was intended as a gift for the church's foundational period (Eph 2:20; 3:5), to encourage her and provide direction during her infancy, then that need has been met, and the church no longer needs that charismatic gift; she has all she needs for her welfare and instruction in the prophetic and apostolic Scriptures. The Gospel and the full counsel of God are proclaimed through preaching and teaching from the Scriptures. And if the Pentecost Day tongues signified that the Gospel was for all nations and languages, and that those who mocked the Spirit of Christ (1 Pet 1:11) would be under judgment, then their point has been made; the Christian church has long since accepted that her mission is universal. Other signs and wonders, too, which characterized the apostolic age (e.g., healing miracles and miraculous powers) may have been intended simply to confirm the apostolic message (cf. 2 Cor 12:12: "the signs of a true apostle were performed among you . . . with signs and wonders and miraculous powers").

While it is not proper to be dogmatic in an area on which the Scriptures are silent, lest we "quench the Spirit" (1 Thess 5:19), by the same token it would be wrong to claim that the Scriptures promise that the more spectacular spiritual gifts are intended for all places and all periods of the church's history. A more balanced approach would grant the possibility that the Spirit may increase or decrease gifts in accord with the needs of the church.

Paul's concern that the language used in worship be intelligible to the hearers has a timeless relevance. Just as Luther insisted on the basis of 1 Corinthians 14 that any public reading of the Scriptures in Latin (a sixteenth-century practice which he compared to speaking in tongues) should be followed by a sermon explaining the text in German (AE 53:11), so the contemporary church should ensure that the language used in preaching, teaching, liturgy, and hymnody benefits and edifies the whole congregation. That is not to suggest an avoidance of biblical and ecclesiastical language, but Paul's mandate for intelligibility does require diligent catechesis so that the biblical treasures of the church's historic theology become the vernacular of God's people in each generation anew.

THE SPIRIT AND HIS GIFTS ARE GIVEN IN BAPTISM (1 COR 12:13)

Christians disturbed by the Pentecostal insistence on a second spiritual experience after conversion and Baptism need to be assured that they have already been given everything in Baptism. Their Baptism with water and the word of God (the triune name in Mt 28:19) was their Baptism in the Spirit. That Baptism is when "we all were baptized with one Spirit into one body, . . . and we all were given to drink one Spirit" (1 Cor 12:13). That Baptism poured out the Holy Spirit in all his fullness and with all his gifts. For that reason, Paul said to the Corinthians who had been baptized (1:12–17), "You were enriched in [Christ], in all speech and all knowledge. . . . Thus, *you are not lacking in any gift of grace*" (1:5–7). On that day, the gentle Spirit descended on the baptized as he did on Jesus at the Jordan, and the Father's declaration "This is my beloved Son, with whom I am well pleased" (Mt 3:16–17) became a personal assurance to the baptized child of God as God's son or daughter (Gal 3:26–28).

1 CORINTHIANS 12:12–26
THE ANALOGY OF THE BODY

TRANSLATION

12 [12]For just as the body is one and has many parts,
but all the parts of the body, although being many,
are one body, so also is Christ. [13]For also we all were
baptized with one Spirit into one body, whether Jews
or Greeks or slaves or free, and we all were given to
drink one Spirit. [14]For indeed the body is not one
part, but many. [15]If the foot should say, "Because I
am not a hand, I do not belong to the body," it is not
for that reason any less [a part] of the body. [16]And
if the ear should say, "Because I am not an eye, I do
not belong to the body," it is not for that reason any
less [a part] of the body. [17]If the whole body were an
eye, where would be the hearing? If the whole were
hearing, where would be the sense of smell? [18]But as
it is, God has placed the parts, each one of them, in
the body just as he wished. [19]If all [the parts] were
one part, where would be the body? [20]But now there
are many parts, but one body. [21]Yet the eye cannot
say to the hand, "I have no need of you," nor again
the head to the feet, "I have no need of you." [22]On
the contrary, the parts of the body that seem to be
weaker are indispensable, [23]and the parts of the body
that we consider less honorable we clothe with greater
honor, and our unrespectable parts are treated with
greater respect, [24]but our respectable parts have no
need [of this honor]. But God has blended the body,
giving greater honor to the inferior part, [25]in order
that there be no division in the body but that the
parts should show the same care for one another.
[26]And if one part suffers, all the parts suffer together;
if one part is honored, all the parts rejoice together.

COMMENTARY

The remainder of 1 Corinthians 12 falls into four units: 12:12–13, which introduces the metaphor of the body of Christ; 12:14–20, which addresses members of the body who feel inferior to others and may be inclined to be jealous or resentful; 12:21–26, which speaks to those who feel superior to others and then urges all to avoid "division, schism" (12:25) and to care for one another; and 12:27–31, where Paul applies the analogy of the body to the Corinthian church and its use of spiritual gifts. His argument in 12:12–13 flows naturally from the preceding section, where he stresses that the same triune God has given a variety of gifts to individual Christians for the common good. Not only should the Corinthians' concern for Christian unity be grounded in their understanding that all their gifts come from "the one and the same Spirit" (12:11); they also need to be mindful that by Baptism in that same Spirit they have all become members of one and the same body (12:13). Theirs is a deep organic unity in Christ (12:12).

BAPTIZED INTO ONE BODY (12:12–13)

The image of the body was often used by Greco-Roman authors concerned for the unity of the body politic. Here, Paul's concern is the unity of the church. The analogy of the body and its members was a favorite of his (Rom 12:4–5; Eph 1:23; 4:4, 12, 16; 5:23, 30; Col 1:18; 2:19; 3:15). The unity of the body of Christ is grounded in its members' Baptism into that body (1 Cor 12:13; Gal 3:27–28) and their constant reception of Christ's body and blood in the Lord's Supper (1 Cor 10:16–17). The sacramental body unites the ecclesiastical "body."

Just as the human body is a unit, a single entity comprised of many parts, "so also is Christ" (12:12). We would have expected Paul to conclude the sentence, "so also is the church." But he is using metonymy, a shortened way of saying "so also is the church, which is the body of Christ" (cf. the juxtaposition of "body of Christ" and "the church" in 12:27–28).

The basis for the unity of many diverse parts within the body of Christ is their common Baptism "with one Spirit into one body" (12:13). Paul has in mind here the Sacrament of Christian Baptism, whereby a person is incorporated into the body of Christ (Gal 3:27–28).

Those who object to this natural, literal understanding of the text (1 Cor 12:13) base their argument on a skepticism toward Baptism, an a priori assumption that Baptism cannot actually accomplish what Scripture says it accomplishes. Baptism—Christian Baptism with water in the triune name of God (Mt 28:19)—grants the forgiveness of sins and the Holy Spirit, and incorporates the baptized believer into Christ and the Christian church, Christ's body (Acts 2:38–41; Rom 6:1–4; Col 2:11–13; 1 Pet 3:21). Indeed, to come to any other conclusion about the meaning of "baptize" here in 1 Cor 12:13 is to fly in the face of the text and its close parallel in Gal 3:27.

Here in Baptism (12:13) is the most basic foundation for the church's unity, a unity which transcends traditional divisions between Jews and Greeks, slaves and free people, and (as Gal 3:28 adds) between men and women. On the basis of one Baptism (Eph 4:5) in *one* Spirit, *all* are "*one* in Christ Jesus" (Gal 3:28; cf. Jn 17:21). The word "all" occurs twice in 1 Cor 12:13; the word "one" occurs three times: "we *all* were baptized with *one* Spirit into *one* body, . . . and we *all* were given to drink *one* Spirit." There is nothing in the text about a second experience of "Spirit baptism," an experience granted only to some consecrated believers, which is subsequent and superior to water Baptism. That Pentecostal doctrine of a second baptism is, by its very nature, divisive, because some believers then consider themselves to be on a higher spiritual level than other ordinary Christians. It leads to arrogance and to despising brothers and sisters who are equals in Christ. Paul's teaching, on the other hand, stresses what *"all"* Christians have in common by virtue of their one Baptism. That simple Baptism with water and God's Word is the powerful Baptism in the Spirit.

The final clause in 1 Cor 12:13 ("we all were given to drink one Spirit") runs parallel to "we all were baptized . . . into one body." In Baptism, all are given to drink in the living water of the Spirit (cf. Jn 4:14; 7:37–39) which is poured out on the baptized.

"INFERIOR" MEMBERS OF THE ONE BODY (12:14–20)

In the next unit (12:14–20), Paul stresses the necessary diversity within the body of Christ. Every part of the body, no matter how insignificant it may seem, has a vital role to play in the healthy functioning of the whole.

Paul presents an imaginary conversation among the parts of the body. The spokesmen are those parts of the body who may be inclined to make invidious comparisons with other parts that seem more important. So the foot, depressed by its comparatively lowly status and the drudgery of its work in supporting the whole body, compares itself with the more versatile and skillful hand; the ear becomes discontent with its simple and less prominent function and compares itself with the more attractive eye. In their depression and jealousy, the foot and the ear are tempted to opt out, discontinuing their faithful service to the body.

But Paul insists they cannot opt out. Their only proper place is within the body. If everyone could have his wish and become the eye, we would have a grotesque situation, a body consisting only of an enormous eye. In that case, how would that fantastic organism hear? And if the whole body were an ear, where would be the sense of smell? But leaving fantasy aside, Paul returns to the realities. As a matter of fact, God has set each individual part in the body "just as he wished" (12:18). Their distinctive functions are part of his perfect plan for the whole, a plan which the individual believer should accept humbly, without jealously eyeing what another has been given.

Paul now summarizes his response to those who feel inferior by repeating the illustration used in 12:17, but this time in general terms: if the whole body consisted of one part, there would no longer be a body, but some useless monstrosity. The fact of the matter, however, is that there are many parts in the one body, diversity in unity. The body is like a choir or an orchestra, where each singer or musician has an assigned and vital role in producing a pleasing result.

"SUPERIOR" MEMBERS OF THE ONE BODY (12:21–26)

Paul now, in 12:21–26, appeals to those members with a "superiority complex." Those who had been endowed with more obviously important or spectacular spiritual gifts were tempted to look down on the less gifted. But their position, Paul insists, is untenable. The eye simply cannot do without the hand, nor can the head dispense with the feet. Even though the hand and the feet have more menial tasks, they are still indispensable to the smooth functioning of the whole body. A city can survive without artists, but it cannot survive without tradesmen. The quiet worker may be disregarded by the "movers and shapers," and yet be making a greater contribution to the life of the church. Christ's power is made perfect in weakness (2 Cor 12:9). No one's service is insignificant. On Judgment Day, the contribution of each laborer will be tested by fire and revealed (1 Cor 3:10–15). When evaluated by God, a great reversal of many will take place: "many who are first will be last, and many who are last will be first" (Mt 19:30). Those accorded the greatest human praise may find that those whom they looked down upon receive the greater commendation from God.

In Paul's metaphor in 1 Cor 12:21, the "head" appears to be another member of the body that is prone to sinful pride. The picture here, therefore, is different from that in Eph 5:23; Col 1:18; 2:19, where Christ is the "head." Here the "head" may represent church leaders who glory in their authority to command the "feet"—those below them. But while the "head" is above the members, the "feet" support the whole body, which would topple over without the feet.

The hand and the feet are respectable enough not to need covering. Other less sightly parts of the body, however, such as the arms, the chest, and the legs were normally covered by the tunic and cloak. And even greater care was taken to provide a modest covering for the sexual organs and the buttocks. A feature like the face, however, needed no covering.

Paul concludes his remarks to those who feel superior in 1 Cor 12:24–26. Echoing his earlier statement on the Creator's sovereign role in designing the body according to his own blueprint (12:18), he now uses a different verb to speak of God's activity in blending the parts into a harmonious whole (12:24). To bring about this harmony, he had given more honor to the inferior parts. His concern was to prevent the organism from tearing itself apart as members jostled with one another for the places of honor. Again, as in 1:10–12, we hear Paul's concern for the congregation's oneness in the Gospel. God had set the example by his composition of the body; Christians should follow their Creator's lead by outdoing one another in showing honor to those they deemed inferior (Rom 12:10).

Instead of nurturing divisiveness, the various parts of the organism should be anxiously and thoughtfully concerned about one another (1 Cor 12:25). The heart should care for the kidneys, the kidneys for the lungs, and so on, "for we are members of one another" (Rom 12:5). Paul's own pastoral care for his people in Corinth formed the pattern (2 Cor 11:28–29). In his emphasis on caring for one another (1 Cor 12:25), Paul is laying the groundwork for 1 Corinthians 13, his great chapter on love. Self-centered individualism can only prove destructive for the welfare of the whole; love, on the other hand, always builds up.

Paul adds a final observation about the body in 12:26. Whenever one part of the body is suffering, that affects the person's whole sense of well-being. A toothache makes one feel miserable all over. The philosopher Plato remarked that "when one's finger is hurt, one does not say, 'My finger is in pain,' but 'I have a pain in my finger'" (*Republic*, 5.462). And the presence of pain causes the whole body to react, releasing adrenaline. When a runner has one inflamed Achilles tendon or one pulled muscle, even if the rest of his body yearns for exercise, he must wait until the one injury is healed.

On the other hand, when a part of the body that has been suffering finds relief, the whole body shares that sense of relief. And when a part of the body is honored (e.g., "you have a beautiful smile"), the whole person basks in the glow of the compliment. What Paul is observing about the facts of our physical experience, he implies, should be characteristic of our life within the church. The Christian should "rejoice with those who rejoice, and weep with those who weep" (Rom 12:15). He should not be indifferent to the welfare of others but should seek and rejoice in the good of all.

1 CORINTHIANS 12:27–31

Application: Gifts and Offices in the Church

TRANSLATION

12 [27]Now you are the body of Christ, and members
each for his part. [28]And God has placed in the
church first of all some as apostles, second prophets,
third teachers, then [those with] miraculous
powers, then gracious gifts of healings, helpful
deeds, [gifts of] leadership, various kinds of
tongues. [29]Are all apostles? Are all prophets? Are
all teachers? Are all [people with] miraculous
powers? [30]Do all have gracious gifts of healing?
Do all speak in tongues? Do all interpret? Surely
not! [31]But strive for the gracious gifts that are
greater. And I show you a still more excellent way.

COMMENTARY

With an emphatic "now you are the body of Christ" (1 Cor 12:27), Paul brings his extensive picture of the human body (12:14–26) to bear on the Corinthian church. Everything he has said about the need to avoid a sense of inferiority and jealousy on the one hand, and a sense of superiority on the other, about the indispensable role of each part, and the need for mutual sympathy and care, applies specifically to the Corinthians. They are the body of Christ in Corinth, the church of God which finds full expression in that place (1:2). They are not merely a part of Christ's body. Rather, the "one holy catholic and apostolic church" (Nicene Creed) is fully exemplified there in Corinth, and each individual believer is a vital part of that great entity.

This one universal church has received a great variety of gifts. All of them come from God, who has assigned to all of them their role and function in accordance with his sovereign will (12:28; cf. 12:18, where we find the same verb as in 12:28, "has placed"; cf. also "has blended" in 12:24). The following list begins with three kinds of persons whom God has assigned to serve the church and then proceeds to enumerate various kinds of gifts. The first three groups are listed in descending order of importance.

"First" come the "apostles" (12:28). They were a unique group. The "apostles"—in the specific and narrow sense—existed only in the early church. The normal qualification for the apostolate consisted in having been with Jesus from his baptism by John until his ascension. Above all, an apostle had to be an eyewitness of the resurrected Lord (cf. Acts 1:21–22; 1 Cor 15:7, 9). Apostles were not "first" merely because they were the ones the Lord called first. Rather, they continued to have preeminent leadership roles in the church as her founding fathers (Eph 2:20; 3:5; Rev 21:14).

In 1 Corinthians, "apostle" usually refers to the Eleven plus Paul and has the specific or narrow meaning of an eyewitness of the risen Christ, who was also called to the office of "apostle" (1:1; 4:9; 9:1, 2, 5; 12:28, 29). In 15:7 (and possibly 15:9), and sometimes in Paul's other epistles (e.g., 2 Cor 8:23; Phil 2:25), "apostle" may have a more general or broader meaning akin to "minister" or "church worker."

Pastors today are not eyewitnesses of the risen Christ (unlike the "apostles," who were), nor do they receive immediate special revelations (unlike the "prophets" who did). But pastors are called to the office of preaching and teaching the Gospel from the prophetic and apostolic Scriptures, which are God's definitive special revelation.

"Second" in importance to the apostles were the "prophets" of the NT period (12:28), who gave vital guidance to the young church at critical moments and shared with the apostles the honor of having a foundational role (Eph 2:20; 3:5). They received special divine revelations. Like the "apostles" in 12:28–29, they were unique to the early church. The nature of their ministry is discussed in greater detail in the excursus "Spiritual Gifts in 1 Corinthians."

"Third" are the "teachers" (12:28). The apostles had an important teaching role (1 Tim 2:7; 2 Tim 1:11). But this third group seems to designate a distinctive kind of church servant, paralleling the fourth group listed in Eph 4:11, those who were both "pastors and teachers." Paul refers to the teaching role of the overseer (Phil 1:1; 1 Tim 3:2; Titus 1:7) and the elder (1 Tim 5:1–2, 17, 19; Titus 1:5) entrusted with the pastoral care of the local churches ("teach," 1 Tim 4:11; 6:2; 2 Tim 2:2). They are to labor hard to promote "sound teaching" (1 Tim 1:10). One of the pastor's chief qualifications is that he be "apt to teach" (1 Tim 3:2; 2 Tim 2:24). Especially since the price of hand-copied books was beyond the reach of most Christians, the pastor-teacher had an important role in publicly reading and expounding the Scriptures (1 Tim 4:13). That teaching office continues to be carried out today by pastors and by Christian teachers and other called ministers of the Gospel.

Then Paul still in 1 Cor 12:28 turns from the three kinds of persons who held specific *offices* to which they were called, to list five *gifts* which could be exercised by various members of the church. These gifts did not necessarily involve a call to a continuing role or office. For example, an apostle remained an apostle for life, but an apostle or any Christian may have been granted the ability to heal or perform a miracle at a specific time or just on a certain occasion (e.g., Acts 20:10). For the first two gifts, "miraculous powers" and "gracious gifts of healings" (1 Cor 12:28), see the discussion of 12:9–10. With "helpful deeds" and "[gifts of] leadership" (12:28), we come to two gifts of a more everyday, non-miraculous nature, neither of which was included in Paul's earlier listing of gifts (12:8–10). The first refers to acts of humble helpfulness, the second to the organizing and leadership capacity to pilot the church through troubled waters. But due to a lack of scriptural information, we cannot be more precise about the nature of these gifts, nor the way they functioned in the life of the early church. Finally, Paul mentions "various kinds of tongues" (12:28; cf. 12:10). In contrast to 12:10, in 12:28 he does not refer to the gift of interpretation, which he no doubt takes for granted. He will refer to those who interpret in 12:30. The list in 12:28 is not meant to be exhaustive. If Paul were to try to list every gift, there might be as many as there are parts of the body.

God had supplied the body with an amazing complexity and diversity. It was not his will that all be apostles or prophets or teachers, nor that all should share the same spiritual gift. "If the whole body were an eye, where would be the hearing? . . . If all [the parts] were one part, where would be the body?" (12:17, 19). By a series of seven rhetorical questions in 12:29–30, each expecting the answer no, Paul drives the point home. Like body parts, these offices and gifts are not interchangeable. If, for example, a person lost a hand, he could not use his ear or eye to carry out tasks that require a hand. The healthy functioning of the body of Christ requires each Christian to carry out the office to which he is called and/or to exercise the gift(s) he has been given. The body of Christ is supplied with a diversity of gifts, some greater, some lesser, but all with a necessary part to play in the body's upbuilding.

Next, Paul encourages the Corinthians to "strive for the gracious gifts that are greater" (12:31). Among the greater gifts, as he will explain later (14:1–25), he counts the gift of prophecy, which he deems superior to the gift of tongues. We may wonder how the Christian can strive for prophecy or anything else which is a *gift*. Lk 11:13 provides a helpful parallel, where the Lord encourages his disciples to pray for the gift of the Holy Spirit. As the Spirit himself is a gift Christians should pray for, so the spiritual grace-gifts are to be prayed and striven for.

Paul now adds a significant point, which serves as the transition to his great discourse on love in chapter 13. To be sure, he has just encouraged the Corinthians to strive for the greater gifts. But he would have them aspire to something higher still. Whatever their gift may be, he would have them exercise it in the superior way of Christian love. Love must characterize everything they do; it must be their whole way of life. For only through love will the whole body of Christ be able to function smoothly and grow (Eph 4:16).

Paul does not classify love here among the spiritual gifts. As we have seen, the gifts are not parceled out equally; one person receives one gift, another person receives something different. But love, as the first and highest fruit of the Spirit (Gal 5:22), transcends all the gifts and is to be cultivated equally by all believers.

13:1–13

The Royal Road of Love

Introduction to Chapter 13

The harmonious functioning of Christ's body, the vital oil which keeps every ligament working smoothly, is supplied by Christian love (cf. Eph 4:16). Without love, even the most extraordinary spiritual gift is worthless—mere "sound and fury, signifying nothing" (*Macbeth*, act 5, scene 5). Thus, Paul's great discourse on love (1 Cor 13:1–13) forms the heart of his discussion of the gifts of grace. It echoes the concern of chapter 12 that each part of the body should show loving care for all the others, so that when one suffers, all should suffer together, and when one is honored, all should rejoice together (12:24–26). And it casts its beams ahead into chapter 14, where Paul will encourage the church to exercise the gifts of tongues and prophecy in loving mutual upbuilding.

Viewed even more broadly, it could be said that chapter 13 crystallizes and encapsulates one of Paul's chief concerns from the outset. All of the congregation's problems are symptomatic of a lack of love: the congregation splintering into factions (chapters 1–4); the Corinthians' tolerance of gross sin (chapters 5–6); their indulgence in sacrificial meat regardless of the damage to their brothers and sisters (chapters 8–10); and their divisions at the Lord's Supper (11:17–34). Paul's consistent teaching has been that faith in Christ crucified (2:2) that is "active in love" (Gal 5:6) is indispensable for the life of the church (see Gal 5:13, 22; Eph 5:2; Col 3:14; 1 Thess 4:9). Christians dare not place their spiritual gifts at the disposal of a personal "quest for power" and prestige. The performance of works not motivated by faith and love would incur the Lord's censure, "I never knew you" (Mt 7:22–23).

Paul's concept of love is not to be equated with the modern sentimental notion of love, which often becomes an excuse for various aberrations. The love romanticized and glorified by modern culture is self-seeking. It is rooted in the self and its needs and emotions. Even in the church, devilishly subtle arguments sometimes twist the concept of love in a self-serving way. The condemnation of favorite sins is "unloving," while a libertine accommodation of sin is "showing Christian love" (contrast that with 1 Corinthians 5). A resolute insistence on biblical truth is "unloving," while doctrinal error is tolerated "in the Spirit of Christ's love."

The royal road of Christian love, on the other hand, is marked by unselfish service in fidelity to Christ and his Word. "If you love me, you will keep my commandments" (Jn 14:15). The loving shepherd (pastor) who tends and feeds Christ's flock (Jn 21:15–17) exemplifies the love of Christ. Whenever Christians follow this royal way, the Spirit manifests his presence, for love is a sign that the Spirit has liberated a person from his ego to be active in love.

The structure of 1 Corinthians 13 can be summarized: the absolute *necessity* of love (1–3); the *character* of love (4–7); the *permanence* of love (8–13).

1 CORINTHIANS 13:1–3

The Absolute Necessity of Love

TRANSLATION

13 [1]If I speak with the tongues of humans and of
the angels, but do not have love, I have become
a noisy brass [gong] or a clashing cymbal. [2]And
if I have prophecy and know all the mysteries
and all knowledge, and if I have all faith so as
to move mountains, but do not have love, I am
nothing. [3]And if I parcel out all my possessions,
and if I give my body in order to boast, but
do not have love, I am profited nothing.

COMMENTARY

The tongues-speakers, it seems, were causing the greatest disruption in the young Corinthian congregation, so Paul begins with them. Rather than confronting them head on, however ("you tongues-speakers are guilty of lovelessness"), he tactfully takes himself as an example. Even if he were the world's most gifted tongues-speaker, able to hold forth not only in human languages but even in the tongues of angels, all would be valueless without love. By "the tongues of humans" (1 Cor 13:1), he does not mean the created capacity to learn other languages; he means the supernatural gift of speaking foreign languages as exercised in Corinth, a gift with which Paul himself was richly endowed (14:18). When Paul adds, "and of the angels" (13:1), the question arises whether some Corinthians actually claimed to speak in angelic languages, or whether Paul is simply using hyperbole ("even if my gift in that area, which exceeds the gifts of everyone in Corinth anyway, actually reached to the extent of being able to use angelic languages").

But even the possession of this gift to the highest degree would be a sham if it were not accompanied by love. A loveless tongues-speaker is no better than "a noisy brass [gong]" or a "clashing cymbal" (13:1)—not melodious but monotonous and annoying to the ear. Corinth was noted for its bronze. But what kind of bronze instrument does Paul have in mind? One plausible suggestion is the bronze vases used as amplifiers in theatres. The clash of cymbals would have been familiar to the Corinthians from the frenzied worship associated with the cults of Dionysus and Cybele.

What applies to tongues applies equally to the greater gift of prophecy. Again, Paul was second to none in receiving revelations from God and in his insight into divine mysteries (2:7; 15:51). But if he or anyone else should claim the gift of prophecy but fail to exercise it in love, he would be worthless (13:2).

Jesus spoke severely of those who would boast on Judgment Day, "Lord, Lord, did we not prophesy in your name?" but whom he will reject as workers of iniquity (Mt 7:22–23). The possession of outstanding gifts was no guarantee of God's approval if they were not exercised by faith active in love.

The same holds true, Paul adds, for wonder-working faith. Jesus had said: "If you have faith like a grain of mustard seed, you will say to this mountain: 'Move from here to there,' and it will move" (Mt 17:20). In an unmistakable echo of his Master's words, Paul asserts that even if he were filled with enough faith to move mountains but lacked love, he would amount to nothing (1 Cor 13:2). His gift would fail to build up the church.

Turning from the more spectacular spiritual gifts to actions of a more practical kind, Paul adds that if he were to follow the example of many early Christians by parceling out his possessions to the poor (Acts 2:45; 4:32), he would still reap no spiritual benefit as long as his actions were not motivated by love. In fact, he would be no better than Ananias and Sapphira, whose behavior was prompted solely by selfish considerations (Acts 5:1–11; cf. Mt 6:2).

All his physical sufferings on behalf of the church would be similarly meaningless if undergone without love. Most English versions, with the exception of NRSV, follow the textual variant which reads "if I give my body so that I will be burned" (cf. Dan 3:19–20). Among the arguments against this option is the fact that the fiery persecutions under Nero were still a decade away at the time Paul wrote 1 Corinthians. Besides, a martyr does not give over his body; rather, it is taken from him. More likely, Paul is reflecting on his own experience. He was enduring all kinds of bodily sufferings for the sake of the Gospel, and rather than boasting in his great spiritual accomplishments and visions, he was resolved to boast only in the Lord (1 Cor 1:31) and in his weaknesses (2 Cor 11:18–30; 12:9). But he knew that without love even the greatest reason for glorying is profitless.

The message of 1 Cor 13:1–3 may readily be applied to the contemporary church. Whenever someone is tempted to become puffed up because of his significant role—as preacher, scholar, evangelist, communicator, administrator, adviser, counselor, motivator, visionary, public relations expert, musician (the list could go on indefinitely)—Paul would call him to consider that if his motivation is to build up his own prestige rather than the church of God, he serves no good purpose.

1 CORINTHIANS 13:4–7

Love in Action: The Character of Love

TRANSLATION

13 [4]Love is longsuffering, is kind; love is not jealous,
love does not brag, is not puffed up, [5]does not
behave improperly, is not self-seeking, is not
provoked, does not keep a record of wrong, [6]does
not rejoice in unrighteousness, but joins in rejoicing
in the truth. [7]Love bears all things, believes all
things, hopes all things, endures all things.

COMMENTARY

This fine paragraph uses fifteen verbs to describe the qualities of Christian love. The first two verbs give a positive description of love's greatest qualities. They are followed by a series of eight negated verbs which express what love is not (in 1 Cor 13:6, the last of these negated verbs is followed and balanced by its positive counterpart). The final four verbs are positive again, each being preceded in Greek by "all things."

Whereas English translations generally resort to adjectives in translating many of these verbs, the Greek has a dynamic quality well suited to the way love expresses itself *in actions* for the benefit of others. Christian love expresses itself in outgoing, self-forgetful *activity.*

Love's first and greatest characteristic is to be longsuffering (13:4). Christian love is marked less by the expression of emotion than by the taming (literally the "lengthening") of emotion. The Christian is not short-tempered, but longsuffering with others. In this, he imitates God, who has always displayed longsuffering in his dealings with his people (e.g., Ex 34:6; Joel 2:13; Rom 9:22; 2 Pet 3:9). Paul was deeply conscious of how much he owed to the perfect patience Christ Jesus had shown in his case (1 Tim 1:16). God's longsuffering with his people is to be reflected, then, in the longsuffering Christians are to show one another (Eph 4:2; Col 1:11; 3:12; 2 Tim 3:10; 4:2). Such longsuffering is not the mere cultivation of self-control. It is a gift from God, a fruit of God's Spirit (Gal 5:22).

In the fast-paced, achievement-oriented world of the third millennium, when the spirit of the age tempts churches to look for quick and impressive results, it is salutary to reflect on the priority Paul accords to the love which expresses itself in being longsuffering, a love that can wait (cf. 1 Cor 1:7; 11:33).

Love's second characteristic is to be kind (1 Cor 13:4). Again, it is God who sets the example by showing unfailing kindness in the creation, preservation, and redemption of his people (Rom 11:22; Eph 2:7; Titus 3:4). His kindness to them should bear fruit in their lives (Gal 5:22; Col 3:12).

Having shown love's most important positive characteristics, Paul throws love into sharper relief by showing what it is not. First, "love is not jealous" (1 Cor 13:4). The Corinthians had fallen prey to jealousy through their competitiveness and warring factions (1:10–11; 3:3). Jealousy is "the green-eyed monster" (*Othello*, act 3, scene 3) which is never content with the gifts it has received, but must be eyeing what others have (Mt 20:15), even trampling over others for advancement and preferment. It is one of "the works of the flesh" (Gal 5:19–21) which make war on the new Spirit-filled life within the body of Christ.

Love also does not behave like a braggart or windbag (1 Cor 13:4). Apparently some of the Corinthians, with their delight in eloquent and impressive speech, had fallen into that trap. Paul had to educate them about the world's false wisdom and eloquence; the world's wisdom is foolishness to God (1:17–24; 3:19), and Paul deliberately avoided superficial eloquence in his presentation of the Gospel (2:1–7, 13; 4:19–20).

Nor does love condone the closely related sin of being inflated with self-importance ("is not puffed up," 13:4). A number of times, Paul has had occasion to chide the Corinthians for being puffed up (in 4:6, 18, 19; 5:2; 8:1) because of factional pride and arrogance, for their toleration of immorality, and for their disregard for his directives as a called apostle of God. Now he points out that ballooned, inflated egos are totally incompatible with Christian love. Egoism fractures the unity of the body of Christ.

Love also "does not behave improperly" (13:5). It is concerned for what is right in the Lord's sight and also takes care not to offend others. See Paul's discussion in chapters 8 and 10 about the need not to offend weaker brothers by compromising with false worship practices (cf. also 2 Cor 8:21). Paul often calls on Christians to conduct themselves in a proper and dignified fashion in various aspects of their lives—in their conduct toward the opposite sex (1 Cor 7:35); in their conduct during worship (14:40); and in proper and responsible ethical conduct in general (Rom 13:13; 1 Thess 4:12).

Nor is love self-seeking (1 Cor 13:5). Paul had admonished the Christians in Corinth not to be self-seeking and not to do everything that may be permissible, but to seek the edification of others (10:23–24). Thus, they would be imitating his example of not seeking his own benefit but the salvation of many (10:33).

Furthermore, love "is not [easily] provoked" (1 Cor 13:5). There was widespread tension in the Corinthian congregation, where the factional rivalry had led to a great deal of provocation. Paul's admonition here is in line with his general concern that Christians control their anger (Eph 4:26, 31–32).

Love also "does not keep a record of wrongs" (1 Cor 13:5). In so doing, it follows the Lord of love, who did not keep a record of people's sins, not even of those who crucified him (Lk 23:34). Our Lord erases the sins of his people from his ledger (Rom 4:8; Col 2:14) so that he remembers them no more (Jer 31:34; Heb 8:12). Love does not nurse a grudge. It forgives, even as Christ has forgiven (Eph 4:32).

Coming now to the eighth and final verb negated by "not," Paul rounds off his list of the destructive patterns which mark unloving behavior: "[love] does not rejoice in unrighteousness" (1 Cor 13:6). Love avoids the human propensity not only to give tacit approval to wickedness but even to delight in hearing about it and perpetuating it (cf. Acts 8:1; Rom 1:18, 32; 6:13). Here in 1 Cor 13:6, "unrighteousness" is contrasted not with "righteousness," but, as often in the NT (Jn 7:18; Rom 1:18; 2:8; 2 Thess 2:10, 12), with "truth." While unrighteousness suppresses the truth (Rom 1:18), God's righteousness is displayed in the truth of the Gospel (Rom 1:16–17; Gal 2:5, 14). This truth means a break with unrighteousness toward the neighbor, and signals the beginning of a life of loving service. In place of jealousy, rivalry, rudeness, pride, and other forms of self-centeredness listed in 13:4b–6a, Christian love leads all members of the body to rejoice together when one of their number is honored (12:26). Instead of placing their bodies at the service of wickedness, they join with others in rejoicing in whatever is true, constructive, and edifying (cf. Phil 4:8).

Paul concludes his description of love's activities with four brief clauses in 1 Cor 13:7 about love's tenacity. The first speaks of the way love bears all things; the last completes the chiasm by speaking of the way it endures. Thus, these final clauses form an inclusio with 13:4a, sounding again the dominant theme of the way love extends itself in longsuffering.

First in 13:7, love "bears all things," that is, it puts up with other people and circumstances which try its patience, just as Paul and his co-workers put up with hard work and deprivation for the sake of the Gospel (9:12).

The second and third clauses in 13:7 introduce faith and hope into Paul's description of love, thus preparing the way for the comment on the triad "faith, hope, love" which concludes the chapter (13:13). To say that love "believes ['has faith' through] all things" (13:7) does not mean love is gullible and always believes other people. Rather, faith generated by God's love in Christ endures in all circumstances. Similarly, love never gives up its hope in God. The same theme is found in 1 Thessalonians, where Paul thanks God for the church's "endurance of hope in our Lord Jesus Christ" (1 Thess 1:3).

Finally, love "endures all things" (1 Cor 13:7). Endurance is one of the great characteristics of life under the cross in Christ's kingdom (Rev 1:9). The verb "endures" is a close synonym of "is longsuffering" at the beginning of 1 Cor 13:4, neatly rounding off the paragraph.

1 CORINTHIANS 13:8–13
The Permanence of Love

TRANSLATION

**13 8Love never falls. But whether prophecies, they will
be superseded; whether tongues, they will cease;
whether knowledge, it will be superseded. 9For
we know in part and we prophesy in part. 10But
when that which is complete comes, that which is
partial will be superseded. 11When I was a child, I
used to speak as a child, I used to think as a child,
I used to reason as a child. When I became a man,
I set aside the ways of a child. 12For now we see in a
mirror indirectly, but then face to face; now I know
in part, but then I will know just as I have been
known. 13So now there remain faith, hope, love,
these three things. But the greatest of these is love.**

COMMENTARY

After his almost lyrical description of love's characteristics (1 Cor 13:4–7), Paul turns to love's permanence and abiding value. He begins with the thematic statement "love never falls" (13:8; see similar statements about the Word of God in Josh 21:45; 23:14). Just as the Word of God never falls to the ground ineffective but always accomplishes its purposes (Is 55:10–11), so Christian love will retain its honored place throughout time and eternity.

By contrast, the spiritual gifts so highly prized by the Corinthians possess only a temporary value (1 Cor 13:8). In this age, indeed, they still have their significance, but the form of this age is passing away (7:31). If the Corinthians would only stay focused on the things that endure, eagerly anticipating the revelation of their Lord Jesus Christ (1:7) and the resurrection of the dead (15:1–58), then from that eternal perspective they would see that even the greatest spiritual gifts lack permanent value. When the last day dawns, the gifts of prophecy, tongues, knowledge, and so on will no longer be necessary.

As Paul explains in 13:9, our knowledge and our prophetic insights are at best only partial. This does not mean that the knowledge provided by divine revelation is false, distorted, or imperfect. Jesus assured his disciples that, by continuing in the Word, they would know the truth, and the truth would make them free (Jn 8:31–32). His words are words of eternal life (Jn 6:68). But while the knowledge we have is liberating and life giving, it is still only partial. Our darkened minds find it difficult to comprehend God's truths. His Word still provides only glimpses of what will be fully revealed in eternity, when we will see "face to face" (1 Cor 13:12).

Certain patterns of speech and of thinking and reasoning are appropriate for a child, and children cannot transcend the natural limitations imposed on them by their immaturity. But as they develop into adults, they become capable of more mature cognitive activity. Their former ways are no longer appropriate once they have grown up (13:11). Similarly, gifts like prophecy, tongues, and knowledge, have their place in the Christian life in this aeon but will become obsolete once eternity dawns.

During our life in this age, we live by faith in the revelation we have been given through God's Word, and we do not yet behold God directly, by sight. This may be compared to looking in a mirror (13:12): what we see is only a reflection of the real thing. Paul is not implying that the mirrors of his day were of poor quality, providing only a flawed image. Indeed, Corinth was known for the fine quality of its bronze mirrors. Rather, Paul is comparing the indirect nature of viewing a face in the mirror with seeing someone face-to-face. An apt modern comparison is between seeing a person in a photograph or on television or in a movie versus seeing the person himself. In eternity, we will see God "face to face" (13:12; cf. Mt 5:8; 1 Jn 3:2; Rev 22:4). Just as the Israelites—with a few significant exceptions, such as Moses (Num 12:8)—could not look on God's face and live (see also Gen 32:30; Judg 13:22–23), neither can the Christian in this life look on the full glory of God and live. That privilege is reserved for the next life. Thus, our knowledge of God in this life can only be incomplete.

Switching back to the first person singular in 1 Cor 13:12b (as in 13:1–3), Paul speaks in a personal way of what this heavenly prospect means for him. *Now* the apostle's knowledge of God and of divine things is only partial (in 13:12 as in 13:9). But *then* his knowledge will be complete, just as God's knowledge of him is complete (twice in 13:12). And God's intimate knowledge of Paul is bound up with his divine love and care for him. One may compare 1 Cor 13:12 to Jn 10:14–15, where the Good Shepherd's knowledge of his sheep is connected with his self-sacrificing love for them.

In conclusion (1 Cor 13:13), Paul asserts that far more important than any spiritual gift or any Christian knowledge is the great triad of faith, hope, and love. Faith in the God who knew and loved his people before they were born (1 Cor 13:12; cf. Gal 1:15), hope in him, and the love which flows from faith and hope—these virtues have supreme and enduring value for the lives of all Christians, regardless of the particular spiritual endowment any individual may possess.

Paul does not mean, however, that these virtues in their present form will all abide eternally. Elsewhere he contrasts "faith," which marks the Christian's walk in this aeon, with the "sight" which will be granted in the age to come (2 Cor

5:7). Moreover, he will write to the Romans: "Hope that is seen is not hope; for who hopes for what he sees?" (Rom 8:24). Faith and hope, then, pertain to this temporary aeon, which "is passing away" (1 Cor 7:31). Love, on the other hand, is greater; it "never falls" (13:8). The loving relationship between the God who *is* love and his people will endure throughout eternity; indeed, in eternity it will become most palpable. This will not only be true of the love between God and his people. It will also, in an almost unimaginable fashion, be true of the relationships that God's people have with each other. Our love for each other will be perfect, because it will flow out from God's perfect love toward us.

But the eternally enduring nature of love is by no means the only reason why Paul calls it "the greatest" (13:13). Clearly, Paul is also praising love because of its inestimable value to the church. The whole aim of his apostolic charge was to produce the love that flowed "from a pure heart and a good conscience and sincere faith" (1 Tim 1:5). Nowhere was a church in greater need of this highest of virtues than the strife-torn congregation in Corinth.

14:1–33A

PROPHECY AND TONGUES

1 CORINTHIANS 14:1–12

Prophecy Is Superior to Tongues Because It Edifies the Church

TRANSLATION

**14 1Pursue love [and] strive for the spiritual gifts—
[and] especially that you may prophesy. 2For the
person who speaks in a tongue does not speak to
human beings but to God; for no one understands,
but by [his] spirit he speaks mysteries. 3But the
person who prophesies speaks to people edification,
encouragement, and comfort. 4The person who
speaks in a tongue edifies himself; but the one who
prophesies edifies the church. 5I want you all to
speak in tongues, but even more that you prophesy.
For the one who prophesies is greater than the
one speaking in tongues, unless he interprets
so that the church may receive edification.**

**6So now, brothers, if I come to you speaking in
tongues, what will I profit you unless I speak to
you by revelation or by knowledge or by prophecy
or by teaching? 7It is the same way with lifeless
instruments producing a sound, whether a flute or
a harp: if they make no distinction in their tones,
how will it be known what [tune] is being played
on the flute or harp? 8For also if a trumpet gives an
unclear sound, who will prepare for battle? 9And
so [it is with] you: if you do not utter intelligible
speech, how will it be known what is being said?
For you will be talking into the air. 10There are who
knows how many different languages in the world
and none of them without meaning. 11Therefore
if I do not know the force of the language, to**

the speaker I will be a foreigner, and to me the speaker will be a foreigner. [12]And so [it is with] you: since you are enthusiasts for spirits, seek that you may excel at the edification of the church.

COMMENTARY

TONGUES COMPARED TO PROPHESYING (14:1–5)

Love is Paul's overriding concern. As in 12:31b–13:13, he again encourages the Corinthians to pursue love. From love, then, will flow a concern to edify the church. In striving for spiritual gifts, the congregation should always be guided by this criterion: what serves best to promote the loving edification of the whole church? Thus, the words *edify* and *edification*, which Paul had used four times in previous chapters, become the theme *(Leitmotif)* of chapter 14. These words occur seven times as the apostle takes up a detailed discussion of tongues and prophecy. "Let all things be done for *edification*" (14:26). In chapter 8 Paul demonstrated the superiority of love over knowledge: "knowledge puffs up, but love builds up," that is, "edifies" (8:1). In chapter 10 he portrayed the priority of edification over exercising one's Christian freedom: "'all things are in my power,' but not all things build up/edify" (10:23).

Whereas 12:8–10 lists nine gifts of grace, and 12:28 adds another five, chapter 14 singles out only two for special attention: tongues and prophecy. Paul recognizes that both have a vital role in edifying the church. But the Corinthians seem to have given undue emphasis to the more spectacular gift of tongues. Thus, Paul's concern in 14:1–25 is to lead them to a healthier and more balanced view of the comparative value of each gift. Nowhere does he disparage tongues or discourage the Corinthians from exercising that gift; indeed, he wants all of them to speak in tongues (14:5a). But a more precise understanding of the respective contribution of tongues and prophecy will, he believes, lead them to give priority to prophecy.

Paul now explains why they should value prophecy above tongues. *His thesis is that tongues do not edify the church as well as prophecy does, because they are not intelligible to others without an interpreter.* The tongues-speaker prays, sings, blesses, and gives thanks to God well enough (14:14–17), but "no one understands" (14:2). He speaks of the exalted "mysteries" of God (14:2). These "mysteries" that comprise the message are aspects of the Gospel of Jesus Christ, which is "*the mystery* of God" (2:1). But the words of the tongues-speaker flow from his innermost being, his spirit, rather than his mind. Likewise, the minds of the listeners cannot engage the foreign tongue, with the result that no one can make sense of the message. On the other hand, the prophet's speech is superior, being intelligible to the hearers, since he articulates the Gospel in the hearers' native tongue. Thus, by prophecy the church is built up (edified) in the faith, encouraged, and comforted (14:3).

For some commentators, 14:2 speaks decisively against the view that the tongues-speaking in Corinth was identical with the Pentecost phenomenon of speaking known human languages (Acts 2). At Pentecost "each one *heard* them speaking in his own language" (Acts 2:6; cf. Acts 2:8, 11). There was no need for an interpreter.

In 1 Corinthians 14 Paul is speaking about the congregation as a whole, and it would be likely that few (if any) of those present in Corinth would know the particular foreign language. On Pentecost (Acts 2), the situation was different. Gathered in Jerusalem were large numbers of people from all over the Mediterranean world, and so the diverse foreign tongues were recognized and understood by at least some of those present.

In 1 Cor 14:4–5 Paul continues his exposition of the comparatively greater value of prophecy over tongues. The Christian who utilizes his gift of tongues without also translating or interpreting benefits only a single individual—himself—whereas the prophet edifies the whole church. One might compare this self-edification to a contemporary pastor who practices reciting out loud Psalm 23 in Hebrew or the Lord's Prayer in Greek. By doing so he certainly edifies himself. But if he speaks the original biblical tongues in the pulpit or in Bible class, even though he may impress the church, unless he also provides a translation or interpretation, he edifies only himself.

That Paul was not opposed to speaking in tongues per se—indeed, was favorably disposed toward it—is made plain in 14:5 (cf. also 14:18). Just as Moses expressed the wish that all the Lord's people would be endowed by the Spirit to be prophets (Num 11:29), so Paul wished everyone in Corinth could speak in tongues. Above all, however, he wanted them all to prophesy. Because the prophet built up the whole church, he was greater than the tongues-speaker, unless the latter provided an interpretation or translation for the church's edification. That elucidation of the Gospel in the common language of the listeners would make all the difference!

THE ANALOGY OF MUSICAL INSTRUMENTS (14:6–12)

Tenderly addressing the Corinthian Christians as "brothers" (1 Cor 14:6), Paul asks them to imagine what it would be like if their apostle made tongues-speaking the centerpiece of his next visit. Such an approach may be edifying for Paul himself (14:4), but how would it benefit them? They would only be benefited if he brought a message that was clear and comprehensible to all. As a modern equivalent, one might ask how it would benefit an English-speaking congregation if a guest preacher on mission Sunday were to preach in Russian or Swahili as he described his missionary work among native speakers of that language. Such a sermon would not build up the faith of the congregation.

Next Paul says that it would be more helpful to the Corinthians if he imparted a specific revelation (14:6). The noun "revelation" is sometimes used for an extended lengthy message, such as "the revelation of Jesus Christ" (Rev 1:1), that is, the book of Revelation. In 1 Cor 2:10 the verb "to reveal" refers to God revealing through his Spirit the Gospel itself. But the noun may also be used more narrowly of a specific "revelation," as when God revealed to Paul that he should visit the apostles in Jerusalem (Gal 2:2). That narrow sense of a brief, specific "revelation" is carried by the noun in 1 Cor 14:26 and by the verb in 14:30.

In addition to revelation, Paul could also benefit the congregation "by knowledge or by prophecy or by teaching" (14:6). There may be a link between the first and third items on the list, "revelation" and "prophecy" (cf. 14:29–30), and between the second and fourth items, "knowledge" and "teaching." The relationship would be as follows. Divine revelation comes to the prophet and then is proclaimed by his prophesying. Similarly, divine knowledge is acquired by the teacher, which he then transmits by his teaching. (Paul speaks of his own reception and transmission of divine truths in 11:23 and 15:3–8.) That relationship might be illustrated in the following way:

revelation———prophet———prophecy
knowledge———teacher———teaching

By way of analogy to musical instruments in 14:7–8, Paul illustrates how useless is the gift of tongues without interpretation or translation. First he draws a comparison to a tune played on musical instruments. If woodwinds or the stringed instruments were to produce only a drab monotone or jangle (as when an orchestra is tuning up), no one could possibly derive any benefit from the music. Music is composed to convey a message (compare, for example, the musical notations in the psalms and the hymnic passages in Rev 5:9–13; 15:2–4). But the kinds of sounds Paul has in mind would be chaotic and meaningless.

Moreover, Paul says in 1 Cor 14:8, an incoherent sound would be disastrous in the case of the battle trumpet. If the bugle gives a feeble and indeterminate note, the soldiers have no idea what is expected of them, and no one will prepare for battle. A forceful and unambiguous message is critical for a successful military operation.

Paul now applies the analogies to the Corinthians' use of tongues (14:9). If their speaking fails to convey a recognizable message, the whole exercise will be futile, amounting to so much "hot air." Paul saw no point in such purposeless and undisciplined activity. Like "beating the air" in 9:26, that kind of speech would be "talking into the air" (14:9).

In 14:10–11 Paul now carries further his argument that a language must be "intelligible" [easily recognizable, clear, distinct] (14:9), if it is to be serviceable to the church. Recalling the familiar babble of languages heard in the streets and public places of cosmopolitan centers like Corinth, he observes: "There are who knows how many different languages in the world" (14:10). Each of them, he adds, is perfectly intelligible to those conversant with that language. But if anyone is not adept in a particular tongue, he will be regarded as a foreigner by anyone who speaks it, while he in turn will regard the speaker as a foreigner (14:11). There will be a barrier between them—a barrier that prevents constructive communication.

In 14:12 Paul draws the final conclusion from his arguments. The flute and the harp need to play a meaningful tune (14:7), the trumpet needs to produce a compelling sound (14:8), and—finally—human speakers need to be intelligible to one another if anyone is to benefit from what they are hearing (14:9–11). Even if the tongues are facilitated by the Spirit, they are useless babble without a translator for those who are not conversant in the particular language. Surely then the Corinthians (14:12), in their enthusiasm for the Spirit and his gifts, would not want to be considered as completely ineffective speakers because of their zeal for foreign languages (tongues), coupled with carelessness about supplying a translation or interpretation. They would prefer to be considered as influential instructors about the spiritual life. Thus, Paul urges them again to make the upbuilding of the church their highest priority: "Seek that you may excel at the edification of the church" (14:12; cf. Rom 14:19). There is no place in the church for showing off one's gifts for the purpose of self-aggrandizement.

1 CORINTHIANS 14:13–19

The Tongues-speaker Must Pray for the Gift of Interpretation

TRANSLATION

14 [13]Therefore let the person speaking in a tongue pray that he may interpret. [14]For if I pray in a tongue, my spirit prays, but my mind is unproductive. [15]What then [is the upshot of all this]? I will pray with my spirit, but I will also pray with my mind; I will sing with my spirit, but I will also sing with my mind. [16]For if you bless in spirit, how will the person who fills the role of the outsider say the "amen" to your thanksgiving? For he does not understand what you are saying. [17]For you indeed are giving thanks well, but the other person is not edified. [18]I thank God, I speak in tongues more than you all. [19]But in the church I prefer to speak five words with my mind, in order that I may also instruct others, than countless words in a tongue.

COMMENTARY

Paul has established the principle that what benefits the church is edification, or upbuilding. With a strong "therefore" (14:13), he begins to spell out how tongues-speakers may begin to make themselves more helpful to the church. As he does so, it becomes apparent that in asking them to seek excellence in building up the church, he is not throwing them back on their own spiritual exercises or ethical resources. No, he means that they should lift up their hearts to God in prayer. Just as Jesus encouraged his disciples to pray for the gift of the Holy Spirit (Lk 11:13), so Paul encourages these saints to pray for a specific gift of the Spirit. It is by prayer that they are to "strive for the gracious gifts that are greater" (1 Cor 12:31). This does not mean that Christians may *demand* a particular gift. In his divine freedom, "the one and the same Spirit" distributes "to each one individually *as he [the Spirit] wishes*" (12:11). But the Corinthian tongues-speakers urgently needed to be freed from their self-centered preoccupation and begin thinking of others. To that end, therefore, each should "pray that he may interpret/translate" (14:13) the language into the vernacular of the listeners. Then he will no longer sound like a "foreigner" (14:11) to his fellow Christians, but like someone who can be genuinely helpful.

As long as he only prays in a tongue, he will only edify himself (see 14:4). That is because only his inner being, or "spirit," is engaged in the activity (14:14). Filled with the Holy Spirit, he is speaking about the Gospel in other languages as the Spirit inspires his spirit to give utterance (as in Acts 2:4). But since his rational mind is "in neutral"—not engaged with his spirit—he is unable to communicate that spiritual utterance in meaningful terms in the language(s) known by the listeners.

As a result, the apostle is resolved to pray and sing not only with his spirit but also with his mind and faculties of understanding (1 Cor 14:15). Again, it becomes evident that tongues-speaking was not primarily a form of teaching, directed to human beings, but consisted of prayer, praise, and thanksgiving addressed to God ("I will pray," "I will sing," 14:15; cf. Acts 2:11; 10:46; 1 Cor 14:2). Nevertheless, as exalted and worthy as such expressions may be, Paul determines to set an example by ensuring that in public worship anything he says in a tongue will be translated for the congregation's benefit.

If the tongues-speaker persists in praising God only in spirit, it will be impossible for anyone not conversant with that foreign prayer-language to adopt and affirm the prayer as his own with the "amen" (1 Cor 14:16). Paul's expression for someone not conversant with the tongue, translated above as "outsider," means a person who is inexperienced or incompetent in a certain skill. The word is used in Acts 4:13, where Peter and John are classed as "common" (ESV) in comparison with the rabbis, and 2 Cor 11:6, where Paul calls himself "unskilled" (ESV) in speech. The outsiders in Corinth (1 Cor 14:16) possessed other gifts of grace, as do all Christians (1:4–7), but could make no sense of uninterpreted tongues. The tongues-speakers may have been showing off their talents by the way they said the table grace/eucharistic prayer before the congregational meals which served as the setting for the Lord's Supper (11:17–22).

No matter how fine the speaker's thanksgiving may be, if it is in a language unknown to others, the only person to be edified is the speaker himself (14:17; cf. 14:4). The others receive no spiritual benefit—no edification—because the speaker's only concern is his private conversation with God.

Paul then clarifies in 14:18 that he is not protesting this misuse of tongues from a sense of "sour grapes." Rather, Paul is thankful to God for enriching him with this gift beyond anyone else in Corinth. Nonetheless, he does not want to parade this gift. While it has its place in private prayer and praise, Paul prefers to concentrate on what counts "in church" (14:19), what builds up the body of Christ. To that end, he regards it as infinitely more helpful to speak five intelligible words with his mind fully engaged—words in the common language that also engage the minds of the hearers—in order to instruct others in the faith, rather than countless words that are meaningless to the hearers.

This is not to advocate a "dumbing down" of the church's language, and even less an abandonment of the church's biblical standards and heritage of liturgical worship. When people do not comprehend biblical and ecclesiastical language (cf. "the outsider" in 14:16), what is needed is catechesis, which Paul calls interpretation and/or translation (12:30; 14:5, 13, 27).

1 CORINTHIANS 14:20–25

Tongues Serve as a Divine "Hardening Instrument"

TRANSLATION

**14 [20]Brothers, do not be children in your minds
but be babies in evil, and in your thinking
be mature. [21]It is written in the Law:**

> **"By foreign tongues and by the lips of foreigners
> I will speak to this people, and not even so
> will they listen to me," says the Lord.**

**[22]So tongues are meant as a sign not for believers
but for unbelievers, but prophecy is not for
unbelievers but for believers. [23]If therefore the whole
church comes together in the same place and all
speak in tongues, and outsiders, or unbelievers,
enter will they not say that you are out of your
minds? [24]But if all prophesy and an unbeliever, or
outsider, enters he is convicted by all, he is called
to account by all, [25]the secrets of his heart become
manifest, and so falling on his face he will worship
God proclaiming, "Truly God is among you."**

COMMENTARY

Before presenting one final argument regarding the comparative superiority of prophecy over tongues, Paul pauses for a moment and appeals to his "brothers" (14:20) to take a more mature approach. To be concerned for the edification of Christ's body is a mark of mature thinking. But to be concerned with vain and competitive displays of one's spiritual prowess through tongues-speaking, with no thought for the effect on fellow believers, is a mark of childishness. Paul wants the Corinthians to press on to the maturity of Christian thought which characterizes the veteran of the cross (see 2:6; 3:1–3).

Paul now asks the Corinthians to give some more mature consideration to another of God's specific purposes in bestowing the gift of tongues. Paul's key text is Is 28:11–12. Through the prophet Isaiah God had been attempting to guide his people into the way of peace and rest, but they had rejected his message as gibberish (Is 28:10). In response God had declared that those who refused to listen to clear Hebrew would be compelled to listen to the Assyrians, "people of strange lips and with a foreign tongue" (Is 28:11 ESV). Thus, Israel would be subjected to the judgment foretold in Deut 28:49: "The Lord will bring a nation against you from afar, . . . a nation whose language you do not understand."

In the NT aeon an outbreak of speaking in tongues continues to signify God's judgment on unbelievers and its hardening effect ("not even so will they listen to me," 1 Cor 14:21). Indeed, a consistent line can be traced from the Deuteronomy and Isaiah texts through the book of Acts to the present reappropriation in Paul. According to Acts, the unbelievers in Jerusalem mocked the Pentecost message proclaimed to them in various tongues, and obstinately concluded: "These men are full of new wine" (Acts 2:13). They would have none of Jesus Christ as the "precious cornerstone" of the church (Is 28:16; Acts 4:11), none of the positive aspect of the tongues-message that the Gospel was for all peoples and tongues. Likewise, Paul declares that the phenomenon of tongues in Corinth was (unlike prophecy) not designed simply as a salutary sign to build up believers in the faith; rather, one of its great purposes was to serve as *a negative judicial sign arousing the hostility of unbelievers* (cf. "a sign that is spoken against," Lk 2:34). Thus, the unbelievers, confronted with tongues-speaking in the assembly, would draw a conclusion similar to the conclusion of the unbelieving Jews on Pentecost Day, "You are out of your minds" (1 Cor 14:23).

In this respect, the gift of tongues served a similar dual purpose to Jesus' parables, which enlightened those to whom the mysteries of the kingdom were given but also blinded the eyes and hardened the hearts of unbelievers (Mt 13:11–17 and parallels). Thus, tongues without a translation or interpretation were not at all helpful in building up the believing congregation; prophecy alone served that purpose.

In 1 Cor 14:23–25 Paul proceeds to paint an imaginary scene to illustrate his point about the respective roles of tongues and prophecy. He first asks the Corinthians to imagine what it would be like if, instead of gathering in their separate house churches, the whole Corinthian church were to come together in one place (14:23), such as the home of his host Gaius, and everyone present were to speak in tongues. That would fulfill the fondest wishes of those who were so keen on tongues. But Paul asks them to consider the likely consequences. What would be the effect if, once they were all in high gear, a group of unbelievers unfamiliar with these languages should suddenly enter the assembly? The visitors would think they had entered a gathering of yet another mystery cult like that of Dionysus or Cybele, with its adherents all carried away by religious mania (cf. 12:2). Thus, their encounter with tongues-speech would be a negative experience, a sign that only confirmed them in their sarcastic unbelief.

Paul then paints a contrasting picture in 14:24–25. If an uninitiated visitor should enter the assembly when everyone was engaged in *prophecy,* he would be overwhelmed by the clear Word of God addressed to his heart in intelligible language. As the call to repentance was a key theme of prophetic speech, he would hear every voice in the room speaking to his conscience. Step by step Paul describes the process through which this person will be led by the Holy Spirit as the great spiritual gift of prophecy takes effect. First, the Spirit will work in the person's heart to convince him of his sinfulness (cf. Jn 16:8). Second, he will hear everyone calling him to account: "You cannot let matters rest. Something has to be done about your sin." Thus, in the third place, the person is led to make confession: the secret thoughts and motives of his heart are exposed by the light of God's truth and then renounced. He who once walked in darkness has now come to the light (cf. the similar terminology in Jn 3:19–21; Eph 5:8–14). Finally, the Spirit leads him to fall on his face and worship, humbly acknowledging that "the God of Israel, the Savior" (Is 45:14–15) is truly present in this Christian assembly. The vision of the prophets was that one day the Gentile nations would be incorporated into the people of God together with Israel (Is 45:12–17; Zech 8:20–23). Paul alludes to that prophetic vision with the quote in 1 Cor 14:25, which draws on Is 45:14 and Zech 8:23. The Christians endowed with the spiritual gift of prophecy now fulfill Israel's ancient prophetic hope.

Thus, by seeking to excel in prophecy, the sign so superbly suited for edifying and enlightening the members of the church, the Corinthians will also be more effective in evangelism to outsiders. Their practice of speaking God's Word in clear, intelligible language will not only strike the visitor as eminently sensible; above all, the Holy Spirit will use the prophecies to convict him of his sins and bring him to the light of Christ.

EXCURSUS

Worship Practice Today

Paul's apologetic for worship to provide a straightforward and uncompromising proclamation of the Word of God—the Law's convicting and the Gospel's pardon—has great significance for the church's worship practice today. In modern "worship wars" the battle lines often are drawn by the answer to this question: what is the primary purpose of worship? Should worship be primarily for edifying those who are already church members (and who presumably are Christian believers), or should worship be designed to attract and recruit outsiders (marginally Christian "seekers" and also unbelievers)? The twofold answer furnished by 1 Corinthians 14 is that *worship should be designed to edify the church, and that such edifying worship is also the best kind of worship for evangelism and outreach.*

The goals of edification and evangelism, when properly framed, are not in conflict with each other, but in harmony. Seven times in 1 Corinthians 14 Paul speaks of edifying or building up the church as the goal and criterion for proper Christian worship. In 14:20–25 he addresses the effect of worship on the "outsider" (14:16, 23–24) and on the "unbeliever" (14:22–24). The same worship that builds up the church also converts unbelievers (14:24–25).

This worship is characterized by a direct presentation of the Law, which accuses and convicts the hearers of their sin (14:24–25; cf. Jn 4:17–18). Worship should not soften or downplay the Law on the grounds that it may offend; it always does and must offend the sinner in each of us! As for offending unbelievers who may happen to be visitors, they especially are in need of the Law's condemnation so that they may be brought to repentance and faith.

This worship must also plainly proclaim the Gospel of the full forgiveness of sins by grace alone and through faith in Jesus Christ alone. A creedal confession about the God in whom we believe—his creation, his redemption, and his uniqueness among all the world's gods—is found in the OT texts to which 1 Cor 14:25 alludes (especially Is 45:12–17; see also Zech 8:20–23). Those OT texts portray the ingathering of the Gentiles to join Israel in the worship of the God who is like none other. In 1 Cor 14:25 the converted worshiper responds with a creedal confession of his faith in the one true God who is to be found among his worshipful people.

Following Paul's terminology, such salutary worship might be called "prophetic." Paul's concern in 14:1–25 has been to demonstrate the superiority of prophecy over tongues in edifying the church at worship. Tongues are fine for an individual's private devotional worship (14:4), but prophecy is what benefits the corporate congregation (14:1–25). "Prophetic" worship then stands in contrast to what might be called "charismatic" or tongues-oriented worship, which gives free (and chaotic) reign to diverse individual gifts and talents. The diverse gifts of the

Spirit are indeed blessings to the body of Christ, but the issue here is the proper exercise of gifts during the church's corporate worship.

The direction of Paul's argumentation in chapter 14 points to an employment of worship forms that have been accepted and practiced by the whole Christian church throughout her history. The historic liturgies of the catholic (universal) church are "prophetic" because they are drawn from the prophetic and apostolic Scriptures and proclaim Law and Gospel uncompromisingly to engender repentance and faith. Paul's emphasis on plain and direct language and his recurring reminders that tongues need translation and interpretation (14:5, 13, 27) suggest the need for catechesis whenever worship language is not readily understood.

Untold damage has been caused to congregations by the reckless and iconoclastic jettisoning of the church's historic liturgies and hymns in the interests of "change." In a turbulent world where people are faced with overwhelming changes, the church should stand as the temple of the unchanging God who is "not [a God] of disorder but of peace" (14:33), the God who offers stability and a safe refuge and anchorage from life's storms (Is 33:6; cf. Is 4:6; 32:2; Heb 6:19; 13:8). Christians should be able to look to the church as a place which treasures her continuity with the communion of saints through the centuries and across national borders, as expressed in her rich international heritage of liturgies, "psalms, hymns, and spiritual songs" (Eph 5:19).

At the same time, the church's worship should never become ossified but should always be open to further enrichment from the fresh contributions of contemporary saints (cf. 1 Cor 14:26). A vibrant church in every age and culture will have musically gifted members who express the faith in new compositions. The best survives, to be shared with others; the rest falls by the wayside.

It would seem to be consistent with Paul's concerns in 1 Corinthians 14 (a) that all liturgy and hymnody, whether ancient or modern, should be based on the Word of God, which convicts worshipers of their sin and comforts them with the Gospel, and (b) that *the whole church* be nourished and edified by the life-giving Word and Sacraments. The church should not focus only on "seekers" at the expense of the regular flock. Nor should the worship be intelligible only to "baby boomers"; things precious to elderly saints should also find an honored place. On the other hand, there should be no rigid adherence to what is old if that means a refusal to make any room for what is both biblical and meaningful to the young. An issue in immigrant communities has often been the adherence to worship in the parents' mother tongue at the expense of the younger generation who needed nourishment in their adopted language. Jesus' words in Mt 13:52 are instructive for those who prepare and lead Christian worship: "Every scribe who has been trained for the kingdom of heaven is like the master of a house, who brings out of his treasure what is new and what is old" (ESV).

Paul will address further worship concerns in 1 Cor 14:26–40. Upbuilding worship will also observe the scriptural guidelines that Paul offers later. His topics in 14:26–39 are propriety and due order in worship, and the observance of appropriate roles. In 14:33–38 he addresses the proper roles for women in public worship and reminds the church of a divine command. It may suffice to say here that edifying and evangelical worship precludes the service of women as pastors, since that is contrary to the express command of the Lord (14:37) and is also contrary to the universal practice of the universal church for almost two millennia. The argument that women should be ordained to allow them to use freely the individual gifts God has given them runs counter to Paul's emphasis in 1 Corinthians 14 that the edification of the corporate church takes precedence over the desire of individuals to exercise their particular gifts. The argument that women should be ordained for the sake of outsiders or potential converts (who may be offended by limitations placed on women's roles) overlooks Paul's thesis that the Christian church's orderly and edifying worship is also her evangelistic worship. A concern for evangelism should not overturn the church's order; the church's order is part of her witness to the unbelieving world. Paul's consistent priority in 1 Corinthians 14 is on fidelity to the Word of God, observance of the divine order, and harmony with the practice of the universal church—all for the sake of building up the church and winning the unbeliever.

1 CORINTHIANS 14:26–33A

GUIDELINES FOR THE ORDERLY USE OF TONGUES AND PROPHECY IN WORSHIP

TRANSLATION

**14 [26]What then [is the upshot of all this], brothers?
When you come together, each has a hymn, has a
teaching, has a revelation, has a tongue, [or] has an
interpretation. Let all things be done for edification.
[27]If someone speaks in a tongue, [let there be]
two or at the most three, and in turn, and let one
interpret. [28]But if there is no interpreter, let him be
silent in church, and let him speak to himself and
to God. [29]As for prophets, let two or three speak
and the others evaluate. [30]And if [a revelation]
should be revealed to another while he is seated,
let the first one be silent. [31]For you can all prophesy
in turn, that all may learn and all be encouraged.
[32]And spirits of prophets are subject to prophets.
[33a]For God is not [a God] of disorder but of peace.**

COMMENTARY

Evidently the Corinthian worship services were characterized by a degree of disorderliness unacceptable to the apostle. The Corinthians' unruliness in worship became apparent in the women abandoning their head-coverings, and the well-to-do members' selfishness at the communal supper which preceded the Lord's Supper (11:2–22). Apparently speaking in tongues had also gotten out of hand (14:23, 27–28), and prophets competed with each other for the floor (14:30). Another concern was the proper roles of women in worship (14:33b–38).

Now that Paul has clarified the role and relative value of tongues and prophecy (14:1–25), he begins to bring his discussion to a close by spelling out the implications for the rubrics of their worship services. All things, he insists, should be done in love, so that the whole body of Christ receives "edification" (14:26, the last of seven occurrences of "edification" and "to edify" in chapter 14).

Again (as in 14:6, 20), he addresses the Corinthians affectionately as "brothers" (14:26). Then he describes some aspects of their worship. When they assemble as a church, many individuals make a contribution to the service. One person brings a hymn that has come into his hands or that he has composed himself (see Lk 1:46–55, 68–79 and 1 Tim 3:16 for possible examples of early Christian hymns; the "hymn" ["psalm" in Greek, 1 Cor 14:26] might be a biblical psalm set to music). Another has a gift for teaching and is prepared to expound a portion of the Scriptures. Another is a prophet and has just received a fresh revelation from the Lord. Another has something to say in a tongue, while another is able to interpret the foreign language. Each of these contributions has its rightful place in the church's worship, as long as each participant remembers to "let all things be done for *edification*" (14:26). Again, Paul declares that the chief guideline must be what is most edifying, what is best suited for building up the whole congregation in the faith.

Paul now adds more specific directions for the tongues-speakers and prophets (14:27–33a). He is happy to include tongues-speaking in worship. As in Acts 2, these tongues are proclamations of God's magnificent deeds in foreign languages. But in keeping with his wish that everything be done for edification he adds three qualifications. (1) He commands that no more than two tongues-speakers, or three at the most, should speak to the congregation at one gathering. Apparently a great number of people had been speaking in tongues at the Corinthian worship services and carrying on at some length. Paul urges restraint. (2) He urges those who do speak on a given occasion to do so in an orderly fashion, each awaiting his turn, rather than speaking on top of one another and trying to drown the others out. (3) They should only speak when an interpreter or translator is available (cf. 1 Cor 14:5, 13). Otherwise the tongues-speaker should remain silent, communicating with his own spirit and with God (cf. 14:2).

The command that the *tongues-speaker* who is unable to supply an interpretation must "be silent in church" (14:28) is the first in a series of three closely-linked injunctions. The other two are (1) that the *prophet,* too, must be silent if another receives a revelation (14:30) and (2) the *women* must be silent in the churches (14:34).

Like the tongues-speakers, it seems the prophets were also vying with one another for the floor (14:29–30). Accordingly, Paul also restricts them to no more than two or three at a worship service. The other prophets should listen attentively and evaluate the message, lest anyone introduce a false prophecy (cf. 1 Jn 4:1–3).

The criterion for evaluating messages is whether they are in harmony with the Scriptures and the apostolic Gospel. The Bereans, many of whom became Christians, evaluated Paul's preaching on the basis of the OT Scriptures and found it to be true (Acts 17:10–12). The test of whether prophecy is true involves whether it comes to pass and whether it is in accord with the words of the great

Prophet (Christ) promised in the OT (Deut 18:15–20). If anyone utters false prophecy or a false "gospel," he is to be anathema (Gal 1:8–9). True prophecy and the correct interpretation of prophecy come about only through the activity of the Holy Spirit (1 Pet 1:10–12). Revelation is the final prophetic book (Rev 1:3; 22:7, 10, 18, 19), and it ends with a dire warning against anyone who adds or subtracts from its prophetic message (Rev 22:18–19). By extension, since Revelation is the last book of the canon, that warning applies to anyone who would distort or detract from any doctrine in all the sacred Scriptures.

Again, the prophets should refrain from speaking on top of one another (1 Cor 14:30). If a prophetic revelation suddenly comes to someone who is seated, the prophet holding the floor should be silent and make way for this fresh word from the Lord.

Paul assures the Corinthians that by restricting them to two or three prophetic messages at any one gathering (14:29) he is not imposing a harsh restraint. In the course of time, everyone with a prophetic gift will have his turn to prophesy (14:31). The goal, after all, is not to stroke the prophet's ego but to edify the church. All need to learn and be encouraged (cf. 14:3). The prophets, then, should patiently wait their turn, for everyone will get his opportunity (14:31).

Moreover, if one truly is a prophet, then he should be able to keep his spirit, his inner self, under control (14:32). After all, self-control is one fruit of the Spirit (Gal 5:22–23). The Christian faith is not a pagan cult which calls forth uncontrolled emotional outbursts. Pagan Greek and Hellenistic prophecy was characterized by madness and a loss of self-control, but prophecy of that sort is not a Christian spiritual gift.

The proper exercise of self-control on the part of tongues-speakers and prophets is in keeping with God's character (1 Cor 14:33a). For, as Paul explains, God is not a God who delights in disorder but is "the God of peace." If the Corinthians wish to be in harmony with their God, they will do all they can to promote peace and good order in the church.

1 CORINTHIANS 14:33B–40

The Lord's Command for Women to Be Silent in the Churches

TRANSLATION

14 [33b]As in all the churches of the saints, [34]let the
women stay silent in the churches. For it is not
permitted for them to speak, but they should
be subordinate, as the Law also says. [35]If they
wish to learn something, let them ask their own
men at home. For it is shameful for a woman to
speak in church. [36]Or did the Word of God go out
from you, or are you the only ones it reached?

[37]If anyone thinks he is a prophet or spiritual,
let him recognize what I am writing to you—
that it is the Lord's command. [38]If anyone does
not recognize this, he is not recognized.

[39]So, my brothers, strive to prophesy and do
not forbid speaking in tongues. [40]But let all
things be done properly and in order.

COMMENTARY

"Let the Women Stay Silent in the Churches" (14:33b–34a)

"God is not [a God] of disorder but of peace" (14:33a). The presence and gifts of the Spirit are manifested whenever the congregation shows a loving concern for mutual edification through orderly and peace-promoting worship (cf. chapter 13 and 14:26c). In the interests of a God-pleasing peace, then, Paul finally adds a third command for silence: "Let the women stay silent in the churches" (14:34).

In 14:33b–37 Paul uses a closely knit argument with a structure similar to the structure in 9:3–14, where he defends his freedom as an apostle. First, he employs an ecumenical argument, appealing to the practice of the universal church: "as in all the churches of the saints" (14:33b; cf. similar appeals in 4:17; 7:17; 11:16). He is reminding the Corinthians that they are not on some spiritual plane superior to that of other churches, but simply an outcropping of the one holy catholic and apostolic church. Second, he appeals to "the Law" (14:34). Third, he appeals to their sense of shame (14:35b). Finally, he cites a specific command of the Lord Jesus (14:37).

The apostle's command is simple and clear: let the women be silent in the congregational gatherings (14:34)! Paul's injunction for women covers any kind of authoritative teaching of God's Word—the leading role in speaking or teaching when the church assembles for worship. Just as clear is the parallel in 1 Tim 2:12: "I do not permit a woman to teach." Here in 1 Corinthians 14 Paul may be focusing primarily on women's participation through tongues-speaking and prophecy. This is confirmed by his use of "to speak" throughout chapter 14. After frequent references to *speaking* in tongues (14:2, 4–6a, 9, 11, 13, 18, 21, 23, 27–28) and three references to *speaking* prophetically (14:3, 6b, 29), practices which must be regulated in an appropriate way (14:27–32), he now adds this further regulation, commanding the women not to "*speak*" (14:34) in church. See the section "The Relationship between 11:2–16 and 14:33b–38" in the excursus "The Ordination of Women" for an analysis of the various ways Paul's prohibition here may be reconciled with chapter 11, and for a discussion of the modern debate on women's ordination, which also entails the roles of preaching and pastoral teaching.

A DIVINE COMMAND (14:34B–35)

Paul hastens to add that this prohibition is not some arbitrary imposition of his own authority. Rather, it is grounded in the divine will. The passive form of the verb "to permit" in the phrase "it is not permitted" (14:34) indicates that God is behind the command, as does the final clause in the sentence, "as the Law also says" (14:34). Behind the apostle's word (cf. 1 Tim 2:12: "I do not permit a woman to teach") stands the word of God.

Rather than speaking, the women "should be subordinate" (1 Cor 14:34; cf. the headship pattern enunciated in 11:3). What Paul asks of the women here is in keeping with his counsel to Christians in other situations in life. By reverent submission the Christian obeys God and gives a positive witness to Christ and the Christian faith (Rom 13:1–7; 1 Pet 5:5–7). Of special importance in this context is the willing subordination of a Christian wife to her husband (Eph 5:24; Col 3:18; Titus 2:5; 1 Pet 3:1). The Christian family under the husband's headship forms the pattern for the Christian congregation (cf. the close connections Paul draws between family and church in Eph 5:22–33). Both at home and at church ("in everything," Eph 5:24) the woman will submit in a self-giving manner to the man's authority. Her submission to the man of the house (her husband or father or other men in authority) does not demean her any more than it demeans husbands to submit to Christ or Christ himself to submit to the Father (1 Cor 11:3; cf. 15:27–28).

Paul's words to the women are backed by God's "Law" in the OT (14:34). Paul appeals to the Torah in a general way, as he often does (e.g., Rom 2:12–27; 3:19–31), but the parallel in 1 Tim 2:11–12 reveals that he especially has in mind the Genesis account of the creation of Adam and Eve and their fall into sin (Genesis 2–3). According to his sketch in 1 Timothy of the creation account, the woman has a subordinate role both before and after the fall. "Adam was formed first, then Eve" as his helper (1 Tim 2:13; cf. Gen 2:18). Thus, the man has precedence as the first person created. Moreover, "Adam was not deceived, but the woman was deceived and fell into transgression" (1 Tim 2:14). Her transgression, according to Genesis, led to the conflict in which her desire (to rule) is over her husband, but he will rule over her (Gen 3:16). Thus, by the order of creation she was subordinated to the man before the fall, and after the fall her subordination was confirmed.

Thus, the man is to exercise leadership in theological speaking, while the woman is to learn "in quietness" (1 Tim 2:11–12). In this manner the church will abide by the order of creation, the divine order instituted from the beginning for human welfare and confirmed by the Gospel. The order of redemption does not abrogate the original divinely willed order (cf. Mk 10:2–9).

Unlike those rabbis who discouraged the teaching of the Torah to women, Jesus and the apostles were happy to instruct women in the Word of God (see Lk 10:38–42; Jn 4:7–30; Acts 16:14–15). But in church they were to listen and learn quietly, and if they had questions, they were to bring them to their men at home (1 Cor 14:35).

Paul does not indicate the precise nature of the women's questions (14:35). However, judging from the use of "to ask" in a significant number of other texts (e.g., Mk 14:60–61; Lk 2:46), it is not unlikely that the questions took the form of interrogation and disputation with the speaker on the grounds that the women wanted to learn. Every experienced pastor and public speaker knows how easy it is for a person in the audience to use a question as an opportunity to instruct, even to undermine the speaker's message.

Just as it was "shameful" for a woman to appear at public worship without a head-covering (11:6), so it is "shameful" for her to assume a teaching role on those occasions (14:35). The formula "it is shameful" covers what is offensive to God as well as what causes social offense (cf. Eph 5:12).

UNIVERSAL PRACTICE (14:36)

With heavy irony in 1 Cor 14:36, Paul challenges the Corinthians' sense of their own importance. Puffed up (4:6, 18–19; 5:2; 8:1) by their spiritual insights and accomplishments, they were behaving as if they were the fount of God's revelation to the world. Were they forgetting that the Word of the Lord had not gone out from Corinth but from Jerusalem (Is 2:3; Micah 4:2; cf. Jn 4:22; Rom 11:18)? Or, if their pride had not carried them away to the extent that they thought they were the source of the Gospel, were they acting as if they were the only church to have received it?

Paul's rhetorical questions apply equally to modern churches that go their own way in the matter of women's ordination, as if their unique cultural situation somehow justified it or they now possessed superior wisdom to the church of previous generations. Again, it must be affirmed that 14:33b–38 is part of the unchanging and authoritative Word of God.

"THE LORD'S COMMAND" (14:37)

Finally, Paul clinches his argument with an appeal to a *"command"* (14:37) of the Lord Jesus (cf. Paul's earlier appeal in 9:14 to Jesus issuing a specific command). Anyone claiming prophetic or spiritual discernment should recognize that to defy Paul at this point is to defy the Lord himself (14:37). Paul's injunction that women should be silent in church is no light matter. It may not be dismissed as a temporary concession to a first-century congregation influenced by Jewish patriarchy. Nor is the authority of the command at all dependent on the prevailing culture; as the excursus "The Ordination of Women" will show, this command of the Lord is *countercultural,* even in its first-century setting, *not* a response to or a result of culture. So far in this epistle Paul has used the word "command" only in 7:19, where he places great emphasis on the importance of keeping the divine directives: "Circumcision is nothing, and uncircumcision is nothing, but [what counts is] keeping the *commandments* of God." Now, in his only other use of "command" in the epistle, he insists that what he is writing about women's subordination at public worship is a divine command to be accepted in the obedience of faith.

Most likely Paul is reminding the Corinthians of a command which came directly from the Lord Jesus himself and impressed itself on the memory of the disciples (although it was never recorded in the gospels). Similar examples of unwritten sayings of the Lord are found in Acts 20:35 and 1 Thess 4:15 (cf. Jn 20:30; 21:25). Alternatively, the phrase "the Lord's command" (1 Cor 14:37) could be synonymous with "the Law" (14:34) and "the Word of God" (14:36), thus underlining Paul's earlier appeal to the opening chapters of Genesis. In that case, the injunction rests on the written text of Genesis, which expresses the words, will, and action of the Lord.

A Permanent "Command"

Some divine commandments may be temporary, designed for a particular time and circumstance. The following examples are found in the NT: (1) Jesus called the divorce legislation in Deuteronomy a temporary concession to the Israelites' hardheartedness, which was superseded by his own command not to rend asunder what God has joined (Mk 10:2–9; see also 1 Corinthians 7). (2) Upon Jesus' descent from the mount of transfiguration, he issued a temporary command: "Don't tell anyone what you have seen, *until* the Son of Man has been raised from the dead" (Mt 17:9 NIV). (3) Jesus received commands from his Father which related to his ministry in a specific time and place (Jn 10:18; 12:49). (4) The epistle to the Hebrews regards the OT ceremonial law as a temporary arrangement, calling its "commands" regarding the levitical priesthood "fleshly" (Heb 7:16) and "weak and useless" (Heb 7:18), since they have been superseded by Christ's eternal priesthood after the order of Melchizedek (Heb 7:4–19). In this category belong other commandments of the Torah (e.g., circumcision, Eph 2:11–15) which applied only to the OT people of God. (5) Although it is not called a "command," the decision taken by the council in Jerusalem may—at least in part—be viewed as a divinely inspired but temporary decree: "it seemed [good] to the Holy Spirit and to us . . ." (Acts 15:28).

Wherever a divine command has only temporary significance there are contextual indicators, for example, "don't tell anyone . . . *until* . . ." (Mt 17:9). However, without such a contextual indication, divine commandments issued or reissued in the NT possess permanent significance. Jesus confirms—indeed, he sharpens—the Decalogue and its individual commands, avowing that until heaven and earth pass away not a jot or tittle of the Law will pass away (Mt 5:17–19). Nor are any limits set to his "new commandment" that his disciples should love one another (Jn 13:34; cf. Jn 15:12; 1 Jn 2:7–11). Similarly, the Johannine commands to "believe in the name of [God's] Son Jesus Christ" (1 Jn 3:23) and to walk "in truth" (2 Jn 4) are open-ended and so apply to all Christians of all times and places.

The context of 14:37 contains no indications that the command for women to be silent was a temporary restriction. (Some interpreters who assert that it may be temporary suggest that it could be a concession to Jewish Christians who had only recently become accustomed to the higher regard in which women were held in Christianity, and who were by no means ready for the further step of seeing women in preaching and teaching roles.) If Paul were asking Gentile Christians merely to make a temporary concession out of consideration for the weaker brother, one would think he would make this plain in his usual fashion (see 8:7–12). All the evidence points to this "Lord's command" in 14:37, like the "commandments of God" in 7:19 (the only other occurrence of "command" in 1 Corinthians), *being a specific divine command of the Lord possessing permanent validity.*

Sometimes it is argued—or implied—that those Christians who would uphold this command are falling prey to a legalism which fails to distinguish between Law and Gospel. This argument suggests that because "we are not under Law but under grace" (Rom 6:15), anything that smacks of being a command no longer has a place in the Christian life. This argument amounts to antinomianism, which is condemned in the Formula of Concord (SD V 15–17). It also operates with a definition of a "command" that is too narrow. As outlined above, the "commands of God/the Lord") cover the whole counsel and will of God as expressed both in Law and Gospel and, above all, the command for faith and love (1 Jn 3:23). They involve teaching Christians "to observe all things that *I have commanded* you" (Mt 28:20; the verb "command" in Mt 28:20 is cognate with the noun "command" in 1 Cor 14:37). In other words, the church is bound to treasure and uphold the entire Word of God, both Law and Gospel. As the Lord of the church, which he has purchased with his own blood (Acts 20:28), does he not have the authority to lay down guidelines for the church's welfare? Dare we criticize Christ himself as being legalistic when he says, "Do this in memory of me" (Lk 22:19), or "Go therefore and make disciples, baptizing . . . teaching" (Mt 28:19–20)?

THIS COMMAND MUST BE RECOGNIZED (14:38)

Paul solemnly warns anyone who refuses to recognize this as the Lord's command that "he is not recognized" by God (1 Cor 14:38). Obviously, such a person is not concerned for the edification, peace, and good order of God's people (cf. 14:26, 33a, 40). Rather, he is "puffed up" by his pretended knowledge (4:6, 18–19; 5:2; 8:1). Although he claims to be "a prophet" and "spiritual" (14:37), that claim is actually null and void in God's sight; his ministry—in contrast to the faithful ministry of Stephanas, Fortunatus, and Achaicus (16:17–18)—"is not recognized" (14:38). Consequently, his "work" will not survive the fire of judgment, though "he himself" will be saved if he repents (3:13–15).

On the other hand, if he persists in flouting the divine will, he may (in light of the broader context) lose God's recognition in a far more serious sense: he may be in danger of falling under the divine anathema, "If anyone does not love the Lord, let him be cursed/anathema" (16:22). Compare also Jesus' condemnation of the false prophets in Mt 7:23: "I never knew you." Whether a person loves the Lord will become manifest, above all, from his attitude to the Lord's commandment (1 Cor 14:37; cf. Jn 14:23–24).

CONCLUSION (14:39–40)

In seeking to correct excesses during worship, Paul has used severe language throughout 1 Corinthians 11–14. Now he changes his tone (cf. 11:33), addressing the Corinthians affectionately as "brothers" (14:39, as he had also in 14:6, 20, 26). His final admonition in chapter 14 echoes his starting point in 14:1: they should "strive to prophesy" and "not forbid speaking in tongues" (14:39). Their overriding consideration, however, should be for what promotes propriety and good order (14:40). It is inappropriate and contrary to good order when too many tongues-speakers dominate a worship service and fail to provide interpretation (14:27–28). It is also unseemly and contrary to good order when too many prophets speak and fail to yield to each other (14:29–33a). Finally, it is unseemly ("shameful" 14:35) and contrary to good "order" (14:40) when the women are unwilling to adopt a quiet, subordinate (14:34) role in the worship service. Instead of all the self-assertion being practiced in Corinth, Paul calls on the congregation to do everything in a becoming, orderly, and loving fashion (cf. 16:14), that others may be edified, that is, built up in the faith (14:3–5, 12, 17, 26).

EXCURSUS

The Ordination of Women

Wherever the Gospel has free course, it has a liberating effect on women (as indeed the Gospel liberates all people, Jn 8:31–36). In the South Pacific nation of Papua New Guinea, for example, where women were traditionally treated as chattels, the advent of Christianity has often brought them a new dignity and respect. Indeed, there are countless societies where many women, once regarded merely as garden beds for raising children—to be discarded if they proved unfruitful—have found their Christian husbands treating them with courtesy and affection.

This Christian regard for women is, of course, inspired by "the meekness and gentleness of Christ" (2 Cor 10:1). Jesus himself set the pattern for his church by his own respect for women, beginning with his childhood submission to his mother (Lk 2:51). To women he extended his healing hand; with women he was happy to converse, to the amazement of his disciples (Jn 4:27); to women and men alike he taught the Word of God. Luke records how on one occasion the Lord took time to teach a class consisting of one woman, Mary, who received his praise because she "chose the best part, which will not be taken away from her" (Lk 10:38–42). Paul commands husbands to love their wives "as Christ loved the church and gave himself up for her" (Eph 5:25). Peter counsels husbands to "live considerately . . . with [their] wives, bestowing honor [on the women] as joint heirs of the grace of life" (1 Pet 3:7). Thus, biblical Christianity elevates women, honors them as equal members of the Christian community, and encourages them to study the Scriptures. The same is true of the Lutheran church in particular. The Lutheran Confessions (Ap XXIII 25) sharply criticize misogyny: "Daniel says that it is characteristic of Antichrist's kingdom to despise women."

Whereas the OT honors women as equal members of the worshiping community (Ex 19:6–8; Deut 29:10–12), rabbinic Judaism during the days of Jesus and Paul was developing in a direction which relegated women to an inferior status. The Tosefta (*Berekhot*, 6.18) includes this second-century AD rabbinic teaching:

> R. Judah says, "A man must recite three benedictions every day: (1) 'Praised [be Thou, O Lord, our God, King of the universe,] who did not make me a gentile'; (2) 'Praised [be Thou, O Lord . . .] who did not make me a boor'; (3) 'Praised [be Thou, O Lord . . .] who did not make me a woman.' . . .

At the opposite extreme from rabbinic Judaism, the Greco-Roman culture of Paul's day frequently allowed women a leading role in religious rites. Whereas the Jewish Torah restricted the priesthood to men, there were no explicit prohibitions of priestesses in other religions. Thus, women priests may be found at any time and in any place in the Hellenistic world.

In the light of the contrasts with its religious environment, the apostolic teaching on the role of women in worship is *countercultural*. Whereas the male chauvinism characteristic of some cultures (in Paul's day and ours) regards women as mere chattels, and rabbinic Judaism tended to treat them as second-class members of the community, the apostles counsel husbands to cherish and honor their wives. On the other hand, in contrast to the permissiveness of pagan religions, which often allowed women to serve as priestesses and instructors in the cult, the biblical revelation does not permit them to serve as priests (Ex 28:1) or pastors (1 Tim 3:2; Titus 1:6). Thus, Paul's command that the women be silent in the churches (1 Cor 14:34) must be understood, in part, as countercultural and antisyncretistic. It is a command that distinguishes and separates the Christian church from other religions. Inspired by the Spirit of God, its roots are deep in the biblical revelation, which always runs counter to the spirit and the wisdom of this world (2:12).

THE SCRIPTURES ARE THE BASIS FOR DECIDING THE ISSUE

There is a broad consensus among those who desire to remain faithful to historic Christianity that the issue of whether or not to ordain women must be decided on the basis of the biblical evidence. There is also consensus that the results of this biblical study will depend on the principles of interpretation (the hermeneutics) employed. Beyond this point of consensus, however, the ways divide. While there is general agreement that different hermeneutical approaches are at the root of the differing conclusions, some maintain that these variations in approach and result should not trouble the church; after all, the divergence is *merely* a matter of hermeneutics and should not be considered church divisive.

Others object that much more is at stake in one's choice of a hermeneutical approach. Not every way of interpreting the Bible is equally true to the Bible's self-understanding and therefore equally faithful to God and helpful in building up the church. No matter what assurances may be given regarding a common commitment to the Bible, it is by no means insignificant that higher-critical methodologies foster a critical stance toward the authority, truthfulness, and clarity of parts of the Bible. Again, the church faces this old question: Is the Bible the Word of God, as a whole and in all its parts (1 Thess 2:13), or does it merely contain the Word of God? And—a corollary to that primary question—is the Bible clear, harmonious, and self-consistent, or does it contain (as critical scholars suggest) divergent theological strands with different, even diametrically opposed, conclusions on the subject of women's ordination. Thus, the issue of women's ordination is no isolated phenomenon. Rather, the church's stance on the issue will be symptomatic of its attitude to more fundamental questions of hermeneutics and the doctrine of Scripture.

The question, then, is whether to adopt (1) an understanding of the entire Bible as the Word of God, together with a hermeneutic which allows Scripture (rather than culture) to interpret Scripture, or (2) whether to follow a critical approach to the Scriptures, which to a greater or lesser extent questions the authority, clarity, and relevance of foundational texts. Related to this matter of interpretive approach is another question: Whether the issue is to be decided by appealing to some overall central message of the Scriptures (such as "the Gospel") or to specific texts that deal with the topic? Expressions such as "proof texts" and "individual texts" have been used, without proper definition, to disparage any appeal to the key foundational texts which have served as the church's basis in determining its teaching and practice. If employing "proof texts" means that a person appeals to biblical texts without regard to their context, then all would agree that this is bad. But what critics of using "proof texts" attack specifically is making too much of those texts that speak directly to the issue.

One must ask: What is wrong with appealing to key foundational texts? Jesus himself, immersed in the Scriptures as he was, constantly appealed to individual texts from the OT as the foundation for his teaching and practice (see the thrice-repeated "it is written" in Mt 4:1–11, for example). A reading of the Small Catechism will show that Luther also uses texts that speak to the specific issue. In elucidating the doctrine of Baptism, for example, he does not appeal in general terms to "the Gospel." Rather, he adduces individual texts that deal specifically with Baptism (Mt 28:19; Titus 3:5–8; Rom 6:4).

APPLYING THE SCRIPTURES TODAY: BRIDGING THE "GAP" BETWEEN THE BIBLE AND THE MODERN WORLD

Advocates of women's ordination see enormous significance in the cultural, linguistic, and historical gaps that divide the first century from the twenty-first. They assert that what the biblical text meant then may be different from what it means today. Biblical texts are said to be "time conditioned" and "culture bound." In view of this gulf between the biblical and the modern "horizons," it should not be surprising (it is alleged) that whereas in Paul's day to have ordained women would have been harmful to the church's mission, in our day it would be helpful to her mission.

We must, indeed, deal discriminatingly with the Scriptures. Not all is on the same level, not all is as equally and directly applicable to the church today. For example, much of the OT law has been fulfilled and thus superseded: the ceremonial law has been fulfilled in Christ, our great high priest; the civil law applied specifically to the nation of Israel, and no longer applies to us. The Ten Commandments, on the other hand, still do apply; Jesus and the apostles constantly confirmed them (e.g., Lk 18:18–20; Rom 13:8–10). And the NT is the authoritative interpreter of the OT. Consequently, we need to be careful before concluding that any NT teaching no longer applies. To be sure, we no longer wash one another's feet (John 13). But that custom is not prescribed in the NT, anyway; Jesus simply refers to it as an "example" or "pattern" (Jn 13:15) of how we are to serve one another in Christian love. What is commanded, *mandated,* is that we love one another, however that love may be expressed in our modern culture. Similarly, in 1 Cor 11:2–16, Paul urges the women to conform in feminine modesty to the custom of their day by wearing a head-covering at public worship. *Customs* of dress may change, but the *principle* of male headship and female subordination (1 Cor 11:3) remains in effect. We have no authority to abrogate a command, a mandate of the Lord. To do so involves disobedience to the Lord of the church.

Certainly the first-century world differed from ours in a host of ways (the practices of foot-washing and head-coverings are but two examples). But the significance of these differences should not be exaggerated. Cultures vary from one another in their surface configurations—thus the fascination of studying other cultures and languages. But the longer one is immersed in another culture, whether ancient or contemporary, the more one realizes that under the surface all human beings have the same desires, weaknesses, aspirations, and so forth. It is a myth that modern men and women are thoroughly different from the people of biblical times. Deep down, all share a common humanity which is far more important than anything that appears on the surface.

And the same Word of God is addressed to all. From one point of view, indeed, there are two horizons; we need to dig into the biblical world and its history and languages if we are to grasp it accurately. But the more we enter that world sympathetically, the more we hear the same Word that was addressed to people of biblical times addressing us today. From the divine perspective, there is really only one horizon. The OT prophets were taken up into God's council (Jer 23:22) and enabled to see past, present, and future from God's vista. Similarly, the apostles and evangelists of the NT are given the Word of the One who sees and foresees all human history. What God said to our forefathers and mothers he still says to us "today" (Ps 95:7; cf. Deut 5:2–3)—unless there are clear indications to the contrary in Scripture. The God in whom there is "no change or shadow of turning" (James 1:17), the Lord who is "the same yesterday, today, and forever" (Heb 13:8), has given the same clear Word to all generations of his church.

THE GOSPEL

Some have argued that the only link between the first and twenty-first centuries that remains unchanged is the Gospel. Indeed, if there is one thing on which both the advocates and opponents of women's ordination are agreed, it is the importance of the Gospel as the great central theme of the Scriptures. In 1 Corinthians, Paul's argument concerning the role of women in the church is embedded in his magnificent presentation of the Gospel. This Gospel is first articulated in his announcement of the epistle's theme—the word of the cross

(1:18)—then reiterated throughout the epistle in keeping with his desire to know only "Jesus Christ and him crucified" (2:2). Finally it is taken up again immediately after Paul's discussion of the role of women as he reminds the Corinthians of their basic lessons in the Gospel: "I delivered to you as of first importance what I also received: that Christ died for our sins . . ." (15:3).

Disagreement begins to arise, however, when we consider the relationship of this fundamental article of the Christian faith to other articles. While we agree that every other article will—if correctly stated—be in harmony with the Gospel, this appreciation of the way the various articles of the faith form one perfect tapestry does not provide a warrant to drain individual articles of their color. Thus, our adherence to the Gospel principle—the centrality of the Gospel—and our appreciation of the new creation in Christ does not warrant reduction and homogenization of other doctrines (most importantly in this context, the ongoing significance of the original order of creation, the fall into sin, the Law, and the doctrine of the ministry) so that these collapse and cease to have significance.

Paul defines and spells out the Gospel of justification in very specific ways and continually highlights it as his great central theme. But he addresses other topics as well and deserves an attentive hearing on each issue. These other topics are relevant for the faith and life of the church, and ultimately they are connected in an organic way to the Gospel, even if they may appear otherwise. Thus, in this epistle we hear him speaking to a great variety of topics, and even making rules and regulations as when he commands the Corinthians to "remove the wicked person from among yourselves" (5:13) or solemnly warns them that wicked people will not inherit the kingdom (6:9). Likewise, this thoroughly Gospel-centered apostle does not see any inconsistency with the Gospel in laying down rules and regulations for the proper conduct of divine worship, using a string of imperatives to demand silence from the tongues-speaker who has no interpreter, from the prophet who finds that another has just received a revelation, and, finally, from the women (14:28–34).

Thus, the advocates of women's ordination must concede that Paul does from time to time use his apostolic authority to lay down rules and regulations. This is not a naked use of authority for its own sake; it always expresses a fatherly concern (4:14–16) for the eternal welfare of the saints. At the same time, opponents of women's ordination must concede, indeed, must wholeheartedly agree that the same Gospel which makes saints is the Gospel which makes ministers. The same "grace of God, richly poured out on all "called saints" in Corinth (1:2–5) had bestowed on Paul and his fellow apostles and pastors the gracious gift and calling which was the basis of their ministry (4:1; 9:1–2). By grace alone a person became a saint; by that same grace some were called to the public ministry. Thus, Paul praises God: "To me as the very least of all saints was given this grace, to preach to the Gentiles the unfathomable riches of Christ" (Eph 3:8; see also 4:7).

But just as not all are apostles, not all are prophets, so not all are pastors and teachers (1 Cor 12:29; Eph 4:11). And not only women are excluded from the pastoral office, but also most men. Most men have not been called to the office, nor have they been given sufficient aptitude in teaching. The ministry can be difficult enough, in these turbulent times, even for men who are "apt to teach" (1 Tim 3:2). This catechetical aptitude is the one qualification on Paul's lists of qualifications for pastors (1 Tim 3:2–7; Titus 1:6–9) which is not required of every Christian man. Since God has called the church into existence through the Gospel, he has every right to select those whom he chooses to be pastors, and to establish such qualifications as he desires pastors to have. Just as in Israel the eleven other tribes had no right to cry foul because God selected only the Levites to serve at his sanctuary, and only the sons of Aaron to be his priests, so Christians have no right to criticize God for limiting the pastoral office to those who meet his qualifications, including that of gender. It is not inconsistent for the God of the Gospel also to establish such an order in his church: "God is not [a God] of disorder" (1 Cor 14:33).

CREATION AND THE NEW CREATION

The relationship between the order of creation and the order of redemption is another key topic where hermeneutical assumptions will lead to certain conclusions relevant to the ordination of women. The order of creation is not merely a construct of theologians but has deep roots in the Scriptures. When Jesus and Paul provide guidance for the proper ordering of marriage and relations between the sexes, they go back to the order of creation set forth in the first three chapters of Genesis. Thus, Jesus, in speaking against lax attitudes toward divorce, says, "In the beginning it was not so" (Mt 19:8), and quotes Gen 1:27 and Gen 2:24 in Mt 19:3–9 and Mk 10:2–12. Paul, in arguing that the woman is not to function as head and teacher of the church family at worship, grounds his injunction "I do not permit a woman to teach . . ." (1 Tim 2:12) in the order of creation and fall established in Genesis 2 and 3: "For Adam was formed first, then Eve. And Adam was not deceived, but the woman was deceived and fell into transgression" (1 Tim 2:13–14). In other words, Adam reneged on his spiritual responsibilities. He failed to exercise his headship by following his wife instead of correcting her after she had given a false lead. Finally, when Paul appeals to "the Law" as the basis for his ruling in 1 Cor 14:34 ("it is not permitted for [the women] to speak . . . as the Law also says"), he almost certainly has in mind the same passages of Genesis 2–3 which he cites in his epistle to Timothy (1 Tim 2:13–14).

In 1 Corinthians, when discussing worship practices and the conduct of women Paul invokes the order of the original creation in 11:7–10. God's activity in creation is in harmony with his activity in redemption (11:11–12). These two activities of God are not in conflict with each other or contradictory; the goodness of God the orderly Creator is manifested also in the order of redemption.

THE RELATIONSHIP BETWEEN 11:2–16 AND 14:33B–38

One of the main questions which must be addressed is the relationship between 1 Cor 11:2–16 (especially 11:5), where Paul seems to accept that women may pray or prophesy in worship, and 14:33b–38 (especially 14:34), where he seems to forbid any speaking by women. Advocates of women's ordination often assert one or more of the following: (1) The two passages simply contradict one another. (2) Since they conflict, the apparently more lenient passage (11:2–16) is to be preferred. (3) By means of a text-critical argument 14:34–35 is deleted as inauthentic. (4) The import of 14:34–35 is reduced to a mere ban on women asking disruptive questions.

The following may be said in response. First, the apparent discrepancy between 11:5 and 14:34 should not be exaggerated. After all, the "heading"—the thematic verse that sets the tone for 11:2–16 (especially 11:3–10)—is the introductory statement on headship (11:3). This headship/subordination theme in 11:2–16 plays in perfect harmony with 14:34. Second, the larger passage which speaks directly to the issue of women speaking in worship (14:33b–38) should be given more weight than 11:5. And third, a number of solutions are at hand which do not assume a contradiction between 11:5 and 14:34.

The following five harmonizations have been proposed by various scholars. They are presented in order from least likely to more probable. This commentary's view is that the fifth explanation is the best. The fourth has much to recommend it, but the second and third are less plausible, and the first is not supported by sound evidence.

Post-Enlightenment exegesis tends to presuppose that contradictions will be found in many parts of the Scriptures. Apparent difficulties and discrepancies are often blown out of proportion, while attempts to supply harmonizing solutions are disparaged. The alternative approach adopted in this commentary is based on the belief that the Scriptures are a unity, the Word of one primary, divine author—the Holy Spirit, speaking through prophets, apostles, and evangelists as secondary authors—and that consequently the Scriptures are all true and consistent. This assumption that the Scriptures possess the integrity, consistency, truthfulness, and authority of God himself legitimizes the attempt to demonstrate their unity and harmony in particular cases. For this purpose it is sufficient to show that one or more plausible explanations exist, even if the state of our knowledge does not permit us to state definitively that one explanation is right and all others are wrong.

1. Many advocates of women's ordination "solve" the "problem" by arguing that the offensive verses in which Paul prohibits women from speaking in church, 14:34–35, are inauthentic. Having eliminated these verses from the picture, it is readily concluded on the basis of 11:5 that Paul is content to allow women to pray and prophesy in church, and generally to take a leading speaking role in worship.

A number of commentators make a similar case with regard to the authenticity of 1 Timothy by classifying it and the other pastoral epistles (2 Timothy and Titus) as "pseudepigraphical" (i.e., forgeries) and thus unworthy of the same regard as the "authentically Pauline" epistles. Thus, at a stroke two of the most significant texts (1 Cor 14:34–35 and 1 Tim 2:11–12) are eliminated from consideration, undercutting the ecumenical doctrine and practice of the Christian church over the last two millennia of not ordaining women.

The problem with this explanation is that the actual manuscript data support the authenticity of 1 Cor 14:34–35. In the overwhelming majority of manuscripts these two verses are found in their normal location between 14:33 and 14:36. In a few manuscripts, however, they are placed after 14:40.

2. A second suggestion is that when Paul insists a woman wear a head-covering (11:2–16), he has in mind private devotions in the home. Thus, there is no conflict between his apparent tolerance for a woman praying and prophesying in that private setting, and his later insistence that she should not speak "in the churches" (14:33). But this solution to the difficulty does not seem tenable. Among the arguments against it, most noteworthy is Paul's statement in 11:16: "We have no such custom, nor do the churches of God." Paul's concern from 11:2 to 14:40 is what happens *in the churches.*

3. A more plausible reconciliation between chapters 11 and 14 is the proposal that Paul expects the women to be silent in church only when it comes to "weighing" prophecies, that is, giving an authoritative interpretation of what the prophecy means for the church's faith and life (cf. 14:29). By no means is the apostle banning the women from any kind of speaking in the assembly. They may, as can be assumed from 11:5, pray and prophesy; they may also speak in tongues. Only the evaluation of prophecies is prohibited. The parallel in 1 Tim 2:11–12 would show that the apostolic injunction in 1 Cor 14:34–35 applies to authoritative speaking, that is, to teaching the Word of God to the assembled congregation ("I do not permit a woman to teach," 1 Tim 2:12). The interpretation of prophecies is a kind of authoritative teaching.

The parallel injunction in 1 Tim 2:11–12 certainly shows that in 1 Cor 14:34–35 Paul is prohibiting women from teaching authoritatively (as a pastor does) in the church's worship. It is also certainly correct that 14:34–35 should not be interpreted so broadly as to prohibit women from joining in the church's prayers, hymns, liturgical responses, and confessions of faith in the worship services.

However, this view suffers from a weakness. If interpreting prophecies (a form of authoritative teaching) were the only restriction Paul had in mind in 14:34–35, it is surprising he did not spell it out: "Let the women be silent in the churches by not weighing prophecies, but let them speak in tongues and prophesy." If this was what the apostle meant, the best that can be said is that he did not express himself—or God's will—unambiguously. Throughout the chapter

Paul has used "to speak" in connection both with speaking in tongues (2, 4–6a, 9, 11, 13, 18, 21, 23, 27–28, 39) and with prophecy (3, 6b, 29). Tongues-speakers may speak if there is an interpreter; two or three prophets may speak if they take their turn (14:26–32). But then Paul declares—and there is no way of getting around the abruptness—that the women are *not* permitted "to speak." There is no exception clause.

As attractive, then, as this proposal may be in allowing women some latitude to speak in the assembly (hymns, prayers, and so on), and in harmonizing 11:5 and 14:34, it does not fit the flow of Paul's argument in chapter 14. Nevertheless, it is one of the most plausible of the solutions that have been offered.

4. A fourth interpretation is that in 14:34–35 Paul is prohibiting women from speaking authoritatively in church. As in 1 Tim 2:11–12, in 1 Cor 14:34–35 Paul prohibits women from preaching and authoritative (pastoral) teaching of the church in worship. Thus, there is no conflict with 11:5, where Paul apparently accepts that women with head-coverings may pray and prophesy in church. This would coincide with 1 Tim 2:12, where he states: "I do not permit a woman to teach."

This view is expressed well in the CTCR document *Women in the Church* (page 33):

> First, that [in 1 Cor 14:34–35] Paul is not commanding *absolute*, unqualified silence is evident from the fact that he permits praying and prophesying in 1 Corinthians 11. The silence mandated for women in 1 Corinthians 14 does not preclude their praying and prophesying. Accordingly, the apostle is not intimating that women may not participate in the public singing of the congregation or in the spoken prayers. It should be noted in this connection that Paul uses the Greek word *laleo* for "speak" in 1 Cor. 14:34, which frequently means to "preach" in the New Testament (see Mark 2:2; Luke 9:11; Acts 4:1; 8:25; 1 Cor. 2:7; 2 Cor. 12:19; Phil. 1:14; *et al.*), and not *lego*, which is the more general term. . . . When *laleo* has a meaning other than religious speech and preaching in the New Testament, this is usually made clear by an object or an adverb (e.g., to speak like a child, 1 Cor. 13:11; to speak like a fool, 2 Cor. 11:23). Secondly, it must be underscored that Paul's prohibition that women remain silent and not speak is uttered with reference to the worship service of the congregation (1 Cor. 14:26–33). . . . Thus, Paul is not here demanding that women should be silent at all times or that they cannot express their sentiments and opinions at church assemblies. The command that women keep silent is a command that they not take charge of the public worship service, specifically the teaching-learning aspects of the service.

According to this view, women may teach as long as they are not occupying the pastoral office, that is, if their teaching is done under the supervising authority of the pastor, or in a private setting. For example, Paul tells Titus to "speak" (Titus 2:1; the same activity women are prohibited from carrying out in 1 Cor 14:34) to the older women so that those women may be "good teachers" who can "advise the younger women to be lovers of their husbands and lovers of their children" (Titus 2:3–4). Older women were to teach younger women, and women were expected to teach children. A woman like Priscilla could also give private instruction in the faith to a man like Apollos (Acts 18:26). Nor should it be understood as an absolute ban prohibiting women from joining in the hymns and prayers, creeds and responses.

A difficulty with this view is Paul's use of "speak" earlier in 1 Corinthians 14 in connection with tongues and prophecy (e.g., 14:2–6, 27–29). One might naturally assume that "speak" in 14:34 refers to the same kind of speaking: to speak in a tongue or to speak a prophecy. In that case, Paul would be telling the women that they cannot speak in a tongue or prophesy in church, in a worship service (that is the next explanation, number 5, below).

However, against that objection, and so in favor of this explanation (number 4), is a different approach to the understanding of the verb "speak." The verb itself can refer to a variety of kinds of speaking. The *kind* of speaking must be determined by the context, the words and phrases used with the verb. In 14:2, "the person who speaks in a tongue" obviously refers to tongues-speaking, while in the next verse, in the phrase "the person who prophesies speaks to people," the same verb is in the context of prophesying. Speaking in tongues and prophesying are distinctly different activities, even though the same verb can be used for either. It entails tongues-speaking in 14:2, 4–6a, 9, 11, 13, 18, 21, 23, 27–28, 39, but prophesying in 14:3, 6b, 29.

In 14:34–35, "speak" is used absolutely; there are no modifying or qualifying words such as "in a tongue" or "a prophecy." The only qualifying phrases are "in the churches" in 14:34 and "in church" in 14:35. This absolute kind of speaking may then be interpreted in light of the similar passage in 1 Tim 2:11–12, which leaves no doubt that the kind of speaking prohibited for women is the authoritative teaching of men. Therefore, 1 Cor 14:34–35 prohibits women from assuming the role of authoritative (pastoral) speaking (preaching and teaching) of the church in worship.

5. A fifth explanation is preferred by this commentary. This explanation assumes that because "to speak" earlier in chapter 14 referred to speaking in tongues and prophesying (see number 4 above), that same verb must entail those same kinds of speaking in 14:34–35. This reading of 14:33b–38 is that here Paul prohibits the women from speaking in tongues, prophesying, and, a fortiori, authoritative (pastoral) preaching and teaching in the worship service. Nevertheless, this should not be understood as a blanket ban on women prophesying or speaking in tongues in *any* context. Philip's daughters, presumably, would still be permitted to prophesy in private (Acts 21:8–9), and Priscilla could still give private instruction (Acts 18:26).

If this interpretation is correct, the question arises why Paul did not make his position clearer back in 1 Corinthians 11, where he seems to allow properly covered women to speak in tongues and prophesy (11:5). Here it may be helpful to consider his pastoral approach in other parts of the letter. A close parallel may be found in his discussion of food offered to idols (chapters 8–10). In chapter 8 he lays the theological foundation for approaching the issue and gently suggests that reclining in an idol temple could be an offense to the weaker brother. Then by way of a lengthy excursus (chapter 9) he points to his own example as the free Christian apostle who has voluntarily given up some of his rights for the sake of the church, including the weak brother. Then he firmly forbids any participation in cultic meals (10:14–22). His position in both chapters 8 and 10 is that the Christian should not partake of meals in pagan temples, but his appeal in chapter 8 is based on Christian love, and he saves his explicit command until chapter 10. A similar dynamic may explain the relationship between chapters 11 and 14. In chapter 11 Paul appeals to the Corinthians on the basis of Christ's headship and their natural sense of propriety and decorum. He calls his description a "custom" (11:16), not a "command" (the word in 14:37 that refers to 14:34–35). Then in chapter 12 he lays the theological foundation regarding spiritual gifts and follows it up with an excursus on Christian love (chapter 13). Paul then concludes the more detailed discussion of tongues and prophecy in chapter 14 with a number of directives regarding the proper role of tongues, prophecy, and the appropriateness of women holding the teaching office.

Paul's approach, then, is a fine example of wise pastoral care. Not everything can be addressed at once. A foundation must first be laid before the more difficult things that must be said can be said. Thus, Paul in 11:2–16 is not yet ready to issue "the Lord's command" (14:37) regarding the women. He restricts himself primarily to the issue of their head-coverings and prayer. Although he briefly mentions prophesying (11:5), he leaves his direct orders regarding the more sensitive issue of their speaking during worship (including prophesying and speaking in tongues) to the end of chapter 14.

OBJECTIONS TO "THE LORD'S COMMAND"

The apostle's injunction in 14:34–35 is encountering more opposition today than at any time since the second century AD. The objections are legion; to respond to them all with any measure of adequacy would require another book. Six of the most significant may be singled out for discussion: the crucial NT passage Gal 3:28; the appeal to justice and human rights; the appeal to "inclusivity"; the appeal to women's giftedness; the meaning of the verb "be subject/be subordinated" in 1 Cor 15:28; and the appeal to the role of prophetesses in both testaments.

Galatians 3:28

Gal 3:28 is the text most frequently cited by the women's ordination movement. While the argument from Gal 3:28 may seem persuasive, if one examines its context even cursorily, it is obvious that Paul is not speaking to the issue of ordination—of women or of men—at all! The topic is the baptismal identity of all believers as God's "sons" and "heirs" of the Abrahamic promise of eternal life in Christ Jesus. The verse must be read in context: "You are all sons of God through faith in Christ Jesus, for as many of you as were baptized into Christ have been clothed with Christ. There is neither Jew nor Greek, there is neither slave nor free, *there is neither male nor female;* for you are all one in Christ Jesus. If you are of Christ, therefore you are Abraham's seed and heirs according to the promise" (Gal 3:26–29). Ordination is another topic, which Paul addresses elsewhere. If Gal 3:28 is taken as the standard for determining who may be ordained, what prevents the church from ordaining incompetent Christians, children, or for that matter, homosexuals? To such questions, proponents of women's ordination often respond that one must then look elsewhere, for example to 1 Tim 3:2, which says a pastor should be "apt to teach." But that is precisely the point: we must look to other passages, not to Gal 3:28, to find the qualifications for ordination. These are set out in 1 Tim 3:1–7 and Titus 1:5–9, where "husband of one wife" (1 Tim 3:2 and Titus 1:6), together with the masculine Greek nouns and adjectives, limits the office to qualified men. That conclusion is corroborated by 1 Cor 14:33b–38 and 1 Tim 2:11–14.

Justice and Human Rights

For some, the case for women's ordination is straightforward: it is a matter of simple justice. The movement toward justice and equal rights for women in the workplace or political arena is taken as a normative signal to the church that Christian women should be eligible to be ordained. Although this argument can appeal in general terms to the biblical theme of "justice," its real impetus is in the secular culture. The church should not be shaped by the world, but by the Word.

Advocates of the ordination of women sometimes draw a parallel between the way the church was slow to recognize the evils of slavery but eventually was led by the Gospel to denounce slavery, and the way the church was slow to recognize the evils of "patriarchy" but is now being led by the Gospel to protest "patriarchy" and the withholding of the pastoral office from women. But the two cases are vastly different. Slavery was a powerfully entrenched system of the Roman state, imposed on Christian and non-Christian alike by Roman society. Yet Paul could say, "But if indeed you are able to become free, by all means make use of [the opportunity]" (1 Cor 7:21b). The headship of the man, on the other hand, applied only to the Christian home and the Christian church, where Christians were free to order their relationships in keeping with the Word of God. Paul never said to the women: "If you can assume the leading teaching office in the congregation, by all means avail yourself of the opportunity." Rather, he insisted that "the Lord's command" (14:37) ruled it out (14:34–38).

Inclusivity

More recently, "inclusivity" often replaces "justice" as one of the movement's buzz words. The ordination of women serves as an important sign of greater openness and inclusivity.

The "inclusivity" slogan confuses the issue. On the one hand, to be sure, the Gospel is inclusive: "God wants *all people* to be saved" (1 Tim 2:4; the Greek term there is inclusive: "people," not just "men"). Through Baptism into Christ *all* Christians share a oneness in Christ Jesus (Gal 3:28). This does not mean, however, that all are called to the public ministry. It is God who calls certain individuals into the pastoral ministry in accordance with his Word; the church has no right to add unbiblical requirements or to abolish biblical prerequisites.

The "inclusivity" argument unfairly brands those who do not accept women's ordination as "exclusive" and narrow minded, in contrast to those who are "inclusive," "open minded," and so on. It is also infinitely elastic and raises these questions: "Whom would you debar from the public ministry? Why not ordain practicing homosexuals, or children, or the intellectually disabled? Where do you draw the line? And on what basis?" All Christians will agree that not *everyone* is fit for the ministry. The question then becomes whether the criteria will be determined by human reasoning or by the Word of God.

The Giftedness of Women

The claim is often advanced that women should be ordained because they, too, have been endowed with the Spirit's gifts and should therefore be given an opportunity to exercise them in the public ministry. The NT does indeed teach that God's multifaceted grace has endowed every Christian with a "gift of grace," either for speaking or for service (1 Pet 4:10–11; see the commentary on 1 Cor 12:8). Christian women also have a station and vocation in life, as do Christian men—in family, church, community, and workplace. As with all Christians, this gives women ample opportunity to speak "the words of God" to others, and to serve "out of the strength which God supplies, so that in everything God may be glorified through Jesus Christ" (1 Pet 4:11). But the gift of the public ministry has not been given to them (nor to most men).

1 Corinthians 15:28

Some proponents of women's ordination point to the use of the verb "be subject" in 1 Cor 15:28. On this matter the following comments can be made.

The Greek verb "to subject" (active) or "to be subject" (passive) occurs nine times in 1 Corinthians. In chapter 14 it refers to the subjection of the spirits of prophets to prophets (14:32), and the subordination of women in the churches (14:34). In chapter 15 it refers first to the Father subjecting everything, including death, to the Son, and then the Son's subjecting himself to the Father (15:27–28).

Finally, in 16:16 it refers to the need for the Corinthian Christians to subject themselves to Stephanas and the other church servants like him.

In Eph 5:21, 24 Paul uses the verb "be subject" in close conjunction with the concept of headship (Eph 5:23). This supports the assumption that his statement about headship in 1 Cor 11:3 ("the head of every man is Christ, the head of the woman is the man, and the head of Christ is God") implies the subordination or subjection of the woman to the man, the man to Christ, and Christ to God the Father.

Given this headship structure, then, it is proper to view the apostolic word on women's subordination in the light of what Paul says in the context (11:3; 15:28) regarding the Son's subordination to the Father. Moreover, this broader context leads inescapably to the conclusion that it is no more demeaning for the woman to be subject to the man than it is for the man to be subject to Christ, and Christ to the Father. Conversely, the man's headship (properly exercised according to the divine order) over the woman is no more oppressive than Christ's headship over the man and the Father's headship over the Son.

To affirm, with the NT, that the Son is subordinate to the Father is not to detract from his full divinity, nor from his equality and consubstantiality with the Father. The mystery of his person can only be described by way of paradox. Jesus could say of himself both "I and the Father are one" (Jn 10:30) and "the Father is greater than I" (Jn 14:28). Likewise, the Athanasian Creed affirms that the Son of God is "equal to the Father with respect to His divinity, less than the Father with respect to His humanity" (*LSB* 320:31). The Son of God submitted himself voluntarily to the Father, delighting to do his will (Ps 40:7–8; Phil 2:5–11; Heb 10:5–10).

Likewise, Paul never calls on the Christian men to make the women submit. There is nothing in Pauline theology providing a warrant for men to be oppressive, dictatorial, or misogynistic. The pattern Paul holds before men is the self-sacrificing love of Christ for his bride, the church (Eph 5:25–33). When he speaks of the submission of women, he always appeals to the women themselves to submit voluntarily (1 Cor 14:34; Eph 5:22–24).

Some may take offense that it is Paul, a man, who demands this submission. However, Paul is not speaking in a private capacity, but as the "apostle of Christ Jesus" (1 Cor 1:1). The Gospel provides the motivation for men and women joyfully to take their appointed places in God's order, especially in the church. It is possible to resist and reject the Gospel, as Paul himself once did, but such rejection is "to kick against the goads" (Acts 26:14). On the other hand, the person of faith—the new creation in Christ—delights in God's order (cf. Pss 1:2; 112:1; 119:16, 24, 35).

Prophetesses in the Old and New Testaments

The occasional references to prophetesses in both testaments have been taken as a warrant for ordaining women. But as has been argued in the excursus

"Spiritual Gifts in 1 Corinthians," we cannot draw a straight line from the office of the prophet to that of a pastor. Unlike pastors, prophets speak on the basis of special revelations. In the cases of the prophetesses Miriam (Ex 15:20), Deborah (Judg 4:4), and Huldah (2 Ki 22:14; 2 Chr 34:22) in the OT, and of Philip's daughters (Acts 21:9) and Anna (Lk 2:36) in the NT, it may be noted that nothing is said of them speaking in public also before men. Specifically, Miriam led a group of women, and to hear Huldah it was necessary to go to her home.

Among the slighter arguments are the appeal to supposed NT precedents in the case of Priscilla, who assisted her husband Aquila in giving private instruction to Apollos (Acts 18:26), or Phoebe, the deaconess at Cenchrae (Rom 16:1), or Junia, whom some take to be a female apostle (Rom 16:7). The comments above apply here too; none of these women preached, led, or taught the church in worship or administered the Sacraments. It may be added that, in contrast to the few women who were OT prophets, all the priests were men. And it may be argued that the priests' responsibilities in teaching the Torah and administering the sacrifices bear the closest relationship to those of the NT ministers of Word and Sacrament.

CONCLUSION

The above will have to suffice in response to the array of arguments advanced by the advocates of women's ordination. None of those arguments stands up to serious exegetical scrutiny. Nor is that surprising, for the movement to ordain women does not really have its starting point in the Scriptures, but in the sociology and spirit of the modern age (cf. 1 Cor 2:12). It is a novelty, an aberration from the Scriptures and from the universal doctrine and practice of the church for almost two millennia.

Thus, the apostolic command that women be silent in the churches (1 Cor 14:34), as it is *"the Lord's command"* (14:37), binds the church's conscience to "the obedience of Christ" (2 Cor 10:5). Christians who submit their thinking and living to this obedience will not be deterred by ostracism and anathemas, even as Luther ignored the papal bull and took his stand on the Word of God.

APPENDIX

On November 11, 1992, at about 4:30 p.m., the Church of England approved the ordination of women to the priesthood. The vote was carried by majorities of over two-thirds in each of the synod's three houses (bishops, clergy, and laity). The earlier part of the day was devoted to speeches for and against the legislation. Of those who spoke against the legislation, one of the most eloquent was Mrs. Sara Low (see *The Ordination of Women to the Priesthood: The Synod Debate*, 42–43). I believe she is an able spokesperson for all Christians who desire to remain faithful to their Lord.

> When I was converted to Jesus Christ in my early twenties and came into the Church of England, I was told by my first parish priest, now

a bishop on these benches, that the Church of England based itself on Holy Scripture, holy tradition and human reason. This legislation gives me the gravest possible concern on all three counts.

One of the things that I have learned in my time as a Christian is that where we are faithful to the revealed truth, there the promises of the New Testament are fulfilled. The Churches that believe this and do it are, in my experience, those that are blessed.

Like many of those here, I have listened for nearly twenty years to this debate. I listened very carefully to the early arguments about Jesus' cultural conditioning and the claim that Jesus did not have the freedom to appoint women. If cultural conditioning was determinative for Jesus, then all his teaching and all his actions are thus heavily influenced. We are no longer talking about the eternal Son of God. Jesus Christ is different today from what he was yesterday, and he will be different again tomorrow. I have listened to the arguments that the early Church was equally unable to make this change, yet, on the contrary, what could have made a bigger bridgehead with the pagan world than the introduction of women priests, with which they were already familiar? I have listened to arguments on St. Paul where one classic quotation [Gal 3:28] has been wrenched out of context, given a meaning that no previous generation of believers has given it, and seen it used to deny the clear teaching on headship in the rest of St. Paul's letters. I have listened to the doctrine of creation being divided into greater and lesser truths, so that the complementarity of male and female has been debased to a banal interchangeability. I have listened patiently to talk of prayerful, thoughtful majorities when surely our problem is that the minority is also prayerful and thoughtful.

These are not comfortable things to say, but they must be said because if the Synod overturns scriptural authority today it will be no good coming back next time and hoping to impose it on other issues. For the Church, the authority of the Scriptures and the example of Jesus has always been determinative; I do not believe that this House has the authority to overturn them.

My second concern is the legislation itself. What of those who dissent? It seems strange, does it not, to call those who faithfully believe what the Church has always believed "dissenters"? Bishops and archbishops may give verbal assurances that there will be no persecution against such priests and laypeople, but it is with great sadness that I have to tell the bishops that I have not met one opponent of the measure who believes them. The reasons are simple. First, no verbal assurance can undo the fact that you are legislating for two classes of Christian; any good intentions that may exist will wither before the law and practice, as in other provinces. Second, in many dioceses the spirit of this legislation has been in operation for some years. Orthodox clergy are excluded from appointments and orthodox laity are made to feel excluded from that warm glow of official approval, as if they are suffering from some embarrassing handicap. I have experienced that myself often enough in these corridors.

However, if the human injustice of this legislation, which eases old men into retirement and condemns others to serve forever under authorities whose primary qualification is compromise, is disgraceful, it is as nothing besides its theological arrogance and blasphemy. The legislation clearly instructs the Lord God Almighty whom he may raise up to lead the Church. The Holy Spirit will be told, "You may choose anyone you want so long as it is one of us." A Church that denies the sovereignty of God is no longer a Church. The fruits of this debate are not the fruits of the Holy Spirit.

What of tomorrow? If you wake in the morning having voted yes, you'll know that you have voted for a Church irreconcilably divided, for whom the revealed truth of God is no longer authoritative. If you vote no, you will wake to tears and a healing ministry, but above all to the possibility of a renewed New Testament Church, for all of us could then be united in encouraging, training and funding the ministry of priest, deacon, teacher, prophet, healer, administrator, spiritual director—all promised by the Holy Spirit.

I urge Synod to vote for the authority of the Word of God, for the unity of Christ's Church and against this ruinous legislation.

1 CORINTHIANS 15:1–58

THE WORD OF THE CROSS IS THE BASIS FOR THE CONGREGATION'S HOPE

Introduction to Chapter 15

15:1–11 The Risen Christ and His Eyewitnesses

15:1–7 The Resurrection of the Dead Is the Foundation of the Gospel

15:8–11 The Risen Lord's Appearance to Paul

15:12–34 The Necessity of the Resurrection

15:12–19 How Can Some Say There Is No Resurrection?

15:20–28 Christ Has Been Raised as the Firstfruits

15:29 Why Baptisms for the Dead If There Is No Resurrection?

15:30–34 Why Endanger Oneself for the Gospel If There Is No Resurrection?

15:35–58 The Resurrection Body

15:35–44a Analogies about the Resurrection Body

15:44b–49 Application of the Analogies: It Is Raised a Spiritual Body

15:50–58 The Mystery of the Transformation

Introduction to Chapter 15

Paul has left some of his best wine till last. His discourse on the resurrection is one of the church's greatest treasures. But as the pearl in the oyster grows because of an irritant, this chapter owes its origin to a serious heresy embraced by some members of the Corinthian church: the denial of the bodily resurrection (15:12). Apparently some had become so self-satisfied with their spiritual riches that they thought there was no longer anything more worth waiting for. As early as 1:7 Paul had reminded them that they still lived in the tension between the now and the not yet, that they should still be eagerly looking forward to "the revelation of our Lord Jesus Christ."

This deficient eschatology on the part of "some" (15:12) in Corinth may have been akin to the gangrenous heresy propagated in Ephesus by Hymenaeus and Philetus, who claimed the resurrection had already occurred (2 Tim 2:17–18). Apparently that heresy also fostered ungodliness and wickedness (2 Tim 2:16, 19; cf. 1 Cor 15:32–34). Puffed up (1 Cor 4:6, 18–19; 5:2; 8:1; 13:4) with their *spiritual* riches in Christ, such people failed to appreciate the significance of *embodied* life here and now. Confident that they were "already" replete, rich, and royal in the Spirit (4:8), they had lost their Christian hope, a hope that does not center on the spirit's sloughing off the shackles of the body (as in traditional Greek thought) but on its being clothed with the glorious resurrection body. Their loss of this *hope* did not necessarily mean that they had already lost their Christian *faith* and salvation, but it certainly posed that threat. The false doctrine, like pernicious leaven, could infect them to the extent that Paul would have to say "you believed in vain" (15:2).

Now at the conclusion of his epistle, Paul spells out in detail the implications of the Gospel for their understanding of the Christian hope. His argument falls into three main parts: (1) his rehearsal of the Gospel of the crucified and risen Christ, together with a summary of the eyewitness testimony to Christ's resurrection (15:1–11); (2) his rebuttal of the skeptics' arguments (15:12–34); (3) his explanation of what kind of body we will have in the resurrection, an explanation which culminates in a crescendo of praise and a final admonition to steadfastness (15:35–58).

15:1–11

The Risen Christ and His Eyewitnesses

1 CORINTHIANS 15:1–7

THE RESURRECTION OF THE DEAD IS THE FOUNDATION OF THE GOSPEL

TRANSLATION

**15 1Now, brothers, I want you to know the Gospel
which I preached to you and which you received,
because of which you are standing, 2and through
which you are being saved. [I want you to know]
in what terms I preached the Gospel to you, if you
are holding fast to it—unless you believed in vain.
3For I delivered to you as of first importance what
I also received: that Christ died for taking away
our sins according to the Scriptures, 4and that
he was buried, and that he has been raised on the
third day according to the Scriptures, 5and that he
appeared to Cephas, then to the Twelve. 6After that
he appeared to more than five hundred brothers
at once, of whom the majority remain alive until
now, though some have fallen asleep. 7After that
he appeared to James, then to all the apostles.**

COMMENTARY

THE RESURRECTION IS OF FIRST IMPORTANCE (15:1–4)

Paul will now show that the word of the cross (1 Cor 1:18–19) is the basis of the resurrection hope (chapter 15). He opens this new topic with a gentle rebuke (15:1–2). There is one more area in which the Corinthians have a lamentable lack of knowledge (cf. 10:1; 12:1; 14:38). This he now intends to remedy. According to reports he has received, some of them had failed to grasp the implications of the Gospel for the Christian's hope. So he recites in creedal form the "ABCs" of the Gospel—the things he had delivered to them as the vital "mother's milk" of the faith (15:3–4)—as if they had never heard it before (cf. 3:1–2; Heb 5:12–13).

Nevertheless, it was the same Gospel which Paul had preached to them some years earlier and which they had embraced at that time. Furthermore, it was to that same Gospel that they owed their present status as Christians (cf. Rom 11:20), and by that same Gospel that their present and future salvation was being secured (1 Cor 15:2; cf. 1:18).

Paul adds that he wishes to make known "in what terms" (15:2) he had preached the Gospel to them. But before doing so, he voices his pastoral concern, saying in effect: "Are you retaining the Gospel? Surely you didn't receive it in vain?" (15:2).

On the road to Damascus the risen Christ had revealed himself to Paul in blazing light from heaven and in a voice calling him to account for his sin (Acts 9:3–5). That personal encounter with Jesus convinced him that the one he had persecuted was the Son of God (Acts 9:20). Of course, the Christian message was by no means entirely new to Paul. After all, he had heard Stephen's address and witnessed his martyrdom (Acts 7:1–8:1); no doubt Paul had learned other details about the faith from Christians he had interrogated. Later, after his conversion, he would have had the opportunity to flesh out his understanding of the basics when he spent two weeks with Cephas in Jerusalem (Gal 1:18). Paul remained adamant, however, that he had not received the Gospel from any human source (Gal 1:11–24) but through God "revealing his Son in me" (Gal 1:16; cf. Gal 1:12). The reception of Christ Jesus as Lord was central (Col 2:6; cf. 1 Cor 12:3).

This Gospel of the living Christ, then, Paul had faithfully transmitted to the Corinthians. What were the main terms of Paul's Gospel (15:2)? Paul summarizes its content in four clauses, each introduced by "that": "*that* Christ died . . . *that* he was buried . . . *that* he has been raised . . . and *that* he appeared" to many (15:3–8).

Among the Gospel's foremost features was, first of all, Christ's atoning death according to the Scriptures. That "Christ died for taking away our sins" (15:3) lay at the heart of the Gospel. These words form one of Scripture's most succinct Gospel statements (cf. Rom 5:8, "Christ died for us"). Thus, in his great resurrection chapter, Paul begins with the sacrificial death of Christ, which he does not see as an event far removed from the resurrection, but as the first act in the drama of our salvation. Here Paul echoes his earlier statements on the Gospel word of the cross as the power of God (1 Cor 1:17–18). Without the powerful death of Christ, we would still be "in our sins" (Jn 8:24).

Christ's atoning death took place "according to the Scriptures" (1 Cor 15:4). No doubt Isaiah 53, which is cited or echoed frequently in the NT (e.g., Mt 8:17; Acts 8:32–33; 1 Pet 2:22–25), would have been one of the chief texts in Paul's mind. But numerous other portions of the OT are cited in connection with aspects of the crucifixion narrative (e.g., Psalms 22; 69; Zech 12:10; 13:7).

According to all four gospels, the account of Christ's burial (1 Cor 15:4) underlines the reality of his physical death on the cross. Both the Apostles' Creed and the Nicene Creed testify that he "was buried." He had truly become a corpse who had to be disposed of in the usual manner.

The sequence of simple past tenses ("Christ *died*," "he *was buried*," 15:3–4) suddenly gives way to a significant and climactic perfect tense: "he *has been raised*" (15:4). From among the corpses Christ has been raised "by the glory of the Father" (Rom 6:4 completes the divine passive by naming God as the agent of the action) and continues to live as the risen one "forever and ever" (Rev 1:18). His resurrection took place "on the third day according to the Scriptures" (1 Cor 15:4). Earlier he had told his disciples that he "must" be killed and rise again on the third day (e.g., Mt 16:21), implying that this must happen to fulfill the Father's will as laid down in the OT Scriptures. The apostles and evangelists found the Messiah's resurrection foretold specifically in passages such as Pss 16:8–11; 110:1; Is 53:10–12; and far more broadly in other passages.

That it would happen on the third day seems to have its roots in Hos 6:2 and Jonah 1:17. What makes the Jonah passage particularly pertinent is that Jesus himself declared that Jonah's three days and three nights in the fish's belly was a prophecy of the Son of Man's three days and three nights in the heart of the earth (Mt 12:39–40). While there is no NT text which directly cites Hos 6:2 as a prophecy of Christ's resurrection on the third day, its wording suggests that the early church may also have found here one of the key OT witnesses.

In raising his Messiah on the third day, God also raises and bestows life on all those who are in Christ. Baptism into Christ's body (1 Cor 12:13) is Baptism into his death and resurrection (Rom 6:1–11; Col 2:11–13).

WITNESSES OF THE RESURRECTION
(15:5–7)

The fourth and final "that" clause in 1 Cor 15:3–5 supplies the supporting evidence that Christ had really risen on the third day. These four clauses state the foundational facts of the Gospel: "that Christ died for taking away our sins . . . that he was buried . . . that he has been raised . . . and that he appeared" (1 Cor 15:3–5) to many witnesses. Luke relates that Jesus "presented himself alive after his suffering by many convincing proofs, appearing to them [the apostles] over a period of forty days" (Acts 1:3). Thus, the church's faith in Christ's resurrection rests on eyewitness testimony.

OT law stipulated that legal evidence should be corroborated by the testimony of two or three witnesses (Deut 17:6; 19:15). The resurrection of Christ is so vital a fact for the Christian faith that God supplied an abundance of witnesses. Fittingly, the first eyewitness on Paul's list is the first of the twelve apostles, Simon Peter or, as Paul calls him by the Aramaic equivalent, Cephas ("stone, rock"; cf. Mt 10:2; Lk 24:34). Christ's appearance to him must have been reassuring to Cephas after his shameful denial, and it prepared him for his leadership role in the days after Christ's ascension (e.g., Lk 22:32; Acts 1:15; 2:14).

Jesus' appearances to "the Twelve" (1 Cor 15:5) took place on the evening of the first Easter Sunday (Lk 24:33–36; Jn 20:19) and again a week later when

Thomas was present (Jn 20:24–29). Although only ten members of the original Twelve were present on the first occasion (Judas Iscariot was dead and Thomas was absent), and only eleven the following Sunday, Paul is using the term "the Twelve" in a technical sense for those who constituted the original apostles whom Jesus called during his earthly ministry (Mt 10:2–4 and parallels).

Continuing in chronological sequence, Paul comes to Jesus' appearance to "more than five hundred brothers" (1 Cor 15:6). Since the evidence of two or three witnesses was sufficient to prove the veracity of an event, the presence of more than five hundred constitutes overwhelming testimony. There is no way of knowing when this event took place. One suggestion which fits the sequence is that it happened in conjunction with Jesus' Great Commission to the eleven apostles prior to his ascension (Mt 28:16–20). Although Matthew does not mention that others were present, it seems that the apostles usually were accompanied by a larger group of Jesus' disciples (cf. Lk 24:33; Acts 1:14–15; 13:31).

If anyone was still skeptical about these appearances of the risen Christ, he could easily check out the story himself by consulting some of these five hundred eyewitnesses. Most of them were still alive, though some had "fallen asleep" in Christ (1 Cor 15:6). This euphemism for Christian death is found again in 15:18, 20, and 51. It should be preserved in English translations because of its allusion to the resurrection.

The Lord's next appearance was to James. This James was his half-brother, the second oldest son in the family (Mt 13:55). James and his younger brothers had initially refused to believe in Jesus (Jn 7:5), but this post-resurrection appearance proved to be a turning point, it seems, not only for James but also for his brothers. Thus, in the days between the ascension and Pentecost they joined the other believers at prayer in the upper room (Acts 1:14). Subsequently, James became the leader of the Jerusalem church (Acts 15:13; 21:18). Paul counted him among the "apostles" (Gal 1:19) and "pillars" (Gal 2:9) of the church universal.

Then Jesus appeared to "all the apostles" (1 Cor 15:7). If this includes "James" (15:7, the Lord's brother) and possibly others in the five hundred, then it was a wider group than "the Twelve." It would be James and the rest of Jesus' brothers and men like Barnabas, Andronicus, Junias, and others able to add their testimony as eyewitnesses of the risen Christ and commissioned to do so (cf. Acts 14:4, 14; Rom 16:7). Paul himself was later included in this wider apostolic group. How he came to be included in their number he will explain in the next pericope (1 Cor 15:8–11).

1 CORINTHIANS 15:8–11
THE RISEN LORD'S APPEARANCE TO PAUL

TRANSLATION

15 [8]**Last of all, as to one prematurely born, he even**
appeared to me. [9]**For I am the least of the apostles,**
one who is unworthy to be called an apostle because
I persecuted the church of God. [10]**But by the grace of**
God I am what I am, and his grace toward me was not
in vain. Rather, I labored more than them all, yet not
I but the grace of God that was with me. [11]**Whether**
then it was I or they, so we preach and so you believed.

COMMENTARY

Paul concludes the list of eyewitnesses who can attest to the fact of Jesus' resurrection, which is the foundation of the Gospel. In deep humility, he finally mentions himself. The Lord had appeared to him "last of all" (1 Cor 15:8). Thus, on one important count he was not qualified to be an apostle in the strictest sense: he had not accompanied the other disciples during the three years or so that the Lord Jesus "went in and out" among them (Acts 1:21–22). Like a "premature birth," he had not had the benefit of a full gestation period; he had been thrown into his apostleship in a sudden and unexpected fashion. Yet even he—a premature birth (1 Cor 15:8), a former persecutor (15:9)—had been given the privilege of becoming an eyewitness of the resurrected Christ.

In 15:9–10 Paul now elaborates on what he has just said about himself as "last of all," a premature birth (15:8). He considered himself the least of the apostles; indeed, in his epistle to the Ephesians, he called himself "the very least of all the saints" (Eph 3:8). To be a Christian at all was a high privilege for one who saw himself as "nothing" in God's sight (2 Cor 12:11; see also 1 Cor 3:7); to be a "called apostle" (Rom 1:1; 1 Cor 1:1) was a sign of unfathomable grace. Like Jacob in his later years, he knew he was not worthy of the least of the mercies God had shown his servant (Gen 32:10).

Paul's consciousness of personal unworthiness was sharpened by the painful memory of the way he had persecuted the church of God (Gal 1:13; Phil 3:6; 1 Tim 1:13). In attacking God's saints, he had attacked the Son of God himself (Acts 9:4). For that affront to the divine Majesty, he knew he deserved death and eternal condemnation. But instead of condemnation, this chief of sinners had been privileged to receive God's astounding grace, mercy, and longsuffering love (1 Tim 1:12–16; cf. 1 Cor 13:4), so that he had become the person he was: not only a saint, but even an apostle. Totally insufficient for these things in himself, the sufficiency of God had conferred this ministry on him and equipped him for it (2 Cor 2:16; 3:5–6; 4:1).

God's unmerited grace toward him had born rich fruit. Indeed, he had labored "more than them all" (1 Cor 15:10). Commentators debate whether this means "more than all the other apostles put together" or "more than any one of them"; probably it is the latter. Called by the One who came to serve and to give his life as a ransom for many (Mk 10:45), Paul devoted long hours to wearisome toil and endured great hardships in his Master's service (1 Cor 4:9–13; 2 Cor 6:4–5; 11:23–27; 1 Thess 2:9; 2 Thess 3:8).

While it was no empty boast but the simple truth that he had labored harder than anyone else, Paul refrains from continuing in this vein (cf. 2 Cor 12:6), lest anyone think he wanted the credit for himself. No, he says that "the grace of God that was with [him]" (1 Cor 15:10) was the master workman laboring alongside him. All the glory belonged to God alone and to Christ, who had worked in him and through him to bring the Gentiles to the obedience of faith (Rom 15:18; Gal 2:8). Apart from God's grace in Christ, Paul knew he could accomplish nothing. In 1 Cor 3:6–7 he stated, "I planted, Apollos watered, but God was giving the growth. So neither the planter is anything nor the waterer, but only God, who does the growing" (cf. Jn 15:5).

Thus, Paul's joy and confidence in the risen Christ had inspired him to fruitful labor in the Lord's service. The chapter ends with his appeal to the Corinthians to follow the pattern he had shown them, abounding in the Lord's work in the confidence that their labor, no less than Paul's, would not be in vain (1 Cor 15:58; cf. 3:12–15).

Paul now rounds off this first section of the chapter in 15:11. The other apostles and eyewitnesses had labored before him; he, as an untimely birth, had joined that great cloud of witnesses and entered into that same labor. So whether it was Paul himself or Cephas or the Twelve or any of the others Paul had listed (15:5–7), they all preached the same Gospel of Christ's death and resurrection (15:3–4). And it was to that common Gospel that the Corinthians owed their faith and hope of resurrection to eternal life.

15:12–34

The Necessity of the Resurrection

1 CORINTHIANS 15:12–19

HOW CAN SOME SAY THERE IS NO RESURRECTION?

TRANSLATION

15 [12]Now if Christ is preached as risen from the dead,
how can some among you say there is no resurrection
of the dead? [13]If there is no resurrection of the
dead, then Christ has not been raised either. [14]And
if Christ has not been raised, then our preaching is
in vain, and your faith is also in vain. [15]Moreover,
we are found to be false witnesses of God, because
we witnessed against God that he raised the Christ,
whom he did not raise if indeed the dead are not
raised. [16]For if the dead are not raised, then Christ
has not been raised. [17]And if Christ has not been
raised, your faith is futile, you are still in your sins.
[18]Then also those who have fallen asleep in Christ
have perished. [19]If in this life only we have hoped
in Christ, we are of all people most miserable.

COMMENTARY

GREEK SKEPTICISM TOWARD THE RESURRECTION

Paul now explains why he has set forth the fundamentals of the faith in such detail. While he and his co-workers are preaching Christ as risen from the dead (1 Cor 15:4), some of the Corinthians are promoting an idea that runs directly counter to the apostles' message.

Their skepticism about the resurrection was typical of Greek culture. Those on the Athenian Areopagus had mocked Paul for preaching the resurrection (Acts 17:32). Commonly the Greeks believed that at death, only a person's soul was taken by the ferryman across the River Styx to the gloomy world of the shades. This animistic idea that only the soul survives death in a shadowy, unhappy existence has been common to most non-Christian cultures, even highly advanced cultures like those of ancient Egypt, Mesopotamia, and Greece. Only Christianity has been brightened by the hope of the resurrection of the body.

The Corinthians may have woven their new faith into the traditional Greek fabric. On the one hand, they had to admit that faith in Christ's resurrection was central to Christian teaching. On the other hand, they may have insisted, in line with Greek tradition, that the only resurrection they would see was a spiritual one, and that this had taken place "already" (2 Tim 2:18). Through their coming to faith in Christ and their reception of the Spirit, they believed that they were now so full of the Spirit's gifts that they "already" enjoyed resurrection in all its fullness (1 Cor 4:8). There was nothing more to look forward to, and certainly no "resurrection of corpses" (alternate translation in 15:12–13).

THE STRUCTURE OF PAUL'S LOGIC

The form of Paul's logical argumentation might be described as links of "if-then" sentences, which together form a chain leading from the Corinthians' false premise to the logical conclusion of despair. First, three "if-then" statements (15:12–15) progress up to a threefold conclusion (15:14–15) about the implications of the Corinthians' denial of the bodily resurrection. The threefold conclusion (15:14–15) is immediately grounded ("for," 15:16) in two more "if-then" statements (15:16–18), the first of which (15:16) virtually repeats the second (15:13) of the three earlier "if-then" statements. In 15:16–18 the second "if-then" statement (15:17–18) offers a further threefold conclusion about the implications of the Corinthians' error. Finally, 15:19 presents a devastating "if-then" summary statement. The logic looks like this:

15:12 *If* Christ is preached as risen from the dead,
then how can some among you say there is no resurrection of the dead?
15:13 *If* there is no resurrection of the dead,
then Christ has not been raised either.
15:14 *If* Christ has not been raised,
then (1) our preaching is vain;
(2) your faith is vain;
15:15 (3) we are found to be false witnesses of God,
because we witnessed against God that he raised the Christ,
whom he did not raise if indeed the dead are not raised!
15:16 For *if* the dead are not raised,
then Christ has not been raised.
15:17 *If* Christ has not been raised,
then (1) your faith is futile;
(2) you are still in your sins;
15:18 (3) then also those who have fallen asleep in Christ have perished.
15:19 *If* in this life only we have hoped in Christ,
then we are of all people most miserable!

This analysis highlights the practical consequences that emerge from a denial of the resurrection of the Christians' bodies on the last day. Carried to its logical extreme, that denial would mean that Paul's preaching is a lie and that the Christian faith is an empty deception that leaves believers still in their sins.

PAUL'S THEOLOGICAL ARGUMENT

Paul asserts that if the Corinthians would only pay attention to the essential message of Christianity, they would realize that their position was untenable. If Christ is preached as raised from the dead, how could anyone claim there is no raising from the dead (15:12)? Obviously there has been at least one great exception! Or, to put it the other way around, if there is no such thing as a resurrection of the dead, then no such thing happened to Christ; he could not have been raised either (15:13).

Consequently, if Christ has not been raised, there is no point to the apostles' activities (15:14). By God's grace, Paul had engaged in strenuous labor on behalf of the Gospel, and he believed that this grace was not "in vain" (15:10). His own missionary journeys were devoted to preaching "the hope of the resurrection of the dead" (Acts 23:6; see also Acts 24:15; 26:6–8; 28:20). But this group in Corinth had struck at the heart of the Christian message. If they were right, then indeed the apostles' activity and their message were in vain, and the Corinthians' faith was in vain (1 Cor 15:14). The whole Christian message was a hoax; all of them, apostles and believers, would be better off abandoning it.

Furthermore, if the Corinthian skeptics were correct, the apostles were guilty of something far worse than merely wasting their time and energy on an empty message. They would have been found out as false prophets (cf. 1 Jn 5:10), men who had misrepresented God by alleging that he had raised the Messiah when in fact he had done no such thing—which would be the case if, as the skeptics claimed, the dead are not raised (1 Cor 15:15–16). The apostles' false witness would have been "against God" (15:15), for it reflected badly on him as one who disappointed those who hoped in him. Similarly, a philanthropist is placed in a bad light when someone claiming to represent him promises a large benefaction but later announces that the promise was void.

In 15:16 Paul repeats 15:13 almost word for word, pressing home the logic of his argument. If the dead are not raised, then the One who was "crucified, died, and was buried" (Apostles' Creed) for our sins (15:3–4) has not been raised either.

1 Cor 15:17 repeats 15:14, except that now Paul says nothing about the apostolic message. His focus is solely on what it would mean for believers if Christ had not been raised. Their faith would be futile (cf. 15:14c), and furthermore, they would still be in their sins. If Christ is not raised, then his death to atone for their sins (1 Cor 15:3) is to no avail.

Furthermore, if Christ has not been raised, not only are the living still in their sins, but their loved ones who have fallen asleep in Christ did not go to be with Christ (15:18). Paul is trying to bring the Corinthians to their senses. They fondly imagined, it seems, that in death the believer's soul would escape the prison of the body and be ushered into a new and more blessed spiritual state. To this delusion Paul responds: "Not so! If Christ is not raised, your loved ones have all perished. They have no future."

Indeed, Paul continues (15:19), if the skeptics are right, Christians have lost both the present and the future. They do not enjoy present forgiveness in Christ, nor do they have any hope that extends beyond the veil into heaven (15:19; cf. Heb 6:18–20). Their hope is only good for this life. Contrary to what Paul maintained in 1 Cor 13:13, hope would not endure and be fulfilled in eternity. With such a limited hope, Christians would be "of all people most miserable" (15:19). They would have staked their lives on a great delusion. (Even more did this apply to Paul and his co-workers; cf. 15:30–32).

PRACTICAL IMPLICATIONS

For Paul, Christ's resurrection is inseparably connected to the future resurrection of Christians; they are two sides of the same coin. Through Baptism Christians have become members of Christ's own body (1 Cor 12:13). Consequently, the bodily resurrection of Jesus guarantees the resurrection of the believers' bodies. That resurrection will be the fulfillment of the gift of salvation accomplished through Christ's death and inaugurated by Christ's own bodily rising.

Here is profound and direct insight for our proclamation of Christ's Easter victory. Easter means that the victory has been won by Christ. At the same time, for God's people the full participation in that victory is yet to be experienced. Easter is, then, an eschatological event with end-time implications that the church must never forget if she is not to lose her hope.

Contemporary Christians, including preachers, sometimes seem to forget that the final Christian hope is not just for the soul to enter Christ's presence after the death of the body. It is surely true that the Christian's soul goes "to be with Christ" immediately upon death (Phil 1:23; see also Lk 23:43; 2 Cor 5:8; Rev 6:9). At times, however, it seems as though this has become the only goal in the minds and hearts of believers, and that the return of Christ Jesus and the resurrection of the body do not play as vital a place in everyday living, believing, and hoping.

But the great hope toward which the church and indeed all creation looks is the renewal of that creation and the resurrection of the body. On that day, God will receive the full harvest of which Christ's own bodily resurrection is the firstfruits (1 Cor 15:20). Without this hope, the Gospel proclaimed by Paul would collapse. Faith would be futile, sin and its consequences would remain, fellow Christians who have died would have perished, and humanity should look upon us Christians as people who are wasting their time.

Paul has led the Corinthians from their view—that there is no final resurrection of the body—to the place of despair to which such a view inevitably leads. Next, with the glorious rhetorical pivot of "but as it is . . ." (15:20) Paul will move them from despair back to hope.

1 CORINTHIANS 15:20–28
Christ Has Been Raised as the Firstfruits

TRANSLATION

**15 20 But as it is, Christ has been raised from the dead,
the firstfruits of those who have fallen asleep. 21 For
since through a man [came] death, also through a
man [came] resurrection of the dead. 22 For just as in
Adam all die, so also in Christ all will be made alive.
23 But each in its proper order: Christ the firstfruits,
then those who belong to Christ at his parousia,
24 then the end, when he hands over the kingdom
to [his] God and Father, when he has destroyed
every ruler and every authority and power. 25 For he
must reign until "he puts all his enemies under his
feet." 26 The last enemy that is destroyed is death.
27 "For he has put all things under his feet." Now
when it says that all things have been subordinated
[to him], it is clear that this excepts the one who
subordinated all things to him. 28 So when all things
are subordinated to him, then also the Son himself
will be subordinated to the one who subordinated
all things to him, that God may be all in all.**

COMMENTARY

Leaving behind the depressing hypotheses which filled the previous paragraph (1 Cor 15:12–19: "if there were no resurrection of the dead . . ."), Paul gives a ringing affirmation: "But as it is, Christ has been raised from the dead" (15:20). The Corinthians should never doubt this basic tenet of their creed, nor should they doubt its implications for their own resurrection. For the risen Christ is not the only one who would rise; he is the "firstfruits of those who have fallen asleep" (15:20; cf. Rev 1:5). Just as the Israelites brought the sheaf of firstfruits to the Lord on the "Sunday" ("the day after the Sabbath") after Passover as a sign that the whole harvest belonged to him (Lev 23:9–15), so Christ's resurrection was the pledge that all who had fallen asleep in him would be physically raised as he was.

Through one man's disobedience, the tragedy of human suffering and death had become the common lot of all (1 Cor 15:21–22). It was fitting, then, that it would be through the obedience of another man, the second Adam, that resurrection and life would come to all men. Later, Paul would spell this out more fully in his epistle to the Romans (5:12–21). Here he sketches the Adam-Christ typology in the briefest terms. Just as Adam's sin and death affected not only himself but all humanity, so the Corinthians needed to appreciate that Christ's resurrection was not only for his own benefit; through this Man the resurrection from the dead had become the destiny of all believers. Just as Adam was the head of the old humanity, so that his fall left a legacy of sin and death to all, so Christ stands as head of the new humanity to be made alive in him.

The clause "so also in Christ all will be made alive" must not be understood in a universalistic sense. Only "those who belong to Christ" (15:23) through baptismal incorporation ("we all were baptized with one Spirit into one body," 12:13) and by faith will receive the gift of resurrection to eternal life. Unbelievers, too, will be raised bodily but then will be cast into the lake of fire, which is "the second death" (Rev 20:14–15; cf. Dan 12:1–3).

Paul goes on to encourage the Corinthians to be patient (1 Cor 15:23–24). The end is not yet; their loved ones must still rest in the grave for a time. But everything will surely happen in its proper order. Christ's resurrection is the great first step, the firstfruits holding the promise of everything else. *Then* those who belong to him will be raised when he descends from heaven on the Last Day (1 Thess 4:16). At no point in 1 Cor 15:20–28 does Paul refer to the fate of unbelievers; his concern is to bring comfort and hope to the believers (cf. 1 Thess 4:18).

At the appointed time, *then* Christ's second coming will usher in the consummation of the age (1 Cor 15:24). The conjunction "then" (15:24) does not necessarily indicate that there will be a marked interval between his return and his handing over the kingdom to the Father. Rather, the triumphant Messiah may be compared to a nobleman who had journeyed to a far country to receive a kingdom and then to return (Lk 19:12). All authority had been entrusted to him for this assignment (Mt 11:27; 28:18). In the course of his campaigns against the enemies of the kingdom, he had bound up the "strong man" (Satan) and plundered his goods (Mk 3:22–27), so that Satan's former possessions now belong to the conqueror. Then he hands over his people to his God and Father, having deposed all spiritual and temporal authorities and powers (1 Cor 15:24).

The texts parallel to 15:24 make it clear Paul has in mind primarily *hostile spiritual* powers: the devil and his forces (Eph 1:21; 2:2; 3:10; 6:12). But his terminology is comprehensive, and he may well have been thinking also of *hostile human* authorities: kings, rulers, and all anti-Christian forces who under the influence of demonic forces range themselves against the Lord and his Anointed.

Christ's triumph over these powers (1 Cor 15:25) fulfilled God's plan as it had been laid down in Ps 110:1. David says:

> The Lord says to my Lord:
> "Sit at my right hand,
> till I make your enemies
> your footstool."

Paul cites the psalm freely to show the divinely ordained necessity that Christ should triumph over death and ascend to the Father's right hand, where he is enthroned and rules in the midst of his defeated foes (Ps 110:2). His regency would continue until *all* his enemies had been subjugated completely. Paul adds "all" to the quote in 1 Cor 15:25 and places "all" first in the Greek of 15:27 to emphasize it.

The last enemy to be destroyed is death (15:26). A little later Paul will call death an "enemy" with a vicious "sting" (1 Cor 15:56). Humankind fears death as a hostile and destructive force (Heb 2:15) and the punishment for sin (Rom 6:23). As long as people continue to die as the wages of their sin, God's good and gracious will for his creation is not yet brought to completion. But after all Christ's people have been raised to life at his second coming, there will be no more death (Rev 20:14; 21:4).

The fact that death is our spiritual enemy has immense significance for Christian existence and Christian funerals. Sometimes at funerals one hears comments such as these: "We shouldn't be sad; we should only rejoice. This is a victory celebration." To be sure, there is a sense in which that is true. But death, the last enemy and sign of sin's universal dominion over fallen humanity, will not be swallowed up until the Last Day (1 Cor 15:54), and Christians are free to grieve at the death of their loved ones. God never intended the pain of separation and the heartache that attends death. That sharp pain of grief can be an entirely appropriate manifestation of the biblical understanding that death is the enemy that has not yet been fully overcome. And so Christians may and should mourn at funerals—but not as those who have no hope (1 Thess 4:13–18).

Reflecting further on the defeat of all Christ's enemies, in 1 Cor 15:27 Paul cites another psalm in support of his argument. Ps 8:6 speaks of the dominion given to man/the Son of Man "over the works of your [God's] hands; you have put all things under his feet"—all sheep and oxen and so forth. This citation of Psalm 8 continues the Adamic typology of 1 Cor 15:21–22. Just as Psalm 8 referred to the reign of the first Adam over all things of this creation, so now Christ, *the* Son of Man, reigns as the Second Adam over all things in the new creation (cf. Heb 2:8). His resurrection from the dead proves that God has subjected all things, even death, to him. There is a beautiful parallel in Phil 3:21, where Paul says that at his final coming Christ "will change our lowly body to be like his glorious body, *by the power which enables him even to subject* [the same verb used three times in 1 Cor 15:27] *all things to himself*" (RSV).

There is one exception, of course, to this subordination of everything to Christ: God the Father himself, the one who is subordinating all things to Christ, does not lose his superordinate position (15:27b). Once the Son of God's victory is completely implemented, he will hand over the kingdom to his "God and Father" (15:24a) and submit himself to the Father's authority (15:28). Having come into the world to do the Father's will (Heb 10:7–9), when his mission is fully accomplished he will submit voluntarily to the one who sent him. Thus, God—Father, Son, and Holy Spirit—will be "all in all" (1 Cor 15:28; cf. Rom 11:36).

Paul's vocabulary here must be interpreted in context. Paul's theology here is that of the Athanasian Creed, which distinguishes between the Son's inferiority to the Father *with respect to his manhood,* and his equality to the Father *with respect to his Godhead:* "equal to the Father with respect to His divinity, less than the Father with respect to His humanity" (*LSB* 320:31). At the same time, that creed also affirms that "the Godhead of the Father and of the Son and of the Holy Spirit is one: the glory equal, the majesty coeternal" (*LSB* 319:6).

Chemnitz (*The Two Natures in Christ*, 275) amplifies:

> In Scripture the Father is not only called the Father but also the God of Christ (John 20:17; 2 Cor. 11:31; Eph. 1:3; Col. 1:3). That He is the God of someone involves the idea of greater and lesser, superior and inferior. Christ, therefore, is lesser or inferior to the Father in glory, not however according to His deity but according to His humanity (1 Cor. 11:3). The husband is the head of the wife, but the Head of every man is Christ. Indeed, He is Head of all the angels (Eph. 1:21–22). But God is the Head of Christ. However, according to His deity the Father is not the Head of Christ, for Christ is equal with God (Phil. 2:6). Paul thus shows that the human nature in Christ has been exalted above all creatures, but is below or lower than God. . . .
>
> In 1 Cor. 15:28 Paul also shows that the human nature in Christ is below or less than or inferior to God, not only when in the state of humiliation He says, "My Father is greater than I" [John 14:28], or when after the resurrection He says, "I ascend to My Father and your Father, and to My God and your God" [John 20:17], but even after the Last Day when He will have handed over the kingdom to God and His Father.

This theme of the Son's subjection to the Father reflects their distinctive roles in carrying out the divine plan of salvation. The Father sent the Son; the Son subordinated himself in willing obedience to the Father, who sent him; and finally, at the glorious consummation of his mission, the Son will deliver the kingdom into the hands of his Father. In no way does this distinction in roles detract from the Son's eternal divinity or his full equality with the Father (cf. Jn 1:18; 5:19; 10:30; 14:11). Nor does it mean that at the consummation the Son will relinquish his dominion. Christ's kingdom, in conjunction with the Father's, will never end (Lk 1:33; Eph 1:21; Rev 22:3).

1 CORINTHIANS 15:29

Why Baptisms for the Dead If There Is No Resurrection?

TRANSLATION

15 [29]Otherwise what will those people do who
are being baptized on behalf of the dead?
If the dead are not raised at all, why indeed
are they being baptized for them?

COMMENTARY

Since the beginning of the chapter Paul has been preaching the bodily death and resurrection of Christ and what his victory over death means for all believers. In 1 Cor 15:28, Paul's argument closed on a doxological note, praising the all-conquering Son and the Father to whom the Son will submit. Now Paul suddenly switches his focus from Christ to the Christian. The practice he is about to mention makes no sense if the dead are not raised.

1 Cor 15:29 is one of the most obscure passages in the NT. The phrase "those . . . who are being baptized on behalf of the dead" seems to imply a kind of baptism otherwise unknown in the history of Christianity. The dozens of suggestions advanced to explain this apparently eccentric practice may be summarized in six categories.

1. Most scholars think Paul is speaking of a vicarious form of baptism in which living Christians were baptized on behalf of persons who had already died. If this majority view is correct, then Paul is referring to a form of baptism, which as far as can be determined, was without historical or biblical parallel. Some of the Corinthians seem to have been so concerned about relatives and friends who had died before receiving Christian Baptism that they were having themselves baptized (or rebaptized?) on behalf of the dead.

2. Some take "those being baptized" metaphorically. Paul is not speaking about people who were receiving Christian Baptism. Instead, he is speaking about "those being *destroyed*" (referring to the apostles).

3. A related interpretation which attempts to fit 15:29 into the epistle's broader context is the proposal that Paul is speaking about regular Christian Baptism, but "the dead" refers not to deceased persons, but to the living apostles.

4. Another view is that the phrase usually translated "the dead" must instead be taken adjectivally: "those who are being baptized for their [own] dying bodies."

5. Some approaches postulate a different understanding of the Greek preposition translated above as "on behalf of." Luther suggested that it must be understood locally, "baptized *over* the graves." Luther considered the Baptism to be regular Christian Baptism and explained that the purpose of the practice of baptizing over the graves of deceased Christians was to strengthen the faith of the Corinthians in the reality of the bodily resurrection (AE 28:150–151).

6. A similar view considers the verse to be speaking about regular Christian Baptism and renders the prepositional phrase as "with a view to the dead" (meaning deceased Christians). The baptism, life, and death in faith of the now deceased Christians furnish the motive for the living to receive baptism for the same purpose.

It seems that the Christians in Corinth, having been instructed regarding Baptism, considered it necessary for salvation. As Peter says, "Baptism now saves us" (1 Pet 3:21). In 1 Cor 12:13 Paul stated that Christian Baptism is the Sacrament that incorporates one into Christ's body and gives one the Spirit to drink. He also refers to Baptism in 1:13–17 and alludes to it in 1:9–10. But the discussions of Christian Baptism by Paul and the other NT writers never suggest that there could be a legitimate practice of vicarious baptism that would be efficacious, availing for the dead.

Although Paul—for some inexplicable reason—does not explicitly censure the group that is practicing this kind of baptism, neither does he approve of this eccentric practice. He merely asks, in effect: "What would be the point of these baptisms if the dead are not raised?" (15:29). In his epistles to the Romans and the Colossians he will expand on the significance of Christian Baptism as a participation in the death and burial with Christ in order that the baptized Christian may also be raised to new life with Christ (Rom 6:1–4; Col 2:11–13). That new life begins at Baptism and continues throughout the Christian's present life (Rom 6:6–23), but it will be fully realized only in the resurrection. Note the change from the perfect (past) tense to the future tense in Rom 6:5: "If we *have been* joined together [in Baptism] to the likeness of his [Christ's] death, then also we *will be* [joined in the likeness] of his resurrection."

1 CORINTHIANS 15:30–34

Why Endanger Oneself for the Gospel If There Is No Resurrection?

TRANSLATION

15 [30]And why indeed are we in danger every hour? [31]I
die daily, by our pride in you, brothers, which I have
in Christ Jesus our Lord. [32]If humanly [speaking]
I fought wild beasts in Ephesus, what gain did I
have? If the dead are not raised, "let us eat and
drink, for tomorrow we die." [33]Stop being deceived:
"Evil associations corrupt good habits." [34]Sober
up, as you should, and stop sinning, for some have
ignorance of God—I tell you to your shame.

COMMENTARY

Paul now takes himself and his colleagues as a further example. If the dead are not raised, then the apostles would have to reconsider their whole way of life. Paul had described the sorry lot of the apostles, in contrast to the pampered life of the Corinthian Christians, in 1 Cor 4:8–13. Why should Paul and his fellow apostles be in daily peril of their lives? His whole ministry was a catalogue of hardship, opposition, and persecution (2 Cor 4:7–18; 6:3–10; 11:23–33). Daily he lived in the shadow of death. He could testify to that just as surely as he could testify to his great pride in the Corinthians for the grace that had been poured out on them. Ultimately, he is quick to add, his boasting in them is a boasting in Christ Jesus (1 Cor 15:31).

What comes most vividly to his mind as he writes are his recent and present dangers in Ephesus (1 Cor 15:32). He compares what befell him there to fighting wild beasts. The expression must be figurative, for as a Roman citizen Paul would not have been condemned to fight wild animals in the arena; furthermore, if that unlikely event had happened, he would probably have died. Rather, Paul is speaking in terms similar to those used later by the imprisoned Bishop Ignatius of Antioch (Ignatius to the Romans 5:1): "From Syria all the way to Rome I am fighting with wild beasts, on land and sea, by night and day, chained amidst ten leopards (that is, a company of soldiers)."

Most likely the "wild beasts" (15:32) Paul has in mind were hostile Jews who threatened his life from the beginning of his ministry in Ephesus and continued to hound him later (see 16:8–9 and 2 Cor 1:8 for other general references to his suffering in Asia, and Acts 21:27; 24:19 for specific complaints about Asian Jews). Toward the end of his time in Ephesus he also ran into fierce opposition from Gentiles, who stormed into the theater protesting against the Christian missionaries (Acts 19:23–41). This was the incident which forced Paul to leave the city. However, there would have been no time after the riot to pen this epistle. Probably, then, it is some earlier occasion when he encountered fierce opposition from Jews that leads Paul to speak of fighting wild animals.

Again, Paul asks in effect: "What is the point? If the dead are not raised, what good does it do me to live in daily fear of my life?" (1 Cor 15:32). It would make far more sense, he continues, to get the most out of this life, like the Israelites in Isaiah's day who saw the Assyrians at the gates of Jerusalem, but instead of weeping over their sins said to one another: "Let us eat and drink, for tomorrow we die" (Is 22:13). In this pithy quotation Isaiah and Paul depict the hedonism and Epicureanism of secular people, both ancient and modern, "without hope and without God in the world" (Eph 2:12).

It seems that their lack of hope in a future resurrection was one reason why so many in Corinth had a lax attitude about moral matters and needed stern warnings (1 Cor 15:34; see also, e.g., 1 Corinthians 5; 6:8–11, 18). False doctrine fosters loose morals. Paul urges them to stop being deceived, and quotes a pagan poet to indict their pagan thinking and pagan ways. A fragment from the comic poet Menander contains the proverb "evil associations corrupt good habits" (15:33). If the Corinthians continued to associate with pagans or paganized fellow Christians in idol temples (1 Corinthians 8 and 10) or consort with prostitutes (1 Corinthians 6), they would reap the corruption they had sowed (Gal 6:7–8).

Finally, Paul commands the Corinthians to "sober up . . . and stop sinning" (1 Cor 15:34). Too many of them were "on a high," intoxicated with their spiritual gifts (1 Corinthians 12 and 14), and insufficiently concerned with sound teaching on the resurrection (1 Corinthians 15) and other issues. In order to shame them and bring them to their senses, Paul has to tell them: "Some [of you] have ignorance of God" (15:34). The skeptics in the congregation had forgotten that their God was a God of righteousness, holiness, and great power.

Since the Corinthians were enchanted with their supposed "knowledge" (1 Cor 8:1, 7, 10, 11) and Paul began his epistle by portraying Christ as the incarnation of God's "wisdom" (1:24, 30; 2:6–7), his statement that some possessed "ignorance" (15:34) was a direct affront to their pride. Paul is calling them to repentance with the strongest possible language. He intends to make them ashamed (15:34, cf. 6:5).

15:35–58

The Resurrection Body

1 CORINTHIANS 15:35–44A

Analogies about the Resurrection Body

TRANSLATION

15 [35]**But someone will say: "How are the dead raised?**
And with what kind of body do they come?" [36]**Fool,**
in your own experience, what you sow is not made
alive unless it dies; [37]**and what you sow is not the body**
that is to come into being, but a naked seed, perhaps
of wheat or of something of the others. [38]**But God**
gives it a body as he has determined, and to each of
the seeds [he gives] its own body. [39]**Not all flesh is**
the same flesh, but there is one flesh of humans, and
another flesh of animals, and another flesh of birds,
and another of fish. [40]**And [there are] heavenly bodies**
and earthly bodies. But the splendor of the heavenly
bodies is different, and that of earthly bodies is
different. [41]**[There is] another splendor of the sun, and**
another splendor of the moon, and another splendor
of the stars, for star differs from star in splendor.

[42]**So [it is] also [with] the resurrection of the dead:**
It is sown in corruption, it is raised in incorruption;
[43]**it is sown in dishonor, it is raised in glory;**
it is sown in weakness, it is raised in power;
[44a]**it is sown a natural body, it is raised a spiritual body.**

COMMENTARY

Paul knows there are some in Corinth who will still not be satisfied with his arguments for the resurrection of the dead. They claimed they could not grasp the mechanics of the resurrection—how a corpse which had been reduced to dust or ashes could be raised to life again. For the Greek mind such a concept was a sheer impossibility, and a number of the Corinthians, like the Athenians (Acts 17:32), were inclined to scoff.

Paul's response stresses both the *continuity* of the resurrected body with the believer's earthly remains, and their remarkable *transformation* into a glorified, spiritual body. In essence the resurrected body remains the same body, but it will become gloriously different. Thus, Jesus, as the firstfruits (1 Cor 15:20, 23), will be the pattern for all believers. His body was raised with his flesh and bones and the marks of the nails and spear, testifying to the *continuity* with his body as the disciples had known him before Easter (see Lk 24:39–40; Jn 20:20, 24–29). But his body was also transformed into a glorious, spiritual body. So, too, the Savior will transform the believer's humble (or humiliating!) body and bring it into conformity with his own glorious body (Phil 3:20–21).

Paul's argument in the remaining part of the chapter falls into three parts: First, from our common experience of the created order he shows that the wonderful change anticipated in the resurrection is not really surprising. After all, the transformation of our bodies has analogies in the planting and sprouting of grain, the wide variation in the flesh of the various creatures, and the varying brilliance of the heavenly bodies (1 Cor 15:36–44a). Second, he points again to Christ as the second Adam, the "life-giving Spirit" (15:45) who is the heavenly prototype of the new creation (15:44b–49). Finally, he concludes on a note of triumph, praising God for our victory over death in Jesus Christ and encouraging the Corinthians to stand firm in the faith (15:50–58).

Thus, Paul reminds the Corinthians that they must be patient in hope (1 Thess 1:3) and stop thinking they already possess spiritual existence in all its fullness. Their bodies are not merely encumbrances to be sloughed off at death, whereupon they finally become fully spiritual. Rather, their bodies have a glorious future in Christ. The doctrine of the resurrection of the body affirms and complements the doctrine of creation. Our created bodies, corrupted by sin, will be given new life through faith in the One who is "the resurrection and the life" (Jn 11:25).

Paul now responds to those Corinthians who had raised questions about the mechanics of the resurrection. His sharp reply ("fool") in 1 Cor 15:36 indicates that these questions were not innocent requests for information; rather, they stemmed from a deep skepticism disposed to mock the very idea of a resurrection (cf. 2 Pet 3:4). These people wanted to know how a disfigured and decomposed body could possibly rise again.

Such a questioner, Paul says, is no better than the "fool" who "says in his heart there is no God" (Pss 14:1; 53:1). The question is a further indication that some of the Corinthians have "ignorance of God" and his power (1 Cor 15:34). Again, Paul is speaking to shame them (15:34). Then he asks the inquirer to consider himself and his own experience. Literally Paul's words read: "[As for] you, what you sow is not made alive unless it dies" (15:36). The emphasis falls on the personal pronoun "you." Paul is saying: "From your everyday experience in horticulture you can observe the necessary cycle that a seed must first die before it is made alive." His words echo Jesus in Jn 12:24: "Unless a grain of wheat falls into the ground and dies, it remains alone; but if it dies, it bears much fruit."

Paul now develops the thought further (1 Cor 15:37). That seed of wheat or other grain which is sown in the ground and dies bears no resemblance to the plant that will one day emerge. Despite the continuity between the seed and the plant, they bear such a different shape and form that Paul can say that the seed is *not* the same body as "the body that is to come into being" (15:37). So it will be, Paul implies, with the believer's body. (With the term "*naked* seed" (15:37), he foreshadows the imagery in 15:53–54 of putting on clothing.)

Everything Paul has been describing depends on God's *gift* and his *free will.* He "gives" each naked seed its own distinctive "body" in keeping with his freely willed determination (15:38) to make everything reproduce according to its kind (Gen 1:11). Human beings cannot fathom how God can make a seed sprout and grow into a mature plant (Mk 4:26–29); there is a mystery about the whole process which points to the generous and almighty hand of God. In the same mysterious manner, Paul is suggesting, God will give every believer a new body in keeping with his gracious will.

Paul moves now from his consideration of vegetation to an analogy from the creation of living creatures (1 Cor 15:39). Just as plants appear in an enormous variety of forms, so there is great variety among the animals which God brought forth on the fifth and sixth days of creation (Gen 1:20–28). Paul describes them in the opposite order from the Genesis account, beginning with human beings and ending with the fish. Each of these categories—humans, domesticated animals, birds, and fish—has its distinctive physical constitution ("flesh") which places it in an entirely different order from the others.

Having considered vegetation and living creatures, Paul continues to move up the scale, drawing a third analogy from the "heavenly bodies"—the sun, moon, and stars (1 Cor 15:40–41). Not only do the "earthly bodies" (15:40)—the plants, human beings, and other creatures—display an enormous diversity in their physical forms, but the "heavenly bodies" (15:40) must also be taken into account. These have a brilliance different from and far superior to any earthly body. Moreover, among the "heavenly bodies" there is as much variety to be found as among the "earthly bodies" (cf. 15:39): the sun is brighter than the moon, the moon is brighter than the stars, and one star is brighter than another (15:41). Could anyone doubt that the Creator, with his proven capacity to form such a variety of bodies, would be able to find a suitable new form for the believer's resurrected body?

In speaking of "heavenly bodies" (1 Cor 15:40) Paul has already foreshadowed what he will say later about the nature of the Christians' resurrected bodies. They, too, will enjoy the glory of being "heavenly" (15:48) when they have been set free from the corruption and weakness of earthly bodies and will bear the image of the Man from heaven (15:42–49). Thus, Daniel's prophecy will be fulfilled: "Those who impart wisdom will shine like the shining of the firmament, and those who lead many to righteousness [will shine] like the stars for ever and ever" (Dan 12:3).

Just as everyday experience shows how God brings naked seeds to life in an amazing variety of botanical forms and creates the wonderful heterogeneity among "earthly" and "heavenly bodies" (1 Cor 15:35–41), "so" Paul concludes, "it is also [with] the resurrection of the dead" (15:42). The God who can confer such a variety of physical forms on his creation is able to give "as he has determined" (15:38).

Returning to his analogy of the seed and the plant (1 Cor 15:35–38), and taking that as his framework ("it is sown . . . it is raised," 15:42–44a), Paul contrasts the wretched condition of the "naked" (15:37) body that is sown with the glorious condition of the body that will be. The four short sentences (15:42b–44a) in which he draws this contrast have a rhythm that evokes that of seedtime and harvest.

The first sentence (15:42b) provides the pattern and is primary, for Paul picks up the terminology of "corruption" and "incorruption" again in 15:50, 53, 54. The body that is sown in the ground is decaying and breaking down. But this process will be gloriously reversed when it is raised imperishable (cf. Rom 8:21). Then the believer's body will be conformed to that of his Lord, whose body never saw corruption (Acts 2:27, 31; 13:35–37).

The second sentence (1 Cor 15:43a) speaks of how in death a person's body is stripped of all dignity, despite efforts at beautification. But though it is buried "in dishonor" and humiliation, it will be raised glorified and radiant like Christ's glorified body (cf. Phil 3:20–21; Col 3:4).

The third sentence (1 Cor 15:43b) adds the assurance that no longer will the risen body be subject to "weakness," illness and weariness.

In the fourth sentence (1 Cor 15:44a) Paul explicitly calls what is sown a "body" and contrasts the "natural body" that is sown with all its limitations to the supernatural (literally, "spiritual") body with which we will be vested in the resurrection. The risen body will no longer be subject to the earthly limitations and mortality that result from the fall, nor to the tug-of-war with the sinful flesh, but will be wholly enlivened and pervaded by the Holy Spirit.

1 CORINTHIANS 15:44B–49

Application of the Analogies: It Is Raised a Spiritual Body

TRANSLATION

15 [44b]If there is a natural body, there is also a spiritual
body. [45]And so it is written: "The first man, Adam,
became a living soul"; the last Adam [became] a life-
giving Spirit. [46]But the spiritual [did] not [come]
first but the natural, then the spiritual. [47]The first
man [is] of the earth, made of dust; the second man
[is] from heaven. [48]As [is] the man of dust, so also
[are] those [who are] of the dust; and as [is] the man
of heaven, so also [are] those [who are] of heaven.
[49]And as we wore the image of the man of dust, we
will also wear the image of the man of heaven.

COMMENTARY

1 Cor 15:44b–49 may be viewed as an extended meditation on the depiction in Gen 2:7 of the formation of Adam, balanced and amplified by Paul's reflections on the role of Christ as second Adam. Sentence after sentence has a nice balance between a statement about Adam in the first part (15:45a, 47a, 48a, 49a) and about Christ in the second part (15:45b, 47b, 48b, 49b).

Whereas some in Corinth were denying the resurrection of the body, Paul now assures them that just as surely as there is a natural body, so surely will there be a spiritual body (15:44). Scriptural proof for this statement he finds in Gen 2:7c, where the Lord God breathes into the man's nostrils the breath of life, thus animating the body he had formed from the ground, "and man became a living being." In 1 Cor 15:45a Paul has added two words, "first" and "Adam," to the quotation, thus making explicit the Adam-Christ typology which he first introduced in 15:21–22.

After the Genesis citation Paul balances the sentence with words of his own composition referring to Christ as "the last Adam" and the "life-giving Spirit" (1 Cor 15:45b). No other human being will appear after Jesus with the same significance for the whole human race. He stands as the second and *last* Adam, the head of the new humanity, as the first Adam heads the old humanity. Whereas the first Adam was merely a life-receiving human, the last Adam is the life-giving Son of God. As his risen and ascended body is enlivened by the Spirit, so he will pour out the life-giving Spirit on the bodies of believers.

Paul now underlines the proper historical order: Adam precedes Christ; the natural body precedes the spiritual body (15:46). According to that order, Adam, the first man, was formed from the *dust* of the earth (Gen 2:7a) and after his fall into sin came under this condemnation: "dust you are, and to dust you will return" (Gen 3:19). The stress at the end of 1 Cor 15:47a falls on the term "made of dust." Adam's origin is in the dust; dust and corruption form his destiny (cf. 1 Cor 15:42). On the other hand, the second man's origin and destiny is heaven. The stress at the end of 15:47b falls on "from heaven." In Johannine terms, the Son of God came down from heaven to do the Father's will, and once his mission was accomplished he returned to the Father (Jn 3:13, 31).

Adam is the head and representative of the whole human race. Just as he is "the man of dust," so all human beings born in the ordinary course of nature are people "of the dust" (1 Cor 15:48). Adam has set his stamp on them. Adam's first children were conceived and born "in his image, after his likeness" (Gen 5:3), and all his subsequent descendants shared in his human frailty. By the same token, just as Christ is "the man of heaven" (1 Cor 15:48), so all those who belong to him by baptismal incorporation into his body (12:13) and by faith are people "of heaven" (15:48). As citizens of heaven, they enjoy the great confidence expressed in John's first epistle: "When he appears we will be like him, for we will see him as he is" (1 Jn 3:2; cf. Phil 3:20).

Maintaining the pattern of balancing a statement about Adam with a statement about Christ, Paul concludes his reflections on their comparative significance for humanity with these words: "And as we wore the image of the man of dust, we will also wear the image of the man of heaven" (1 Cor 15:49). Noteworthy in this final comparison is the change to the first person plural, "*we* wore . . . *we* will also wear" (15:49). The apostle is now applying the general statements of 15:44b–48 to himself and to all Christians personally, including the Corinthians, assuring us of the blessed destiny in store for us (cf. similar first person plural assurances in 1 Thess 4:15–17). Paul thus anticipates the first person plural verbs of 1 Cor 15:51–52, "we will not all sleep, but we will all be changed."

The first part of the comparison (15:49a) gathers up and reaffirms the sobering theme of human frailty and corruptibility that has been developed in 15:42–48. Here, in this life, we have all worn the garment of human flesh, a garment subject to the "corruption," "dishonor," and "weakness" (15:49) of fallen human nature. As Seth bore the image of his father Adam (Gen 5:3), the man formed from dust in the image of God but then condemned to return to dust because of his sin (Gen 3:14–19), so all of us in subsequent generations have borne the image of that first frail man of dust.

But, Paul promises his readers, just as surely as our lives here are stamped by frailty and decay, so surely "we will . . . wear the image of the man of heaven" (1 Cor 15:49b). Restoration of the divine image comes through Christ, who is the man of/from heaven (1 Cor 15:47–49) and who is the "image of the unseen God" (Col 1:15). In his later epistle to the Romans Paul will explain that "those whom God foreknew, he also foreordained to be conformed to the *image* of his Son" (Rom 8:29). This conforming takes place through reading and hearing the Scriptures in faith: "We all, beholding the Lord's glory with unveiled faces, are being conformed to his image from glory to glory, which comes from the Lord, who is the Spirit" (2 Cor 3:18). That same connection between God's *glory,* the image of Christ, and the work of the *Spirit,* through whom God brings about the glorious transformation to eternal life, is evident in 1 Cor 15:42–49. The Christian's body will be raised "in *glory*" (15:43). We will fully bear "the *image* of the man of heaven" (15:49), and so our eschatological state will be "*spiritual*" (15:44, 46).

1 CORINTHIANS 15:50–58

The Mystery of the Transformation

TRANSLATION

15 [50]Now this [is what] I am saying, brothers: flesh and
blood are not able to inherit the kingdom of God,
nor does corruption inherit incorruption. [51]See, I
am telling you a mystery: we will not all sleep, but we
will all be changed, [52]in a moment, in the twinkling
of an eye, at the last trumpet. For the trumpet will
sound, and the dead will be raised incorruptible
and we will be changed. [53]For it is necessary for this
corruptible [body] to be clothed with incorruption,
and for this mortal [body] to be clothed with
immortality. [54]And when this corruptible [body]
is clothed with incorruption, and this mortal
[body] is clothed with immortality, then there will
come into effect the word that has been written:

> Death has been swallowed up in victory.
> [55]Where, death, is your victory?
> Where, death, is your sting?

[56]Now the sting of death is sin, and the power of
sin is the Law. [57]But thanks be to God who gives
us the victory through our Lord Jesus Christ.

[58]So, my beloved brothers, be steadfast, immovable,
always abounding in the work of the Lord, knowing
that your labor is not in vain in the Lord.

COMMENTARY

OUR CORRUPT, MORTAL BODIES WILL BE CLOTHED WITH INCORRUPTION AND IMMORTALITY (15:50–57)

The scoffers in Corinth had demanded to know this: "How are the dead raised? And with what kind of body do they come?" (1 Cor 15:35). They could not conceive that God would take any further interest in the disfigured human corpse; in fact, they found the whole idea abhorrent. In response to these skeptics, Paul has been contending that there are many kinds of bodies. No one should imagine that the almighty Creator of the immense variety of earthly and heavenly bodies would be limited to resuscitating our bodies in the same form in which they were buried. The body that will be raised will not be "the same flesh" (15:39) but radically "different" (15:39, 41).

Paul now sums up his argument as he moves toward the triumphant climax: "This [is what] I am saying, brothers" (15:50). Of course, the skeptics are right in thinking that flesh and blood cannot inherit God's kingdom. For ever since humanity fell into sin, "flesh and blood" marks what is most perishable about us, designating our natural limitations and weaknesses as human beings, our frailty as people "of dust" (15:47–48; cf. Heb 2:14; 4:15), who are doomed to die (Gen 2:17) and return to dust (Gen 3:19). Thus, the phrase "flesh and blood" in 1 Cor 15:50a parallels "corruption" in 15:50b. Flesh and blood, corruption, dishonor, weakness, and natural limitations (cf. 15:42–44) characterize our lives in this fleeting world (7:31). They belong to the order of things that comes "first" (15:46), under the headship of Adam, "the man of dust" (15:47–49). But they have no place in the coming eschatological order under Christ. Through Holy Baptism the Christian is "baptized . . . into one body" (1 Cor 12:13)—Christ's body—and so the Christian will be raised bodily even as Christ was. Only after his old flesh-and-blood self has been "washed," "sanctified," and "justified" (6:11) and clothed with incorruptibility, glory, and power, will he be able to enter his heavenly inheritance.

Twice in 15:50 Paul states that the believer's place in God's kingdom is something he will "inherit." The verb underlines that the believer receives eternal life purely as a gift. Just as Israel received Canaan as an inheritance, so believers receive new spiritual bodies and enter the kingdom not as something they have earned but as God's gracious gift to his children (cf. Mt 25:34; 1 Pet 1:4). In 1 Corinthians 15 Paul does not develop the implications of "inherit." Other passages in Scripture connect the reception of the inheritance to the express will of the testator (cf., e.g., Genesis 27; Numbers 36). The Lord's institution of "the new *testament* in my blood" (1 Cor 11:25) may be connected to the idea of inheriting the kingdom in the resurrection in 15:50–58. The faithful reception of the body and blood of the crucified and risen Christ promises the communicant a share in the resurrection and in the heavenly inheritance guaranteed by Christ's death and resurrection.

With the exclamation "see!" in 15:51, Paul signals that he is about to say something of great significance. What he will tell them is a "mystery," something that can only be known by divine revelation (15:51; cf. 2:7; 13:2; 14:2; and also Rom 11:25–36). In contrast to the similar revelation in 1 Thess 4:15–17, where "the word of the Lord" assures the congregation that those who die in the Lord will not be at a disadvantage in the parousia, here Paul's concern is with those who are still living on earth when Christ returns. If the living cannot enter the kingdom in their corruptible flesh and blood, what will be the fate of those who are alive when the Lord returns? Some commentators have thought that the first person plural verbs in this text indicate that Paul expected Christ's return in his own lifetime, but this is not necessarily the case. He may simply be identifying himself with those Christians who will be alive at that time. Not every Christian will fall asleep in Christ; some will still be alive when he returns.

But whether "we" are alive or in the grave on that day, "we will all be changed" (1 Cor 15:51). This verb echoes 15:39 and 15:41 in a fine play on words: just as God's ingenuity and his lavish generosity in creation has arranged for there to be one flesh of humans, "another" of animals, "another" of birds, and "another" of fish (15:39), and for the sun, the moon, and the stars each to have "another" brilliance (three times in 15:41), so by that same divine provision (note the divine passive, which implies that God is the agent) we will all be made totally "other" (an alternate translation for "changed," 15:51).

The transformation will take place in a flash (15:52). Paul uses colorful language to describe how instantaneously our bodies will be changed. The first phrase in 15:52, "in a moment," literally denotes an instant of time that is indivisible. The second phrase in 15:52, "in the blinking of an eye," or as most English translations have it, "in the twinkling of an eye," denotes a movement of the eye that is so rapid it is almost undetectable.

Paul then adds a third phrase, "at the last trumpet" (15:52). At Mt. Sinai loud trumpet blasts from heaven signaled the Lord's descent to the top of the mountain and his proclamation of the Ten Commandments (Ex 19:13, 16, 19; 20:18). Later, Israel would advance through the desert and march against her enemies upon the signal from the two silver trumpets. These were also blown on days of rejoicing in God's redemption (Num 10:1–10). When God finally subdues all the enemies of his people, including death, "the last enemy" (1 Cor 15:26), and confers on believers the redemption of their bodies (Rom 8:23), it is fitting for the great moment to be heralded by a trumpet blast (cf. Mt 24:31; 1 Thess 4:16).

Paul explains that God's trumpet will indeed sound and rouse the dead from their sleep. Their bodies, corrupted in the grave, will then be raised "incorruptible" (1 Cor 15:52). Furthermore, Paul assures the Corinthians again, "we"—that is, all Christians, whether dead or alive at the last trumpet—"will be changed" (15:52).

After all, this transformation "is necessary" (15:53). It has the divine mandate. God's plan to overcome death and restore his creation by first raising his Son and then raising believers is laid out in the OT Scriptures, and therefore *must* (15:53) be fulfilled. According to this plan, "it is necessary" that there be continuity between God's original creation and our newly recreated bodies. Almost as if he is regarding his own body as he speaks, four times in 15:53–54 Paul uses the demonstrative pronoun "this." It is precisely *this* perishable, mortal body of dust (15:47–49), the subject of so much weakness, humiliation, and affliction (cf. 2 Cor 12:7–10), that must be endued with "life and immortality through the Gospel" (2 Tim 1:10).

Thus, when he is roused from sleep at the dawning of God's kingdom, the believer must be clothed with the new outfit which goes with life in the eternal kingdom—a new spiritual body that is incorruptible and immortal (1 Cor 15:53–54). The God "who alone possesses immortality" (1 Tim 6:16) graciously confers immortality on his people. Freed now from the groaning and anxiety which have weighed them down as long as they lived in their earthly "tents," they see their mortality finally "swallowed up by life" (2 Cor 5:1–4).

When this investiture takes place, the prophecy of Isaiah will come true: "Death has been swallowed up in victory" (1 Cor 15:54, drawing on Is 25:8). The original prophecy has "the Lord of hosts" (Is 25:6) as the subject of this sentence: "He will swallow up death for ever, and the Lord God will wipe away tears from all faces" (Is 25:8; the latter part is quoted in Rev 21:4). But Paul inverts the grammar by making death ("the last enemy," 1 Cor 15:26) the subject, thus bringing it into sharper focus as the evil force which will at last be swallowed up. Christ has won the final victory over death, bringing about its total subjugation and extinction. Therefore, "there will be no more death" (Rev 21:4; cf. 2 Tim 1:10; Heb 2:14).

Paul now sings a taunt song over this defeated opponent in 1 Cor 15:55, saying in essence: "Where, death, is all your power now? Where, death, is your ability to cause people so much pain?" His words are freely adapted from Hos 13:14. Christ has removed the sting of this malignant enemy; it is no longer able to harm Christian people.

Why, it may be asked, is death so painful if it is nothing but the transition to immortality? Paul explains in 1 Cor 15:56 that it is the power of sin that makes death a bitter "enemy" (15:26) which rules the human race with an iron hand. Sin stings the conscience of the dying person and is responsible for the painful breakdown of his body. The very separation of body and soul is an assault on our humanity, for human beings are not essentially only a body or a soul, but both, joined together. Later, Paul would write to the Romans: "The wages of sin is death" (Rom 6:23). The Christian knows that death came into the world through Adam's sin and has spread to all people, including himself, because all have sinned (1 Cor 15:21–22; see also Rom 5:12). However, while the Christian must still suffer the physical consequence of Adam's sin, he does not die "in" his sins (1 Cor 15:17; cf. Jn 8:24). He dies absolved. Since the Christian is reckoned as sinless for Christ's sake, death cannot hold him.

In addition to sin, the other power that drives the engine of death is the Law (1 Cor 15:56). God's Law, as Paul will insist in the letter to the Romans, is "holy and just and good" (Rom 7:12). The Law holds up a mirror to reveal to us our sins (Rom 7:7). Moreover, it actually arouses and stimulates sinful passions within the fallen person, giving them a bridgehead within a person's heart (Rom 7:8–11). This rearing up of sin, in turn, arouses God's wrath and condemnation (Rom 2:12; 4:15).

Nevertheless, Paul continues, these grim forces themselves are doomed: God has been victorious over them. Through the death and resurrection of Jesus Christ he has swallowed up death forever (Is 25:8). Death's stinger has been withdrawn. Just as death can no longer harm Christ, so it cannot permanently harm those who are in Christ, for God has transferred the benefits of Christ's conquest of death to us. Thus, God "gives us the victory through our Lord Jesus Christ" (1 Cor 15:57; cf. 1 Jn 5:4). Thus, Paul breaks out in doxology: "Thanks be to God!"

A FINAL APPEAL: BE STEADFAST! (15:58)

A strong "so" introduces the final verse of 1 Corinthians 15, inviting the reader to reflect on everything Paul has taught concerning the resurrection and to draw the proper conclusions. If Christ is risen, and your bodies are also to rise, "what kind of people ought you to be?" (2 Pet 3:11). Appealing to them tenderly as "my beloved brothers" (1 Cor 15:58), Paul exhorts them to be steadfast, in words very similar to Col 1:23: "Continue in your faith, founded and steadfast and not moved from the hope of the Gospel." He is concerned for them because their skepticism about basic doctrines like the resurrection has inevitably led to instability (cf. Eph 4:14). The Christian hope should provide them with a firm anchorage for their souls (Heb 6:19).

Furthermore, the Christian hope should foster fruitful service of Christ and the brother. Picking up themes from earlier in the chapter, Paul calls the Corinthians to be "always abounding in the work of the Lord, knowing that your *labor* is not *in vain* in the Lord" (15:58; cf. 15:10). In imitation of the apostle's own pattern, the Corinthians are not to spend their days being "disorderly" or "idle, lazy" (1 Thess 5:14) as frequently happens when Christians lose their eschatological vision (cf. 1 Thess 4:11–18; 2 Thess 3:6–13), but to devote themselves wholeheartedly to loving service of the Lord and others (cf. 1 Cor 16:10, 13–14; Col 3:17). The hope of the Gospel should energize them to labor diligently in their respective vocations, serving their families and neighbors wholeheartedly. The final phrase is significant: labor done "in the Lord" (1 Cor 15:58) is never in vain. The Christian on earth may not ever perceive the fruit of his labor. Hard and faithful work may go unrecognized by the church. But the Lord knows the labors of each of his servants, and the day is coming when each faithful servant will receive the commendation of his Lord and the eternal reward by grace (3:10–15).

1 CORINTHIANS 16:1–24

CONCLUSION

16:1–4	The Collection for the Saints in Jerusalem
16:5–9	Paul's Travel Plans
16:10–12	Concerning Timothy and Apollos
16:13–14	Marching Orders
16:15–18	Recognize Stephanas and Others like Him!
16:19–24	Greetings, Anathema, Maranatha, Benediction

1 CORINTHIANS 16:1–4

The Collection for the Saints in Jerusalem

TRANSLATION

16 1 Now concerning the collection for the saints: just as
I directed the churches of Galatia, so you should do
also. 2 On the first day of every week let each of you
put [something] aside for safekeeping in proportion
to his income, so that when I come no collections
need to be made then. 3 And when I come, those
whom you approve I will send with letters to carry
your gracious gift to Jerusalem. 4 And if it should be
appropriate for me to go too, they will travel with me.

COMMENTARY

In this concluding chapter Paul turns to a number of ways in which the saints in Corinth, Paul himself, and his co-workers can show themselves to be "steadfast, immovable, always abounding in the work of the Lord" (1 Cor 15:58). First, he points to the collection for the saints in Jerusalem and urges the Corinthians to give that project special attention (16:1–4). Then he speaks of the itinerary he has planned through Macedonia and Corinth, but says he cannot embark on his journey as yet because of the door, great and "effective" (16:9—from the same Greek word family as "work" in 15:58), that stands open to him in Ephesus (16:5–9). Then he turns to his co-workers: Timothy, engaged in the "work" of the Lord (16:10–11); Apollos likewise (16:12). Next he exhorts all the saints to be strong and loving as they go about their work (16:13–14), and he calls for the Corinthians to be subordinate to all who, like Stephanas, "work together" (16:16—from the same word family again) and toil (16:15–18). The chapter closes with a series of greetings (16:19–24).

THE COLLECTION (16:1–4)

One excellent avenue for the Corinthians to abound "in the work of the Lord" (15:58) presented itself in a project dear to the apostle's heart, the collection for "the poor among the saints in Jerusalem" (Rom 15:26). In his second epistle to Corinth he will devote considerable space to the final preparations for the collection (2 Corinthians 8–9), encouraging his hearers to develop a self-sufficient attitude so that they "may abound in every good work" (2 Cor 9:8; see also 2 Cor 8:7). The collection was a broad interchurch project, involving the churches of Galatia and Macedonia in addition to Corinth and the other churches of Achaia. Thus, Paul was able to stimulate a friendly rivalry, holding up the example of their sister churches to urge the Corinthians to a greater effort (2 Cor 8:1–6; 9:2–4).

The Corinthians had asked Paul for further clarification "concerning the collection" (1 Cor 16:1). They were already familiar with the project but needed more information on how to proceed. The money was "for the saints" (16:1). From 16:3 and other texts we know that Paul did not mean their fellow Christians in general, but those members of the mother church in Jerusalem who had become impoverished (cf. Rom 15:25–28). Why they had fallen into poverty we can only speculate. All we know for certain is that the church had a large number of widows (Acts 6:1–6) and had suffered from famine (Acts 11:27–30). Paul believed the newly founded daughter churches in Macedonia, Achaia, and Galatia, who had reaped spiritual benefits from the mother church in Jerusalem, were indebted to minister to their mother in her physical needs (Rom 15:27). He had already directed the Galatian churches (1 Cor 16:1), the fruit of his first missionary journey (Acts 13–14), to pave the way. Now the Corinthians were to follow.

Paul now outlines the procedure (1 Cor 16:2). Every Sunday ("every first day after the Sabbath," the literal meaning of 16:2), each member of the congregation, no matter how poor, should store up (literally "treasure up") in his home an amount in keeping with how well he had fared during the week. Paul wanted the Corinthians to give only what they could spare (cf. Acts 11:29). As he assured them in his second epistle, "I do not mean that there should be relief for others and pressure on you, but it is a question of a fair balance between your present abundance and their need" (2 Cor 8:13–14 NRSV). Paul may also be suggesting that by this unselfish action the Corinthians will be storing up treasures in heaven (cf. Mt 6:19–21, where "store up treasure" [the same verb used in 1 Cor 16:2] and the noun "treasure" are used).

The small amount each person would set aside each Sunday would soon accumulate to a significant sum, so that when Paul arrived in Corinth, together with delegates from Macedonia, he would find the gift ready and waiting. This would spare Paul and his companions, not to mention the Corinthians, any embarrassment. Thus, Paul would be spared the need to exert personal pressure by making a last-minute appeal, and the Corinthians would be spared having to rustle up in haste whatever they could find (2 Cor 9:3–5).

In 1 Cor 16:3 Paul refers to his impending visit (as he did in 4:18–21), the details of which he will spell out in the next paragraph (16:5–9). When he comes to Corinth, he will supply the congregation's chosen representatives with letters of introduction to the church in Jerusalem (16:3). Such references were a regular part of business practice in the ancient world. The plural "letters" may suggest that each member of the delegation carried a personal recommendation from Paul. Paul is careful to entrust the collection and conveying of this gracious gift to the church's representatives. At no time would he touch any of it with his own hands. Thus, no one could accuse Paul of defrauding the church (2 Cor 12:17–18). Moreover, it was fitting that the Gentiles' gift be carried to the mother church by Gentiles.

Paul is still undecided whether or not to accompany the delegation. It depends on whether it would be "worthy" or "fitting" (1 Cor 16:4). It is unlikely this means that Paul is waiting to see whether the gift is substantial enough to make it worthwhile for him to go along. More likely he is concerned to find out if the Corinthians think it "proper" for him to join them in conveying the gift. After all, it is their gift, not his (16:3). He does not want to participate without their consent (cf. Philemon 14).

Moreover, it is significant how the apostle takes up this issue without pressure, gimmicks, or emotion. The contrast with many highly visible campaigns for money is noteworthy.

1 CORINTHIANS 16:5–9

Paul's Travel Plans

TRANSLATION

**16 [5]I will come to you when I travel through Macedonia.
For I am traveling through Macedonia, [6]and if
possible I will remain with you, or even spend the
winter with you, so that you may send me on my way
wherever I may go. [7]For I do not wish now to see you
in passing, for I hope to remain with you for some
time if the Lord permits. [8]But I will stay in Ephesus
until Pentecost, [9]for a door has opened up for me,
great and effective, and there are many opponents.**

COMMENTARY

Paul's discussion of the arrangements for the collection led him to touch on his travel plans (1 Cor 16:3–4), which he now proceeds to spell out in more detail (16:5–9). First he explains that he will not be able to visit the Corinthians immediately. When he does, it will be by the land route through Macedonia, the route he had followed on his second missionary journey. He hopes to set out soon after Pentecost (i.e., late spring) and spend summer and possibly the early part of fall strengthening and encouraging the Macedonian churches (Philippi, Thessalonica, Berea). After writing this epistle, his anxiety for the Corinthian church prompted him to formulate a plan to visit the Corinthians first, and then visit them again after his time in Macedonia. Thus, they would have "a double favor" (2 Cor 1:15–16). Upon more mature consideration, however, Paul reverted to his original plan outlined here. He traveled from Ephesus to Macedonia, and then spent three months in Corinth (Acts 20:2–3).

Paul assures the Corinthians that he does not want to make merely a fleeting visit; he hopes to stay with them a significant amount of time (1 Cor 16:7). Envisioning that he would arrive in the fall, he had thoughts of even spending the whole winter with them, since further travel during that season would normally be out of the question. That would depend, of course, on the Lord's will (16:7; cf. Acts 18:21; James 4:15). Paul knew he was not the master of his fate. Indeed, he had experienced how the Lord could block his plans and send him in another direction (Acts 16:6–7). But if the Lord permitted him to spend some time with the Corinthians, this would give them ample opportunity to provide him with the necessary food, money, and traveling companions for the next stage of his missionary work (1 Cor 16:6). Having earlier refused to accept any assistance from the Corinthians, in order to make it crystal clear that his Gospel came free of charge (1 Corinthians 9), Paul now graciously offers them an opportunity to share in his ministry.

He was still not sure where the Lord would lead him after his stay in Corinth (cf. 16:4). It is likely that places such as Illyricum and Spain were at the back of his mind. But soon after writing this epistle he "resolved in the Spirit" that his next destination should be Jerusalem (Acts 19:21).

In the meantime, however, he informs the Corinthians (1 Cor 16:8) that he will continue his ministry in Ephesus until Pentecost (May/June). His three-year ministry in that prominent city had resulted in many residents of Asia, both Jews and Greeks, hearing the Word of the Lord (Acts 19:10; 20:21, 31). The Word had grown mightily and prevailed (Acts 19:20). The Lord had indeed opened for him a "great and effective" door (1 Cor 16:9) for the Gospel, in accordance with the prayers of Paul and his fellow believers (2 Cor 2:12; Col 4:3). Whereas human efforts per se are totally ineffective in bringing people to faith, the Lord provides open doors and opens hearts and eyes as he wills.

The other side of the coin is that wherever there are great opportunities for the Gospel, there great opposition arises (1 Cor 16:9). Paul had experienced this from the beginning in Ephesus (Acts 19:9). Whether he is writing before or after the great riot in the Ephesian theater (Acts 19:23–40) we do not know, but the incident gives us an impression of the volatile situation. By the time he wrote 1 Corinthians his opponents' attacks had become so severe that he testified, "I fought wild beasts in Ephesus" (1 Cor 15:32; cf. 2 Cor 1:8). The apostle's experience parallels that of his Lord, whose fruitful ministry was carried on in the face of many opponents, and the common experience of other faithful pastors. But Paul did not allow his opponents to frighten him (Phil 1:28); in proclaiming the gospel, the places of greatest risk are sometimes the places of greatest opportunity.

1 CORINTHIANS 16:10–12
Concerning Timothy and Apollos

TRANSLATION

**16 [10]Now when Timothy comes, see that he comes to
you without fear, for he is doing the Lord's work
as I am. [11]So let no one despise him, but send
him on his way in peace, that he may come to me.
For I am waiting for him with the brothers.**

**[12]Now concerning Apollos the brother, I strongly
urged him to come to you with the brothers. And
yet it was not at all [his] will that he would come
now. But he will come when he has an opportunity.**

COMMENTARY

TIMOTHY (16:10–11)

Earlier Paul had informed the Corinthians that he had sent Timothy to them. Timothy, his "beloved and faithful child in the Lord," would remind them of Paul's ways in Christ Jesus (1 Cor 4:17). The younger man now making his way to Corinth was engaged in the great work of the Lord (16:10) no less than the apostle who was so actively engaged in Ephesus (16:9; cf. 15:58). If the Corinthians were to create difficulties for Timothy, they would be obstructing the work of the Lord. Thus, they should welcome him as they would welcome Paul, their father in the faith (4:14–15).

Paul had grounds for concern on Timothy's behalf. Timothy seems to have suffered from a timid disposition, which caused stomach trouble and other ailments (1 Tim 5:21–23; 2 Tim 1:6–8; 2:1, 3, 15; 4:1–2). Moreover, he was a young man, perhaps still in his twenties. Several years later Paul still felt the need to urge him, "Let no one despise your youth" (1 Tim 4:12). There were a number of arrogant people in Corinth (1 Cor 3:1–3; 4:18; 5:2) who were probably not above treating a young and timid pastor with contempt. Especially was this likely to occur if some had taken offense at the apostle's latest epistle and were inclined to take out their resentment on his representative. Paul attempts to forestall such attacks with his word of warning, "Let no one despise him" (16:11).

Rather, the Corinthians should give him a warm welcome, which would allay his fears, and send him on his way back to Paul in peace (16:11). This serves as a gentle reminder that Timothy will be reporting back to Paul. Whether Paul comes to the Corinthians "with a stick, or in love and a spirit of gentleness" (4:21) will depend to no small extent on how they treat Timothy.

According to one possible reading of 16:11, Paul could be expecting Timothy to be accompanied by some brothers. From Acts 19:22 we learn that Timothy had set out for Macedonia and Corinth with Erastus, but no other brother is mentioned there. Paul may have sent some unnamed Christians from Ephesus along with Timothy and Erastus, or he may have been expecting Timothy and Erastus to return with brothers from the Corinthian church. But another way of understanding the phrase "with the brothers" (1 Cor 16:11) is to connect it with Paul, the subject of the sentence, as in the Jerusalem Bible: "the brothers and I are waiting for him." That connection would reinforce to the Corinthians that Timothy is a representative of the larger church. If they mistreat Timothy, he will report this not only to Paul, but also to these other brothers, who would lend their weight to appropriate corrective measures.

APOLLOS (16:12)

Paul comes now to the sixth and final topic raised in the Corinthians' prior letter to him: the question of when they could expect a visit from Apollos. Paul speaks of his co-worker affectionately as "the brother." There is no jealousy or rivalry between the two men. If there were, Paul would not have been so keen that Apollos join "the brothers" (16:12) Stephanas, Fortunatus, and Achaicus (16:17) when they returned to Corinth, for that would give the eloquent Alexandrian a chance to increase his personal following. But Paul considered Apollos to be a faithful servant of God who had "watered" the Corinthian congregation which Paul had "planted" (3:6), and Paul stated that he and Apollos were "one" (3:8).

Apollos, however, had insisted that he would not go to Corinth at the present time; "it was not at all [his] will" (16:12). The tense of the Greek verb for "it was" probably indicates that Apollos was no longer with Paul at the time of writing. If Apollos were still in Ephesus, presumably Paul would have added a greeting from Apollos in 16:19–24.

We can only guess why Apollos was unwilling to visit Corinth at that time. He may have been too busy with new tasks in another area, or he may have feared that the faction in Corinth which claimed him as their leader (1:12; 3:4–6, 22; 4:6) would make too much of him at the expense of the church's unity. Whatever the reasons, he had assured Paul that he would visit the congregation as soon as he found a suitable opportunity.

1 CORINTHIANS 16:13–14
MARCHING ORDERS

TRANSLATION

16 [13]Be watchful, stand in the faith, be manly, be strong. [14]Let all you do be in love.

COMMENTARY

Paul moves swiftly to conclude the epistle. Almost in the fashion of a general, he issues five crisp commands to his hearers. His words do not come totally out of the blue, however; they echo and reinforce 15:58: "Be steadfast, immovable, always abounding in the work of the Lord."

The first four commands use imagery from warfare (cf. 1 Macc 12:27; Eph 6:10–17) to urge the Corinthians to be Christian soldiers who stand in constant battle readiness and conduct themselves in a courageous manner on the field. Like ancient Israel in the wilderness (e.g., Num 1:3), the church is an army on the march. The final command (1 Cor 16:14) reminds the Corinthians that an army cannot be divided against itself; it must be cohesive and united in its campaign, which in the case of the church is driven by God's "love" (16:14) in Christ Jesus.

Paul's first admonition is to "be watchful" and alert (16:13), which is the antonym of being asleep or drunk (1 Thess 5:6–10; Ignatius to Polycarp 1:3). It includes watching for the day of the Lord, lest that day come upon the believer unawares (Mk 13:33–37), and watching against the devil, false teachers, and various temptations (Mk 14:38; Acts 20:31; 1 Pet 5:8–9).

Second, the Christian should continue to "stand in the faith" (1 Cor 16:13). Earlier Paul had reminded the Corinthians that they were standing in the Gospel (15:1), but now he urges them not to become slack and weary in the struggle. The antonym would be to fall from grace by abandoning the faith. "Let him who thinks he is standing watch that he doesn't fall" (10:12). Instead of slouching, the Christian soldier should "stand" his ground (Eph 6:11, 13–14; cf. Rev 14:1), refusing to give an inch as he stands in the Lord (1 Thess 3:8) and contends for the Gospel (Jude 3).

Then Paul urges the Corinthians: "Be manly, be strong" (1 Cor 16:13). These two imperatives are paired together in the admonitions in Ps 27:14 and Ps 31:24. But such admonitions were also common in the exhortations that preceded Israel's holy wars. In Hebrew the imperatives "be strong" and "be courageous" are paired in exhortations for Joshua and Israel not to fear the Canaanites, but to fight and conquer the Promised Land, confident that the Lord will fight with and for them and fulfill his covenant promises (Deut 3:28; 31:6–7, 23; Josh 1:6–7, 9,

18; 10:25). God's people are not to let their hearts shake "as the trees of the forest shake before the wind" (Is 7:2). Rather, with firm confidence in the Lord, they are to acquit themselves in a manly fashion on the field of battle, letting the Lord strengthen them in the inner man (Eph 3:16).

Finally, with the fifth imperative of 1 Cor 16:13–14, Paul urges the Corinthians, "Let all you do *be* in love" (16:14). His call for manliness and courage should not be taken to mean they were at liberty to be aggressive and abusive toward others. No army can function if the troops are constantly fighting among themselves (cf. Gal 5:15). From the beginning of the epistle, his major concern has been to promote Christian love and unity (1 Cor 1:9) in the face of divisive, arrogant, and inconsiderate tendencies within the congregation. This culminated in his great chapter in praise of Christian love (13:1–13). Everything God's people do in the work of the Lord should bear the imprint of that love.

1 CORINTHIANS 16:15–18

Recognize Stephanas and Others like Him!

TRANSLATION

16 [15]I also urge you, brothers—[for] you know the
household of Stephanas, that it is the firstfruits of
Achaia and they have set themselves to serving the
saints— [16]to set yourselves in subordination to such
people and to everyone who works together and toils.
[17]But I am rejoicing in the presence of Stephanas and
Fortunatus and Achaicus, because these men have
made up for your absence. [18]For they have refreshed
my spirit and yours. Therefore recognize such people.

COMMENTARY

This paragraph serves as a letter of recommendation for Stephanas, Fortunatus, and Achaicus, who would bear 1 Corinthians back to Corinth. Paul urges the congregation to continue to hold these men in high honor for their service.

The household of Stephanas had been "the firstfruits of Achaia" (1 Cor 16:15), just as Epainetus' household had become the firstfruits of Asia (Rom 16:5). According to Acts 17:34 the Athenians Dionysius the Areopagite, a woman called Damaris, and "others with them" had come to faith before anyone in Corinth. Stephanas and his family may have been among those "others," if they were living in Athens at the time (see the commentary on 1:16 for a discussion of that possibility). Whether he was resident in Athens or elsewhere, he must have been the first convert in Achaia to bring his entire household to Baptism (1 Cor 1:16). The whole family, then, together with the servants, set themselves to the service of the saints.

The expression "set themselves" (16:15) means that they ordered their lives and routines to function as a unit which served that one great purpose. Paul does not spell out what their service to the saints consisted of, but undoubtedly it included above all the ministry of the Gospel together with constant acts of Christian love and helpfulness. It may not be far off the mark to see here the ideal picture of a pastor's household, ordering itself so that it can best provide for "the work of ministry."

Since the members of Stephanas' household have ordered their lives to serve the saints, it is fitting that the saints in Corinth give proper recognition to their service and subordinate themselves to them and to anyone else who works and toils in the Christian ministry (16:16). Paul's words reflect his earlier letter to the Thessalonians: "Now we ask you, brothers, to recognize those who labor among you and are over you in the Lord and admonish you, and to esteem them very highly in love because of their work" (1 Thess 5:12–13; cf. 1 Tim 5:17; Heb 13:17).

Paul adds his personal expression of joy that Stephanas and his two companions, Fortunatus and Achaicus, had been able to spend some time with him (1 Cor 16:17). Fortunatus ("fortunate one") and Achaicus ("man for Achaia") were probably slaves or freedmen who were attached to Stephanas' household and had received spiritual formation under his tutelage. Now this delegation had filled Paul's need to enjoy again the love, warm fellowship, and encouragement of the saints among whom he had spent eighteen months of his ministry.

Stephanas, Fortunatus, and Achaicus had performed this service to the apostle in rich measure, for their meek and humble ministrations had refreshed his spirit (16:18) in a way that reflected the ministry of their Master (Mt 11:28–29; cf. 2 Cor 7:13). But this would be no surprise to the Corinthians, who had often experienced how their own spirits were refreshed by these men. Accordingly, Paul appeals to the congregation to give such men the recognition they deserved.

1 CORINTHIANS 16:19–24
Greetings, Anathema, Maranatha, Benediction

TRANSLATION

16 [19]The churches of Asia greet you. Aquila and Prisca, together with the church in their house, send you many greetings in the Lord. [20]All the brothers greet you. Greet one another with a holy kiss.

[21]The greeting is in my own hand—Paul's. [22]If anyone does not love the Lord, let him be cursed. Marana tha! [23]The grace of the Lord Jesus [be] with you. [24]My love [is] with all of you in Christ Jesus.

COMMENTARY

Paul closes his letter with a series of greetings (1 Cor 16:19–21), followed by a solemn "anathema" on anyone who does not love the Lord (16:22a), a prayer for the Lord's return (16:22b), and a gracious benediction on the congregation (16:23–24).

GREETINGS (16:19–21)

The greetings serve as another gentle reminder that the Corinthians are not an isolated group free to go their own way; they belong to the wider communion of the church universal, which extends to them its warm affection and solidarity.

The first greetings come from "the churches of Asia" (16:19). The word "Asia" does not have its modern connotation of the vast continent by that name. Rather, it denotes the Roman province of Asia, which comprised the western third of the peninsula now known as Asia Minor or Turkey. Ephesus was the province's largest and most important city during the Roman period, with a population estimated at 200,000 to 250,000. During Paul's three-year residence in Ephesus, the Word of the Lord had radiated throughout the province (Acts 19:10)—to Colossae, Laodicea, Hierapolis (Col 4:13), and no doubt other centers. All the churches now send their greetings to their older sister in Corinth.

Especially warm greetings came from Aquila and Prisca and the church which met in their home. Aquila and Prisca had been Paul's hosts and fellow tentmakers in Corinth (Acts 18:2–3). This outstanding Jewish-Christian couple had come to Corinth from Rome, after the emperor Claudius had ordered the expulsion of all Jews from Rome. Upon the conclusion of Paul's eighteen-month ministry in Corinth, they had accompanied him as he sailed for Syria. Paul left them in Ephesus (Acts 18:18–19), where they again played a prominent role in the young church and opened their home for worship. Later, we find them back again in Rome (Rom 16:3–5; 2 Tim 4:19), with the church gathering in their home. Apparently they were a wealthy couple, with a home large enough to accommodate a house-church gathering and with the means to sustain their frequent moves from city to city. They were a capable couple, able to give Apollos the more accurate private instruction he needed in "the Way" (Acts 18:26). It has been suggested that Prisca (or Priscilla, as Luke calls her) was a particularly outstanding person, for her name is given first on four of the six occasions when the couple is mentioned.

Since Paul has already passed on comprehensive greetings from the Asian churches, the additional greetings from "all the brothers" (1 Cor 16:20) at first sight may seem redundant. But most likely it means "all the brothers of the church in Ephesus," that is, not only Aquila and Prisca and their circle, but every Christian in the city.

Just as their fellow Christians in Asia have lovingly expressed their warm affection for the Corinthians, so the Corinthians in turn should show that same affection to one another, putting behind them the frictions of the past and greeting each other "with a holy kiss" (16:20). The practice of God's people greeting each other with such a kiss has its roots in the OT, where family members and friends would greet each other or say farewell with a kiss (Gen 27:26–27; 31:28; 31:55; 45:15; Ex 18:7; 1 Sam 20:41). A kiss could also be a sign of reconciliation (Gen 33:4). The NT indicates that a similar practice existed at least among some Jews and Christians (Lk 7:38, 45; 15:20; 22:47–48; Acts 20:37). Paul calls this expression of Christian love a "holy kiss" to distinguish it from an erotic or romantic kiss and perhaps also from the treacherous kiss of a Judas.

If it may be assumed that Paul's letters were intended for reading in worship, then the holy kiss which he recommended may have followed immediately as part of the congregation's response to the reading. A century later Justin Martyr (*First Apology*, 65.2) testified that the greeting of peace followed the prayers in the common liturgy in Rome. No doubt Paul's words had great influence in shaping the development of this and other liturgical practices.

It is reasonable to suppose that 1 Corinthians was intended to be read at a congregational gathering, and that the gathering would have concluded with the kiss of peace and Holy Communion (note also the use of "maranatha" in the post-communion prayer of Didache 10:6). We should bear in mind the role of the apostle himself in instituting the liturgical forms practiced in Corinth (11:2, 23), and his constant concern throughout the epistle that the Corinthians' worship remain pure. It would therefore not be surprising if his closing words echoed formulas from worship which were so familiar to his hearers and to himself. Furthermore, there do seem to be some remarkable parallels between 16:20–24 and elements of later liturgies.

The final greeting (16:21) and the final pithy sentences (16:22–24) are penned by Paul himself with his own hand. Not only did this gesture add a personal touch at the end of a letter that probably was mostly in his secretary's handwriting (presumably Sosthenes, 1:1), but it also certified that the letter genuinely came from Paul. In 2 Thess 3:17 the apostle explains, "I, Paul, write this greeting with my own hand. This is the mark in every letter of mine; it is the way I write" (Cf. Gal 6:11; Col 4:18; 2 Thess 2:2; Philemon 19).

ANATHEMA (16:22A)

In issuing this strong injunction in the form of an anathema (1 Cor 16:22a), Paul seems to be casting his eye back over all the sorry divisions and disobedience to the Lord that have been the burden of his epistle. The Corinthians' love of human power and wisdom rather than the power and wisdom of the Crucified One (chapters 1–4), their love of worldly pleasures—the case of the incestuous man (chapter 5), the wrangling over property by means of lawsuits (6:1–8), the resorting to prostitutes (6:9–20), the reclining and eating in heathen temples (chapters 8 and 10)—and their desire for spectacular gifts (chapters 12 and 14), all amounted to human pride and love of self rather than love for the Lord. There were some in the congregation who lacked "the obedience of faith" (Rom 1:5).

Paul insists that anyone who does not love the Lord should be "anathema" (1 Cor 16:22a; cf. Rom 9:3; Gal 1:8–9). Thus, the apostle places anyone who persists in his proud, puffed up, and loveless attitudes into the hands of the living God, that he may be subject to the divine curse. "He [the Lord] repays fully him who acts proudly" (Ps 31:23). The anathema, followed as it is by the "marana tha" (1 Cor 16:22), clearly has this eschatological ring. In addition, it may also imply that Paul would direct that the congregation carry out a preliminary judgment by excommunicating such a loveless person, as in the case of the incestuous man (5:1–13). He should be regarded as one who is "cut off from Christ" (Rom 9:3) and excluded from the Christian fellowship (cf. Rom 16:17–20; 1 Cor 12:3; Gal 1:8–9). What this means for the church's practice Paul spells out in 2 Thess 3:14–15: "If anyone refuses to obey what we say in this letter, note that man, and have nothing to do with him, that he may be ashamed. Do not look on him as an enemy, but warn him as a brother." This would also mean that he could not receive the Lord's Supper until such time as he might repent and be restored to the church's fellowship.

MARANATHA (16:22B)

On the other hand, those who love the Lord and rest their hope in him may be courageous and strong, having nothing to fear from his second coming (Ps 31:23–24). Those who love the Lord love and long for his appearing (2 Tim 4:8). Thus, Paul now cries to the Lord from his heart (cf. Ps 31:22), using the language of his heart, his mother tongue, Aramaic: "Marana tha! Our Lord, come!" (1 Cor 16:22b).

Like other Aramaic or Jewish words that became common coin in the early church ("amen," "hallelujah," "hosanna"), "maranatha" seems to have been a beloved expression because of the way it gave voice to the Christian expectation and hope. Thus, Paul sounds again, and in a particularly emphatic and memorable way, the eschatological note with which the epistle began ("as you eagerly await the revelation of our Lord Jesus Christ," 1:7). This intense Christian expectation of the end is intended to help the over-excited Corinthians sober up as they wait and watch (16:13). They do not have everything "already" (4:8); the best is yet to come. Meanwhile, every celebration of the Lord's Supper takes place in eager anticipation of that day, as the church proclaims the Lord's death "until he comes" (11:26).

Paul's prayer ("marana tha," 16:22b) expresses his personal longing and the longing of all the saints. Their prayer is voiced again in the final chapter of the Bible, where John depicts the Spirit and the whole church, the bride of the Lamb, saying, "Come!" (Rev 22:17), and John himself, in response to Jesus' assurance "Surely I am coming soon," adds his firm "Amen, come, Lord Jesus" (Rev 22:20). Thus, the whole church fixes all her hope on the grace which is to be brought to her at the revelation of Jesus Christ (1 Pet 1:13).

BENEDICTION (16:23–24)

The church's longing for that ultimate grace colors and inspires Paul's final benediction: "the grace of the Lord Jesus [be] with you" (1 Cor 16:23). Until God's saints receive that final gracious deliverance, they will live by the grace of the Lord Jesus, and by his grace alone. Thus, the epistle ends as it began, with words of gracious benediction (see 1:3: "Grace to you and peace …"). Everything the Corinthians have is by grace. There is nothing which they have not received as a gracious gift from the hand of God (1 Cor 4:7). No one is more conscious than the apostle himself that everything he is and has as a Christian and as an apostle is by the grace of God (15:9–11). In humble reliance on this grace, Paul prays, as he does at the end of all his letters, that "the grace of the Lord Jesus" (1 Cor 16:23) may continue to be with the Corinthians.

God's inexpressible love toward him inspires Paul's love for his fellow saints. Paul now adds a closing verse which is unique to 1 Corinthians: "My love [is] with all of you in Christ Jesus" (16:24). Despite the harsh things he has had to say, he is still their father in Christ (4:15), and he still regards all of them as his "beloved children" (4:14) in Christ. In this final expression of his love for them, Paul models what he has just preached: "Let all you do be in love" (16:14).

The apostle's fatherly love for his children is "in Christ Jesus" (16:24). Fittingly, the name of Jesus becomes the last word in an epistle devoted to restoring the church's faith and fellowship in him (cf. 1:9).